The Ultimate Crosswords Omnibus

Edited by Mel Rosen

COURAGE BOOKS

AN IMPRINT OF RUNNING PRESS
PHILADELPHIA • LONDON

9 8
Digit on the right indicates the number of this printing.

ISBN 0-7624-0182-6

Cover design by Diane Miljat

Published by Courage Books, an imprint of
Running Press Book Publishers
125 South Twenty-second Street
Philadelphia, Pennsylvania 19103-4399

FOREWORD

Crosswords first appeared in the *New York World* beginning in 1913 and gained much popularity in the 1920s. They are a natural choice of pastime for those who like to challenge their wit, word-knowledge, and wisdom of the world.

From that time onward, crosswords have undergone many changes. Two of the most important standards established over the years are symmetrical patterning and "total interlock" (each letter must have an across word and a down word crossing it). Later came the elimination of two-letter words because they were usually too easily solved.

Gradually, the *New York Times* crosswords editor assumed the role of "guru of cruciverbalism." First it was Margaret Farrar in the 40s and 50s, and then Will Weng. Eugene Maleska became editor in 1977, and among his earlier style innovations were the "stepquote" and the use of phrases as answer words.

By the 80s, the crosswords scene was ripe for a change of content—constructors began to get away from the dictionary-based literalism that had long predominated. Composers such as Henry Hook and Merl Reagle used cleverness and contemporary topics in their clues and answers. Editors such as Will Shortz, Stan Newman, and Mel Rosen began to eliminate stale crosswordese, incorporate more pop-culture items, and promote more interesting word play. Classical and historical references were replaced by more modern allusions. A fresh sense of wittiness pervaded the construction and presentation of puzzles. A growing and changing audience became devoted solvers. And ultimately, crossword puzzles became more stylish, more challenging, and more fun.

The puzzles gathered within this book were originally constructed in 1987 and 1989, and all of them were edited by Mel Rosen. His longtime association with wordplay of all sorts in the National Puzzlers' League placed him in good standing as he edited these puzzles. With a Rosen-edited puzzle, "Flower" can mean "that which flows" (as a river) in addition to "blossom." The answer for "Start over" could be "more" (as in "moreover") instead of the more usual "redo." And naturally, "The end of time" may have nothing to do with apocalyptic visions, but instead with "less," "piece," or "share."

His enthusiasm for sports means that you can expect to make the acquaintence of several Hall-of-Famers, and his fondness for the sea means that an occasional "Ahoy" or "Avast" will certainly be either fore, aft, or abeam.

It was around the time of the original publication of these puzzles that the changes that began to stir in the early 80s really started to take hold and to flourish. You can sense, while solving these puzzles, the excitement of people who were breaking away from the norm and heading into uncharted territory. Compare these puzzles to today's and notice the similiarities, but also the differences which link these puzzles to the past.

And by the way, a *cruciverbalist* can mean either a constructor or a solver of crosswords. So sharpen your cruciverbalist skills on these cruciverbalists' puzzles, and enjoy!

—Daniel and Roslyn Stark
Editors of the *Crosswords Challenge* series

PREFACE

Charles Caleb Colton, an early-19th-century English clergyman, sportsman, wine merchant, and author, wrote: "Many books require no thought from those who read them, and for a very simple reason: they made no such demands upon those who wrote them. Those works, therefore, are the most valuable that set our thinking faculties in the fullest operation."

There is no evidence, of course, that Colton had foreknowledge of the crossword puzzle, but his words seem somehow related to this collection. The puzzle creators used their thinking faculties to build these entertaining challengers. Now it's your turn to operate your thinking faculties. Savor the exercise.

—Mel Rosen, Editor

Harp Lesson?   by Donna J. Stone

As usual, advice from Laurence J. Peter is pithy and succinct.

1

Across

1 One of a mixed bag?
7 Diluted
11 Balmoral
14 Knock stopper
15 Angelic topper
16 ____ Speedwagon
17 **Start of lesson**
20 Perennial flower
21 Fencing weapon
22 Laborer
25 Upright
28 A word to the wretched
29 Sprightly, to Solti
31 Auto feature
33 Head of state headdress
34 Cruising
35 **Middle of lesson**
40 "Beetle Bailey" character
41 King bound to a wheel, in myth
44 Cane cutter
48 Auto feature
50 Say it again. . .and again. . .and again. . .
51 Up
53 Pop
54 Irish isles
55 ____ a time
57 **End of lesson**
64 Fatal conclusion?
65 Crossword opera?
66 "L.A. Law" divorce specialist Becker
67 Tailless tail?
68 *Very* revealing picture
69 Message holder

Down

1 Bully
2 Essen exclamation
3 Berkshire home
4 Carmen's number
5 Slaughter
6 Hose
7 Reporter's question
8 Canal zone?
9 Hgt.
10 Prince Andrew's onetime playmate, ____ Stark
11 Increase by 200 percent
12 Dido's darling
13 Mr. Mussorgsky
18 *Very* impressive sandwich?
19 Adrenaline catalyst
22 Contrived
23 Whitney
24 Canute's foe
26 Alternative to plastic
27 End-of-year purchase
30 Marquisette
32 Cuomo
34 From ____ Z
36 "____ Smile Be Your Umbrella on a Rainy Day"
37 Very French?
38 Real
39 Rural tower
42 Ref. rm. treasure
43 Blue Eagle legislation, for short
44 "Yellow Submarine" villain
45 Puzzling direction?
46 Amulets
47 Whetstone
48 ____-Japanese War
49 Quickie quarters?
52 Now
56 Coif
58 Wicked stuff?
59 Publicize
60 Cereal box abbr.
61 Decay
62 Addition
63 ETO monogram

Originally published in 1987

Tongue Sandwiches *by Richard Silvestri*

This theme has a lot of bite to it. Here are three possibilities.

2

Across

1 Dressed
5 Maundy money
9 Original
14 Bridal shower?
15 Fastidious
16 Light but strong beam
17 Short-long, in verse
18 Film alternative
19 Cordial flavoring
20 Pan
23 Diplomacy
24 Ponderosa papa
25 Vince Coleman specialty
28 1936 Olympics hero
31 Gray monogram
34 Like some tea
36 Census datum
37 Incite to action
38 Pane
41 Pinocchio's polygraph
42 Bee follower
43 Place for an ace
44 Compass pt.
45 Square one
47 Pullman berth
48 Skater Babilonia
49 "Ta-____-Boom-De-Ré"
51 Pain
58 Audible water?
59 Grad
60 ____ facto
61 Crop up
62 1948 Hitchcock film
63 Tree house
64 Grew dim
65 Exploit
66 Heredity factor

Down

1 Baby bed
2 Tall tale teller
3 Height
4 Moot
5 Bit of buffoonery
6 Simple shelter
7 Glove compartment items
8 Footfall
9 Dogfight duo
10 Busted
11 Wife of Osiris
12 Screening
13 Afore
21 ____ Lama
22 Doubleday and Li'l
25 Stand out
26 Grand ____ National Park
27 Clear the slate
29 Thin snack
30 Part of the psyche
31 Inch along
32 Vino variety
33 Abacus user
35 Relating to milk
37 Girding up
39 Teachers' gp.
40 Book jacket words
45 Used emery cloth
46 Acting company
48 It can be perfect
50 Set for battle
51 ____ song; cheaply
52 Rack's partner
53 Stony
54 Arctic sight
55 Rapier's relative
56 Org.
57 Be lavish with affection
58 Apothegm

Dogmatic View *by Peter Swift*

Herein, H.L. Mencken's definition of Puritanism.

Across

1 Eat soup boorishly
6 Hounded
12 Certain horses
18 Atelier appurtenance
19 ——-down cake
20 Three sister goddesses
21 **Start of definition**
24 Warm
25 —— clear of; avoid
26 Source of energy
27 Essence
30 Perishes at sea
32 Cupid
35 Bring to bear
38 Droop
39 Hammarskjöld
42 Needlefishes
43 Casinos, for example
46 Enlist again
48 Also-ran
50 **Definition, part 2**
52 Dictum
53 Wears away
55 Pharaohs, for example
57 Yesterday, in Tours
58 Atomic number 50
59 Compete
61 Reality, old style
62 Buffalo Bill's promoter Buntline, and others
63 Advances obliquely
66 Francesca's lover, in Dante's "Inferno"
68 Rapidly
71 Smooth fabric
74 Consider again, in court
78 **End of definition**
82 Laundry worker
83 On cloud nine
84 Emanate
85 Schuss experts
86 Satan's little helpers
87 Regattas

Down

1 Bristle
2 "Oz" costar
3 Secondhand
4 Prepared for opening night
5 Factory
6 Roll of hair
7 Quick to learn
8 Fertility goddess
9 Hair dye
10 Sharpened
11 Put off
12 Tom Kite's org.
13 Prepared for
14 Suffragist Carrie's in-laws
15 She pined away for Narcissus
16 Enlarge a hole
17 Atl. crossers
22 Complete
23 Son of Aphrodite
28 Tomahawks
29 Put down a new lawn
31 Kind of correspondent
32 Shoelace part
33 Native New Zealanders
34 Welles
36 New York city
37 Ringlet
39 Calf, on the range
40 Intended
41 Snarls
44 —— Gigio, mechanical mouse on Ed Sullivan's show
45 Be a busybody
47 "From the Terrace" author
49 Critic
51 Ms. Kett of the comics
54 Caesar
56 —— up; add support
60 Otherwise
63 Display of temper
64 Like some seals
65 Stone tablet
67 "The Merry Widow" composer
68 Sale stipulation
69 Kind of barrel
70 Mine, to Yvette
72 Moslem scholar
73 One alliance with Eur.
75 Beowulf, for one
76 Church projection
77 Sandwich loaves
79 Time periods: Abbr.
80 Japanese coin
81 Police anti-terrorist gp.

3

All Puffed Up   *by Martha J. De Witt*

And no place to go.

4

Across

1 Our 27th President
5 Small poisonous snakes of Egypt
9 Pant
13 —— podrida
14 Courtly
15 Throe or throb
16 Endure
17 Syrian religious sect: Var.
18 Highlander
19 Inflated
22 Eden's mistress
23 Historical period
24 Tormenter
26 Belief
31 Withered
32 Arnie Becker's Gal Friday ("L.A. Law")
33 Hardly enough
35 Novelist Ngaio ——
38 Moscow's man on the street
40 "The Sons of Katie ——"
42 Tomcat or drake
43 Fathered, old style
45 Doles out
47 Wine cask
48 Small weight
50 They testify
52 Ship
55 Annoy
56 Peace's opposite
57 Inflated
63 Girasol
65 Hand-holder
66 Can
67 Actress Moreno
68 Kind of beaver?
69 Comedian —— Wilson
70 Sketched
71 Tatum's father
72 Method: Abbr.

Down

1 Start of Hamlet's soliloquy
2 TV's Trebek
3 Level
4 —— and feathered
5 Vibes
6 Vending machine fooler
7 Leaning Tower guide, perhaps
8 Prospects
9 Xenon, for one
10 Up rate or amount
11 What push comes to
12 Detective Lord —— Wimsey
14 Make headway
20 God of 56 Across
21 Abound
25 Three scruples
26 Where baby sleeps
27 Wander
28 Inflate, in a way
29 Still
30 Over
34 Antoinette lost hers
36 Legato symbol
37 Scarce as —— teeth
39 Asta's mistress
41 Complaining one
44 Pack down
46 Alphabetize
49 Business union
51 Light rowboats
52 Excalibur, for one
53 Tropical ungulate related to the horse
54 Type of race
58 Roman robe
59 All tied up
60 Slick
61 He wrote "Topaz"
62 Mo. in which the Gregorian calendar replaced the Julian
64 Binding rule

Observances   *by John R. Prosser*

Observances on the calendar.

5

Across

1 Rush hour vehicles
5 The baddest of the bad
10 Wicked
14 Thanks ____
15 Poetry inspiration
16 "____ flim-flam stories, and nothing but shams and lies." (Cervantes)
17 Hawaiian fete, 3rd Saturday of September
19 Needle and wheedle
20 Letter closing word
21 Lagos native
23 Give a helpful hint
24 Anser mister
25 Where some foes meet
27 Western highlands
31 Compassionate
35 Explosive stuff
37 Missile in a pub
38 Shielded from
40 Queen of the fairies
42 Go round and round in a pipe
43 Ceiling
45 Sam "____" Malone of "Cheers"
46 A certain button
48 Jewish ceremonial dinner
50 Try on for size
52 "Through the Looking ____"
57 Coastal region
59 Keep an ____ the ground
60 Places
61 May 1, by act of Congress
63 Often-discordant grp.
64 Oat genus
65 Popular PBS show
66 "The Way We ____"
67 Dittos
68 "____ 'ow!" (toast from Andy Capp?)

Down

1 Tumbrels
2 Argus-eyed
3 Outcast
4 Fusty
5 Hose down
6 Bowl made in Miami
7 In high spirits
8 Like some ponds
9 Fooled with
10 May 24, in England
11 Vague actress?
12 Golf club
13 Took first place
18 Simon Legree, for one
22 Sleep-student's initials
26 Fishing pole device
28 True grit
29 Operatic solo
30 Remain
31 Play a broken record?
32 Covering for the pupil
33 Cruel
34 ____ Day, now Veterans Day
36 "It's Howdy Doody ____"
39 Shoot full of holes
41 Quarry
44 Put off
47 Rumpleteazer or Old Deuteronomy
49 Franklin ____ Roosevelt
51 Mouthy grinder
53 NFL great QB Bobby ____
54 Passion
55 Barrel part
56 Some beans
57 Move like a deer
58 Cake decorator
60 Juliette ____, founder of the Girl Scouts
62 ____ Palmas, Canary Islands

Originally published in 1987

The Sky's The Limit   by S.E. Wilkinson

Hitting the high spots.

6

Across

1 Burgle
4 Country music's Ernest
8 Place for dressing
13 Walking stick
14 Words of understanding
15 Took down
16 Rarely
19 Poet Edna
20 In addition
21 Consecrate
22 Louis Armstrong
27 Dismantled
29 A judge of Israel
30 Wash out
32 Gable and Grable
35 Health professional: Abbr.
36 Pen point
37 Churchill's gesture
38 Undecided
43 Sleeveless top
44 Are you a ____ mouse?
45 Eat
47 Gray, for example
49 Overlook
52 Actor James
54 Prey on the mind
55 1950 Swanson film
60 Team or team up
61 Solitary
62 Wishing will make ____
63 Roc group
64 Breaks off
65 Jell

Down

1 Arrested
2 Ecstatic
3 Direct route
4 "A Christmas Carol" character
5 "Born in the ____"
6 Nixon's friend Rebozo
7 Carillon
8 "____ every sound. . ." (Tennyson)
9 Hand holder
10 Card game
11 From ____ Z
12 Cozy room
13 Robin Cook novel
17 "____ my Annabel Lee." (Poe)
18 Grammar concern
23 July clock setting, in Ill.
24 1980 epic western film
25 Dictates of society
26 Start
28 Finished
30 Amusement park ride
31 Frighten
33 By way of
34 Short citation
39 Strong ale
40 Arm muscle
41 Attacks
42 Waves
43 Opposite
46 Hard blow
48 Eating place
50 Fly apart
51 Old name for Tokyo
53 High time?
55 Rel. degree
56 Tell's canton
57 Neither's partner
58 Turf
59 And, to Wagner

Travelogue *by Thomas W. Schier*

A challenger. Note the stacked full-width answers

7

Across

1 Hint
4 The Bard's river
8 Orchestra section
13 Car traveler's path
15 Sacred writings
16 Mechanical traveler
17 Change travel plans
20 Whirlwind traveler's state?
21 Extravagant
22 Where _____?
23 Certain undergarment
25 _____ Mahal
27 New: Pref.
31 Traveler in a UFO
32 In-one song
33 Nigerian tribe
34 Actress Taylor, to friends
35 In opposition to

38 Travel _____ and wide
39 "If _____ a wiz there was. . ."
41 Top-notch
42 Fishnet fiber
44 Evening, to a Rome traveler
45 Length measures: Abbr.
46 Mingles thoroughly
47 Brat
49 Having a rough surface
50 Big-spending travelers?
57 Route of an "organic" traveler?
58 Tablecloth fabric
59 Life's lot
60 Ballet skirt
61 Adolescents
62 Derisive cries
63 Sitcom final scenelet

Down

1 Fairway bunker
2 Eurytus's daughter
3 Sponsor
4 _____ santé
5 Ground
6 Music halls
7 Soccer orgn.
8 Halloween traveler's vehicle
9 Habitual method
10 Hillside shelter
11 Passable
12 British machine carbine
14 Transfer
18 Eye membrane
19 Musical key
23 Grows ashen
24 Animated
25 Small cities
26 Wings
28 Crazy

29 Article of food
30 Gumbo ingredients
32 Did the smithy's job
36 _____ Springs, Florida
37 Central Mexican native
40 Cable hands
43 Allows access
46 Wooden obstructions
48 Bearings
49 Jollity
50 Soda shop order
51 Tennist Nastase
52 From end to end in the Rose Bowl
53 Advise: Abbr.
54 Very narrow shoe width
55 . . .I could _____ horse!
56 Musket ball

Back To Back *by Ernie Furtado*

Short mirror fugues from a master composer.

8

Across

1 Wife of Sir Geraint
5 Pert
9 Who —— that lady?
12 Resort name
13 Rhône feeder
14 English spa
15 Start of a pun game
17 Magazine for *femmes*
18 Lamprey
19 Roadway sign
20 Land of *vino*
22 Hit musical based on poetry by Eliot
23 Writer, with 6 Down
24 Partial refund
27 Like some news
30 Reputations
31 Curl
32 Mary —— Retton
33 Resumés
34 Western cinematic classic
35 Facile
36 Building extension
37 Cuffed
38 Terminate
39 Popular summer place
41 Glare
42 Flirt chaser
43 "My Name is ——"
44 Innate ability
46 Cupid
47 —— carte
50 Double-reed instrument
51 Hip '40s expression
54 Humble
55 Actress Burstyn
56 —— noire
57 Stand-in
58 "The —— Hunter"
59 Note part

Down

1 Sommer of film
2 Baseball team
3 Billy of rock
4 What's up, ——?
5 Data
6 See 23 Across
7 Dick and Joanna Loudon's Stratford ——
8 Small dog
9 City in SE Washington
10 Gudrun's mate
11 Home of the Mets
13 Take after Katarina Witt
14 Rhythms
16 Famed poet
21 Aunts, to Charo
22 Train units
23 Coeur d'——
24 Togae
25 Roman magistrate
26 Yale song
27 Babble
28 Din
29 Potato, for instance
31 Anagram for north
34 Mollified
35 Math. branch
37 Tibia
38 Barton or Bow
40 Pilot
41 Plaint
43 Caution light
44 Outdoes
45 —— Ben Adhem
46 Competent
47 Encourage
48 Stringed instrument
49 Attention getter
52 Diminutive suffix
53 Small shot

Letter Perfect   by Norma Steinberg

Your initial reaction is probably correct regarding this composition.

9

Across

1 Wherewithal
6 G sharp
11 Parts of prescriptions
16 Musical based on a comic strip
17 Honker
18 "____ Care," Eva Tanguay's trademark tune
19 Peter Jennings, e.g.
21 Actress-singer Lenya
22 Pizza sauce ingredient
23 A ____ of his word
24 French philosopher and writer
25 Ogles
26 Ms. Verdon
28 Sun.'s preceder
29 Olive ____, Popeye's lady
30 Hideaway
31 ____ a nice day!
32 Aglow
36 Large trucks
37 "____ Done Him Wrong"
40 Entertainer Channing
41 Early legislator
42 Polite term of address
43 Mickey Mantle in 1962, e.g.
47 Filmdom's Turner
48 Horror/Sci-fi film
49 Henry ____ Lodge
50 Compass dir.
51 Farmer's concern
52 Mistaken belief
54 Responsibility
55 "____ 18," Uris novel
56 Pub order
59 Get hitched
60 Parking lot mishap
61 Twosome
65 Tennis shot
67 Pot cover
68 Kitty on "Gunsmoke"
70 Perfume oil
71 Wm. Casey, for one
73 Mick Jagger
74 Greetings!
75 Stallone's "Rocky" costar
76 Having a slight tint
77 Ruhr valley city
78 Revenue source

Down

1 Flat finish
2 Ambassador
3 "What's in ____?" asked Juliet
4 Little girls in Madrid
5 Bloc
6 History book word
7 Ex
8 Miller's Salesman
9 Strong ____ ox
10 Decimal system base
11 Widens
12 Scent
13 ____ voce
14 ____-level job
15 Pittsburgh product
20 Paul ____, Crocodile Dundee
24 Kind of grace
27 "Rug"
28 South Pacific islands
30 Caron role
31 Singer Reddy
32 Climb
33 Esther's foe
34 Peaceful name
35 Mrs. Nick Charles
36 Foot parts
37 Canasta variation
38 Pandemonium
39 Drained
41 Clips
42 Supper, for example
44 Gleason's second banana
45 Spoken
46 The Pac. Ten's "Bruins"
51 Shrank
52 Fiver
53 Church table
55 Butt in
56 Hey! on board
57 Game of chance
58 "Crocodile Rock" singer John
60 Radio parts
61 Summer cottage for Gorbachev
62 To that time when
63 Love
64 Takes a chance
66 Lois or Abbe
67 Tales
69 42 Down, West Point style
71 Sr. Guevara
72 Charged particle

The Big Loser   by H.P. Burchfield

This and the next puzzle feature opposing sides of a famous historical event. Fittingly, the composer used the same diagram for both puzzles.

Across

1 Less experienced
6 Hard to get through
11 Try
16 Dodge
17 Florida city
18 Expenditure
19 Malodorous
20 Profound sleep
21 Adjust a skirt length
22 Public warehouse
24 Mark doubtful statements
26 At some distance
28 Knobby
30 "___ Kapital"
31 One sign of summer
34 Keys
36 Bovine deli?
38 Scattered about
40 Weaver's machine
41 Bribes
44 Chem. endings
45 Secret
47 Teacher's org.
48 Ottoman officers
49 Dusk on June 17, 1815
52 Cinema's Diana
54 Prefix for phyte or prene
55 Much smaller
59 Student pilot's big moment
60 Bad place for a cinder
62 Algonquian
63 Second man on the moon
65 Joplin jazz
66 Bread under the table
68 Cribbage scorekeeper
69 Forty winks
71 Formal
73 Like a book on next season's list: Abbr.
74 Swedish academic center
77 Paid attention
79 Tara resident
81 TV announcer Don
83 Catch one's breath
86 Loser's successor
87 Misbehave
88 Maori gods
89 Where loser's nephew was captured, 1870
90 Garden starters
91 George Washington ___ here

Down

1 KO counter
2 Hail!
3 Arena, June 18, 1815
4 Go over a manuscript
5 Monomorium pharaonis pest
6 Medicated
7 Prefix for system or sphere
8 The big loser
9 Oscar, but not Felix
10 Like mature cornstalks
11 Verb form denoting action
12 Canal of note
13 Loser's exile, 1815-21
14 Bronze or Iron
15 ___ Kippur
23 Aussie occupation
25 Lad's date
26 Kind of clerk
27 Wet
29 Vestment
32 Lambs' dams
33 Switch settings
35 Loser's title
37 Sweep
39 Governor's jurisdiction
42 Inst. at Storrs, CT
43 Smart
46 Boob tubes
48 Tap stuff
50 Cold feet
51 Pad for a Native American
52 Welfare
53 Loser's stalwarts
56 Loser's nemesis
57 Wriggling
58 ". . .they shall ___ the whirlwind." (Hosea 8:7)
59 Nerd
60 Belonging to Ms. Claire, the actress
61 Alter ___
64 Hurting
67 Adjusts to
70 Irene of "Zorba the Greek"
72 Boutiques
75 South Seas sailor
76 "Arsenic and Old ___"
78 Horizontal bar
79 Hydroxyl compound endings
80 Haw's companion
82 Loser
84 Small taste
85 Winter clock setting in Tampa: Abbr.

10

The Big Winners   *by H.P. Burchfield*

Completing the theme set forth in the previous puzzle.

11

Across

1 Kind of pin or rod
6 Idea, in Platonism
11 Flower part
16 Cognizant
17 Winner's son
18 Lift up
19 Legendary creatures
20 Treaty signer
21 Fabricates
22 Turn into law
24 Calabar bean extract
26 Condensed ed.
28 Krypton and xenon, for example
30 Lush
31 Where Celtics meet Lakers: Abbr.
34 Rhythmic swinger
36 Captain's diary
38 Dirty old man
40 Oceanic ice
41 Easy-gaited horse
44 ____ and file
45 Festooner
47 49 Across activity
48 Gold or silver fabric
49 June 18, 1815 scene
52 Stumble
54 Adjective suffix
55 Interminable
59 Flightless bird: Var.
60 Having no heir
62 Within: Comb. form
63 "Old Wine in New Bottles" columnist Ben Ray ____
65 Gymnast's feat
66 Zeus or Aton, for instance
68 Americana or Britannica: Abbr.
69 Tomcat
71 Aztec people
73 DJ's discs
74 Declaiming
77 ____ Centauri
79 Manner

81 "The Love Boat" on land?
83 Between puddles and lakes
86 Cave
87 Soap substitute
88 Provide; put on
89 Foundations
90 Splits violently
91 Adjust, as a watch

Down

1 Every dog's due
2 Be in the red
3 June 18, 1815 locale
4 Winner's birthplace, poetically
5 French dramatist (1668-1747)
6 Fixes up for publication
7 ". . .and ____ the opposite shore will be. . ." (Longfellow)

8 The big winners
9 Galena and cinnabar
10 Saddle ____
11 Middle Easterner
12 Dash; verve
13 Winner's wife, nee Kitty ____
14 Consumed
15 "____ Girls"
23 Wall-to-wall item
25 ____-poly
26 "A," in communications
27 Picture, in Plauen
29 Building wing
32 Nota ____
33 Biblical refuge
35 Rare-earth element 65
37 Tennis's Steffi
39 Held close
42 Even: Pref.
43 Inland Indians
46 23 Down quality
48 Honorary deg.
50 Gaunt

51 Imbue with spirit
52 Fed. agents
53 Winner's stalwarts
56 Belonging to the victorious country
57 Arrest
58 Lawns
59 Before
60 Agitated state
61 Pollution monitoring org.
64 Some marbles
67 Asta at the water dish
70 Indian state
72 Drags
75 Laugh, to the loser
76 Alaskan cape
78 Sharpen
79 Bill
80 Double helix, for short
82 Antiquity, in antiquity
84 Owing
85 Tennis unit

Map Flap *by Peter Swift*

"I am a little world made cunningly
Of elements, and an angelic sprite." – Donne, "Holy Sonnets"

12

Across

1 Dry run
5 Certain pols.
9 Flat; insipid
14 Scold
15 Feverish state
16 Roof of the mouth
17 Shalom
18 Knitting stitch
19 Agitate
20 Dutch duplicity?
23 Links starting point
24 Aphrodite's mother
25 State of agitation
26 Ottoman Empire bigwigs
27 "___ Little Indians"
28 Monk
31 Onagers
36 Stitch
38 Roof worker
40 Teemed, like bees
43 Sign at a garage sale
46 Pretoria coin
47 California spice?
50 About
51 Bartlett, for one
52 Parasite of a sort
53 Sources
55 Summon
57 ___ out; extirpates
58 Actor Knight
59 Time periods: Abbr.
62 Vatican name
65 Operatic highlight
66 Dominique's relative
68 Trevino's org.
71 "1812 Overture" feature?
76 Kind of battle
77 Salute
78 Peregrine's claw
79 Plagiarizes
80 Conversational filler
81 Abrade
82 Campus term for a local resident: Var.
83 Minus
84 Word of annoyance

Down

1 Kind of song
2 Cancel
3 School of thought
4 Scottish river
5 Peke or pom
6 Tropical lizards
7 Rangoon burlesque act?
8 Ego
9 Contemptible one
10 High up
11 Singer Anka
12 Frank Capra classic, "___ Wonderful Life"
13 Regard
14 Tiff
16 "Common Sense" author
21 Inlet
22 WWII assault vehicle
28 Part of an I-beam
29 Let
30 Passions
31 Baseball statistic
32 River of song
33 Kind of cow
34 Misplayed
35 Wee, in Dundee
37 Court
39 One of the Forsytes
41 Part of HRE
42 Poor grade
44 DJ's albums
45 Brief swim
48 Pinch
49 Use a scythe
54 With a high-pitched sound
56 Journals
60 Iranian money
61 Salvador or Remo
63 Certain kin
64 Actor Erwin
65 Pakistani or Thai, for example
67 Organic compound
68 Kind of whale
69 Vendor's assets
70 Actress Meara
71 Plant disease
72 ___ no good; making trouble
73 Display, old style
74 Hockey's Esposito
75 Ms. Teasdale

Author! Author! *by Jeanne Wilson*

Ms. Wilson got three of them, at least, to put in an appearance.

Across

1 Brushing sound
6 Sign of battle
10 Old card game
15 Mixed (Ital.)
16 Szczecin residents
18 Emergency vehicle attention-getter
19 Belief in Allah
20 Naomi, to Ruth
21 Mushroom stalk
22 Bret rats on Poe?
25 Bring joy
26 Thai language
27 Common abbr.
29 Andy and Oliver
32 Novice
33 Bristle
34 Period
35 Gujarat garment
38 Taxonomy abbr.
40 Australian state: Abbr.
41 Pungent
44 ___ over; persuades
46 On the ___; fleeing
48 Oscar phones London?
54 OB's guess?
55 Fuss
56 Nantes's river
57 Cleo's finish
60 Containing nitrogen, in combinations
62 Words of understanding
64 First st.
65 Lugosi
67 Range dividing Asia and Europe
69 Joe E., Katharine, and Diana
72 Toenails, in Madrid
73 Fleur-de-___
74 Laissez-___ doctrine
76 Charles Edward serenades Dickens?
82 "Thereby hangs ___."

83 Certain exams
84 Nevada resort lake
85 Took into account
86 Vikings
87 More than one opus
88 Three-spots
89 Let it stand
90 Smells

Down

1 Hit, old style
2 Birthday-cake ritual
3 Tropical spot
4 Set forth, formally
5 Plain, plus
6 Don't cry over ___ milk
7 Short adventure story
8 ___ breve; cut time
9 Honestly?!
10 Greek peak
11 Carpenter's corners
12 Composer Benjamin ___
13 Says again and again
14 Chem. ending
17 Curses
23 Dundee dolly
24 Major ___ of "Our Boarding House"
28 What there oughta be!
29 Vehemence
30 Paris landmark
31 Undercooked
32 Wrapping material
36 Cobbler's tool
37 "You're a ___, Alice!" (Kramden)
39 Ratchet engager
42 Jewel thief's term
43 Computer input or output
45 Flags: Abbr.
47 "O Sole ___"
49 Lapis ___
50 Rake's cousin
51 Covers

52 Endure, in Scotland
53 Lampreys
57 ___ Simbel; Ramses II temple site
58 Biden or Dole, in 1987
59 Mollify
61 Prayer
63 Sevareid
66 Scarlett's love
68 Houston ballplayers
70 Daniel Webster, for one
71 Mexican wrap
74 Like some eyelashes
75 Good looks, for one
77 Beatty film
78 Shopping locale
79 Former Korean statesman
80 Famed WWI Sergeant
81 Meadows
82 Rubber tree mover of song

13

Am. Lit. 201   *by Joy L. Wouk*

A collection of stories and plays by American writers.

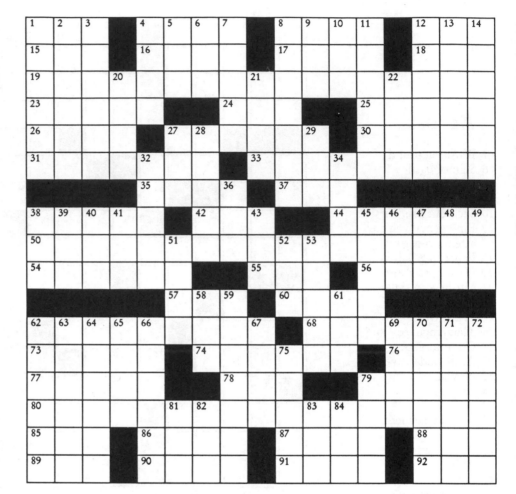

Across

1 Ending for Japan or Canton
4 Colorful fish
8 Need
12 Computer terminal, for short
15 Mata Hari, for one
16 Former NFL QB George ——
17 Hautboy
18 TV control knob
19 O'Neill play
23 Sun: Comb. form
24 Harem room
25 Fruit meats
26 Goddess of discord
27 Outdoes
30 Everything, in Bonn
31 Steinbeck's "The ——"
33 Cather book
35 Hun king: Var.
37 "—— Can't Take It. . ." (Kaufman and Hart comedy)
38 Valuable possession
42 Prefix with sphere or system
44 Go back on a promise
50 Wolfe book
54 Most competent
55 Stowe heroine
56 T.H. White's "The —— in the Stone"
57 Owns
60 Feed the kitty
62 Sinclair Lewis book
68 Poe's "The ——"
73 Author Jong
74 Creator of Natty Bumppo
76 —— does it!
77 Proscenium
78 Hawaii's Mauna ——
79 Kitchen device
80 Saroyan play
85 Actor-singer Linden
86 "High ——" (Grace Kelly film)
87 Yugoslavian leader of many years

14

88 Weight
89 Ship's timber curve
90 Roman clan
91 Corrida calls
92 Word in Napoleon's supposed palindrome

Down

1 Old Testament heroine
2 Province
3 Lash bearer
4 Melville book
5 Brooch
6 Neighbor of Bol.
7 Play —— with; ruin
8 With faithfulness
9 Saudi robe
10 Gear tooth
11 Persist in
12 Very spiny cactus
13 Gamboled
14 Having lots of hair

20 Computer language
21 Concert halls
22 Shuck
27 Tolkien creature
28 Woody tissue
29 Michigan-Ontario region
32 Vows
34 Voiceless
36 Arctic sight
38 In the mode of
39 Kind of sister
40 Musical syllable
41 Supplement
43 Be in debt
45 Studio feature
46 Compass dir.
47 Self
48 Neighbor of Den.
49 Antiquity
51 Friend of Nero
52 A Gardner
53 Kitchen feature
58 Circle part
59 Strawberry plant runners

61 Maxwell Anderson's play, "High ——"
62 "—— boatman takes no bribe. . ." (Horace)
63 Elinor Wylie's "The —— Angel"
64 In an urgent manner
65 Glaswegian
66 Like the moon, every month
67 Horseshoe site
69 Distribute
70 White or yellowish mineral called heavy spar
71 Have no ——; dislike strongly
72 Leatherneck
75 Words on a check face
79 Cons' opposition
81 One Stooge
82 Long time
83 Lubricate
84 Shoshonean

Back To School *by Roger H. Courtney*

To math class, specifically.

15

Across

1 Edmonton's prov.
5 Turkish city
10 Old slave
14 At ___ for words
15 Build the troops up again
16 Department of France
18 Procreate
19 Like 10ˣ
21 Actress Hagen
22 "___ It Romantic?"
24 Masculine
25 Shakespeare sharpened it
26 Scarlett's plantation
28 Center of activity
29 Kind of will
30 Wight, for one
31 Static force
34 Lily
36 Blend color again
38 Vane letters
40 Patriot Hale
44 Respires in part
46 Holy woman: Abbr.
48 Check casher
49 Summa ___ laude
50 Modern dress?
53 Earlier than, in combinations
54 Short shrub
57 Copycat
58 Data, on "Star Trek, the Next Generation"
61 Flinch
63 Sandy's comment
65 Musical compositions
66 Bivalve mollusk
68 Like cocoa powder
70 ___ facto
73 West of Hollywood
75 Old Roman household god
76 Geraint's wife
79 "___ Bravo," John Wayne movie
80 Fishy organ
81 ___ fixe
83 Mary of stage and film
84 With sides having the same length
87 Analysis
89 Irene, the actress
90 Recite dramatically
91 Oliver, Rex and Donna
92 "The Razor's ___"
93 Went to Sardi's, perhaps
94 ___ majesté

Down

1 Prince Valiant's wife
2 Relating to "number power"
3 Half an African fly
4 Italian wine center
5 We ___ alone!
6 Starchy substance with many uses
7 Rock musician's elec. gear
8 Ruth's mother-in-law
9 Chronicles
10 Trigonometric relationship
11 Superlative ending
12 Part of Santa's sleigh rigging
13 Delicate
14 Juxtapose
17 North Sea feeder
20 Actress Drew
23 Check one's ID
27 Crossworddom ox
30 Least bit
32 Photo lab product: Abbr.
33 Complements of queries
35 Cumberland ___
36 Kitchen implement
37 Habituate
39 H, to a Hellene
41 Certain triangle sides
42 Lofty perch
43 Exigencies
45 Rodgers's score, "Victory at ___"
47 Gabor
51 FDR grp.
52 Guarantee
55 Designer Chanel
56 Be indisposed
59 Confer knighthood upon
60 Stir up
62 Vampire
64 Leafy
67 Certain milk drink
69 Served soup
70 Provoked to anger
71 Nettle
72 ___ off; air a beef
74 Yellowish resin
77 Turkish ruler's decree
78 Former Algerian governors
80 Type of club
82 Nobleman above a viscount
85 Gerund finisher
86 Reagan, to friends
88 Holy ___

XXXX *by Louis Sabin*

Hugs and kisses from an expert.

Across

1 Dinner course
6 Mosel feeder
10 Capitol go-fer
14 Runs off to wed
16 The fur of furs
17 "____ Old Cowhand" (Crosby hit)
18 Romberg-Hammerstein song popularized by Rudy Vallée
21 Charge for services
22 Sitarist Shankar
23 Magazine entry
24 Vulpine
26 Shea franchise
28 Member of the wedding
29 Cartoon shriek
31 Triton
33 Harrow hedgerow
34 Ladder unit
36 Position
38 Off-the-wall
42 Kind of fink
43 Ground cover
45 Yeats's home
47 "Beautiful ____" (1918 song)
48 "You ____ Love" (Kern song)
49 1978 song by Lionel Richie, Jr., and others
52 Wapiti
53 Nerd
55 Merchandise
56 Kind of bulb?
57 Thrush Peggy
58 Thor, Odin, and the rest
60 Social reformer and writer Jacob August ____
62 Stretch autos
64 Silent indication
66 Yonder
68 Murray Schisgal play
69 Finishes
72 Party rouser
74 ____ Bingle (Crosby)
76 Mosque tower
78 Mrs. Shakespeare, ____ Hathaway
80 Sheriff Andy Taylor's aunt
82 Rod McKuen song
85 Followers
86 TV's "Kate & ____"
87 Place of many wives
88 Studies
89 TV's Carter
90 Duded up

Down

1 Ego
2 Lotion additives
3 "____ in the Sand" (Pat Boone 1957 hit)
4 Echo, in a way
5 Earl ____ Biggers, creator of Charlie Chan
6 Therefore, to Angus
7 Top-grossing rock group
8 Tocsin
9 Headmaster
10 Neck
11 Soap source
12 Winning hit
13 Compass dir.
15 Con game
16 Conks, biblically
19 Pottery producer
20 Upped, as a check
25 Winner's vote
27 1979 Susan Collins song
30 "Rock 'n' Roll All Night" was a hit for them
32 Shadow
34 Rangoon garb: Var.
35 Spats
37 Walked
39 TV sitcom
40 Roof cover
41 Burden
42 Punjab prince
44 "Bambi" cast
46 Impishness, plus
50 Director Kazan
51 Early film actor Jannings
54 Affection
59 Bonheur, and namesakes
61 Cruel
63 Sprinter's problem
65 Indian Ocean port
67 Henry ____, 3,000-meter steeplechase champion
69 Chew the scenery
70 Author of "The Moon's a Balloon"
71 Elizabethan period playwright George ____
73 Adam's grandson
75 Pay
77 Famed archer
79 Actress Barbara
81 Hard to get hold of
82 Skimmer
83 Zippo
84 Choral syllable

16

True Grit *by Kathryn Righter*

Life is a beach.

17

Across

1 Andean relatives of the camel
7 Half a Latin-American dance
10 Burn the surface
14 Atrium of a heart
16 God of love
17 Word with brew, coming, or plate
18 Sleepy-time visitor
19 Young seals
20 Space
21 Take to court
22 Completion
23 &
25 Drag behind
27 Greek letters
28 Twig broom
33 Manipulate; control
35 Selects
39 King Arthur's paradise
41 Between sunrise and sunset
42 Desires
43 Shorebird
45 Crumpled mass
46 Shoe width
47 High-tech albums
48 Negative conjunction
49 Male child
50 Beret
51 Young animal
52 Wager
53 Abrasive material
56 Lustrous concretions
58 Ventilate
59 Strict; harsh
60 High nest
61 Bowler's test
63 Taut
64 Coloring agent
66 Detective Spade
68 Safari hazard, in B movies
72 Coral, Red, or Black
74 Baseball stat.
77 Put back to rights
78 Arboretum specimen
79 Tot's play place
81 Roman road
82 Not so much
83 Exalt
84 Tailless amphibian
85 Ogee curve
86 Sight, taste, and touch

Down

1 Glasgow girl
2 Hawaiian feast
3 "Rule Britannia" composer
4 Central
5 Pinnacle
6 Approach
7 Friable
8 Moved like 84 Across, perhaps
9 Balance sheet item
10 Frame
11 Israeli dance
12 So be it!
13 Peruse
15 Provide funds for
16 Fed. clean-up org.
24 Swift
26 Broader
28 Some coll. degs.
29 Displaced person
30 River navigation hazard
31 Famous name in the auto industry
32 Swab
34 Sensory organ
36 Reduce the value of
37 Zoo attendants
38 Compass dir.
40 Baseball teams
42 Batons
44 Saucepan's relative
45 Hit the jackpot
49 Indian garments
50 Spelunker's interest
51 Busy one in early Apr.
52 Dreary
53 The S of RSVP
54 Dog or cat
55 Female ruff
57 Parachutist's need
58 Fitting quality
61 Traps
62 Cup, in Paris
65 Tough fiber
67 Ways and ___ Committee
68 Cease
69 Golden rule word
70 Notion
71 French article
73 Queen of England, 1702-14
74 Wanes
75 Play part
76 Woodsman's tools
80 Put on

Escort Service *by Sidney L. Robbins*

"They are never alone that are accompanied with noble thoughts."
– Sir Philip Sidney, "Arcadia"

18

Across

1 Like one who's seen it all
6 —— facto
10 Major work
14 Stand
15 Turn into law
16 It can be stuffed
17 Dance comment
20 Math subj.
21 Used up
22 Combo with the goods
23 Seabird
24 Agitates
25 It may keep you in stitches
26 Weapon for one on the fence?
27 Soak
28 Sightseer's bus
34 "—— *Kapital*"
37 Region of northern France
38 Challenge
39 Not perm.
40 Goad offensively
41 Plain surface of a triglyph
42 Song parodied by Spike Jones
43 Goes astray
44 Theban deity
45 Bray
46 Lair
47 Eng and Chang
49 Barge into
50 Greek letters
51 Crouches
54 Blemishes of a sort
56 Health resort
59 Game
60 Boxes lightly
61 Tsk, tsk!
62 Joint attempt
65 "—— the accomplice of love." (Rémy de Gourmont)
66 Full
67 Came up
68 Youngster
69 Like an oldster
70 Sot

Down

1 Tan
2 Sooner's alternative
3 Chemistry Nobelist, 1922
4 Tailor's pride
5 Wapiti
6 Put away, in a way
7 Minor chess pieces
8 Citizen of Edinburgh
9 Baseball's Mel
10 Chicago airport
11 One of Columbus's ships
12 Prodded
13 Mod. plane design
15 Discerned
16 Act shocked
18 Belonging to Lauder
19 Natural pigment
24 Acrobatic feat
25 Kilmer's poem
26 Lustrous blacks
28 Stale
29 "—— Ben Jonson"
30 Reversal of direction on the road
31 Swelling
32 Rebound
33 Coin of Denmark
34 City of India
35 Sir Edwin Arnold's characterization of mortal life as the wind
36 Throws out
39 Physical strength
41 Mutilates
42 Equatorial constellation south of Pisces
45 Somber vehicle
47 Woodland deity
48 Ogled
49 Does a fall chore
51 Germ cell
52 Cite
53 Loosen
54 Malice
55 —— in; collapsed
56 Sailing vessel
57 Describe grammatically
58 Pink flower
59 Beat it!
60 Cousin of 5 Down
61 Continental prefix
63 —— matter of fact. . .
64 Lard

Farmfoolery *by Ernie Furtado*

Animation by an expert.

Across

1 Chess piece
4 At some distance
8 Bk. addendum
11 "___ old cowhand. . ." (Mercer)
15 What's the ___?
16 Language of Pakistan
17 Hasten
18 Contend
19 Rwy. depot
20 Zilch, to Lucy of "101 Dalmatians"?
22 Ages
23 Gobs
25 Reach for
26 Stretch
27 Tad
29 Stop
31 "___ *Misérables*"
32 Russian film director Tarkovsky
35 Headdress
37 Antique car
38 *La* ___, where divas deliver
42 Poetic
46 Units of energy
48 "The Big Chill" actor Kevin ___
50 "___ With Judy," 1948 musicomedy
51 Kind of bag
52 Liberty and Rose
54 Nice summers?
55 African antelope
57 Unclad
59 Cellular stuff: Abbr.
60 Play the closing theme
63 Happen again
65 Peer Gynt's mother
66 Above it all
68 Flatfoot
70 Musical talent
73 Dallas native
75 Slide
76 Final rehearsal
78 Some are Dutch
80 Bon mot
84 State of agitation
85 Quoth the raven, "buttercup"?
87 Map abbr.
88 "___ *Kleine Nachtmusik*"
89 Debtor letters
90 Astringent stuff
91 Rep.'s epithet
92 Wolf's wink
93 A.B.A. member
94 Bugler's "good-night"
95 Compass dir.

Down

1 Necessity
2 Nick Charles's pet
3 Close by
4 Summer mo.
5 Kermit's swimming style?
6 Worship
7 Deer genus
8 Have ___!
9 Queue for Salomey or Arnold?
10 Cribbage scorekeeper
11 "Happy Birthday" writer, perhaps
12 Fable lesson
13 Swiftly
14 Fledgling homes
21 Flow's partner
24 Orch. section
26 ___ firma
28 "___, We Have No Bananas"
30 Starr of song
32 Mountain ridges
33 Perfume ingredient
34 ID for Sandy?
36 Lent a hand
39 Yugo.'s neighbor
40 Detroit footballer
41 Sadat
43 Forty winks for Felix?
44 Bilko command
45 The preferred evil
47 Small Persian rug of fine weave
49 Actress Sommer
53 Jiffy
56 Dullards
58 Pushover for Donald?
61 Goliath, to David
62 Dance for Reynard?
64 *Vive le* ___!
67 Like, wow, man!
69 ASAP
70 Ford flop
71 Golfer with a loyal army
72 Spouse of 64 Down
74 York or Mexico preceder
75 Old robe
77 Old or young follower
79 "'Twas ___ oyster. . ." (Pope)
81 Encourage
82 Put ___ my tab
83 ___ le Moko
85 Covert grp.
86 Logos: Abbr.

19

Choices *by Bill Leonard*

There were no good alternative titles for this one.

Across

1 Not open or ajar
5 Xenon or oxygen
8 Point or critique
12 Pkg. carrier or switch settings
15 Misplace or get beat
16 Pecan or enthusiast
17 Writer or ex-Met
18 Mesh or profit
19 Lost or cruising
20 Pother or bother
21 Pompous or high
22 Paid athlete or for
23 George or Ira
25 Rear or produce
27 Bonnet or bunny
29 Head, in France or Benin
30 Straight or curved lines or geometric patterns
33 Teddy and Alice, or Franklin and 44 Across
38 Sirius or Procyon
41 Lincoln or Burrows
42 Modifier for body or place
43 Merino or Cheviot mama
44 Powell or Parker
46 Barbara or Anthony
47 Before cheese or puff
48 Some African or Asian rulers
51 Rigel or headliner
54 Social facade or rector
56 Lamb's or ram's call
59 Soupy or revenues
61 Benz or hex finish
62 Chatters or gripes
64 Tarpans or mustangs
67 Whence much Greek art or literature came
68 Suds or TV sitcom
69 Nightclubs or dances like Travolta
72 Cronkite and Rather, or Huntley and Brinkley
75 Old maid or yarn maker
79 Verb or land measure
80 HST or DDE
82 Coarse fabric or pat
83 Spear tip or fish
84 Yellow ocher or Ag
85 Kiln for hops or malt
86 Hitherto or before
87 Sign or bad vibes
88 Goddess of the underworld or dead
89 Innkeeper, to Luigi or Mario
90 Buttons or crimson
91 Quiz or grill

Down

1 Kind of glass or sand
2 Stockings or fireman's gear
3 Addict or employer
4 Posers or imps
5 Harasses or chews
6 Review or strong brew
7 Pit remover or rock thrower
8 Wink or club
9 Culture medium or actor John
10 Tell or interact
11 Trust or think
12 With or without skin
13 Illinois or Indiana city
14 Street or light
24 Fedora seller or lone miner
26 Dock workers or Allen and Martin
28 Sheepskin or horse
30 Keats or Pindar work
31 Bam! or stalag resident
32 Bronze or Stone
34 Bassoon's or English horn's relatives
35 Discourse or homily
36 Three, in Milan or Rome
37 Fake or like: Abbr.
39 Pub order or English festival
40 Harvester or grim one
45 Ratifying or concluding words
47 Beliefs or sung confessions
49 Balin or Claire
50 Share or allot
51 Dir. from Dallas to San Antonio or Chicago to Memphis
52 Pacific porgy or Indo-China native
53 Watch's cry or part of a Shakespeare title
55 Donna or Rex
56 Franklin or Jonson
57 Onassis or "Exodus" hero
58 —— rule or Judah king
60 Hair cleaner or Beatty film
63 Sot or lush
65 Horse and soap, or "Tosca" and "Aida"
66 Nun or "toots"
70 Tire or bowling score
71 Quoted or ticketed
72 Ogden or old car
73 Canal or Lake
74 Home or kind of egg
76 Newsmagazine or noon
77 Gets by or supplements
78 Opening or payment
81 Jeanne or Cecilia: Abbr.

20

Do It My Way! *by Jeanette K. Brill*

Keep in step.

21

Across

1 Director of "It Happened One Night"
6 Poet Teasdale
10 James Bond foe
14 Stranger
15 Club where Miami's major PGA tournament is held
16 Up the —— without a paddle
17 Chastity's father
18 True
19 1952-3 TV adventure hero played by Jon Hall
20 What some wagerers raise
21 Sea duck
22 Where Greeks met
23 Conform
26 Yannick of tennis
27 Luges
30 African antelopes
34 Two below par
37 Greek letter
39 18th century Spanish missionary in California
40 "A —— of Honey"
41 Mine, in Metz
42 Conform
46 Forearm bone
47 Pat or Daniel
48 Related on the mother's side
49 Common Market initials
50 Houston athlete
51 Fervent
53 He wrote "The Cloister and the Hearth"
55 Over, in Oberammergau
56 Conform
63 Show scorn
66 Control tower devices
67 Gave the pink slip
69 Chief Anglo-Saxon god
70 Twenty: Comb. form
71 Former baseball star Tony
72 Gossip column twosomes
73 1988 Olympics host
74 Took charge
75 Cures leather
76 Chem. lab endings
77 Youngsters

Down

1 *Señorita*'s house
2 "Take Me ——"
3 Bean or pony
4 Vitalize again
5 Indefinite number
6 Clayey soil of poor productivity: Var.
7 Math.
8 Maharajah's lady
9 Like a good sentry
10 Small, round, silver cake decoration
11 San ——, Italy
12 At hand
13 Soup ingredient
15 Russian villas
16 Baby's bed
21 Old portico
24 Relative by marriage
25 The British ——
28 Humble
29 Ermines
30 Offspring
31 Whimpering one
32 "Purple Rain" star
33 Weapon for Juan
34 "Jack Sprat could —— fat . . ."
35 Wimbledon winner Arthur
36 NYSE giant
38 —— Semple McPherson
40 Norse god of war
41 English composer (1710-1778)
43 Author of "Hedda Gabler"
44 Wee one
45 Tropical fish
50 Decks out
51 European peninsula
52 Word with print or paper
54 Revokes
55 Decrees
57 Three-wheeler
58 Georgia city
59 Worship
60 Asset
61 Banish
62 Number of Rome's hills
63 Actress Loretta
64 —— care in the world
65 First garden spot
68 Fathers
71 Table scrap

Clues In Reverse *by Bill Leonard*

Some of these definitions are more commonly seen as answers.

Across

1 Six ____ a-laying
6 Bench warmer
9 Arroyo
15 "Star Wars" weapons
17 Pitcher's stat.
18 Reckons
19 Alum
21 Past, present, and future
22 Gore
23 Particle
24 Interjections of reproof
26 Gelderland commune
27 Place
28 GI's overseas address
29 Recent: Comb. form
30 NFL scores
31 Pause
33 Comedian Wil
35 Cossets
38 Tearful
42 Father, to *fils*
45 Of flight, in combinations
46 Stabilize
47 Guinness
48 New Jersey city
51 James Bond's school
52 Candidate lists
54 Argyll island
55 On-the-hour summary
56 Domesticates
57 Rasps
59 In a royal way
62 Not so much
65 Distance measures: Abbr.
67 Former Korean president
68 Inquire
70 Gumshoe
72 Louis XIV, *par exemple*
73 Actor James of "The Godfather"
74 Not well

75 Peter, Paul, and Mary, for example
76 Ark's Mount
78 Yaws
81 End
82 Landing-time guess, for short
83 Vend
84 Peter and Paul
85 Strong drink, in Puerto Rico
86 Fine-grained silt

Down

1 Lens
2 Egg-hunt time
3 Manor
4 Yugoslav
5 Assam silkworm
6 Observed
7 Coffee container
8 Rams
9 Putrid
10 "Planet of the ____"
11 Bordeaux, in Bordeaux
12 Map detail
13 Requires
14 To be (Lat.)
16 Cut
20 Sentimentality
25 Prefix with form or verse
28 One ____ time
29 Narrative
30 Sham
32 Shades
33 Withered
34 Maa-maa mama
36 Gym pads
37 Via
39 Diminutive suffix
40 Farm implement
41 Itches
42 Bygone
43 Miss Phant, Soupy Sales's unseen girlfriend
44 Paper quantity

46 Cinch
49 Conservative, British style
50 "____ Bicycle Built for Two"
53 Naut. dir.
57 Lean
58 Wapiti
60 Rasps
61 Gotcha!
63 Oarsman's action
64 Fishing nets
65 Divided nation
66 Florida city
68 Mr. Baba
69 It can be grand or small in bridge
71 Purchase prices
72 AM-FM units
73 Dramatis personae
74 Lendl
75 Novice: Var.
77 ____ Tin Tin
79 Ike's command
80 1960-61 chess champion

22

Originally published in 1987

Different Strokes *by Thomas W. Schier*

A unique blend of the usual and the unusual.

Across

1 Deceives
6 Fortune-telling card
11 Fraudulent operations
16 City on Ishikari Bay, Japan
17 Love, in Lyons
18 Of a classical order of architecture
19 Difference
21 Me, too!
22 Actress Sue ___ Langdon
23 Surprised exclamation
24 More isolated
26 Show a good time
28 1982 growing-up film
29 Mao ___-tung
30 "Boys Town" star
31 Actor Richard ___ of TV's "Redigo"
33 One of the "Little Women"
35 Some hockey outcomes
38 The Boston Garden, for one
41 Alphonse-Gaston phrase, French style
44 Expedient
46 Want
47 Eliminate a squeak
48 Go one better
49 "___ Misbehavin'"
50 Operational cessations
52 Differences
54 President of Turkey, 1938-50
55 "___ Shout" (1962 Isley Brothers song)
57 Ban: Var.
59 Interrogates
60 Coffee break hr.
64 Get a lode of this!
66 Lightheartedness, songfully
68 Fender material, once
69 Cole's girl of song
71 Et ___; and others
73 Corp. execs.
74 Fred's sister
75 Differences
78 Bowler's button
79 Gourmand
80 Monetary gain
81 Jaunty
82 Small crown
83 Trusted horse

Down

1 Track vehicle
2 Confessional visitor
3 Mexican unit of land measure
4 Transp. chge.
5 It ___! (undoubtedly!)
6 Fictional plantation
7 In the course of
8 Shad product
9 Silhouette
10 Use experimentally
11 Expressed in relation to constellations
12 Rattlesnake's pose
13 Holding different views
14 Small insects
15 Twenty
20 Ripen
25 Bird's bill
27 ___ strange way; behaved oddly
28 Irrigation projects
31 Conceited person
32 Frenchman
34 Three-stamened plant
36 Cry at Pan's parties
37 Newscast segment
39 "___ to Five" (Parton song)
40 Stamp and Homestead
41 "___ Love Her" (Beatles' hit)
42 Hammer part
43 Indifference, perhaps
45 Vision: Comb. form
48 Type of force
51 Difference
52 Traveler's need, on occasion
53 Where some social insects live
56 Arizona Indian
58 Swiss canton south of the Lake of Lucerne
61 Greenhorn
62 Electrical unit
63 ___ up; botched
64 Sharif and Bradley
65 ___ horse; practiced dressage
67 It's on the plus side of the ledger
68 Org. of moles and covert operations
70 Pub brews
71 Tennis player with an unreturnable serve
72 Money for Craxi
76 Transp. abbr.
77 Nonsense!

23

Critters Everywhere! *by Peter Swift*

These four are troublemakers.

24

Across

1 Takes on
7 Appraise
12 Amusingly outlandish
16 "—— the Jabberwock" (Carroll)
17 Doughy pastry
18 Woodwind
19 Imperfection
22 There are two in Mecca
23 Hires
24 Subside
25 ". . .for dust thou ——. . ." (Gen. 3:19)
26 Discontinue
28 Muck
29 Indonesian island
30 Food fowl
32 Selfish person
38 Astaire and namesakes
39 Goods for sale
40 Aphorism
42 Narrow street
43 European finch
44 Bandleader Shaw
46 Little island
47 Fine-grained clay
48 Quaker
49 Loony
53 Pile up
54 Suits to ——
55 More tractable
57 Clio and her sisters
59 Feminine ending
62 Kind of point
63 Cheese or chard
65 Chief of the Near Islands
66 Potential disaster
70 Leader, in France
71 Mother-of-pearl
72 Musical interval
73 Thirst quenchers
74 Animal's track
75 Sniveling one

Down

1 Fiber called Manila hemp
2 Submit
3 Young bird
4 Is profitable
5 Three: Pref.
6 Japanese coin
7 Ruins
8 Locale
9 Sweep's concern
10 Tropical blackbirds
11 Longing
12 Carding wool
13 Nautical direction
14 —— Carlo
15 The "Our Gang" dog
20 "The Orient Express," for one
21 Claw
26 Shrewd
27 Belonging to actor Wallach
28 Certain baths
29 Tree trunk
30 Moderate red
31 Word of approval
32 Extemporize
33 Gamma chaser
34 Aviary sounds
35 Grating
36 Organic compound
37 Wet
38 Drivers' org.
41 Join together
43 Start of a D.H. Lawrence title
44 City on the Rhône
45 Abounding
47 Ananias
48 Gala
50 Mexican dishes
51 —— a rat
52 Some opera voices
55 "And so ——." (Samuel Pepys's diary)
56 Kind of accent
57 Prefix with film or wave
58 Escort
59 Patriot Allen
60 Range
61 Apt. mgr., to tenants
62 —— morgana
63 Cinch
64 Baylor University's site
65 Italian wine region
67 Officeholders
68 Pronto!
69 Kiel cry

Jewel Collection *by Manny Miller*

Another gem from Mr. Miller.

25

Across

1 Iridescent gem
5 British good-byes
10 Principal parts
15 Ms. Bryant
16 Decree
17 Actress Dickinson
18 Dressed to the ——
19 Mother: Pref.
20 Oyster's contribution to this puzzle
21 Small one
22 Corundum varieties
25 Means of comm.
26 Tooth covering
28 Scatter, as grass
29 Actress Jean ——, who married Howard Hughes
31 Folding money
33 Home of the sol
34 Kind of flight
37 Chrysoberyl or chalcedony
41 Outer garment
45 Doing an imitation of
47 Unit of heat
48 Of same qty.
49 Hard to get to
50 Geological time
51 Charlotte ——
52 Rugged ridge
53 Critical
55 Revolving part
56 Starchy root
57 Hope, for one
59 "—— It Romantic?"
60 Musky-odor perfume of ancient times
62 Tops
64 Movies
67 Org.
70 Sewing box item
74 Chihuahua cheer
75 Crystallized quartz stones
78 Crewman's need
79 Quartz variety
81 Slants
82 Fails to use
84 Maternal kinsman
85 Excellence
86 Real estate notice
87 Kind of bar
88 Eyeglasses
89 Semiprecious layered stone

Down

1 Edible bulb
2 One of Columbus's ships
3 Broke bread
4 California peak
5 Supplemental worker
6 Conform
7 Tax of a sort
8 Caustic
9 Agitate
10 One who forfeits
11 Chem. suffix
12 Fine-grained chalcedony
13 More grim
14 Retails
15 Cost
23 Sir —— Guinness
24 Fencing weapon
27 Translucent feldspar
30 Sky-blue gemstone
32 Brooded, as a hen
33 English Parliamentary statesman (1584-1643)
34 Nasser's successor
35 "The Magic Flute," for example
36 Solid hit, in baseball
38 Zoological case or sheath
39 Body fluid
40 One of the Muses
42 Expels
43 Buffalo player
44 Turn outward
46 Opposite of haw
48 Blunder
53 Assistance
54 Incr.
57 Small amount
58 Force
61 Surprised
63 16th century Spanish explorer
64 Sheep shelters
65 Actress Massey
66 Home of the highest mountain
67 Precipitous
68 Chicago airport
69 Skeptic
71 Lacy napkin
72 Milky plant fluid
73 Before the present time, formerly
76 Shade trees
77 Transatl. jets
80 One —— time
83 Cal. column

Wearabouts *by Norma Steinberg*

There are no duds from Ms. Steinberg, even though these entries may not be cloaked in secrecy.

26

Across

1 Con game
5 Drop in
10 Egyptian viper
13 Swiped
14 Rich Little's homeland
15 Lumber
17 Choir part
18 Gilbert and Sullivan opus
20 Throw a tantrum
21 Moves easily
22 Infantrymen
23 Tina Turner's ex
24 The 24 in 36-24-36
25 Ledge
26 Fortune-teller
28 "Oh, ___ in England. . ." (Browning)
29 Polly on "Alice"
32 Grandiloquize
33 People
34 Uproar
35 Walk like a drum major
37 Chiropractor's concern
38 Dry
39 Sugar shapes
40 Playing the ___
41 Make butter
42 Cain's victim
43 Gold touch king
44 River Styx region
45 Brooks or Gibson
46 Less covered
47 Lamb Chop's Lewis
49 Cal. clock setting
50 Commits perjury
51 Spotted cat
54 Zephyr
55 Consumers
57 Recent: Pref.
58 Maroon
61 Go in
62 Cook's measures: Abbr.
63 Cogitation headgear
65 Donnybrook
66 Transported
67 Brownies who "fly up"
68 Works on a leaky boat
69 Brit. sports cars
70 Gives a party
71 Elec. units

Down

1 T-bones and sirloins
2 Assembly line mover
3 Skin cream ingredient
4 *Mal de* ___
5 Sirens
6 Map detail
7 Fall guys
8 Infamous Amin
9 Real
10 Horrible
11 In a second
12 After-dinner wine
13 Denude
14 "Sophie's ___"
16 ___ Moines
19 French city
21 *Café* whitener
24 "___ up, Doc?"
25 Sensible
27 Inhumane
28 Labors
29 Verbal faux pas of a sort
30 "The Mask of Dimitrios" lead
31 Runner Jesse
33 Asparagus piece
35 Rascal
36 London subways
37 Walls
38 Opposite of flat
40 Canned
41 Total unpredictability
43 Entree
46 Double wink
47 Catches some z's
48 Mister, in Munich
52 Wards off
53 Medicinal measures
54 Hankers
55 In its full form, as a movie
56 Figures, for short
58 They often cross aves.
59 Those folks
60 Call up
61 "Me-generation" concerns
62 Sports group
64 MSgt., for one
65 Yuppie's deg.

Orderly Starts   by Richard Silvestri

The four long entries are orthographically interesting.

27

Across

1 Salary
6 One of Whitman's bloomers
11 Blueprints
16 Radio/early-TV sitcom "___ With Judy"
17 Empty
18 Lured
19 Obsequious
21 Old violin
22 Folklore figure
23 Summer snake?
24 OCS grads
26 Actor Beatty
27 Low-pitched
29 Transmits
31 Idle
33 Capsize
35 ___ hand; abjectly
37 Guard details
40 Airborne crime
44 Future oaks
45 Of an hour
46 Part of a franc
47 Horse follower
48 Shipworm
49 Distribute
51 Bi- plus one
52 North and South
53 Lawyer's patron
54 CGS unit
57 Sea air?
58 Amalgamate
59 Take as a tenant
60 Rustler's target
63 Go-devils
65 Yep canceler
69 "___ Buttermilk Sky" (Carmichael-Brooks song)
70 CIA forerunner
72 Wax grandiloquent
74 Taxco two
75 San Antonio shrine
77 Undersized condition
80 Mislays
81 Home on the range
82 Golden egg producer
83 Garbo, for one
84 Wooden Mortimer
85 Coastal raptors

Down

1 Walked through water
2 An Astaire
3 Blunder
4 When Nancy gets hot
5 Immunity fluids
6 Basswood trees
7 Mean
8 Scottish landowner
9 Literary snippets
10 Clone unit
11 Formative
12 Moon vehicle, for short
13 Hersey's bell town
14 Makes special mention of
15 Nasty
20 Late '50s flops
25 Bottom-line figure
28 Siamese sounds?
30 English counties
32 What a squid squirts
34 Cake from corn
36 Not quite shut
37 Trattoria staple
38 Sour-tasting
39 Pick-me-up
40 Biblical mount
41 Key
42 Daytime TV Emmy winner Kathleen
43 Full of pluck
45 Role for Rathbone
48 Italy's shape
49 Verbalized sigh
50 Sheets, pillowcases, and so on
52 Layers
53 Virtuous
55 Three strikes
56 Set free
57 Tranquilized
59 "My Fair Lady" lyricist
60 Newcastle superfluities
61 Give permission
62 Tantalize
64 Jeweler's magnifying glass
66 Greek theater
67 Sheriff's men
68 Mississippi quartet
71 Transatl. flyers
73 Move little by little
76 Smaller than lge.
78 Time for a scholar?
79 Negative conjunction

This Old Rag? *by Lois Sidway*

Step lively!

28

Across

1 Unheeding
5 In the midst of
10 Coarse and vulgar
16 Like an unusual avis?
17 Wild
18 Soft palate parts
19 He wrote "Charleston Rag"
21 He wrote "He's a Ragpicker"
22 Decorate
23 Chicago's Mrs. O'____
25 Tattered's partner
26 *Mal de* ____
27 Pat
30 Brit. combat medal
31 Disorderly
32 Lothario
34 Tear jerker
36 Ragtime's close relative
39 Zola novel
40 Aves.
43 Composer of "Rule Britannia"
44 Artist's medium
46 Embroidery yarn
48 Restaurant worker
49 "____ Street Rag"
52 Raja's missus
53 American League manager of the 1980s
55 Gaming cube
56 Egyptian deity
57 Printer's measures
58 German song
61 Film popularizing "The Entertainer" rag
64 She was all tears
65 Skirmish
66 Hot beverage
69 Harvest goddess
71 Specs support
72 To the ____ degree
75 Mideasterner
76 Make ____ of; jot down
78 Ciao's Pacific cousin
80 "Maple Leaf Rag" composer
82 Like all ragtime music
85 Turmoil
86 Singer John
87 "Leave ____ Beaver"
88 All sorts of racket
89 San ____ Padres
90 Horse color

Down

1 King had one
2 ____ cologne
3 Bower
4 Rather pretty
5 B-52's home: Abbr.
6 Brooks or Tillis
7 Spoken
8 Like a jaybird?
9 Star of "The Hustler"
10 Precious stone
11 "____ Got a Secret"
12 A Taylor ex
13 Permit
14 Scottish landowner
15 Bulldog Drummond's butler
20 Bequeath
24 Columnist Barrett
28 "I ____ Camera"
29 Not up to
31 Sound from Simba
32 Smells something frightful
33 Muskogee native
35 Move by degrees
36 Hidden loot
37 "____ Without Windows"
38 Has learned
40 Pundit
41 It needs a mortise
42 Throw
45 Atty.'s degree
47 Calliope's sister
49 Piano, bass, drums
50 Tiny tantrums
51 Giggle
54 Director Kazan
59 Black, in poetry
60 Ousted from power
62 Greek vowel
63 Band
64 Titled ones
66 Southern cooking style
67 Maine campus site
68 "Isle of ____"
70 Phonograph needles
72 ____ worry!
73 Greek letter
74 Wore
76 Picnic pests
77 Being (Sp.)
79 Bear's bedroom
81 British verb ending
83 Gear tooth
84 Yoko ____

Open Season *by William Canine*

. . .on a wide range of subjects.

29

Across

1 USPS letters
4 British title
8 Catchers' gear
13 ". . .after they've seen ____."
15 Belonging to actress Rowlands
16 Neutral, in a way
17 Notions
18 Occasion
19 Former GPU chief: Var.
20 "The Vision of ____," long Middle English poem
23 Sort of photo
24 "Hannah and Her ____"
25 Turmoil
26 Halfback's gear
27 Cry of disappointment
28 Sanction
31 They try harder, so their ads said
33 Semisoft cheese
34 Tilled the fields
38 ____ de mer
39 Rapscallion
41 Inimical
42 Commit a foul, in hockey
43 Horn aplenty!
44 Dutch master
45 Leo "the ____" Durocher
46 Brooder
48 Hard to please
49 Book of folded pages: Abbr.
50 Spring observance
51 Demur
52 This stuff is for the birds
53 Unbending
55 Le Moko or Le Pew
57 Walk sidewise
60 "Ask ____ what your country. . ."
61 Cardinal's topper
64 Anteroom
65 Ruth stood amid this, according to Keats
68 Soul singer Shirley
70 Circuit
71 Decorous
72 Direction
73 Foots it
74 Irritable
75 "The Playboy of the Western World" dramatist
76 Joint
77 Mail carrier's abbr.

Down

1 Rays
2 Members of a mid-1800s political party
3 Famines
4 "Whip It" rock group
5 Over again
6 Not natural
7 A Mexican state
8 Marble
9 Amateurish
10 ____ firma
11 Musical chord
12 Supports
13 Gladys Knight's backers
14 Site of the Krupp works
15 Sets
21 Major leaguer
22 Great coal port
28 Columnist Bombeck
29 Pinch
30 Fresh
31 Chemical compound
32 Empty spaces
33 Papoose
35 "The Timid Soul"
36 In the inner circle
37 Terminus
39 Bucephalus, for one
40 Cassis ingredient
41 Potboiler's author
44 Sword's haft
47 Horse's accommodation
48 Criticize severely
51 Justine of "Family Ties"
52 Ghost
54 Five Nations member
55 Shoofly, for example
56 Film director Lubitsch
57 The mating game
58 Ninth inning effort
59 Edgar ____ Poe
61 Little pieces
62 Overworked
63 Golfer Bean
66 Dextrous
67 The same as
69 Jeanne or Marie: Abbr.

Arbor Special   *by Manny Miller*

More than a dozen examples for your stroll in the forest.

30

Across

1 Willow family member
7 Donkey's cry
11 "Animal House" college
16 Idle
17 Part
18 Statesman Stevenson
19 Trees used for cabinetwork and ornamental carving
21 Novelist Hobson
22 Exact
23 Time —— half
24 Trees with trembling leaves
25 Dine
26 Grape residue made into brandy
28 Worries
29 Showy, early spring trees
32 Paid beforehand: Abbr.
35 Mysterious
38 —— voce
39 Heraldic band
40 Gazed dreamily
41 City in France
42 Destroyed building
43 Green shots
44 Anka and Lynde
46 Tropical "chocolate tree"
47 Blues singer James
48 Word often confused with fewer
49 Catch, as in a clock
50 Old autos
51 "—— is not builded in a day. . ." (Lindsay)
53 "—— Fideles"
54 Ending for east, west, north, or south
55 Tree with aromatic bark
57 Alcott's "Little ——"
60 Large metal vat
61 Deserter
64 Iced drink
66 Praise
68 Republican of note
69 Teenage toughs
70 Sycamores
73 Where 19 Across may be found
74 Signs up for mil. service
75 Aggressive insect
76 Patients
77 Member of the lily family
78 Also-rans

Down

1 Appointments
2 Hokkaido port city
3 Popular barracks picture
4 Metallic deposit
5 Quiet —— mouse
6 Cath. or Prot.
7 Denver's NFL team
8 Crucifix
9 Actor Alan
10 Affirmative word
11 Erroneous
12 Make suitable
13 State trees of Colorado
14 Deserve
15 Inlets
20 Alert
24 Felony involving fire
26 Horses' heavy hair
27 Up in years
28 Goddesses of destiny
29 Huge rays
30 Trees with white flowers and hard wood
31 Florence's lang.
33 Supple
34 Indicate
35 Electrical unit
36 Furrowing tool
37 Rapidly growing trees with luxuriant foliage
39 Declaims
44 Nut tree
45 In its present condition
46 Tree of Lebanon
48 Kind of beam
49 Be bold enough
52 USSR's second-largest administrative unit
56 Generic dog's name
58 Hit song of long ago
59 Western highlands
61 Television's Arledge
62 Birch-family tree
63 Examines
64 Smart
65 Mrs. Chaplin
66 "Clair de ——"
67 Salt tree
68 Diana of films
70 Barbara —— Geddes
71 Where Bruins meet Nordiques: Abbr.
72 Try to win, in a way

Letter Bank *by Kathryn Righter*

No special theme. . .just 96 questions and answers.

31

Across

1 Spate
6 Spouse
10 TV service
15 Sri ____ (Ceylon)
16 City on the Po
17 Allium family member
18 Awed, and then some
20 Book of maps
21 Eden
22 Flower part
24 Allow
25 Carnation color
26 Delta material
29 Walked barefoot
33 Formal farewell
34 Recent: Pref.
35 Medicinal plants
36 Poker pile
37 Walk unsteadily
40 Vessel similar to a ketch
41 Ditto
42 Stylish
43 Infinitesimal
47 Dairy product
49 Bok ____
50 Zola novel
53 "____ the Wind"
55 Little devil
56 Author of "Wild Animals I Have Known"
57 Dined
58 Sign of the zodiac
60 Aquatic mammals

61 London district
63 Large casks
64 Timetable abbr.
65 Go up
67 Swimmer's hazard
72 Terra-____
74 Practical and realistic
76 Intertwined
77 Burdens
78 Commonplace
79 Fundamental character
80 Therefore
81 Indian infantryman in the British army

Down

1 Dud; fizzle
2 It's making Hawaii larger
3 Unique person or thing
4 Gumbo ingredient

5 Loiters; dallies
6 Symbol of stubbornness
7 Limb
8 Item of jewelry for a man
9 Concluding passages
10 Garment
11 Those opposed
12 Abusive language
13 Hawaii's Mauna ____
14 Nav. officer
16 Challenge
19 Ran off quickly
23 Superficial
25 Strengths
27 Dregs
28 Colonial loyalist
29 Settle a debt
30 ____ mode
31 Toper's toast
32 Expunge
33 Lake of northern Italy
36 Like some poker

hands
38 Fatima's husband
39 A booby is one
41 Mark with furrows
44 Dry: Pref.
45 Electrical units
46 Go one better
47 Oblique; diagonal
48 Preposition
51 Conjunction
52 Reply to a ques.
54 Move on wheels
56 Thoroughfares
59 Not alfresco
60 Church calendar
62 Bone: Comb. form
64 Hill dwellers
66 Bounders
67 Open a package
68 Uncommon
69 Junket
70 Director Preminger
71 Milk serum
72 Small: Suff.
73 Cereal grain
75 Comic

Pure Poetry *by Arthur W. Palmer*

No trouble. On the double. Hurry, hurry, mustn't worry.

32

Across

1 Billiards shot
6 Put in a lawn
12 Moby Dick's pursuer
16 Revere
17 In cahoots
18 European sheep dog
19 Heavy coach
21 Eye amorously
22 Item for Nicklaus
23 Plow sole
24 Thief of birds' unhatched offspring
25 Vitality
28 Prophets
29 Barley bristle
32 In the center of
33 Landlord's income source
35 Of an earthquake
37 Quiet's companion
38 Heap of hay
41 Type of grass or fox
42 Zaragoza's river
43 California's —— Woods National Monument
44 Fashionable resort on Lake Geneva
45 Bogs down
47 "Taps" instrument
48 ". . .not one —— for tribute."
49 Dining utensil
50 Tall drums
51 ". . .that —— men's souls." (Paine)
52 There'll be Hell ——!
53 Striking; essential
54 Made thick soup
56 Transport
57 Rtes.
58 Fashion design
60 Upstanding

62 Settle a bill
63 Like Leo's domain, perhaps
65 I, to Nero
68 *Café au* ——
69 Driving mishap
73 Best, for one
74 Greek goddess
75 Paris's river
76 Votes from the antis
77 River formations
78 Carrying bags

Down

1 Haul
2 Together
3 The Eternal City
4 Symbol of authority
5 Tillis and Tormé
6 Devilish
7 Avoided
8 Fudd of the comics
9 Knucklebone, in the game of jacks

10 Slithery one
11 ETO commander
12 Apex
13 Secrecy; confusion
14 To go, in Gascony
15 Coffin stands
20 Oleoresins
24 Villa d'——
26 Relative of a loon
27 Months and months
29 Appearance
30 Loom user
31 Affectedly refined
32 To ——; unanimously
34 Sgt., for example
36 Tiff
37 Chipper
39 —— vinegar dressing
40 Distorts
43 Actor who won an Oscar as Louis Pasteur
45 Light vehicle
46 Turkish decree

47 Daring
49 Opponent
50 Relating to Cambridge University
52 Waste allowance
53 Mexican matrons
55 Hall-of-Fame quarterback
56 Samantha's look-alike cousin on "Bewitched"
58 Composer Harold
59 You can —— horse. . .
61 West Point student
64 Take a break
65 Prepare for publication
66 Heredity factor
67 Pay dirts
69 Hula-Hoop or copper bracelets
70 Summer, in Paris
71 Islanders' org.
72 Recent: Pref.

Prison Terms *by Cathy Millhauser*

You should have no trouble filling every cell of this block.

33

Across

1 Dark, lush fur
6 McIntosh center
10 Attempts
15 Standard
16 Done in, as a dragon
17 Fragrant flower
18 Hop of the 1930s
19 19th century French landscape painter
20 Liqueur flavoring
21 Was chief
22 Facility
23 Emulated Sebastian Coe
25 One, in Worms
26 Words hang-up?
31 Pick and battle
32 Dogma
33 "____, *Brute!*"
35 Vitamin bottle initials
37 Saws
41 Entangle
42 Like soap operas
44 Afore
45 Abuse of a typewriter shift key?
49 Put away, in a way
50 More gruesome
51 A camel would walk miles for these
52 Car dealer's turnover
55 Uneven
56 They're next to none
57 Jargon
59 Similar
61 Punctuation on trial?

69 Modern art?
70 Arrest
71 Quantity of quires
72 Double-helix letters
73 Balance
75 Fair-haired
77 Elliptic
79 Ferber and namesakes
80 All the manor lord surveys
81 Grimace of pain
82 Puccini pauses
83 Roe upon roe
84 Microsurgery aid

Down

1 Flowerpot holders
2 Amie's farewell
3 Yields
4 Stripling
5 Isle of ____, Cambridgeshire
6 Neck and neck

7 Had a row?
8 It's Grande
9 Menu word
10 Biased
11 Pewter component
12 E.T. was one
13 Computer language
14 A part of the act
16 Tons
22 Ethyl's end
24 Historical records
27 "*In nomine* ____ *et filio.* . ."
28 Rejoice
29 Class of glass
30 Zeta-theta link
33 Female relative
34 Records
35 Censure
36 Ancient Celtic priest
38 Honkers
39 Osprey's cousins
40 Makes waves?
41 Cicatrix
42 "Gimme a brake,"

on a road sign
43 Ditty
46 Meeting points
47 Water pipe: Var.
48 Impressionist Edouard
53 Ms. MacGraw
54 Elsa of "Born Free"
58 Talk turkey
59 Fills with film
60 Unisys competitor
61 Term after term
62 Wear down
63 Shoemaker's controls
64 Plug part
65 Tears apart
66 Press agents?
67 Chilling words
68 Noted consumer advocate
74 Became a chairperson?
76 Fall back
77 Who says hoo
78 By way of

Shade Plants *by Martha J. De Witt*

Ms. De Witt has chosen a cool, muted palette for this canvas.

34

Across

1 Moon's age in days at new year, for determining Easter's date
6 Condition of sale
10 Roof of the mouth
16 Skull seam
17 Kansas county
18 Reworded
19 Eva Gabor's sitcom
21 Like some small tables
22 Thoroughfare
23 Somber mood
25 Narrow passage
27 Treats for Trigger
28 Saga
31 One ___ million
32 Like Tonto's friend
33 Normal
36 Devoured
37 Litigate
38 Air
39 Mock
40 Paddy wagon
43 Shade
45 Hawaiian verandah
46 Gay
48 Common refrain
49 Jean Giraudoux play
51 Intellect
53 Bolivian Indian tribe
54 Vientiane's country
56 ___ Alamos, New Mexico
57 Terminus
58 ___ es Salaam
59 Monsieur, in Munich
60 Actress Arthur
61 Mid-March, in old Rome
62 Yawn
63 Go to bed
65 Sulphur-bottoms
69 Box in
73 Archimedes' shout
74 Caution signal
76 Originated
77 X may mark it
78 ". . .lovely as ___." (Kilmer)
79 Abandon
80 Oriental sauce
81 Calendar cycles

Down

1 Units of energy
2 Role
3 Mimic
4 Photographer's "smile now" word
5 Precept
6 Rainbow
7 Belgrade's republic
8 Not participating
9 Indifferent
10 Ball-park souvenirs
11 "___ Fideles"
12 Shopper's reminders
13 Westernmost Aleutian Island
14 ___ off; irate
15 Whirlpool
20 Inner court
24 Pull it over one's eyes
26 Close by, to Wordsworth
28 Scandal sheet
29 Emory University's city
30 Hero's lover
32 Climbing vine
33 Stole
34 City 145 miles WSW of Fort Worth
35 Delays progress
37 Hide
38 Members of a certain club
39 Encircled
41 Seth's sib
42 Severity
44 School orgs.
47 Tenth President
50 Kind of seal
52 Pained one, from the sound of it
55 Neighborhood
59 Pushcart pusher
60 Waiter's waiter
61 Provoke
62 Ninnies
63 Andante or allegro
64 Decorative adornment
65 Necklace unit
66 Bait
67 Author Leon ___
68 Colleen
70 Taj Mahal site
71 Persian tiger
72 Summers, on the Riviera
75 Sched. abbr.

Reasoned Rhymes   *by Elizabeth T. Holcomb*

This time clues rhyme.

35

Across

1 Neighbor of Oreg.
6 Plant-disease spot
10 Drench
15 African bearded sheep
17 Drink excessively
18 Force out
19 Foot comforter
20 April 13, to Caesar
21 Organization legislation
22 Clear, as profit
23 French city
25 ——-de-vie
27 Of each, to a druggist
28 Mortality normality
31 Laser, for example
34 Hessian expression
35 WWII monogram
36 Supreme, for one
37 Excommunication proclamation
41 Star or spice preceder
42 More sensible
44 Full of fissures
48 Turf grippers
50 Buddhist sect
52 Gaelic hero
53 Seize for ransom
54 Norse goddesses of fate
56 On-——; gossip
57 Phone zone
60 Moslem decree
62 Taro dish
64 Returned Letter Office: Abbr.
65 Ring-shaped
67 Gentility responsibility
71 Beer's cousin
72 Feline sign

73 Desert transport
74 Keats form
77 Type of hepatitis
79 Complete defeat
81 Kind of acid
83 Reconcile
84 Structurally related: Comb. form
85 Puzzler
86 Head Red, 1917-24
87 Lamp gas
88 —— up; excited

Down

1 Original criminal
2 First-rate
3 Zest
4 Wedding days phrase
5 Momentary luminary
6 Fence steps
7 Manuscript volume
8 O'Neill's hairy one

9 Implore
10 Gentry entry
11 Moron preceder
12 Higher region
13 Apparition exhibition
14 NFL quarterback John
16 Idolize
24 Lake Geneva, to Pierre
26 River in Hades
28 Actor Chaney
29 One way to stand
30 Revolutionary Sam
31 Taken ——; surprised
32 Stringed instruments
33 Irritated; agitated
38 —— Percé
39 "There —— atheists in the foxholes." (Cummings)
40 Evolutionary intermediary
43 Defame

45 Looking like, in combinations
46 Lebanese seaport
47 Use the door
49 "For want of ——. . ." (Herbert)
51 Wooden-shoe sailor
55 Kingdom
58 Election loser
59 Runner Sebastian
61 Regret
62 Refined
63 Titania's spouse
66 Nephew's sister
67 Of the fleet
68 Actress Burstyn
69 Eye: Comb. form
70 Relay-race rod
74 Extreme indulgence
75 Kind of novel
76 Organism modified by environment
78 American cuckoo
80 "Aye!" cry
82 Word with beam or line

Literally So by Norma Steinberg

Clowning around with the clues.

36

Across

1 Angler's gear
6 Loon family member
11 Milk, in Mexico
16 Separate
17 Adam's rib, so the story goes
18 Somehow or ___
19 TEN FOUR
22 Health resort
23 Scout's shelter
24 Symmetry
25 Sing, in a way
26 Chat
28 Cpl. or Sgt.
31 Michael Caine role
34 Actor Elliott
36 Contemporary of Jung
38 Weaver's machine
39 Puppeteer Lewis
40 Outran
41 Mr. Grant
42 Embryonic oak
43 Like ___ of bricks
44 SEE CHE
49 Breathe heavily
50 "___ at Sea"
51 It's hell, said Sherman
53 Strip
56 ___ Pyle
57 Ventilated
58 ___ we devils?
59 Sudden blows
60 Slant
61 ___ none
62 Dog without papers
63 LLD holder
64 Book of maps
67 Fair
69 Inspired poetry
72 AN ANT MATH
77 South American mountain chain
78 Inventor Howe
79 Celebrity's bit part
80 He followed Washington
81 Kind of rocket
82 Pitchers

Down

1 Thailand's neighbor
2 ___ and away!
3 Pro ___
4 Goof
5 "The Kiss," for one
6 Ms. Verdon
7 Cheer for
8 Large, flightless bird
9 College degs.
10 Hug
11 "Hawaii Five-O" star
12 Diminutive ending
13 Agitated
14 Layer in a coop
15 Before
20 Precious stone
21 Mork's home planet
25 That guy
26 TO U
27 Ms. MacGraw
29 Fast Eddie's stick
30 Unusual
31 Winner's take
32 Chicago area
33 Quartet
34 ___ of a chance
35 Paddles
36 Floating ice masses
37 Old mysterious letter
39 Aroma
40 Anesthetic
42 ___ of thousands
43 Pinnacles
45 Unwrap
46 Not quite dry
47 Gulp
48 ___ of Sandwich
52 Deli choice
53 Small amount
54 Lyricist Gershwin
55 Open porch
56 Understood, finally!
57 Hill dweller
59 George Armstrong ___
60 Now!
62 Rug
63 Words in a simile
65 Those folks
66 Highland honey
67 Play the lead
68 "Ish"
69 For the life ___!
70 Antlered animal
71 Aphrodite's son
72 Sheepcote sound
73 Connecting word
74 Beer's relative
75 Secondary coll. basketball season finale
76 Caught sight of

TV Guise by M.R.

Look for these on your fall schedule. Or maybe not.

Across

1 Pack away
5 Steep slope
11 Hard to find
17 Fabric feature
18 Artful dodger
19 Horse operas
20 Fallout measures: Abbr.
21 Soap opera for Carson and Rooney?
23 Wrath
24 Charged
25 Wildebeests
26 Lamb's ma'am
27 Chatterboxes
29 "Your ___ Too Big"
31 Normandy town
32 Musical sound
33 Old Greek woodland deities
35 Covered market, in France
36 Explorer Sebastian
38 Pinocchio's sitcom?
40 At ___ for words
41 Greases the car
42 On the lanky side
44 Cheer
45 More like Stephanie of "Newhart"
46 The height of hot air
49 Korean GI
50 Cloyed
51 Descartes and Coty
52 Paddle
54 Hackney coaches
56 Neuters
57 ___ Domini
58 Workers' equity benefit: Abbr.
59 "Pomp and Circumstance" composer
60 Duncan Renaldo, "The ___ Kid"
61 Detective show for Beetle Bailey?
64 Zodiac sign
65 Plains animal
68 Records
69 Bottom of the barrel
70 Premed course
71 "The Man in the Gray Flannel Suit" author Wilson
72 Just
75 Librarian's warning
76 Regimen
77 Mournful jazz
79 Cravat
80 Sitcom for Don Rickles?
84 Simple Simon's want
85 Off-target
86 May and Stritch
87 "Picnic" author
88 Commences
89 Like a raccoon's tail
90 Matures

Down

1 Shoot
2 Small crown
3 Cop show for Jimmy the Greek?
4 Guitarist Montgomery
5 Cowgirl Dale
6 Protein bean
7 Old burial chamber
8 Pother
9 Ump's cousin
10 Children
11 Fern spore-cluster
12 Crow's cries
13 When lunch hour ends?
14 Show
15 Embroidery yarn
16 Old ascetic
18 Saw
22 To the time that
24 Carries on
28 Give a leg up
29 Pilot
30 Lampreys
31 Electronic keyboard brand name
33 Fries lightly
34 Surround closely: Var.
35 "For ___ broke loose in Georgia" (Benét)
36 Singer Vikki
37 Offish
38 Galway's instrument
39 Keys
43 Detective show for Neil Armstrong?
45 Wristbones
46 Fastens, at sea
47 Wrestling's "___ the Giant"
48 John ___ Garner
50 Be derisive
51 Kingly
53 Aussie jumpers
55 Would you care for ___ of tea?
56 Ascertain
57 Buenos ___
59 Historic volcano
60 Has empathy
62 Parking attendant
63 One more
65 Wild parties
66 Sunday newspaper flyer
67 African region
69 Attire
71 Prepares flour
72 Melted together
73 Vassal
74 Affirmative words
76 Word of warning
77 Naval jail
78 Rural road
81 Patriotic org.
82 Actor Wallach
83 Food container
84 Singer Zadora

37

Leftovers   *by Clare T. Smith*

Odds and ends from the Mountain State.

Across

1 Dog in "The Jetsons"
6 Slow movers
12 Antiquated
17 Architectural brace
18 Transitory
20 Underwater sandbank
21 Merry fellow
23 Cooking term
24 "____ My Children"
25 Bizarre
26 Pipsqueak
28 Muscle spasm
29 Cry from the kennel
31 Drone or worker
32 Misrepresent
34 Excite
35 Parched
37 Strike out
38 Vaudeville
   presentations
39 "The Merchant of
   Venice" heiress
42 Stringed instrument
43 Smite
44 Sidestep
45 Forbidding
46 Auto mechanic, at
   times
48 "The Misadventures
   of Sheriff ____"
49 Greek philosopher
50 Small window
52 Deception
53 Central trends
55 ____ Vegas
57 Dribbled
59 Therefore
60 Quote
61 More genuine
62 Pismire
63 Unreasoning terror
64 Highlands hillside
65 Icy rain
66 Shameless
67 Tallow
68 Enigmatic creature
70 Narrow opening
71 Suppress
72 Fold
73 Lubricate
74 Christmas and New
   Year's, for two
78 Helper for 21 Across
79 Celt
80 Actor Flynn

38

82 Alcoholic beverage
83 Coral reef
85 Barrister
89 Small olive-gray
   insectivorous bird
90 Formal meeting
91 Indian tribe
92 Bestow
93 Buttons at the lanes
94 Show scorn

Down

1 Analysis
2 See 12 Across
3 Warble
4 Hose mishap
5 Suave actor Kruger
6 Nettled; vexed
7 Mother-of-pearl
8 Tennis champion
9 Equal: Comb. form
10 ____ Abner
11 Rover, when riled
12 Attention-getter
13 Gotcha!

14 Fort Sumter site
15 Fullness
16 Designates
19 NASA garment
22 Crocheted scarf
27 Wedding
   announcement word
30 Place for a cookout
32 Engaged state
33 Ardor
34 Ridges
36 Clear
37 Regimens
39 Lose effectiveness
40 Egg-shaped
41 "The Natural" star
42 Position
43 Basks
45 More crafty
46 Leaf part
47 Metallic fabric
49 Indistinct
50 Doctrine
51 Morning prayer
53 Grimace
54 Quill feather

56 Clan
58 Harangue
60 Bill of fare
62 "On the Waterfront"
   director Kazan
63 Paid performer
64 Inherent
65 Hangar
66 Admixture
67 Pulley wheel
68 Mineral spring
69 Guilty and not guilty
70 Charmers
73 "To be ____ to
   be. . ."
75 Price
76 Bring cheer
77 Underground conduit
79 Flush
80 American lake
81 Drinks like Fido
84 Astrology's lion
86 Mao ____-tung
87 CIA predecessor
88 Dreyfuss-DeVito film
   "____ Men"

Calorie Counter   by Robert A. Sefick

Incorporate a higher percentage of these selections in your diet, and you'll be able to tighten your 31 Down.

39

Across

1 Prepare to drive
6 One gender: Abbr.
10 Twosome
15 Shell carrier
16 Tropical dog
17 French Open tennis stadium, ___ Garros
19 A pound has 112
20 A cup has nine
22 Rome wrecker
23 Memory jogger
25 Spritely
26 Thanks a ___!
27 Elevator name of fame
29 Mardi Gras monarch
30 Serge suit bane
31 What backups do with time
32 Answer
34 Come back
37 ___ to; cite
38 Followed
40 Scottish two-handled bowls: Var.
41 Suppress a story
42 Sandwich choices
44 Braz. coins
45 Spiritual shepherds
48 Two have only 38
52 Wrong-tree sound?
53 Pale
54 Medical suffix
55 Some brands have none
57 Of aircraft: Pref.
58 Zilch
59 Carolina rail
60 A cup has about 130
62 Sullivan's collaborator
64 Cellular stuff: Abbr.
65 Arizona town
66 ___ Marquette
67 Max and Buddy
69 Actress Mason
73 Main man
75 Realtor's sign
77 Wisconsin town
78 Hades' euphemism
79 Studies
80 "College Bowl" point-getter: Abbr.
82 Some car lights
83 Sort
84 Sinks
86 Some parting words
88 Bow-and-arrow grp.
89 Chewing one uses up more than it has
92 A cup has 92
94 Weakness
95 Gemologist's display
96 Once and twice
97 *Populus tremula*
98 Sky speeders: Abbr.
99 Forest fire debris

Down

1 A pound has 117
2 Blunder
3 School founded by Henry VI
4 Jupiter "the Avenger"
5 Hassle
6 ___ *de mer*
7 Sheltered
8 Four ounces has 127
9 Funeral chests
10 Naval station of France
11 "Portnoy's Complaint" author
12 Hgt.
13 A cup has about 30
14 Scramble
15 Make tight
18 Get in the way
19 Task
21 "The Swedish Nightingale"
24 Part of CEO
28 Drinks noisily
31 Girth girder
33 Of French rock 'n' roll
35 Parts of the spinal column
36 Salad herbs
37 Dare
39 Bemoan
41 Russian desert
43 Good-time Charley
45 ___-walsy
46 ___ avis
47 Nose-in-the-air person
48 Cycle
49 Needle case
50 These contain about eight each
51 Marshall Plan agcy.
52 Neck nicety
56 Santa ___
57 Mite or tick
59 Thrall
61 Swedish liquid measure
63 Bask in Glasgow's sun
64 A pound has less than 300
67 Medium sized tunas
68 Thin board
70 A cup boiled is 36
71 Deference
72 Vase grips
73 Madrid miss
74 Montana city
75 Heraldic band
76 Portrays
79 Israeli soldier-statesman Moshe
81 "Magnificent Obsession" director
84 Soft cheese
85 Word to a feline
87 Canyon mouth
90 Ruler, briefly
91 Cubic measures: Abbr.
93 Repeat, in music

Updating The Atlas *by Jeanne Wilson*

Maybe it should be distributed in loose-leaf notebook form.

Across

1 Catch on
6 Cremona craftsman
11 Angels
18 Loren's hubby
19 Lethargy
20 Brandy flavoring
21 Bob Steele's milieu
22 Positive pole
23 Address the main issues
24 CEYLON
26 "___ men declare war." (Hoover)
28 Embers do; ashes don't
29 Small case
30 Assist
31 Employers
32 CPA's concern
35 Prefix for plasm
37 Double helix, for short
38 Cessna dial: Abbr.
39 MESOPOTAMIA
41 Brezhnev
43 "The Bathers" painter
46 Smaller than small
48 "Hathaway" on Steve Allen's show
49 Dispense with this
51 New Zealand aborigines
53 SYENE
55 College protest grp.
56 Singer Helen
57 Circle segment
59 Mine product
60 Play a part
62 Springtime in Paris
63 EDO
65 VIP before Gutenberg?
67 Grabbed
71 Conger
73 Type of kick
75 Some drums
76 Like hot pink
78 PERSIA
79 Delhi or Mexico
80 Loser to DDE
81 Carroll and Carrillo
83 AMA constituency
84 Confound
87 Long, long ___. . .
88 Signs scalpers love?
90 ___ au rhum
91 Houston ballplayer
93 CONSTANTINOPLE
97 Sorry souls
99 Trim; adorn (Fr.)
101 Arledge of TV
102 Furrowed
103 Rainbow: Comb. form
104 Undermine
105 Plantations, for instance
106 Francis ___, 1922 chemistry Nobelist
107 Automobile bargains

Down

1 They get letters: Abbr.
2 Bellow
3 He opposes a pro
4 Marker
5 Teach, for instance
6 High ___
7 Miss Lisa?
8 GI's address
9 Fuss
10 EIRE
11 ___ Alaska
12 Little, for one
13 Make tears
14 PORT ROYAL
15 The Sorbonne, for one
16 Stator's partner
17 Flight attendants
25 Cores
27 Passing through: Comb. form
31 Radius's neighbor
32 Purpose
33 Black Sea peninsula dwellers
34 Anka or Trebek
36 Oven (Brit.)
37 Passes on
38 NRC's predecessor
40 Jail, in British slang
42 New York town
43 Descartes and Coty
44 "Superman" intro phrase
45 Pencil wood
47 Essay
49 Patriotic org.
50 Q-U connection
52 Fills
54 Cyrano, for one
56 "6 ___, Riv Vu"
58 Taylor of "The Time Machine"
60 Sea eagle
61 Effective at a specified time, in law
64 Affirmative votes
66 Pal
68 GERMAN EAST AFRICA
69 Algonquian language
70 Sculpt
72 Not like Abner, really
74 Printer's measures
76 IBERIA
77 School year segment
80 He gets 10 pct.
82 Used thermal currents
84 Put down
85 Two Dillons
86 Scrub a mission
87 Onagers
89 Sound most deny
91 "Laugh-In" regular
92 Sculls
93 ___-European languages
94 Taylor-Burton bomb?
95 Destroy
96 Peggy and Brenda
98 Ingest
100 Slow down, in mus.

Do Tell! *by Peter Swift*

A mature observation.

Across

1 Urchins
5 Twilled fabric
10 Fidel's former aide
13 Hits
17 Brook
18 Growing outward
19 Poet's contraction
20 Quod _____ demonstrandum
21 **Start of the quote**
23 Egypt, formerly: Abbr.
24 _____ morgana
25 Certain oceanic movement
26 Pielet
28 Recurrent theme
29 His, in Nice
30 **Quote, part 2**
32 Mr. Hurok
35 Close relatives
38 Jacket features
39 Elevator man
41 Give _____ to; express
43 Málaga Mrs.
44 Haggard novel
47 **Quote, part 3**
51 Persian king, 522-486 B.C.
54 Frighten
55 Wild animal's trail
56 Memorable periods
57 Toward the back, on a boat
59 Narrow grooves
61 Command to Fido
62 Runaway of a sort
65 Ananias and others
67 Plutocrat
71 Spanish dance
72 **Quote, part 4**
74 Seed's sit-out round
75 Before omega
77 Aria
78 Black, to Donne
79 Easily bent
83 Farm animals
85 Understand
86 **Quote, part 5**
89 "On _____ Blindness"
91 Diamond area
92 Baseball family name
93 Was
98 Beethoven's birthplace
99 Expert
100 **End of the quote**
102 Whilom laborer
103 Debussy's "La _____"
104 Occur subsequently
105 Libertine
106 Legal document
107 Those holding power
108 Chalcedonies
109 Requisite

Down

1 Niblick
2 Hidden explosive
3 Legal move
4 Insults
5 Scoffing
6 Wife of Geraint
7 Cathedral section
8 Native of: Suff.
9 Hostess Perle's family
10 Niceness
11 Plant native to moors
12 Go astray
13 Muddles
14 Address a multitude
15 Terrace
16 Executive's aides
22 Hwys.
27 One ocean: Abbr.
28 Murray of silents
31 Skirts
32 Turfs
33 Of the ear
34 Singer-actress Kirk
36 Takes a chance
37 Cuts
40 Predicament
42 Play the flute
44 _____ semper tyrannis
45 Whadja say?
46 Feminine word ending
48 Point
49 Waterwheel
50 Pipes
52 Mime's forte
53 Take turns
58 _____ of Capricorn
60 Cartoonist Peter's kin
62 Fall back
63 Actress Myrna
64 Cry of approval
66 Farm structure
68 Hope and White
69 Musical instrument
70 Nota _____
72 Slandering ones
73 Not anywheres
76 Ancient Arab
79 Won like Hulk Hogan
80 Hallucinogen, for short
81 Papal name
82 Chopin compositions
84 _____ with; support
86 Enclose firmly
87 Lasso
88 Hollywood's Irene
90 Unyielding
93 U.N. member
94 Sail before the wind
95 Western Indian
96 Gloomy
97 Flirted
99 Jacques's friend
101 Three men _____ tub

41

Taking Flight *by Dorothea E. Shipp*

A feather to tickle the intellect.

42

Across

1 Stun
6 Fall flower
11 Money in Iran
16 Charm
17 Like the king of beasts
18 Shaped like the earth
20 Asparagus, regionally
22 As one
23 Engine noises
24 Hovel
25 College founded in 1440
27 Hot singer Turner
28 Snick's tag-along
29 Fundamental
31 Freed
32 ____ de plume
33 Fast ____, role for Paul Newman
35 "It is ____ stay out than get out." (Twain)
39 Styptic stuff
42 Entered a marathon
43 Maniples
47 Fonteyn's milieu
51 Excavated
52 Lighter fuel
53 Comic actor James
54 Jelled garnish
56 Family member, familiarly
57 ____ up; excited
58 Major Houlihan's nickname
61 Washington's bill
62 Briefly
64 Aug. clock setting in Boston
65 Never, to Hans
66 Alan and Cheryl
68 Prod
69 Emulating a kitty
71 Metric capacity meas.
72 One with superbly keen vision
75 Film star Renée
76 Country stopover
77 North Sea hazard
78 Mexican woody herb
81 Anticipate
85 Call-up org.
88 Catch 40 winks
89 Actress-singer Anton
92 1104, to Trajan
94 Coup d'____
96 Snare
98 Pig's digs
99 Nutmeg or cinnamon
100 Spud
102 Defenseless targets
105 County Kerry seaport
106 ____ sides; everywhere
107 47 Across, for example
108 Make bread
109 Stairway post
110 Trapshooting

Down

1 Mountainous
2 Made smooth
3 Cleared of guilt
4 Airport info
5 Composer Delibes
6 Cattle breed
7 Minor attack
8 TV listing initials
9 So what ____ is new?
10 Make one's racket like new
11 Type of tournament
12 ____ Saud
13 Got down
14 Language for the masses
15 Office worker
16 Relatives of adders
19 Cheese
21 "Scots ____ hae. . ."
26 Goose, on the Seine
29 Actor Lugosi
30 One, two, three, *etc.*
34 Adjectival suffix
36 Was rude to
37 Framework part
38 Meal grain
40 Edict
41 Middle: Pref.
44 Punjab city
45 Zip
46 Seat
47 Outline
48 Like a forest
49 Play part
50 Lon ____, Cambodian honcho
55 Warsaw's country
56 Cordage fiber
59 Tube or man
60 How some walk
63 Tint
67 C-G fill-in
70 El line
71 Main organ stop
73 ____ extra mile; be very helpful
74 Fictional detective Archer
79 GRF's V.P.
80 Steal cattle
82 Medicine container
83 Winter sight
84 That's the ____!
85 Labor Day mo.
86 Baby bringer
87 Mephistopheles
90 Yet
91 "Atlas Shrugged" author Rand
93 Suit part
95 Yarn
97 Conifer
99 Pierre's loc.
101 Lapsang souchong
103 Shooter marble
104 Literary monogram

Creeping Urbanization *by Bert Rosenfield*

Annexation vexation.

Across

1 Mud and meat
5 Key letters
9 Where Alexander beat Darius
14 MCD halved
17 PBS or IBM
18 Cape ____, New Brunswick
20 Marker
21 A liquid ester
22 BLUENOSE CITY
24 ____ and Pythias
26 Bay
27 Jewish months
28 Andy's radio partner
30 Prefixes meaning "half"
32 Tiberian procurator
34 SCENIC CITY
38 Indian hill dweller
39 Not "fer"
40 Home office
41 100 centesimi
43 Ending for defer
44 Rodeo appurtenance
46 As sick as ____
49 Needlefish
50 One trillionth: Pref.
51 Issued a fiat
53 CHANEL'S CITY
55 Precursor
56 Natives of: Suff.
57 Honorific letters for Elizabeth
58 Veneration
60 Anatomical loop
63 NANETTE'S CITY
66 Undivided
70 Table salt in the lab
71 Kant's study
72 "Cielo ____," "La Gioconda" aria
74 "____ Danaos et dona ferentes." (Lat. caveat)
75 Hugh Johnson's org.
76 Tartan pattern
78 ____ de mer
80 Suffragist Elizabeth ____ Stanton
81 ____ part; dissembles
84 DISCOVERY CITY
88 See you later
90 "American Buffalo" playwright
91 Missile housing
92 Tiger pitcher Frank
94 Ecclesiastical caps
96 "____ of God"
99 EDITH BUNKER'S CITY
102 Leeds' river
103 Q-U filler
104 "Redeem'd I was ____." ("Henry VI Part 1")
105 Carry on
106 Singer Sumac
107 Rope, to Dennis Conner
108 Spring-ahead phenomena, for short
109 Chemical endings

Down

1 Answered a charge
2 New Rochelle college
3 Citizen Kane, for one
4 WISE CITY
5 Score six per TD
6 Pueblo resident
7 What to rule with
8 Happy one
9 Introduce gradually
10 Brand of oil additive
11 Capital of Valais canton
12 Reveal
13 Prevails, as the grippe
14 PRINCESS CITY
15 Bennett or Talmadge
16 Bovine bubble gum?
19 Oleoresin
23 Tra chasers
25 And not
29 Triste
31 Irish bay or port
33 Singer John
34 "Put 'er thar, ____."
35 1958 fiction Pulitzer winner
36 Honey wine
37 Mouthward
42 Indo-Iranian
45 Paten veil
47 Eight in Oaxaca
48 Eydie the singer
50 ESTHETIC CITY
52 Laborers of yore
54 ____ lab; RPI locale
59 Half or dim follower
60 Sten and Christie
61 Drug addiction
62 ELLA'S CITY
64 S-molding
65 Insect's dorsal surface
66 Caspian Sea feeder
67 Warlike
68 Paper the walls
69 Dunce
73 Walker Cup players, for instance
77 Fish catcher
79 Cruces or Palmas
82 "Who?", "Why?", or "Where or When"
83 Climbing perch genus
85 Dubai and Sharjah bosses
86 Type of scar
87 Actress Farrow
89 Grind the teeth
93 Go for ____; play it safe
95 "____ Ideas," 1951 hit tune
97 North Ireland river
98 ____ store by; believes
99 Thirsty
100 Dryden oeuvre
101 Meese and Asner

43

Such Grammar! by Lois Sidway

Yesterday I couldn't spell "cruciverbalist." Today I are one.

Across

1 Like a wet rag
5 Soapstone
9 May honorees
13 "Bye-bye"
17 Seaweed product
18 Bombay nursemaid
19 Once more
20 Yours and mine
21 How ____?! (triumphant expression)
25 Nodded off
26 Goofs
27 Stashed away
28 "____ Misérables"
29 Manitoba Indian
30 Hawaiian seaport
31 Thrashed
34 Slay
35 Weight unit
39 Winged
40 1942 Abbott and Costello film
42 NOW goal
43 Jewelry piece
44 Utter confusion
46 Unites
47 "Oh! What ____ Was Mary"
48 Endangered Florida cat
50 Feeling poorly
51 Honeymoon island
52 Number from "Ain't Misbehavin'"
57 Nation allied with Satan (Rev. 20:8)
59 Size above med.
60 Remainder
63 Thanks ____!
64 Matchmaker Dolly ____
66 Calvin of golf
68 In the manner of
69 High time for Di
70 "The ____, a idiot" said Mr. Bumble ("Oliver Twist")
72 Lace mishap
73 Some people go to them
75 Scottish hill
76 Gear for the Mets
77 Roman road
78 1984 Peace Nobelist
79 ____ ordinaire
80 Richard of "Family Feud"
83 Unless, in law
84 Salesman of a kind
88 Sportin' Life's song

91 "____ Free"
92 "CHiPS" star Estrada
93 Dry
94 Ms. Bombeck
95 Play stoolie
96 "What's My Line?" host John
97 Africa's long river
98 Consider

Down

1 Shane portrayer
2 Frankenstein's aide
3 BLT spread
4 Potential thief
5 Stories
6 Surrounded by
7 "Mighty ____ a Rose"
8 Merry adieus
9 Skier Steve or brother Phil
10 Change for a five
11 Hebrew letter
12 Zanzibar natives
13 Boss
14 "____ Lang Syne"
15 Corner
16 Group: Abbr.
22 Not new
23 General direction
24 Cockpit VIP
29 Type of salmon
30 Sped off
31 Mammy Yokum's creator
32 Inter ____
33 Kids are her specialty
34 Miniature
35 Genuflected
36 Offensive
37 Fahd, for one
38 Actress Powers
41 Birds of prey
44 ____-a-lug
45 That girl
47 "Manon" highlight
49 Spree
50 Follower: Suff.
51 Competent
53 "The King"
54 Shield
55 Fat, plus
56 Cereal grain

57 One of a matched pair
58 Karras of "Webster"
61 Coagulate
62 Vittles
64 Regretted deeply
65 Pitcher
66 Democrat or Republican
67 Biblical brother
70 Admit
71 Mistreatment
72 Lit
74 On the increase
76 Skirt length
78 ____-tacky
79 Mesa ____
80 Chooser's word
81 Thine, to Dumas
82 Alert
83 Simon or Armstrong
84 Jack and Jill's container
85 Harp's predecessor
86 Salinger girl
87 Gad about
89 New Deal letters
90 ____ Lanka

44

Improperly Put *by William A. Smith*

Wrong, but right. Depends on how you look at it.

45

Across

1 Yegg's targets
6 Mexican blanket
12 Serious plays
18 Juan's friend
19 Substitute for the name of God
20 Snappy comeback: Var.
21 Lengthy separation?
23 Small tropical American tree: Var.
24 Guido's high note
25 Proverb
26 Japan's principal commercial port
28 Fussy old woman
29 Volcano goddess
31 Pertaining to: Suff.
32 If ____ could kill. . .
34 Withered
35 Trivially debatable
37 Stallone film
38 King when Christ was born
39 Stress
42 Oval nut
43 Singer Perry
44 Hawaiian tree
45 Lebanon port
46 Pine or spruce
49 Gil ____
50 Hue's kingdom
51 Did a "Steve Brodie"
52 Arafat's grp.
53 Threatened shade tree
54 Small Navy lass?
56 "Come and get it!"
57 Fall guy's sentence
58 Mineral vein
59 Less feral
60 Set a trap
61 Chicago newspaper
63 Intolerant one
64 Carried
65 Not an imit.
66 Breed of cattle
67 Kind of angel
68 Moffo and Held
70 Ship-launcher of epic beauty
71 Capture
72 Price
73 Family members
74 "Mighty ____ a Rose"
75 "Pygmalion" playwright
79 Initials honoring the Queen
80 Speck
81 Buenos ____
83 This ____ fine how-do-you-do!
84 Tennis star Sanchez
86 Litigant in suspense?
90 Logarithms inventor
91 NFL's Forty-____
92 Indian, for one
93 Ancient ascetic
94 Accustoms: Var.
95 ____ Haute

Down

1 Orchid tubers used as food
2 Soap plant
3 Last
4 Incite to action
5 Kind of ash
6 Scholar
7 Italian river to the Adriatic
8 Stood
9 Black cuckoo
10 Kung ____ Chicken
11 One-grained wheat
12 Dribs and ____
13 Russian hemp
14 Shrink's org.
15 Mrs. Bailey?
16 Of a star: Comb. form
17 Crocked
22 Dummy
27 Quebec Trappist cheese village
30 Kin of the ostriches: Var.
32 Crazy incentives?
33 Site of Dunstaffnage Castle
34 Kind of trailer
36 Three ____ match
37 Kind of closet
38 Whet
39 Victoria's consort
40 Salt or wine follower
41 Cup-winning vessels?
42 ____-nez
43 Nightclub charge
45 Sarcastic
46 Desire inordinately
47 Galahad's mother
48 Decayed
50 In the company of
51 Pythias's friend
55 Hitch it to a star
58 Ex-pitcher Tiant
60 Tree trunks
62 Hard-to-handle kid
63 Lugosi
64 Catch
66 Estate
67 One who pretends
68 Buttercup, for one
69 Talmadge and Shearer
70 Fedora
71 Pat; stroke
73 Grace or Garry
74 Cuba ____; bar drink
76 Personnel manager
77 "____ is Born"
78 John, "The Duke"
80 Bearing
81 Can.'s neighbor
82 Name for a firehouse dog
85 Golfing situation
87 Genealogy abbr.
88 Burmese statesman
89 Unreturnable serve

Wolf! *by Alfio Micci*

There's a lesson here.

Across

1 Lacking, in Lyons
5 Walden, for one
9 Vicinity
13 Israelite
16 Work the land
17 ___ Ben Adhem
18 Obligation
19 Recital piece
20 **Start of the lesson**
23 With 63 Across, famed Australian racehorse
24 Spate
25 Actress Anderson and namesakes
26 Rocker Joplin
27 Arizona State locale
28 Close, to Carew
29 One of the "few good men"
30 Palindromic preposition
31 **More of the lesson**
33 Endure
35 Fish catch
36 *Amo, amas,* ___
37 Arrest
38 Spirits
40 Certain hairdo
42 "___ corny as Kansas. . ."
46 Brooklyn trailer
47 Sailor's saint
48 Tough
49 Dregs
50 Maroon
52 Not a person
54 **More of the lesson**
55 Leaning
56 Deli order
57 Brogue
59 Stolen diamonds
60 Undiluted
61 Florist's need
62 Elate
63 See 23 Across
64 Berate
66 Kadiddlehopper
67 "___ for All Seasons"
69 **Source of the lesson**
74 Bee: Pref.
75 Skulls
76 Trick's alternative
77 Err
80 Water buffalos
81 Violinist Isaac
82 Convent dwellers
84 Prie-___

85 **End of the lesson**
87 Part of RPI
88 Once, once
89 Hibernia
90 Pine
91 Ten-percenter: Abbr.
92 Fabrication
93 West Coast team
94 Thirteen Vatican leaders

Down

1 Tiff
2 Divide
3 *Bête* follower
4 Abounded
5 Oklahoma Indian
6 Final notice
7 Lon ___ of Cambodia
8 Reason for sharpening
9 Lord, in Judaism
10 Withdraw
11 Regresses
12 Had a nosh

13 King of Portugal, 1640-56
14 Screenwriter May
15 Deteriorate
19 Trunk item
21 Act as 91 Across
22 Yule music
26 Flapper Era popular song
28 Certain mollusks
29 Interoffice note
32 Diverge
33 Jericho or New Orleans
34 European peninsula
35 Kind of steer
37 Seventh Hebrew month
39 Used
40 Rhône tributary
41 Least wilted
43 Luzon port
44 School of American artists
45 Bo-Peep's charge
48 Court

49 Remedial expert
51 Man on the moon
53 Galena, for one
54 ___ is me!
56 Time and a ___
58 Work on a skirt
61 Traveler's need
62 Soap
65 Sacred bull
66 Cratchit, for one
68 Violent wind of France
69 Louisiana parish
70 Sinner's activity
71 Most reasonable
72 Declare
73 Murmur
74 City on the Somme
78 It's often wild
79 Proper: Comb. form
81 Agile
82 Wedge
83 "___ a Latin From Manhattan"
85 Theology sch.
86 La-la lead-in

46

Originally published in 1987

That Goes Ditto! *by Bert Rosenfield*

Twice-told tales.

Across

1 One Dumas
5 Burgos buddies
11 Alfie's abode
14 Blanc or Tillis
17 Large inland sea
18 Conrad or Klein
19 Purview
21 Early Gershwin musical
23 Got up
24 Poetic garland
25 Chiton-like robe
27 Kay-en connector
28 Soup veggie
29 Boyer's "Algiers" role
33 Communications logo
35 "M*A*S*H" key GI
40 Sad letters for footsore theatergoers
41 Holiday eve, in Tel Aviv
42 Mysterious Gardner
44 Disabled, in a way
46 New York lake
49 Island near SE end of the Panama Canal
50 Philadelphia's "Spectrum," for one
51 Cinema's Robert De ____
52 Union, to Greeks and Cypriots
54 "Adam ____"
56 Tumbler
61 Shrink
62 Space pioneer
64 Oat genus
65 Blankety-blank
67 *Huhn* products
68 Yellowish browns
69 Whit
71 Traffic jam
73 NASA vehicles
74 Curio
78 "Excelsior," for one
79 Garfield's canine patsy
80 Leave out
81 Giant reed
83 Heavy eight-iron
85 Statute
86 Broadway role for Hepburn
90 Vacationer's goal
92 Kind of jerk
93 Garner
96 Mother of St. Augustine
99 Having eyelashes
102 She sang Musetta at the Met
104 Resolve
105 ____ customer
106 Lotion ingredient
107 Distress signal
108 Bee, in combinations
109 Most recent
110 Jan. hrs. in Jackson and Joplin

Down

1 White House pooch
2 Caviar exporter
3 Humdinger
4 Plow sole
5 Portland sago
6 Indian footwear, for short
7 Egret's cousin
8 Mazuma
9 Lowest ship's deck
10 Arrow shafts
11 Lt. factory in WWII
12 Turnpike turnoff sight
13 Nellie's man in "South Pacific"
14 Istanbul's sea: Var.
15 Canton or Brooklyn ending
16 Psychedelic letters
20 Upcoming Dr.
22 Regan's father
26 Forestage
30 Infinitely long-lasting
31 Beer container
32 67 Across, to Augustus
33 Extends a subscription
34 Combiner meaning skull
36 Woe is me!
37 Blue-blood's org.
38 Specimen on a slide
39 Misplay at hearts
43 Ruhr city
45 Klee's art cult
47 Grampus
48 US-Canada air-space shield
53 Rubber or ink
55 Heretofore, in poesy
57 Convex molding
58 "Rio Rita" costar
59 Sallow
60 Body armor plate
62 ____ jam; fouled up
63 Steaming
66 Ruler: Abbr.
68 Location for a bump
70 Yoga posture
72 Ended a career: Abbr.
74 Sinbad's bird
75 *Amas* preceder
76 Caustic Don
77 Lack of stress
82 1973 Oscar winner
84 School founded by Henry VI
87 Brazilian state
88 In a tizzy
89 Cleo or Frankie of song
91 ____ Day, April 25th, down under
94 Merganser
95 Locale
96 Grinder's grist
97 Agglomerate
98 Pub pours
99 Metric liq. amts.
100 Worker's grp.
101 Carp or tome starter
103 Elsie's genus

47

Collaborations *by John R. Prosser*

Unlikely titles from unlikely collaborators.

Across

1 Dreyfus's defender
5 Untouched attic items
11 Nebraska's largest city
16 Aesop's ending
17 What's ____ to do?
19 Plug away at
20 Movie by Čapek, Hodgson, and Kafka?
23 Make a lap
24 *Roi*'s lady of the house
25 Columbus's ship
26 Smite a knight
27 New Mexico pueblo dweller
29 Fish noted for its liver
30 Low pained sound
31 Seasonal dress lengths
32 Toast edges
34 Sonny's ex
35 Laurel and Hardy, for one
37 Meadow
38 Go from curb to curb
39 Offense, chess-wise
43 Longshoreman
46 Party thrower
47 Noshed
48 Careered along
49 Slipped up
50 Lamb seasoning
51 Hurry-scurry
52 One and only
53 Book by the Grimm brothers and Stoker?
57 Rural hotels
58 Furthermost part
59 Seasoned sailors
60 Established
61 Silly Putty container
62 Vacation time for *un étudiant*
63 Bullfight arena (Sp.)
64 Dentists with drills
65 More profound
67 Pickets
68 Kick oneself
69 Author Levin
70 Greek war god
71 The yet unborn
74 ____ for; chooses
77 "____ Your Wagon"
79 Inventor Whitney
80 Animal wrap
82 Show disapproval
83 Ahab's father, in the Bible
84 Equally
86 The night before

87 Boxing match by Marlowe, Nash, and Freeman?
92 Torrefy
93 More anguine
94 Copycats
95 Abated
96 Pulls in laboriously
97 Coverings

Down

1 Where Leo and Scorpio are found
2 Declaimer
3 On the ____; running
4 Winged
5 Airs on the air
6 Redact
7 Hate's opposite
8 Citizen of: Suff.
9 Heels of the hands, at times
10 Firstborns
11 Bane for *el toro*

12 Vitiate
13 Consent to
14 Nonsense
15 Ali Baba and his friends
16 Spar
18 East Indian prince
21 Bee's treat
22 Edict issuer
28 They pout
30 Ibsen-Galsworthy advertisement?
31 "Some Like It ____"
33 Squalid
34 Witch
36 Shoshonean
38 Youngling
40 Electrify
41 Phone user
42 Prepares dough
43 Scoffed at
44 The navel is one
45 Quail; fawn
47 Totals up
50 Leo's neckpiece
51 Some hairstyles

52 Find, with effort
54 Dog, cat, or skunk
55 Watering holes
56 More or less
62 Always, to Longfellow
63 Amusement area
64 Boston's hockey team
66 Circumference ratios
67 Tournament matchup
71 Dusts the cake pans
72 Tottered
73 Young eels
74 Way overweight
75 Speakers' platforms
76 Municipalities
78 Writer Kingsley ____
79 West German city
81 Homophone for tease
84 Kiri te Kanawa forte
85 Of a historical period
88 Ripen
89 Certain baron's color
90 ____ out; make a living
91 Prefix for gram or dermis

48

The Stage Is Set   *by Arnold Moss*

Mr. Moss, a stage and film actor of many years, focuses on his special field
for this opus.

49

Across

1 Tibetan gazelle
4 Type of type: Abbr.
8 Israel's Meir
13 Black
17 Height: Pref.
18 Scarlett's home
19 Skull part
20 Dry: Pref.
21 Kind of horse or lion
22 Border on
23 Star of "Our American Cousin"
25 1913's Count of Monte Cristo
28 Hamster's cousin
29 Menuhin's violin teacher
30 Stagger
31 Woman of letters
32 Small crown
33 Starr of the NFL
34 Billboard
35 ". . .*in corpore* ____"
36 "My Gal ____"
37 Entrée for Diamond Jim?
39 Bark cloth
43 Gray, in Grenoble
45 Actor Bridges
46 Mermaid's cot?
48 Jolson's original first name
51 Urgency
53 Campus org.
55 ____ apso
56 Her corn was green
58 Rip Van Winkle, 1865
60 Mild oath
61 Have a late bite
62 "Hamlet" role
63 That, in Ponce
64 Garland
66 Stage designs
68 U.S. stage org.
70 ____ amandine
71 Musical prelim
73 Heston role, El ____
74 Igneous rock
78 Surgical needle
79 Cattle prod
81 Forestage
82 African capital
86 Presidential candidate, 1900-20
87 ". . .the ravell'd ____ of care." ("Macbeth")
88 African antelope
89 "Kismet" star, 1912
91 Famed Hamlet
94 Shake ____; hurry!
95 Half a play title
96 Comic Jay
97 On mother's side
98 Saturday night ritual
99 René's pal
100 Helper: Abbr.
101 Pan, for one
102 Place ____; gamble
103 Sparks of the silents

Down

1 19th century footlights
2 "South Pacific" locale
3 Ancient Syrian language: Var.
4 Lake ____, Mississippi source
5 No-no
6 ____ for one's money
7 Gridiron pass
8 Holmes portrayer
9 ____ fours; crawling
10 B'klyn campus
11 Dung beetle
12 Interpretations of Scriptures
13 Wield
14 Journalist Lucius
15 Avifauna
16 December songs
24 Lament
26 Sukkoth citron: Var.
27 Cash or court finish
31 Wardrobe mistress's standby
33 Pinza and Ramey
34 Pickles
36 Brynner's "kingdom"
38 Minstrel-show instruments
39 Himalayan goat
40 Degrade
41 Tijuana "brass"
42 "A Bell for ____"
44 June, moon, spoon
45 Signal device
47 Exclusive group
48 Eastern church titles
49 What Ado Annie couldn't do
50 Wine-cask deposit: Var.
52 Monopolistic corporations
54 Frightened
57 Kind of awakening
59 Discovery
65 Germs
67 Unanimous
69 Ski resort
72 Greek letters
73 Melon
75 Khomeini, for one
76 "They have ____ to jealousy." (Deut. 32:21)
77 Kind of barometer
78 Age
80 Geisha's sash
81 Get off
82 Wolf-pack leader in "The Jungle Book"
83 Bodies of ore
84 Grads' wear
85 Dodo
86 Lamour, to Hope?
87 Settlement of monks
90 Thick bacon slice
92 ". . .sat ____ tuffet."
93 Cereal grain

Footnotes *by Jim Page*

"A pretty foot is a great gift of nature." – Von Goethe

50

Across

1 Bogart film
7 MCCLXXV doubled
11 The Rhine divides it
16 Lacking creativity
18 Stiller's partner
19 Grayish-white
20 Sailor's garment
21 Ta-ta, French style
22 Went undercover
23 Icelandic letter
24 Shearer of "The Red Shoes"
26 Drill instructor's concerns?
28 Flatfish
31 Reach the bar?
32 Shopworn
34 ____-mo (instant replay)
35 Ada of the theater
37 Rocker part
40 Symbol of bigness
42 Chronic
44 Richmond defender
45 Ooze
46 Rightos
48 Neat as ____
49 Polanski film of 1979
50 Deep blue: Comb. form
52 Smoker attendee
53 Major blood vessel
54 Acid in milk
56 Certain grads.
57 TV trial-shows
59 Shore or Washington
60 Lotto kin
62 Mine entrance
63 "Thou the ____; I the throng." (Gilbert)
64 Cancel
65 Jonson's "____ to Himself"
66 Did the butterfly
70 Tack on
71 Fraud
74 Drawing back
76 Soapmaking stuff
77 Magnetic-induction unit
78 Actress Farrow
80 Sole proprietor
81 Chip cover
82 Cauldron ingredient, in "Macbeth"
85 Shoe lift
88 Open to bribery
89 Palm leaf
91 Moslem spirit
92 More unsound
94 Giggles
97 Hit musical
98 Home-stretch sounds
99 Formal letter
100 Fortification
101 Proofer's term
102 Authorities

Down

1 Taxonomic category: Abbr.
2 To ____; exactly
3 "Wall Street Lays An Egg," for one
4 Constituting a model
5 "The Road to ____"
6 *Populus* tree
7 Purple Heart, for instance
8 Actress Zetterling
9 Number before *vier*
10 Canaveral site
11 Loose stitching
12 Seat of Pitkin County, Colorado
13 "Lollipop," for one
14 Sediment
15 Limit
17 Some collars
18 Color similar to cranberry
25 Cruise stops
27 Burma tribe member
29 Call ____ cab
30 Does like Krakatoa
32 Recipe amt.
33 ____ anemone; woodland plant
36 Silkworm
37 Lively
38 Caesuras
39 Tableland
41 Points of complexity
43 Film featuring a German submarine
47 Promote, in a way
49 Sweetheart
51 Utmost degree
53 Ringleader?
54 "Out of Control" author
55 Battery terminal
56 ". . . ____ down beside her. . ."
58 March period
59 Clock face
61 Organic compound
65 Neighbor of Taurus
67 Bird appendages
68 Prop finish?
69 Dugout VIP
71 Naples native
72 Warm up to
73 Arabian princes: Var.
75 Mount ____, Jordan, where Aaron died
79 ____ worse than death
81 Actress Berger
83 Unhidden
84 Some mixed drinks
85 Honey house
86 Tennyson heroine
87 Connect points on a graph
90 Woody's son
91 O.T. book
93 New Guinea port
95 Aunt (Sp.)
96 His, in Nice

Originally published in 1987

Tandems *by Dorothea E. Shipp*

Ms. Shipp put an additional restriction on herself for this version of the name game.

Across

1 Ground grain
6 Sch. orgs.
10 Nile dam site
15 Like a solarium
17 Flirt; tease
19 Emulated the sun
20 Bacterium
21 Baltimore player
22 Spanish dramatist (1843-1920)
23 Film stars meet
26 Uncle, in Veracruz
27 The square root of one hundred
28 Red or India substance
29 Character in "The Tragedy of Julius Caesar"
33 Fury
36 Writer Fleming
38 Blood pressure raiser
42 Singers meet
46 Place for "the lowing herd"
47 Notion
48 Cruising
49 Caricaturist
50 Ait
52 Swimmer's trips
53 Confined
54 Balaam's mount
55 Bet
56 Beverage, French style
58 Police blotter notation, for short
59 Jason's mate
62 Cosby-Culp series, "I ____"
65 Forest denizen
68 Chore
72 Obie, for one
73 "Blessed ____ the pure. . ."
74 The other spread
75 Pac. Ten school
76 Congeal
77 Actors meet
81 Egyptian goddess of nature
83 Encountered
84 Actress Barbara
85 Certain reminders
86 Whelm
88 Ref. work
90 Alter ____
92 Actors meet
100 Afghanistan's capital
101 Lumberjack's warning
102 Secondary Hebrew priestly official
104 Cove
105 Directs
106 Joined Weight Watchers
107 Prepares lemon zest
108 Della's creator
109 London streetcars

Down

1 Youth org.
2 Sorry one
3 Japanese box
4 Oscar of "The Odd Couple," for instance
5 Lama follower
6 But, in Barcelona
7 Unclean
8 Worship
9 Poisonous alkaloids from the nightshade family
10 Ski resort
11 Arab leaders
12 ____ of mouth
13 Dill herb
14 Pince-____
16 Actress Garr
17 Site: Abbr.
18 Sparks or Beatty
24 Knobbed
25 Hollywood crossing
29 Line a roof
30 Actor Alan
31 Pace
32 Furniture protector
34 "Two Owls and ____. . ." (Lear)
35 Pesty insect
37 Movie star Gardner and namesakes
39 Film star Nazimova
40 Vichyssoise ingredient
41 Actress Sharon
43 Mock
44 Time period
45 Stunt man's worry
51 Importance
57 Pilgrimage
58 Splittable thing
59 Gaspar and Melchior
60 Fold inhabitants
61 "Crucifixion" artist
62 Ditto
63 Verb tense
64 Agreed!
65 Weeded, in a way
66 Talaria
67 Junket maker
69 ____ de naissance, birth certificate, in Nice
70 Error
71 Midwest st.
78 Iowa city
79 Loudness measure
80 Rise ____ all; surmount difficulties
82 Johnson or Goldwyn
87 Thrashing results
89 Parent, re newborn
91 Norman crown tax
92 "Plain" one
93 Ready, willing, and ____
94 Dollar parts, for short
95 "Breathless" star
96 Some cits.
97 Eternally
98 Film star Naldi
99 Hold back
100 Gymnast's maneuver
103 MSS readers

51

Just Enjoy It *by Alfio Micci*

Anything else, and it's a clear case of "analysis paralysis."

Across

1 Skilled
5 One parallelogram
10 Little emulators
15 Bind
16 Gods of the Norse pantheon
17 Earth, for one
18 **Start of a quote by Ned Rorem**
21 Admiral type
22 Pedro's "Ahoy!"
23 Entangles
24 Annoy
26 Common connector
27 Dusks, to Donne
28 Pierre's aunt
29 Conductor Rapee
30 Argue
32 Rome's port
33 Spinning
34 **Quote, part 2**
38 Confused
40 Limb
41 "Deathtrap" author
42 H.H. Munro
43 "Ile" author
46 Saul's grandfather
47 Bacheller's "____ and I"
50 Arctic sight
52 **Quote, part 3**
54 Annul
56 "____ as a Stranger"
57 Some earthlings
59 Modified gene
61 Roll-call answer
62 Fungal affliction
64 LP hole?
65 Did an electrician's job
66 **Quote, part 4**
70 Coeur d'____
72 Autocrats
73 Kind of top
76 Rover's pal
77 Dixie side dish
78 Neat
80 Pub order
81 Spigot
82 Anyone
83 Wedge up
84 Basic ballet move
85 **End of the quote**
89 Orientals
90 "Family Ties" mom
91 Garner's "Maverick," and namesakes
92 Robe for Calpurnia

52

93 At ____ and sevens; in disorder
94 Saloons

Down

1 Greek goddess of wisdom
2 Stomach, familiarly
3 Cowardly Lion portrayer
4 Ecol. dept.
5 Gaseous element
6 Cads
7 Thessaly peak
8 With, in Wittenberg
9 Acid salt
10 Formal avenue
11 Chums
12 Tolkien creature
13 Takes back on the payroll
14 "Sentimental Journey" author
15 Fine fiddle, for short
17 Already shared
19 Statesman Syngman's folks
20 Roof ornament
25 "____ Nidre"
27 Henri ender?
28 Cooking meas.
29 Green land
31 Of a dry region
32 Metallic element
33 Burning
35 Summer acquisition
36 City near Provo
37 Evident
38 A ____ apple
39 Tijuana tidbit
43 ____ can of worms; seek trouble
44 Baton Rouge inst.
45 Chemist's paper
47 Double-visored cap
48 Hard to find
49 "____ Three Lives"
51 Vestment
53 Fires
55 Small bottle
58 Atomic particles
60 First quiz question: Abbr.
62 ". . .a ____'clock scholar. . ."
63 Italian hill town
65 "Batman" sound effect
66 Canopy support
67 ____ words; retract
68 North or Miniver
69 Ape's kin
70 Fore's counterpart
71 Vines
74 Writers George and Thomas Stearns
75 Coral structures
77 Accra's country
78 ____ were the days
79 Stands
82 Body politic
83 River of Hades
84 Almost, in combinations
86 "O Sole ____"
87 To him (Ital.)
88 Wane

Renaissance Man *by Yvonne R. Helms*

He's a composer, a serious actor, a jazz pianist, and a quick-witted comedian and television host. He writes, too.

53

Across

1 Don't ___ boy to. . .
6 Without missing ___; in perfect time
11 Greek cheeses
16 Indian or Pacific
17 Funny Radner
18 Steinways
20 Short stories by Steve Allen
23 Opposed
24 Crossed out
25 Neither's follower
26 Yours and mine
28 Negative word
30 Leaning
32 Philippine mahogany
33 Book by Steve Allen
40 Arnie's secretary on "L.A. Law"
41 Let
42 Take off pounds
43 Attorney's deg.
44 Skull protuberance
46 H, H, H, H
48 ¿*Cómo* ___ *usted?*
49 Road curve
50 Caviar source
52 Ornate container
53 Bookworm
55 "___ of Laura Mars"
56 Hip retellings by Steve Allen
60 ___ *homo!*
64 Warm up
66 Chit
67 Circus performers
69 On the ___; punctual
72 Capri or Wight
74 "Damn Yankees" character
76 Welfare handouts
77 Prize, for Cortés
78 Sharp
79 "Mule Train" singer
81 City of Nigeria
82 Book by Steve Allen
87 Looks like a lecher
88 Confident
89 Ger.-It. confederation of many years
90 Before: Comb. form
91 Stand for, oddly enough
92 Roofing material
94 Neck area
98 Mystery by Steve Allen
104 Legislative body
105 Giggle
106 Court order
107 Extend a subscription
108 Abalone
109 Slam-dunk targets

Down

1 Divan
2 GNP-student's major
3 Not masc. or fem.
4 Not staid
5 Hill-dweller
6 Author of "A Death in the Family"
7 Tie
8 Woodsy sprite
9 Substitute name of God, in Hebrew scriptures
10 Fortune-teller's cards
11 Mil. mail drop
12 German article
13 Asian language
14 Formerly, Portuguese West Africa
15 "Be it ever ___. . ." (Payne)
19 Ambles
21 Laud
22 Electronic component
27 Prunes, in the highlands
29 Monkey's cousin
31 Subordinate
32 Perfume essence
33 Cleveland's baseball team, familiarly
34 Hives give you this
35 Napoleon, once
36 Relative of ette
37 "Two-bounces" call, in tennis
38 Miniature
39 Give another exam
45 Remove forcibly
47 Slow mover
51 Insulting one
54 Slightly-used car
57 Young hooters
58 Yale word of cheer
59 Jewish ceremonial palm branch
61 "Variety" biggie
62 System of beliefs
63 English county
65 Walks in the woods
68 "Here is ___ and true industrious friend." (Shakespeare)
69 Old Spanish gold coin
70 Situates oneself properly
71 In harmony
73 Put into a shell
75 Ditty
80 Statesman of India
83 Lorne or Graham
84 Privileged class: Comb. form
85 Lower
86 Treelike: Comb. form
92 Ultra-cute
93 Part of U.S.A.
95 Of flight: Pref.
96 Kind of school
97 Shops; stores: Abbr.
99 Summer shade
100 Took tiffin
101 ___ Wallace, author of "Ben Hur"
102 Electrical unit
103 Stadium roar

Literary Diversions *by William Canine*

Open to interpretation.

Across

1 Delta debris
5 Shrine
10 NFL linemen
13 Task
16 Major Bowes's medium
17 Cuban martyr-hero
18 Period
19 Self-esteem
20 United Nations headquarters?
23 Stitch
24 Bedstaff
25 "A Passage to ___"
26 Sheer fabrics
28 Nibble at
30 Yosemite peak
32 Compass pt.
33 Pickford sampled the kabob?
41 Debussy's sea
42 Kidney: Comb. form
43 Dr. Huxtable's son
44 Nobelist Wiesel
45 Jones or Swift
46 Virginia City neighbor
48 Patterns
51 Rustle
54 Dried orchid tuber
57 Most recent
58 Nero Wolfe and Archie?
62 Lofts
64 Phantasm
65 Decree
68 Absorbs
71 Glance through
73 A pittance in Paris
74 Private eye
75 Metric weight unit
78 Author Bagnold
80 Levy
81 Kiss Edgar good-bye?
86 Old car
87 Papa, on "I Remember Mama"
88 Actress Merkel
89 People settled far from their homelands
93 Tidal flood
96 "Martha the Mouth"
100 Plunder
101 Rebecca at her most obstreperous?
104 Hooter
105 Scuttle
106 Blackthorn fruits
107 Small songbird
108 Cough up
109 Beale, Basin, etc.
110 Singer Lena
111 Stravinsky

Down

1 Comic commentator Mort
2 Notion
3 Roadside eyesore
4 Besides
5 Hemsley sitcom
6 Garnish
7 Vehicle for Zhivago
8 Blameworthy
9 Tease
10 Singer McEntire
11 Humperdinck heroine
12 Salty
13 Banter
14 S-shaped curve
15 Acknowledges applause
16 Privileges: Abbr.
21 Languish
22 Lets up
27 Chose
29 Scottish seaport
31 Fed. med. research org.
33 Feline plea
34 Truce
35 "I will build me ___ on the greatness of God." (Lanier)
36 Alice's cat
37 Child
38 Some psychiatrists
39 Wire measures
40 Defeat
41 McKinley, Hood, Washington, etc.
47 Music to Escamillo's ears
49 Antiquity
50 Identify
52 Rotters
53 Rhine wine
55 "The Gold Bug" monogram
56 Paid performers
59 American seagoing letters
60 Keepsake
61 ___ out; making do
62 Computes
63 Journey
66 Cover
67 Short dinner jacket?
69 Exclamation of disgust
70 Attorney's undergrad designation
72 ___ de Cervantes
76 Turkish title
77 Dark red cherry
79 Persecute for payment
82 Undersea measures
83 ___ to handle
84 Boy's given name
85 Insect
89 Plummet
90 The Hawkeyes
91 With skill
92 Rose's team
94 Verdon
95 Get up
97 Prefix with gram or drome
98 North Sea feeder
99 WWII area
102 Somewhat: Suff.
103 506, to Caesar

54

World View *by Ronnie K. Allen*

Globetrotters should find nothing unfamiliar here.

Across

1 Love, Latin style
5 Priestly title
9 Promise
13 Crosstie cross
17 Vesuvius output
18 Anna's kingdom
19 Rose's mate
20 Within: Pref.
21 Roquefort
24 River or monster
25 Foot components
26 Hair color
27 Raised
29 Biddy
30 Coin producer
31 Big wheel
32 Crazy, in the westerns
35 One of the seven dwarfs
36 Foil for West
37 NOW goal
38 Gruyère
42 Med. plan
45 Washington group
47 Leo's locution
48 Chunk of dirt
49 Idolize
50 Prone to gossip
51 Was able
52 Survive
54 Mad. or 5th
55 "Credulity is. . .the ___ strength." (Lamb)
56 Sheer fabric
57 Stun
59 "We ___ Overcome"
60 Part of QED
61 Emporium
62 Ballet maneuver
65 Kurosawa epic
66 *Arroz*
69 Knot addendum
70 Bye-bye
72 Ingest
73 "Auld Lang ___"
74 Building dome
75 Chowder ingredient
77 Cleopatra's snake
79 This evening, informally
80 Set down
81 Director's call
84 ___ boy!
85 Auditor, in Peking?
89 Encounter
90 Emanation
91 *Raison d'* ___
92 With 75 Down, Clinton's ditch
93 Villa d' ___
94 This color's just ducky!
95 Pigeon- ___
96 Pearl starter

Down

1 TV alien
2 *Femme*'s partner
3 Microwave
4 Spanish spread
5 Pale
6 "One spade" and "two clubs"
7 Cheers, for one
8 Ipecac and similar agents
9 Common contraction
10 Final notice?
11 ___ Tin Tin
12 June awards
13 Esteem
14 "Too-Ra-Loo-Ra-Loo-Ral"
15 Runs in neutral
16 Insert a bullet
22 Fidel's lieutenant
23 It's original in the Bible
28 Perry's creator
30 North side plant
31 Aflame
32 Bandleader Brown
33 Mother lode
34 *Coucher du soleil*
35 Disastrous
36 Accomplishment
38 Boutique
39 Sported
40 Haberdashery items
41 Nighttime soap
43 Penicillin without a pedigree
44 Betting parameters
46 No longer a minor
48 Mattress parts
50 Romantic isle
51 Pursue
52 ___ and anon
53 "Heartburn" author Ephron
55 In vogue
57 Communal community
58 Sharp pain
59 Narrow cut
62 Metric weight
63 Oxford academician
64 Lamb's mom
66 Vegas machine
67 Cowboy's lowlife
68 Walkman part
71 Sedative
73 Rosemary and basil
74 Pigeon holes?
75 See 92 Across
76 Golfer's position
77 Felt pain
78 Sault ___ Marie
79 Digital display
80 Milanese money
81 160 square rods
82 Stew vegetable
83 Nuremberg negative
86 ___ and cry
87 DDE's arena
88 Comic Skelton

55

Nonesuches *by William Lutwiniak*

Out of the limelight.

Across

1 Padlock site
5 "___ on first?"
9 Bonkers
13 Got credit
17 Proceedings
18 Nonesuch Harris character
20 Aggrieved
21 Nonesuch flying ace
23 Fed
24 Baja blankets
25 Journal finish?
26 Of an eye part
28 Garden area
29 Accumulation
30 Tract conclusion
31 Dark
34 Jabber
35 Toughening
38 Extension cord
39 Nonesuch British traitor
42 Teachers' org.
43 Hoo-ha
44 On earth
45 Dairy case grouping
46 Tie up
47 Gossiped carelessly
49 Bylaws
50 ___ Hopkins
51 Diving position
52 "Olympia" artist
53 Lunar feature
54 Number four wood, once
56 TV's Williams
57 Christen
60 Barbecue favorite
61 Give ___; heed
62 Laurels
63 A Harrison
64 "The cruelest" mo.
65 Nonesuch Goya painting
67 Floribunda
68 Cried
70 Vote against
71 Small change
72 Small cities
73 Ball club
75 Machine part
76 Bogus
77 Yore, of yore
78 Coin-in-slot eatery
82 Discard
83 Nonesuch Flaubert novel
87 Spanish painter
88 Nonesuch Rosalind Russell role
89 Patron of Tasso
90 Similarly
91 Zeno's portico
92 Mex. mamas
93 Timetable, briefly

Down

1 Millinery
2 Yearning
3 Gang follower
4 Moral message
5 Tried the surf
6 Centers
7 ___ shoestring
8 Uneven in quality
9 Chromosome units
10 Soul, in Soissons
11 Astronaut Grissom
12 ___ shootin'
13 Bony
14 With 79 Down, nonesuch Dumas novel
15 Of a time
16 BSA subunit
19 Author MacDonald
22 Fencer's blade
27 Regard
29 Crafted
30 D'Artagnan's friend
31 Mop up
32 Radames's love
33 Nonesuch literary family
34 Gridiron gain
35 Dessert
36 Downtown light
37 Hiatuses
39 Scallion kin
40 "The ___ the Baskervilles"
41 "Gasoline ___"
44 Yokel
46 Separate
48 Lodge income
49 ___ seed; deteriorated
50 Mock
52 Stuck in the mud
53 Family member
54 Seafood
55 Chinese poet
56 Dessert grouping
57 Handle gently
58 Pizzazz
59 Former spouses
61 Spindle tree
62 Swindle
65 Super Bowl unit
66 Garlands
67 Takes out
69 Jinx
71 Roman historian
73 Contemporary of Edison
74 Peace Nobelist Wiesel
75 Dice
76 Comedian Silvers
78 Start of "The Aeneid"
79 See 14 Down
80 TV's Johnson
81 Laundered ore
82 Wee, in Dundee
84 Neighbor of Que.
85 Sgt.
86 Nasser's creation, for short

56

The Deuce, You Say! *by Elizabeth Arthur*

One for Old Harry.

Across

1 Loud
7 Nuisances
12 Swapped
18 Spain and Portugal
19 High home
20 Other, in combinations
21 "Papillon" setting
23 Airplane control surface
24 Happy, to a Scot
25 Blasting stuff
26 Dejected
28 Carrot-family herb
29 It's often to the ground
30 The long way around
33 Kind of pilot
35 Golfer Trevino
36 Eurorail vehicle, in Italy
38 English Channel feeder
39 Acids + alcohols
41 Took the car
43 Narrow shoes
45 Show off
47 National Monument in Wyoming
50 Vincent Lopez's theme song
52 Dress tops
55 Winged
56 Demolished
57 Brewed beverage
58 Maine city
61 Act like Douglas or Webster
63 Gabor
64 Fastener
66 Insider of a sort
68 Water-wand user
70 Utterly wicked
71 Dice
74 "Mama" Cass ____
76 Hosea, in the Douay Bible
77 Change
80 Granada misters
82 Too
84 Pink table wines
86 Queen of the fairies
88 Leave out
89 Not too neat
91 Highlander's cap
92 Of the early Precambrian era
94 Satan's form, at times
96 Valley, to Franz
97 Leslie Caron role
98 Appear suddenly
100 Fail completely
104 Soluble salt
105 Accustom
106 Stun and confuse
107 Sycophant
108 Church confab
109 Libra's symbol

Down

1 Sally Field's TV role
2 Héloïse's lover
3 One who adores
4 Rainbow: Comb. form
5 Part of RSVP
6 Waste-maker
7 Bucolic
8 Lamprey
9 Seville lady: Abbr.
10 Soho cans
11 Calm
12 Common article
13 Storyteller
14 Have you two fives for ____?
15 Thirteen, to some
16 Irregular
17 Gift recipient
22 "____ each life. . ." (Longfellow)
27 Bandit
30 Pigeon home: Var.
31 Merkel and O'Connor
32 Gaucho's rope: Var.
34 Night-light?
37 Central points
40 Frog genus
42 "If ____ I Would Leave You"
44 "The Man From U.N.C.L.E." role
46 *Ecole* student
48 Kind of exercise
49 Paint or path leader
51 Hebrew month
52 Like one cupboard of rhyme
53 Martini fruit
54 Decks of playing cards, to some
56 Boistrous merrymaking
59 Thanksgiving mo.
60 Stew
62 Louise or Turner
65 Model MacPherson
67 Maxwell and Lanchester
69 Ratio words
71 Condemn
72 ____ one's soul, like Faust
73 Intoxicated
75 Flu-shot substances
78 Summery
79 Understand
81 Puts on
83 Brilliantly colored fish
85 Some clowns put them on
86 Asian peninsula
87 Organic compound
90 Lower classes
93 Muslim priest
95 Theater award
97 Mother of Castor and Clytemnestra
99 Kind of money
101 Large cask
102 Gold, to Pedro
103 Xmas mo.

57

Recklessness *by William Canine*

The circled letters spell out a relevant song title.

Across

1 Cleave
5 Senator Thurmond
10 Ridicule
17 Maureen O'___
18 Persian
19 Sewing machine part
20 Prorate
22 In a stack
23 Nova Scotian
24 Labrador hunters
26 Relocate
28 USN rank
29 Start of Vallée's theme song
30 From ___ Z
31 "*Après moi* ___." (Louis XV)
35 Compass pt.
36 On the way
39 One, to Verdi
40 "Sport" for the foolhardy
45 Give directions
46 Sharp ridge
47 NFL official
50 Judge
53 Son of Zeus and Hera
56 Ben Nevis, for one
57 Troy, N. Y., sch.
58 Rhine tributary
59 Bucksaw parts
61 Thwart
62 Carriage
63 Query
66 ___ *majesté*
67 Franklin, our 14th
69 Heat meas.
70 Sometime Verdi librettist
72 Halftone, for instance
74 Act without thought
79 ___ *generis*
80 Board Amtrak
81 Rubbish!
84 Shakespearean knave
88 Op. ___
89 "Vengeance ___ . . ." (Romans 12:19)
92 Clay, today
93 Manner
95 Penmen
96 Uncountable amount

100 Cinder
102 Circumference
103 Bound
104 Gland: Comb. form
105 Fashion magazine
106 Planters
107 Picnic umbrellas?
108 Proofer's mark

Down

1 Crevasses
2 Jack and Bill
3 Sooner ___
4 Corsican patriot
5 Tastes
6 Prefix with corn or pod
7 Skater-actress Vera
8 Sixty minutes
9 Skirt length
10 Enounce
11 Curve
12 Cartoonist Gardner
13 Blighter

14 Bye, in Bordeaux
15 Jargon
16 Civility, to Burns
21 Pro ___
25 Pee Wee and Della
27 French blossom
30 Peak in Turkey
32 Caused by
33 Record
34 He fled Sodom
37 Never, in Nuremberg
38 Cheers! and Skoal!
41 Manipulative one
42 Blvds.
43 Court call
44 Misplay
48 Wagner's "Ring," for example
49 Tickler of a sort
50 Kuwaiti
51 ♣s or ♠s
52 Show indifference
54 Lend again
55 Shoe width
60 Jitterbugger
61 Holiday

63 Concerning
64 Balkan capital
65 Drug-induced state
67 Summer excursion
68 Sign
71 Larceny
73 *Le* ___ *Soleil*
75 CIA predecessor
76 USN rank
77 Flying plate
78 Advance a basketball
82 Politician Tip
83 Quiz taker
84 Daunts
85 Straighten up
86 Medieval Flemish capital
87 Wards off
90 Sp. spouse
91 Played charades
94 Fervor
95 Sell-out signs
97 Stripling
98 Mobster's diamonds
99 ___ hill and dale
101 Chemical ending

58

Originally published in 1987

M*A*S*H NOTES *by Ronnie K. Allen*

Recalling 251 popular episodes.

59

Across

1 Johnny's bandleader
4 Tom Jones's hit, "____ a Lady"
8 Desktop computers, popularly
11 Attack
16 Christian or Victorian
17 Mrs. Fred Flintstone
19 Deteriorate
20 Composer Copland
21 The padre
24 Palm leaf
25 Mah-jongg pieces
26 Cut of meat
27 Actor Michael, and family
28 Off the beaten path
30 ____ d'oeuvre
31 Animal house?
32 Rex and Donna
33 Surgeon from Crabapple Cove
38 Chessmen: Abbr.
39 Rosie's, and others
40 Can. province
41 Musical talent
42 Modern Olympian
45 Ten-speed
47 Wagnerian work
49 Easily handled, as a vessel
50 ____ de soie; dress fabric
51 Plumbing and carpentry
52 Spin-off subject
57 Most like a day in June
58 Latin lesson word
59 Julio Iglesias hit
60 ____ nous
61 Church corner
62 Former
65 ____-fi
66 Bud's buddy
67 ". . .the ____ of March"
68 Vote in favor
70 The colonel
75 ____ on; encouraged
77 Seep out
78 Proverbial predecessor to riches
79 Towheads
80 "Killing Me ____"
83 Tex-Mex sandwich
84 Stallone character
85 Epic of Troy
86 Radar
90 Type size
91 Nothing's alternative
92 Enjoy the taste
93 Promissory note
94 Won, at chess
95 Limit, in the saying
96 Authors
97 Hole punch

Down

1 NFL platoon
2 ____ pro nobis
3 Most prone to gossip
4 Ocean movements
5 Signed on
6 "Desire Under the ____"
7 TX school
8 Laud
9 Famed counsel Roy
10 Hog's haven
11 Trek after animals
12 Branch of biology
13 Mangle
14 Whole step, musically
15 Targets for Marino
18 Permits
22 Hastened
23 Irish bottle stop?
27 Rank for 33 Across, e. g.
28 Biblical refuge
29 Greek cheese
30 Fabled also-ran
31 Nota ____
33 Abominating one
34 Abner of the comics
35 Sounding thin
36 One who nurses
37 Wipe clean
39 Tours topper
43 Bouncing off the walls
44 Temporary failure
45 Writer Brendan
46 Fleming, and others
47 Believe it ____!
48 Fatherly prefix
50 Apple or pear
51 New York City Square
52 Lock of hair
53 Mink, house, or dressing
54 Clarinetist Shaw
55 Bottleneck
56 Worker in rattan
61 Best, to Lloyd's
62 Pindaric poetry
63 Southern flower
64 Gave the once-over
66 Goldbricking
67 "And So ____"
69 MS markers
71 Turn on an axis
72 Like some Jell-O salads
73 By mouth
74 Diplomatic forte
75 "____ Tune"
76 Mongolian desert
79 Snoopy's aviator enemy
80 Setting for 89 Down
81 Gymnast Korbut
82 Decree
83 Donahue's stock-in-trade
84 Wander about
86 Existed
87 Seance sound
88 Overnight temperature, usually
89 "The King and I" king

Candidly Speaking *by Bill Leonard*

There's nothing covert here. It's all out in the open.

60

Across

1 Black-tie affairs
6 More secure
11 On high
16 Bullrings
18 Dodge
19 Stab in the back
21 Gift of the Magi
23 Kind of valve for fuel
24 Rooter
25 Gleeful
26 Shows approval or drowsiness
28 Teachers' org.
29 Old dagger
31 W-4 perpetrators
32 Drought-resistant ornamental evergreen
33 Lampoon
34 Dream state
36 Flaming
38 Broaches
39 Tranquility and Clouds, on the moon
40 Legion
41 Architect Sir Christopher
42 Floats
45 Arm (Fr.)
46 Top-drawer
48 ___-ski clothes
49 Field laborer
50 Kismet
51 Cruise or Hanks
53 Eye drop
54 Candor
56 Dancer Kelly
57 Taloned flier
58 Vivid
59 Origin
60 Zodiac sign
61 Lean, plus
63 "___ of the Flies"
64 A bunch of smarties
65 Enemies
66 Letter opener
67 Mitch Miller's instrument
69 Cut back
71 Realm
72 Immensely
75 Towel word
76 White with age
77 See 77 Down
78 Leak out
80 Correct for place and time
81 Spoils
82 Protects
85 Pitch
86 Farmer, in planting season
88 Old Blue Eyes
91 Deserved
92 Bizarre
93 Special aptitude
94 Former Moscow rulers
95 Obligations
96 Analyze, in a way

Down

1 Hooks
2 Brazen; out-and-out
3 Near-miss, in horseshoes
4 Lee ___ Meriwether
5 Purpose
6 Factions
7 Away from the wind
8 Reserve
9 Asner and Begley
10 End of the ride, for Sally Ride
11 Dwell
12 Camera part
13 Polo Grounds star
14 Mary Shelley novel, commonly
15 Swindle or shelter
17 Quartz makings
20 Irish poet William Butler ___
22 Nostrils
27 Aficionado's cheer
30 Springtime observance
32 Goals
33 Graf ___
35 "The Untouchables" leader
36 Moses's brother
37 Capital of Kentucky
38 Trieste liquid measure
41 Gagsters
42 Charge
43 Copycats
44 Weiners
45 Orson ___
46 Swift
47 Musical sounds
49 Quarry
50 ___ off; repulse
52 Tableland
54 Bogs
55 Scandinavian
56 Welcomes
58 Joint at risk on the gridiron
60 Hoople of "Our Boarding House"
62 Charged particles
63 Fish-story teller
66 Having workers
67 Sets of 6 or 8 balls bowled, in cricket
68 Brigand
69 Aspect
70 Iterate
71 Nearest star
73 Missive
74 Aspires
76 Groups
77 Rests a bit, with 77 Across
79 Jabber
81 Aristocrat
82 Raiment
83 Entity
84 Click
87 Heredity transmission stuff, for short
89 Female ruff
90 Montgomery's st.

Round The Wheel *by Kathryn Righter*

And the crayon box.

Across

1 Naples staple
6 Like Parmesan cheese, often
12 Card game for two
15 Ford's predecessor
16 Entertains
18 Biblical name
20 Reading at the prime meridian
22 Walks along the beach
24 Shoe width
25 Seasonal visitor
26 Tunic of the eye
28 Stadium cheer
29 Belgrade native
31 Words of consent
32 West Flanders casualty of 1914-17
34 Term of address
35 Girl
37 Calm
38 Novelist Ferber
39 Least colorful
42 More repugnant
43 Goddess of discord
44 Faulty
45 Macho
46 Rabbit fur
48 Cook's containers
49 Ancient: Comb. form
50 Stormy outbursts
52 Social insect
53 Grimm heroine
55 Garden tool
57 Montana's ____ National Park
60 "The Subject Was ____"
61 Desirable
62 Live
63 Scuba user
64 On the length of
65 Competent
66 Rescues
67 Span
68 Cleaving tool
69 "____ of the Pack"
71 Raised
72 ____ a bet; wagers
73 Church feature
74 "Exodus" character
75 Some rulers: Abbr.
79 Wane
80 Grandiose
81 Disconcert
83 Brazilian macaw
84 Uncivilized places
86 Louis Hayward swashbuckler of 1948
90 Mongrels
91 Most unworldly
92 Renter's agreement
93 Hurricane center
94 Jousting weapons
95 Carried

Down

1 Capitol Hill employees
2 Concur
3 Derisive expression
4 Golfer's gadget
5 Grain bristles
6 Reduces to fine particles
7 Right-hand page
8 Turkish title
9 Sylvester, to Tweety Pie
10 Hebrew judge
11 More decorous
12 Musical sound-effect
13 Att.'s org.
14 "Little ____," nursery tale
17 Number of the Pleiades
19 Catches on
21 Hourglass figure feature
23 New York stadium
27 Compass dir.
30 Consecrate
32 Hwang Ho
33 Victim of the hunt
34 Canary-like finch
36 Onager
37 Tendon
39 Family member
40 Surrounded by
41 He slept under a haystack
42 Courage
43 Tome or gram start
45 French painter
46 Subsequently
47 Stores brandy or Scotch
49 Greek letters
50 Ascends
51 Influential Chinese family of recent times
54 Fly like a hummingbird
56 Rim
58 Shafts; spindles
59 Abbrev. in French company names
61 Slide
63 1920s art form
64 Part of "to be"
65 Kind of numerals
66 Suitcase
67 Short and sweet
68 Took off
69 Part of a race
70 Choice
71 Leaves
74 Humiliate
76 Corday's victim
77 Ordinary writing
78 Cut
80 Being (Lat.)
81 Guinness
82 Sentry's cry
85 Arid
87 Historical period
88 Storage place
89 Old car

61

Originally published in 1987

Daily Routine *by M.R.*

Early Wynn, a Hall-of-Fame pitcher whose reputation was "tough guy," comments on aging athletes.

Across

1 Soothed
7 Dinette piece
12 Two-timers
16 Musical passage
17 Desperate
19 American playwright
21 **Start of quote**
23 Jack Sprat's dietician's warning
24 Gladden
25 Confirmation: Abbr.
26 ___ Tracy of the comics
28 Baseball stat.
29 Call-up org.
30 Quiet!
31 Missile housing
32 Fire
33 **Quote, part 2**
38 Indulgent
41 Desert nobleman: Var.
42 June words
43 Humiliated
44 Farm beasts
45 Margin for error
48 ___ on; played grandma
49 Who's sorry now?
50 Paddles
51 Sleep-student's initials
53 See 87 Down
54 **Quote, part 3**
56 "I Remember ___"
57 DDE's command
58 Fido's feet
59 Round: Abbr.
60 Diver's delight
61 Shows scorn
63 Red tape perspective
64 Idiot ___
65 Fond du ___, Wisconsin
66 ___ Lisa
67 Málaga moola
68 **Quote, part 4**
73 Horse color
74 Sailor's saint
75 "Peggy ___ Got Married"
76 Charge
79 Capone and Kaline
80 Contemporary of Agatha
81 Deity
82 Casa rooms
84 Repulsive, in a way
86 **End of quote**
90 "Come up and ___ sometime."
91 Hi-fi
92 Lombard
93 ___ Scott decision
94 Mortimer ___
95 Eats away at

Down

1 Diners
2 Seedcases
3 Milan money
4 The lion's share
5 Italian noble name
6 Period
7 Stylish
8 Baseball's Aaron
9 S. Amer. country
10 Notorious Amin
11 More red-complected
12 Cosh
13 Fuss
14 Triumph over
15 Laundry additive
18 French soldier
20 Ante
22 Common contraction
27 Office machines
30 Transmit
31 Outer covering
32 Kind of job
33 More sagacious
34 Obey
35 Pliable
36 Typical stuff, here
37 March time
38 Soup spoon
39 Small Brit. gun ships
40 Canada or Japan
44 Yours and mine
45 Not clerical
46 Ark's resting place
47 Soo's role on "Barney Miller"
49 Tiffs
50 Fairy-tale monster
52 Soda shop orders
54 Infantryman, at times
55 Hyderabad sovereign
56 Man with a van
58 Fuel
60 Instance (Ital.)
62 Verve
63 Single: Comb. form
64 Dry
66 Occasions
67 Bluenose
68 Orchestra section
69 Turned over
70 Not so hard
71 Cinders and Fitzgerald
72 Crustacean of a certain order
76 Swamp
77 Bald or golden
78 Road curves
80 Gave the once-over
81 Theater patron
82 Headliner
83 One hairdo
85 Sra., on the Seine
87 See 53 Across
88 Charlemagne's realm: Abbr.
89 Diamonds, in caper movies

62

No Riders *by Louis Sabin*

Perhaps Mr. Sabin prefers the horse-and-buggy era.

Across

1 Actress Irene
6 Shakespearean
12 Peru natives
17 "____ of Two Cities"
18 May or Stritch
19 Go by balloon
20 Wheelless chap in Durham?
22 Spitball
23 Type
24 Gave a PG or an R
25 Dick Tracy's wife
27 Manx or Persian
28 Highland host
30 Japanese payment
31 Play the fool
33 Flavor
34 Copyist
36 Sluggish
37 Initiate
38 Old boxing glove
41 In an off-the-wall way
42 Anodyne
43 Ready for use
44 Turn inside out
45 Large stork
48 Masque
49 Break off
50 Marriage, for example
51 Electrician's mantra?
52 Latin lesson word
53 Shrinking NBAer?
55 Kindergarten break
56 Gehrig
57 Holiday preceders
58 Corner
59 Adriatic port
60 Warbled
62 Find new tenants
63 Turkic language
64 Preserve
65 Airport agreement
66 "Honor Thy Father" author
67 Spokes
69 Renowned statue
70 Ergo
71 Eager, plus
72 Quay
73 "Le Coq ____"
74 Hebrew letter
78 Diver's perfect score
79 Mystic letter
80 Dude's problems
82 Trireme hand
83 Visible missile
85 Short 1971 Ann-Margret film?
89 At an angle
90 Sidesteps
91 She preceded Ginger
92 Retreats
93 Scottish stripling
94 Tough problem

Down

1 Wall Street worry
2 Bikini, for one
3 Cold-weather wear
4 High, to Solti
5 Very, in Munich
6 Merman was one
7 Outsider
8 Fan dancer Sally
9 Cicero's 502
10 One ____ million
11 Millenium segment
12 "Our Man in Havana" actor
13 Zip
14 Plant ash shortage?
15 NFL strikers of 1987
16 Davenport's cousin
19 Church extension
21 Watering holes
26 Superlative ending
29 Brazilian port
31 Man who took a shortcut to success?
32 Yield
33 Syllables that trip off the tongue
35 Young komondor
36 That is, to Galba
37 Editor's mark
38 Silver-white metal
39 Captivate
40 National League team with no drive?
41 Tracks
42 Wash
44 Hunted lampreys
45 Power
46 Maureen and Scarlett
47 Diamond decider
49 African feline
50 Chef's tool
53 Melvin at the bar
54 Ticked off
59 Model wood
61 Placed
62 Gad
63 Cross
65 "Show Boat" character
66 Cast
67 Wicker
68 Disinclined
69 Study
70 Muscular
72 Angler's come-on
73 Cartoon tyke
75 Ore veins
76 Philadelphia flyer?
77 More liberated
79 Short agents?
80 Losing streak
81 Kind of hockey shot
84 Sleeping unit
86 Ms. Gardner
87 Israeli landing place
88 Old name for Tokyo

63

Dilemma *by Sidney L. Robbins*

Except for 1 Across, every clue defines two words. Decide which word goes in each of the identical halves of the grid. The solution is unique!

Across

1 Comfy
9 Trig functions/ Calculation
10 Self/Self
11 Aleutian isle/ Containers
12 Ebb or neap/Ogle
13 Projectionist's need/ Pub drinks
14 Takes off/Taken off
16 Slips up/Tradition
19 *Raison d'* ___/ An inning has six
20 Secede/Recently
24 Poet's Muse/ "___ Irish Rose"
25 Stan "the ___" Musial/Baden-Baden, for one
26 Care for/ Wind direction gadget
28 ___ and robbers/ To laugh, in Paris
30 Always/Terminates
32 Single/Aid
33 Mature/Fix over
35 Angers/Clean house
37 Clean the deck/ Petticoat
38 Curtain edging/Row
41 Sink, like the sun before dusk/Unlike baby, usually

43 Gush/Decorate
44 Senior/Bill attachment
46 Past/Crimson
48 Love, Italian style/Foreign
49 Golfer's peg/ Three: Pref.
50 Swit movie/ Dorothy's dog
51 Belgrade native/ Snoozes

Down

1 Common/Look fixedly at
2 Lass/Observe
3 Speak/Kind of sanctum

4 Frenchman/Renowned loch
5 Humanity/TV soap
6 King, to Pierre/ Observe
7 Representative/Beneath
8 Wild fowl/Drills
15 Yours and mine/ News bit
17 Kid/Paddle
18 Feminine ending/ Get rid of
20 Singer Ethel/ Jimmies
21 Beach feature/ Fork feature
22 Desktop computer brand/Merits
23 Joint/Stinger
27 Sin, for example/ Once more

29 Debt initials/ Poetic contraction
31 D.C. figure/Weep
34 "The ___ and the Pendulum"/ 24 hours
36 *Uno, due,* ___/ D.C. figure
39 Major blood vessel/ Furious
40 Tent caterpillar/ Crawl
41 Dull/Chair
42 ___ Lincoln, film's first Tarzan/ Stir up
43 Plane leader?/ Soothsayer
45 The ___ is cast/ Speck
47 Globe/___ Moines

64

The Write Stuff *by Kathryn Righter*

Ms. Righter, a veteran puzzlewright, writes of writing. Can you get this one all right? All right, then.

65

Across

1 Ginger cookie
5 Units of work
9 Lens type
14 San ____, Italy
15 Short fiber
16 Ancient country, source of Solomon's wealth
17 Stash
18 Make well
19 Harmonize; agree
20 Pictographic writing
23 Use public transport
24 Boy
25 Ointment
27 Body of water
29 Tilt
32 Honored American playwright
33 Diplomat's asset
34 Mrs. Dithers
35 Of writing where siht ekil daer senil in alternation
38 Not so much

39 Potpourri
40 Flavoring source
41 Compass dir.
42 Ancient
43 Coven constituent
44 ____ Angeles
46 Merchandising event
47 Deciphering of secret writing
53 Bea Arthur role
54 Mural location
55 Related
57 Pooped
58 Reside; dwell
59 Needle case
60 Defenses
61 Coin-op feature
62 Moist

Down

1 Grad. class

2 Low country: Abbr.
3 Mine (Fr.)
4 Lacking authority or force
5 Write as a cipher
6 Cosmetic counter purchase
7 Daughter
8 Warp count, in weaving
9 Coffee variety
10 Garden pest
11 Stylish, to say the least
12 Edges
13 Mineral rock
21 Metal fastener
22 Dinnerware item
25 Blackthorns
26 Mistreat
27 Tasty
28 Reverberate
29 Invigorating potion

30 Hibernian
31 Step
32 Competent
33 Kind of bridge
34 Disputed
36 Perch
37 Seven times a week
43 Billfold
44 Groucho's tattooed lady of song
45 Prepares for the business day
46 Artillery offering
47 Ring up
48 Dominate
49 Leatherworker's tools
50 Brad
51 Greek letter
52 Depressed urban area
53 Atlas item
56 Dunk

Intrigue! *by Roger H. Courtney*

Troubled times.

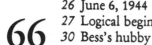

Across

1 Commander in chief, at the time
7 Word often confused with "may"
10 Influential money source: Abbr.
13 List of mistakes
14 To the point
15 Man-mouse connection
16 Lieutenant-colonel in the middle
18 "Y," pluralized
19 Possible advice from a stockbroker
20 Doorway: Abbr.
21 From the time that
23 Kudos upon kudos
26 June 6, 1944
27 Logical beginning?
30 Bess's hubby
31 Golfer's gadget
32 Evergreen tree
33 Kind of code
34 Wheedled
37 Roofer's goo
38 Boarders at the beach
40 Bow ___
41 Party
43 His first novel was "Battle Cry"
44 One of NOW's causes
45 Beatty or Sparks
46 Troll's cousin
47 Ring leader?
48 Guffaw
50 Mathematical vipers?
52 City in Florida's horse country
54 ___ gehts? (How goes it?)
55 Use a blue pencil
59 "Brother ___," 1938 film with 1 Across

60 Like the 1986 dealings
64 Filmmaker's org.
65 "I'm in charge" Secretary of State
66 Electrical conductors
67 Frequent biblical word ending
68 The one over there, once
69 Calyx leaves

Down

1 Antique autos
2 Perry's creator
3 Seed covering
4 Swedish port
5 Ingested
6 GRF's vice president

7 Bow
8 Op or pop follower
9 Utmosts
10 Onetime national security advisor
11 House palm
12 Former CIA head
14 Administrative "thorn in the side"
17 "___, My God, to Thee"
22 It seemed like a good ___ at the time
24 Hounded
25 Jack ___, gangster film star of the '30s
27 Newts
28 Farewell for Antonio
29 Supportive senator from Utah
31 Restless sleeper

34 Arson, for one
35 Irish republic
36 Turn a ___ ear; refuse to listen
39 Destroyed by degrees
42 Not illusionary
46 King Arthur's nephew
48 Goddesses of the seasons
49 ___ of thousands
51 Pay for a round of drinks
53 Throbbing
56 Merrill of films
57 Part of IBM
58 Dick Tracy's wife
61 Pathet ___
62 Snake turn
63 Ursula Andress film

66

Originally published in 1989

When VIPs Meet *by James E. Hinish, Jr.*

More than forty VIPs surround three apt introductions.

Across

1 Fundamentals
5 Curiosity from China
10 Take —— view of; disapprove
14 Playwright Anita ——
15 George Peppard's TV series, "The ——"
16 PBS science series
17 Welsh poet meets English poet
20 Author of "Fables in Slang"
21 School attended by Anthony Eden
22 Across: Pref.
23 Psyche's love
24 Cooper or Coleman
26 "A Tale of Two Cities" hero
29 Vader's foe
30 Fuss
33 Guinness
34 Runyon
35 Eating apple, familiarly
36 TV actress meets TV actress
40 Merkel of the movies
41 "60 Minutes" regular
42 Miss Kett
43 Calendar abbr.
44 Edison or Eliot, e.g.
45 With 34 Down, author of "Moll Flanders"
47 International relief org.
48 Favorable notice
49 "The Front Page" playwright
52 Singer Perry ——
53 Auden's "always"
56 '30s bandleader meets '30s singer
60 Author O'Flaherty
61 Land of Juan Carlos
62 Actress Merrill
63 The "man for all seasons"
64 "The Duke"
65 Getz or Kenton

Down

1 "M*A*S*H" star
2 Hopalong Cassidy's portrayer
3 "High Society" Porter
4 Agcy. estab. by FDR
5 George C. Scott's memorable role
6 Aramis's comrade
7 Night light?
8 Stop up
9 GP's org.
10 Irate
11 Girl's name
12 Lendl
13 1954 and 1965 MVP
18 Pianist Peter ——
19 Like Charles Atlas
23 Emulate Albrecht Dürer
24 TV's —— Pyle
25 Pseudonym of Charlotte Maria Tucker
26 Author of "The Plague"
27 "Babbitt" star —— MacMahon
28 Summary
29 Soupy ——
30 Cremona's famous son
31 *Divina Commedia* author
32 Of a numbering system based on eight
34 See 45 Across
37 Chartwell, to Churchill
38 "Cowardly lion" actor
39 Coty or Magritte
45 Singer Vic ——
46 Bard's river
47 Sound the hour
48 Substance used by Itzhak Perlman
49 First Ado Annie in "Oklahoma!"
50 Pinza
51 Alexis, for one
52 Ali, formerly
53 Emulate Horace Greeley
54 Novelist Ferber
55 Pat Nixon, née ——
57 Sydney's state: Abbr.
58 Fed. clean water gp.
59 MS polishers

67

Award Ceremonies *by Louis Sabin*

Four winners of two awards, courtesy of a
blue-ribbon New Jersey composer.

Across

1 Shark
5 Role players
9 Wimbledon winner Pat
13 Love, personified
14 Muezzin's deity
15 Medley
16 Award dating from 1901
19 Study
20 Very soon after
21 City on the Loire
22 Gershwin and Levin
23 Kismet
24 1987 recipient of 16 Across
27 1975 recipient of 16 Across
31 Described a curve
32 Lapdogs, in brief
33 Kimono adjunct
34 Bulldogs' school
35 Expressed joy, in a way
36 Pinnacle
37 Hagen onstage
38 Clubs for Tway
39 Embattled Attorney General
40 1963 recipient of 52 Across
42 1984 recipient of 52 Across
43 Bud holder
44 Diving bird
45 Wows the bobby-soxers

68

48 River isles
49 Actress Gardner
52 Award dating from 1947
55 Vocational school tool
56 Former rulers in Tehran
57 Cleveland's waterfront
58 Do lawn work
59 Flew
60 Silent Negri

Down

1 Pride-leader's pride
2 Fukien port
3 Osaka Bay metropolis
4 Valuable vein content
5 Laine and Moore
6 Astronaut Shepard
7 Mil. group headquartered in Nebraska
8 "____ and the Dead"
9 Ophthalmologist's subject
10 Landed
11 Junior or large
12 Gardening gear
14 Dismay: Var.
17 Enticed
18 Byways
22 Words of recognition
23 Gridiron ploys
24 On the ____; rising
25 Nettled
26 Acclaim
27 Rouen's river
28 Vied at the rodeo
29 Beyond overweight
30 December 24th flyer
32 Simple language
35 Most furious
36 Time period: Var.
38 Tabriz native
39 Bullwinkle, for one
41 Brought out
42 Early Teutons
44 Nimble
45 Bird's food receptacle
46 Chased hounds
47 Seep
48 Yonder
49 Drome or plane prefix
50 Colorado resort town
51 Rug type
53 Surprised reaction
54 Sure 'nuff!

Not So Good   *by Bill Leonard*

Depends if Michael Jackson's involved or not.

69

Across

1 Bandanna's cousin
6 Spindly
10 West and Murray
14 Walk-on
15 Took a bus
16 "Dancing Queen" group
17 Willow
18 Lou Costello's confession
20 Hitched
21 Dracula's thing
23 Barbara and Sir Anthony
24 March 15th, for example
25 Applesauce no-no
27 Cold dishes
30 Raillery
34 Bad deed
35 Legion
36 Part of USSR
37 M. Descartes
38 Shopping meccas
39 Disastrous
40 One, in Orléans
41 Dollar fractions
42 Region of Germany
43 Dakota region
45 Cuddle
46 Important work
47 Constructed
48 Monk
51 July 4th sound
52 Likely
55 Net game
58 Bad judgment
60 Auk genus
61 Group
62 Heft
63 Wimbledon rating
64 Griffith of "Matlock"
65 Condition

Down

1 Old tub
2 Item for Perry Mason
3 Right there
4 Sandpiper
5 Proscribed
6 Overworked
7 It might be on the range
8 Mrs. Cantor
9 Its cap. is Lincoln
10 Aggravate
11 Singer Lane
12 Dark color
13 Announces
19 High abode
22 "____ a Miracle" (Manilow hit)
24 Notre ____
25 Sagan and Yastrzemski
26 Tote board postings
27 Brighten
28 Madison Square Garden, for instance
29 Hit straight
30 Hardware store purchases
31 Actor's whisper
32 Pierces
33 Smoothes
35 Staff members
38 Diner's reading matter
39 Challenge
41 Bay of Naples resort island
42 Heckles
44 Appeared imminent
45 Fire
47 Manilow's first hit
48 Men-in-blue gps.
49 Harsh breathing sound
50 Futile
51 007
52 Met air
53 Fort
54 Panther's perch
56 Where Magic and Isiah compete: Abbr.
57 Sunburn's prelude
59 Fink

Originally published in 1989

Seascape   *by James E. Hinish, Jr.*

"An ocean is forever asking questions..."—Edwin Arlington Robinson

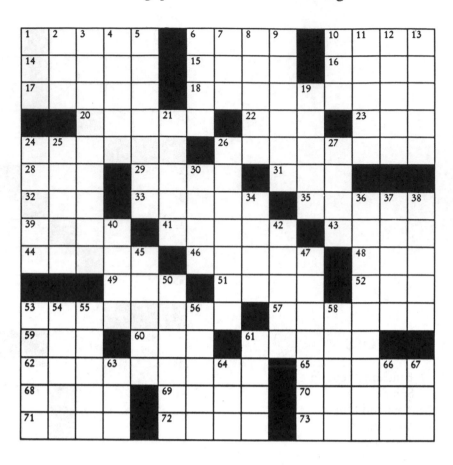

Across

1 Narrow inlet
6 Gaff or yard
10 "Tosca" has three
14 Strait of ____, also called Pas de Calais
15 Diminutive ending
16 Cheer for
17 Slender; frail
18 Chew
20 Spokes
22 Poetic time of day
23 Light touch
24 Chum around
26 Holiday drinks
28 From ____ Z
29 Give up
31 Kicker's device
32 Depot: Abbr.
33 Eskimo vessel
35 Garbage
39 Sea gull
41 Word after postage or gas
43 Aware of
44 "Live Free ____" (New Hampshire's motto)
46 Stalks and ears tied together
48 Hue's partner
49 Baton Rouge inst.
51 Sailor's saint
52 "2001" computer
53 Sailor's guide
57 Turn into
59 Greek letter
60 Corrode
61 Bicuspid's neighbor
62 Trim
65 Prepare to correct
68 "...a ____'clock scholar"
69 Helmsman's direction
70 "Cosmos" writer
71 Cinnabar and hematite
72 Salamander
73 Worries

Down

1 Hyde Park monogram
2 DiMaggio
3 To extremes
4 Fortification
5 Place to repair boats
6 Trucker's trailer
7 School org.
8 Bewildered
9 Examine again
10 Circle segment
11 Raccoon's cousin
12 Sum
13 Paces
19 Map detail
21 Certain girder
24 Must
25 Water mammal
26 Sailor's concern
27 Aviation prefix
30 Changes the color

34 Bottom timber
36 Alaskan city
37 Former NFL coach Hank
38 According to ____
40 River at Thebes
42 Rocky's cousin?
45 Curves
47 Having no enemies
50 Person from Provo
53 Basil-garlic-oil-cheese sauce
54 Unidentical
55 Singer Frankie
56 "And thereby hangs ____" (Rabelais)
58 Jeweler's weight
61 Encounter
63 Not neg.
64 Parishioner's place
66 Noticed
67 Seagoing grad.

Basics *by Ernie Furtado*

Mr. Furtado occasionally likes to do things in a very straightforward manner.

71

Across

1 Halloween wear
6 Kind of school
10 Former tennis great
14 Knock for ——; devastate
15 Explorer De ——
16 Novelist O'Flaherty
17 Purpose
18 **Beginning of a basic series**
20 Clairvoyance letters
21 Boston basketball pro
23 Near East coin
24 **Part 2 of the series**
25 Fencing blade
27 Records
30 Warbler
31 Police-call letters
34 Former Gotham mayor
35 Deborah and John
36 West of Hollywood
37 Belfry denizens
38 **Subset of the basic series**
39 Small bit
40 Before
41 Tangle
42 Thesaurus name
43 Draft gp.
44 Ed and Mel
45 Uses crayons
46 Vb. tense
47 Cipher
48 Actor Davis
51 Finish line
52 FDR agency
55 **Part 3 of the series**
58 Former president
60 Rebekah's son
61 Tiptop
62 Meeting of lovers
63 Former gridder Kyle
64 Has obligations
65 Small and large are two

Down

1 Spice
2 "——, poor Yorick..." ("Hamlet")
3 "Mmm-mmm-good" dish
4 Tyson stats.
5 Skin spot
6 Hymn
7 —— E. Lee
8 Cousin of et al.
9 Seal school
10 1966 Bacharach song
11 Omen
12 Derisive response
13 Arab chieftain
19 Barbara and Anthony
22 Urban rail systems, for short
24 Predicaments
25 Flynn of film
26 Llama land
27 Monastics
28 Approaches
29 Archibald and Thurmond
30 Dams
31 Pancho, to Cisco Kid
32 Mater's mate
33 Borscht base
35 Famed odist
38 Feed the kitty
39 Double agent
41 More tender
42 Squirrels, for example
45 Flatfoot
46 Durable ribbed fabric
47 Grottos
48 Unique person
49 Average
50 Quarrel
51 Call the ——; control
52 **End of the series**
53 Emulate Brinkley
54 They're opposed to syns.
56 —— Paulo
57 Haul
59 A son of Bela

Victors   by H.P. Burchfield

This puzzle and the following one relate winners and losers. Fittingly,
Mr. Burchfield used the same diagram for both puzzles.

72

Across

1 Once a winner, later a loser in his own right
7 Winning side
12 Winners' color
16 Take —— to; befriend
17 Papal vestment
18 Tear
19 Commander on 7-2-63
22 Tired flop
23 Fertility goddess
24 Of days gone by
25 "...the —— of Greece!" (Byron)
27 Broadcast
29 Grads-to-be
30 Pungent root
34 Cosmetics name of fame
36 The Chief
40 Kettle handle
41 Laughing
42 Morass
46 Queen killer
47 Losing charger
50 The Bronx, e.g.
51 Famed electricity explorer
54 Uncanny
55 Trunk
56 One Seminary Ridge defender
60 Matures
61 Some ducks
62 Bond rating
65 Chief's cognomen
66 Jalopy
69 Made a mistake
71 Asian country
72 Military posts

77 Victors road
81 Grain
82 The vanquished on 4-9-65
83 Most optimistically
84 Cemetery Hill defender
85 Never —— moment
86 '80s Attorney General and family

Down

1 Confine
2 Kind of car
3 Japanese measures
4 Auto need
5 The King's ——
6 Sift peas, British style
7 John Brown's necktie
8 Fragrant rootstock
9 Nuclear exposure units

10 Insurance notation: Abbr.
11 Layer
12 "Jacques —— Is Alive..."
13 Clues
14 Beneath
15 Anthony and Barbara
20 —— Blas de Santillane
21 Tasty mushrooms
26 Natty
27 Jeanne's home
28 Altar words
30 Morocco's capital
31 Demean
32 Boring ones
33 Associated with: Suff.
34 Front: Comb. form
35 Vane dir.
37 Twice DI
38 Boot tiers
39 Signed
43 Home

44 Tooth
45 Spoils
48 Tyr, English style
49 Hebrew month: Var.
52 Fall behind
53 Wear away
55 Flower haven
57 San Francisco's —— Hill
58 Maa-maa mama
59 Sweetheart, in Bonn
62 Stalin's successor
63 Sweeper upper
64 Beast
66 Fishing basket
67 Indian carnivore
68 Common arthropod
70 Greek letters
71 Eskimo's pad: Var.
73 Clerical title
74 Entreats
75 Gaelic
76 NCOs
78 La's leader
79 Renowned ref. work
80 Sweet potato

Originally published in 1989

Losers   *by H.P. Burchfield*

Completing the theme set forth in the previous puzzle.

Across

1 Maj. Gen. ___; rear guard commander
7 Losing side
12 Losers' color
16 Arbitrarily penalize
17 Chilean concert pianist
18 Nobel physicist, 1944
19 Commander, 7-1-63
22 Derogatory
23 Wine, in combinations
24 Cemetery Hill loser
25 Dispatch boat
27 Prince Valiant's son
29 But, to Caesar
30 Neotropical rodent
34 Rocket booster
36 The Chief loser
40 Aware of
41 Frost, in France
42 Affix a seal
46 Ten or press follower
47 Roman magistrates
50 Jack ___, Nick Yemana
51 Of the kidneys
54 Provide grazing land for a fee
55 Elbe tributary
56 Cemetery Ridge charge leader
60 Dodge
61 Girls
62 PD alert
65 ___ antiqua (13th century style of music)
66 Boss
69 Read intently
71 Hawaiian goose
72 Saint's day, in Salerno
77 19 Across's final road
81 What's ___ for me?
82 One television signal
83 Get there
84 Singer Abbe
85 Victor on 4-9-65
86 Do a slow burn

Down

1 Chokes or jokes
2 Portent
3 17th century Italian painter
4 ___ Scott decision; *casus belli*
5 Sheathed
6 Educ. soc.
7 Eastern gowns
8 U. of Maine campus location
9 ___ *et orbi*
10 To, in Glasgow
11 Wallace's "Ben ___"
12 Waxed
13 Lung sounds
14 White poplar
15 Give way
20 56, Roman style
21 Kind of racket
26 Precipitation that doesn't reach the ground
27 ___ Khan
28 Gun a motor
30 Lacy
31 Style of writing
32 Frequently
33 Sci-fi vehicle
34 Kind of penguin
35 Questioned, regionally
37 Understand
38 Gerontologist's study
39 Snow on Mont Blanc
43 Residue
44 Malory's "Le ___ d'Arthur"
45 Rhymers
48 Duke U. study
49 Rural crossing
52 Ice or Bronze
53 Dressage movement
55 Informal approvals
57 Primitive propeller
58 Rural rtes.
59 Bus token
62 The cruelest month, wrote Eliot
63 Maharashtra city
64 Bear
66 Fasten again
67 Remove a houseplant from its setting
68 Durocher
70 Cigar or major ending
71 It means nothing to Juanita
73 To be, in Paris
74 Mix up
75 "Jabberwocky" gimbler
76 Fired abruptly
78 Playground game
79 "___ Day Will Come" (Frankie Valli hit)
80 "No ___" (Duran's surrender)

73

Lazybones *by Elizabeth Arthur*

Relax. Take your time. There's no hurry.

Across

1 Turkish bigwig, once
6 Fernando or Lorenzo
11 Commence
16 "Stormy Weather" composer
17 Nimble
18 Make amends
19 Good-for-nothings
21 Former Israeli prime minister Meir
22 Basic root
23 Vein ingredients
24 Shoshoneans
26 Pickpocket
27 Barrel parts
29 Zoo staffer
30 Some execs. have 'em
31 Actor/director Brooks
32 Dillydallyer
35 More competent
38 Railbird
39 Inhabit
42 Doz. upon doz.
43 Asterisk
44 Indigestion relief
45 0
46 Noah's eldest son
47 Monastery brothers
48 Late jazz trombonist Winding
49 Intertwines
51 Freshwater duck
52 A red one isn't worth much
53 Early space station
54 Crow's nest support
55 Charles and Helmer
56 Social whirler
58 Tosspot
59 Letters from Athens
61 One, six, etc.
62 Ancestral emblems
65 Classify someone, slangily
66 Meanie
67 Superior
68 ____ glance; casually
70 House publication
72 Weak; ineffective
75 Minotaur's isle
76 Weather, poetically
77 Trod the boards
78 Lagomorphs
79 Famous Keller
80 Darlings

Down

1 Huff and puff
2 Zones
3 "George Washington ____ Here" (1942 Benny film)
4 "____ First Romance" (1951 O'Brien film)
5 Massachusetts town
6 Noted '30s penologist
7 Ripens
8 Wire measure
9 Detritus
10 Six-lined poem
11 Hunter's limits
12 WWII arena
13 Loafer
14 Bombay's country
15 Some tides
20 Shutout pitcher Hershiser
25 Everlasting
28 Singing brothers
30 Plateau's relative
32 Good potting soil
33 Hockey great
34 Soaks fiber
35 Actress Moorehead
36 Extreme edge
37 Dawdler
38 Canonized women: Abbr.
40 Singer Ross
41 Blue-pencils
43 The whole ____; everything
44 Smell ____; suspect something
46 Great number
47 Gala gathering
50 Woe is me!
51 St. Anthony's cross
52 Animal shelter
54 White wine
55 Steno's need
57 Beet soup: Var.
58 Natives
59 Distinctive time period
60 ____ firma
62 Memento
63 Ray
64 Provide direction
66 Washington bills
67 Summit
69 Provides something more
71 Brunched
73 Be under the weather
74 Chill

Thorough Fare *by Martha J. De Witt*

"...profuse in cautious hints and allusions..."—Bolitho

Across

1 Ransacks
6 Catch
10 Suit
15 Ghana's capital
16 Banff's prov.
17 Buckingham or Windsor
18 Careful
20 Ascended
21 Leaning to one side
22 Requisites
23 —— the finish; there when it counts
24 Concession
25 Pigpen
26 Taverns
28 Girl "sweet as apple cider"
31 Tax mentioned in Leviticus 27:30
33 Cub or eagle
35 Capital of Hadhramaut
36 Careful
38 Antelope
39 Wicket
42 Spruce
43 Defensive diamond statistic
44 Alas, in Essen
45 Muntjac
46 Jamie of "M*A*S*H"
48 Actress Merkel
49 Fast
51 "—— and Janis" of the comics
52 Solicits
53 Yahoo
54 Careful
57 He wrote "Picnic"
58 Long-tailed heavenly mass
59 Concepts
62 Donkey, to a sot?
63 Rooster's topper
64 Fore's opposite
65 Scientist's workshop, familiarly
67 Rat's undoing
69 Asian calculators
72 Actress Raines
73 Earlier
75 Careful
77 Crows
78 Made second base the hard way
79 Carrier's territory
80 Dingles
81 Affirmative votes
82 Ingredients for the pot

Down

1 Lhasa big shots
2 Leopardlike animal
3 Eight-legged creatures
4 Cause to fall
5 USAF division
6 "Roots" author
7 —— vera
8 Poker variety
9 Ardor
10 Stable areas
11 Lamb's alter ego
12 Careful
13 Hard water?
14 ——-gallon hat
17 Rouge
19 Green
25 Haggard novel
27 Pecan, for one
29 Expose sham
30 Bryant and Loos
32 —— Hague
33 Prison
34 Trippet
35 Museum display
37 Choler
38 "—— Town"
39 African republic
40 Squirrel's caches
41 Careful
43 Fruitful
45 Aberdeen's river
46 Campus brotherhood, for short
47 "The Greatest"
50 Abbreviated way
51 Guttled
52 Fruit drink
54 Comedian De Luise
55 Ambassador's office
56 Boston's summer hrs.
58 Vaults
60 Wholehearted
61 Military greeting
63 Wains
64 Litmus reddeners
66 Litmus bluers
68 Tumble
70 Tree trunk
71 Inter ——
72 Harrow's rival
73 Rose garden
74 English river
76 One of the Gershwins

75

Storm Haven *by Bernice Gordon*

"Left" to her own devices, Ms. Gordon prepares a fine mixture.

Across

1 Fashion accessory
6 Estate holdings
11 Insect stages
16 "Pomp and Circumstance" composer
17 Up to now
18 "___ Gay"
19 Steak choice
21 Coverlet
22 "Wheel of Fortune" purchase
23 Merit
24 Neither Dem. nor Rep.
26 Salt Lake City athletes
27 Delaware Indian
29 Flair for music
31 Thaws
33 Betsy or Lanny
35 The Henley, for instance
37 Shorebird
40 Kind
42 Sooner than
43 Roundball, Inc.
46 Toothless
48 Committed money
50 California wine valley
51 The road to Rouen?
52 Supped
53 Drome or plane leader
54 What a high jumper must clear
56 Reneges
58 "Leave ___ to Heaven"
59 Island in the Seine
60 Linden of "Barney Miller"
61 Small egg
62 Drying frames
65 Hibernia
67 1982 Oscar winner
68 Kin of et al.
70 Thrown about
74 College football's ___ Panthers
75 Letters on the Big Board

77 Word of greeting
79 Port of call
80 Mideast chiefs
82 Divvied up
85 Double-reed instruments
86 Canary's relation
87 Magistrate of old Rome
88 Composition for nine
89 Revere
90 Donna and Oliver

Down

1 Flower part
2 Lab creation
3 Smiling, to Tennyson
4 Squeal on
5 City in the Bahamas
6 "Oz" actor
7 ___ person; unanimously

8 Gotham inst.
9 Long for
10 Actress Anna
11 Favorite
12 Not injured
13 "Chortle," for example
14 Amaryllis family plants
15 Adages
20 Charlotte and Norma
25 Snow White's companions: Var.
28 Sports complexes
30 Biblical haven
32 Suit to ___
34 Locate
36 Christian
37 Peasant girl
38 Antarctic cape
39 Exile
41 Knowing look
44 Hard mineral
45 ___ of one's own medicine

47 Judge
48 "___ Camera"
49 Waiter's prop
55 Warbled
57 More corpulent
60 FDR's successor
63 19 Across, perhaps
64 Got
66 "___ True What They Say About Dixie?"
67 Region of oblivion
69 Lofty group?
71 Banks of baseball
72 Exert authority
73 Network intersections
74 Field worker
76 Where to find a *sala*
78 Composer of the oratorio "Judith"
81 Fast Atl. crosser
83 No amateur
84 Beethoven's "___ to Joy"

76

Clues In Twos — *by Manny Miller*

Doubling up on the clues for a singularly good composition.

Across

1 Jack or Clifton
5 Maneuver
9 Borzoi or Bouvier des Flandres
12 Rotating piece
15 Jai ——
16 Knowledge
17 Bring up
19 Chin and Czech
21 Martinique and Cavendish
22 Norm.
23 Fibber McGee specialties
24 Quartz and feldspar
25 Armet and topi
27 Brit. commercial abbr.
28 In a bad way
29 Geologic time divisions
30 Linden or Holbrook
32 —— Canals
34 In —— life; formerly
36 —— forward; volunteers
38 Above
42 Laver and Carew
43 Yawn
44 Scuffled
46 Hermosillo hurrah
47 Yucatán or Iberia
49 Plane or port starter
50 Proust and Marceau
52 City slicker
53 Former pitcher Duren
54 Malicious burning
55 Cacao and baobab
57 Earthquake
58 "Acid"
60 Deuce followers, in tennis
61 Neat as ——
62 New or square policy

65 Throw or area
67 George Washington and London
70 Kudu or bongo
72 Preserve, in a way
73 Johnnie Ray hit
74 Helen and Henry
75 Gallagher and Klein
77 Receiver of property
78 Mont Blanc and Eiger
79 Official order
80 Weaken
81 Ga.'s winter clock setting
82 Kind of case
83 Keats and Pindar works

Down

1 Hall-of-Fame pitcher Ed or actor Raoul
2 Bring joy to

3 Elgart and Alpert
4 Tom Hanks film of 1988
5 Folds
6 Booths
7 Ilmenite and cuprite
8 Affirmative
9 Bookkeeping entry
10 Warner and family
11 Barry or Raymond
12 Erie or Suez
13 —— costs; by whatever means
14 Untidy
18 Different
20 Abounding in: Suff.
24 Fr. miss
26 Peat bog
30 Arizona Indian
31 Modified
33 Hellenic high point
34 Fragrance
35 Kind of bear
36 "Thou —— not then be false to any man" ("Hamlet")

37 Lonigan
39 King or queen
40 Leather straps
41 Pertinent, in law
43 Toothpaste style
45 Diminutive suffix
47 Female swans
48 Takes to court
51 Ursinus or Ursuline
53 Wallace or Tim
56 Fashion
57 Caught sight of
59 Some honeybees
61 Stop
62 Ladies, in Leon
63 "—— Gay"
64 Aweigh
66 Overturn
67 Demotions
68 Banks or Kovacs
69 Estabs.
71 Lois or Penny
72 Porter or Natalie
75 Manx or Russian blue
76 —— Jima

77

New Slants by Arthur W. Palmer

Old wine in new bottles from Michigan.

78

Across

1 "_____ the Lovin'"
6 Savage
12 Pledges
17 Chum
18 Blow up
20 Divert
21 Get a tutor?
23 Damp
24 Consume
25 Chad's neighbor
26 "_____ Camera"
28 Tennis match fraction
29 Sediment
31 Fire, slangily
32 "Beau _____," Cooper film
34 Sarazen, for one
35 Kind of estate
37 Switch- or designated _____
38 Le Mans event
39 College official
42 Incrustations
43 "Elmer's _____," Glenn Miller best seller
44 Type of seal
45 Cultivates land
46 Persuasion
48 Tied
49 Seaweed group
50 Brooke, the Princetonian
52 Charge
53 Avoid retailers?
55 Siouan
57 Parboiled
59 Idaho's largest city
60 Scheme
61 Creator of Prufrock
62 Stage items
63 Decipher
64 Struck, old style
65 Baby carriages
66 Spring bloomers
67 Zeno's bailiwick
68 Like a haunted house
70 Speaker, of baseball
71 Cures
72 Harry
73 Bikini part
74 Son of Aphrodite
78 Housing for certain couples
79 Govt. agt.
80 Pat or Daniel
82 I, in Berlin
83 Wing: Comb. form
85 Santa, to paraphrase Millet?
89 Philippine isle
90 Tess, for Hardy
91 Tuber, country style
92 Famous failure
93 Poetic foot
94 Cognizant

Down

1 Was sore
2 Tuck, for one
3 Linzer or Sacher
4 Dir. from Terre Haute to Indianapolis
5 Some grasses
6 Oligarchic
7 Early Peruvian
8 Dash
9 Deserter
10 Dernier _____
11 Arrogant ones
12 Vasco da _____
13 I love Latin?
14 "Some Like It Hot" cast?
15 Gist
16 Parlor piece
19 Related to mother
22 Ticket
27 Mal de _____
30 Envious
32 "Slow down, fergoshsakes!"
33 Riviera summers
34 Porridge
36 Wide receiver
37 King of Tyre
39 Shoal
40 Overhangs
41 Athenian dupes?
42 Stormed
43 Anagram of 33 Down
45 Naval force
46 Karpov's forte
47 Ceremony
49 Actor Ray
50 Omits
51 Barrel part
53 Move like a butterfly
54 Spacious
56 Wallet items
58 "Wanted" poster datum
60 Balance
62 Lakers, Pistons, and so on
63 _____ Lanka
64 Began
65 Shot out of season
66 Tehran native
67 Cornstarch or flour
68 GC in NYC
69 Australian state capital
70 Mason's tool
73 "By the _____ banks of Clyde..." (Lauder)
75 Gaucho's rope
76 Earth pigment
77 _____ up; support
79 Christmas, in Cannes
80 Harass
81 Miss Kett
84 66, e.g.
86 Pitcher's stat.
87 Certain shoe, for short
88 Hem's partner

Originally published in 1989

A Night at the Operetta *by W. Canine*

Celebrating the work of two famed collaborators.

Across

1 Performance
4 Romaine
7 "Pnin" shelf-mate
10 Domino
14 Pelican or condor
16 Recruiting agent
18 1881 lampoon of Oscar Wilde
20 Smashed particle
21 New Zealander
22 Gilbert's partner
23 Results, as of labor
25 Cranny
27 In a breezy way
28 First-rate
29 Waikiki's island
30 Botha's country: Abbr.
31 Meadow
32 Sea nymph
34 On the ___; fleeing
35 Engrave
37 This ___ way to run a railroad!
38 ___ with the punch
40 "Lohengrin" heroine
44 Nonsense
47 Hem's trailer
48 Resourceful
50 Cuts off
51 "... ___ thieves" (Matthew XXI:13)
53 Get ___ of; sell
54 Residue
55 In Rome, 1102
56 1888 work with Jack Point
60 Cry
61 Nonsense!
62 Relative of "yup"
63 Loveseat
64 Cookie favorite
65 Like some mushrooms
67 Hall or Voight
68 MSS readers
69 Observed
70 Weird, weirdly
71 Unpleasant refuse
73 Main player
76 Hotshot
78 Heirs
81 Hush!
84 Thousands of years
85 Popular vehicles
87 Make beloved
89 "The Pequod," for one
91 Multitude
92 Victoria ___
93 1882 House of Lords ridicule
95 Giselle's aunt
97 Ova
98 Certain operetta fan
99 Presbyter
100 Collie's nickname
101 Jeanne d'Arc *et* Marie
102 Retiring
103 WWII vessel
104 Alums-to-be

Down

1 Sternward
2 Bioflavonoid source
3 Company of actors
4 OSS successor
5 Maine university site
6 Soap opera
7 Recess
8 Family mem.
9 Finally
10 Golda of Israel
11 Verdi's "___ Chorus"
12 Climb up
13 Mombasa's country
15 Film score composer Tiomkin
16 1878 opera satire
17 Famed impresario
19 Of the lower trunk
24 Ballerina's need
26 Comic quality
30 Gusto
33 Tony ___, Wally Cleaver
36 Hollywood heavy Dantine
39 Reluctant
41 Settle
42 Like many churches
43 Sotto voce comments
44 Greek isle
45 Stick fast
46 Herman or Reese
48 One (Scot.)
49 1877 operetta production by 17 Down
52 Hose
53 Fasten again
57 Up-to-date
58 Charge
59 Real
66 Audience's approval
67 Two-year insts.
72 Sidesteps
74 Itsy-bitsy
75 Large vessels
77 Ultimate conclusion
79 Whinnies
80 Advocate Margaret
81 From Geneva
82 Young porker
83 Divide
86 Transmits
88 Grates
90 Vientiane's locale
91 Lamarr
94 Initials for Elizabeth
96 Vietnam holiday

79

'Tis The Season *by Roger H. Courtney*

Wishing you the best.

80

Across

1 Support
6 Theater box
10 Marine hazard
15 Mend a roof
16 "——— to Remember" (Chopin film bio)
18 Ling Ling, for instance
19 People of ancient Dacia
20 Family member
21 Mental concoctions
22 Christmases
24 ——— Tin Tin
26 Actress Sue ——— Langdon
27 Hypnosis starter
28 Mongrel
29 Polaris, now
31 Journalist/reformer Jacob
33 "Moonlight," for one
34 Londoner's resistance
37 Hertz competitor
38 O'Hara's land
42 Spurious
43 Goblet part
44 Musk or water follower
45 Anecdotal collection
46 Gram. gender
48 Ottumwa's state
50 Be indebted to
51 Rainer of "The Good Earth"
53 Broadway light
55 Gladiators' milieus
57 Missile holder
58 Radial
59 Santa's calling card
60 "Notary Sojac" comic strip, "Smokey ———"
62 Adj.

63 Miserly men
66 Actress Hartman
67 Gabor and Le Gallienne
71 Burnsian turndown
72 Canoe implement
73 Hexagonal precipitation
75 Real estate
77 Line of cliffs
79 "——— the Family"
80 Movie Superman
81 Flynn of film
82 Sporting events
83 Anagram for stere
84 Lubricous
85 Famous name in cosmetics

Down

1 Cries like a donkey
2 Broadway show
3 In the slightest degree

4 Worriless
5 Once, once
6 City planner's concern
7 Willow
8 ——— to; attends
9 Bus. ltr. notation
10 Parlor piano
11 "It ——— To Be You"
12 ——— a time; singly
13 Turkish provincial capital
14 A beam
17 Paratrooper's cry
23 Tinsel strand
25 Cantor and Lupino
29 Jack Benny's theme, "——— Bloom"
30 Overfill
32 Silly
33 Posed
34 Hot rod's exhaust system
35 Boredom
36 Unsubstantial
39 Unequaled

40 Dan of "Laugh-In"
41 "Behold I will build me ———..." (Lanier)
43 Cubic meters
44 Stallion's herd
47 Miss ———
49 "——— Concerto"
52 Lukewarm
54 Above, to Tennyson
56 Parsons and Getty
58 Wrap for Nero
59 Ceremonial attire
61 Horn blower
63 Drummer boy's drum
64 Projects for Mason
65 Bowling lane button
66 Sign up: Var.
68 Servant
69 Go fly ———!
70 Horse or common
73 Wrap for Indira
74 Sometimes-fleeting thing
76 Actress Arden
78 ———-Magnon

Put A Lid On It!   *by Isaac Miller*

A top Florida constructor covers things nicely.

81

Across

1 ____ the back; compliment
6 Backward start
11 "____ a man with seven wives"
15 Writer St. Johns
16 "____ with a View"
17 French composer Erik
19 Walking sticks
20 Robert Burns poem
22 Poacher's choice?
23 Took down a peg
25 Blunt
26 Kind of guard or admiral
28 Marche season
29 More offended
31 Aerobics garb
34 Deli offering
37 Fool
39 "Stop Me Before ____!" (1961 film)
41 Offbeat
43 More or less
44 "...waiting for the Robert ____"
45 Jibe
47 Dial
48 Knighthood candidate
51 Ending for some crossword clues
52 Walk the aisles
54 Onetime supporting actor Mischa
55 Woolly
57 "Beulah, peel ____ grape"
58 Dine at home
60 Dominions
61 Like a Turkish bath
63 Metropolitan vehicle
65 Doc or Happy
67 Sun. speech
68 Rich soil
71 Tether
74 Critter
77 Past
78 Santa's overhead?
80 Bitter
82 "Divine Comedy" poet
83 Laughing
84 Scoop for soup
85 Freebie of sorts
86 "With the jawbone of ____..." (Judges XV:16)
87 Photographer Adams

Down

1 Hoosier hoopster
2 Saw
3 Could this prevent a Texas brain drain?
4 Opry adjective
5 Org. with "The Right Stuff"
6 Drumbeats
7 Extinguisher of errors
8 Weighty book
9 Crosses
10 Examples of 12 Down
11 Columbus's backer
12 Meditation muttering
13 Words from Caesar
14 Causes for overtime periods
18 Before, to Blake
21 Of every 60 minutes
24 Happen to
27 Any port in a storm
30 Willow
32 Acknowledge
33 Paint thinner, for one
35 They're the tops at graduations
36 Conceive
37 "____ Scarum," 1965 Presley film
38 Originates
40 Dullea of "2001"
42 Editor's notations
44 Before poise or lateral
46 Friendly
49 Faun
50 Where Mark Twain is buried
53 Rouses again
56 Headache tablet: Abbr.
59 Cremona artisan
60 Lets off the hook
62 Public proclamations
64 Nanking natives
66 Dickensian dastard
69 Nimble
70 Before T or A
71 "Acid"
72 Nipa palm
73 Barrett of Hollywood
75 College sports org.
76 Tra trailers
79 Gun lobby: Abbr.
81 Preserve

Originally published in 1989

Animation *by Melvin Kenworthy*

Half a dozen examples await.

82

Across

1 Heartland units
6 Shepard of "The Right Stuff"
9 —— breve
13 Greek goddess
14 UN subgroup
15 Acidulous
16 Inebriated
17 Launch
19 Into the mind or spirit
21 Remainder
22 Relating to elementary organization
24 Measured step
27 Cheese choice
28 Awarded a PG or PG-13
32 Actress Balin
33 Imitate Francis
34 Beneficial
35 Concealed
37 Pince-—— glasses
39 Admit
40 Michigan county
41 Nary a person
43 Commercials
44 Ear protuberances
45 Regarding
46 Old dirk
47 A single indicator of cold or fear
50 Pays out
53 Small carpet
57 Confirms
59 Most peculiar
60 Shield border
61 Vintage auto
62 Thanks, I —— that!
63 Coward
64 Miami, from Chicago: Abbr.
65 They accompany MSS

Down

1 Bus. letter notation
2 Mess tent grub
3 Provide another title
4 It precedes *febrero*
5 Dude ranch supply house
6 So, in the original
7 Old call to arms
8 Stopover
9 Inhale
10 Clamorous
11 Humdinger
12 Johnson of "Laugh-In"
13 —— was saying...
18 Usually
20 Auto style
23 Hot pepper
24 Slender tube
25 Close, to Thackeray
26 Magna ——
29 Giant
30 Skip over
31 Tightly packed
33 Digital inflammations
36 Jingle
38 "—— the Greek"
42 Nerve cells
45 Editions
46 Gardener's implements
48 Aromas
49 Sorceress of legend
50 Black
51 Dry: Comb. form
52 Wan
54 Explain: Dial.
55 Employs
56 Carrying the mfr.'s backing
58 Digit

Originally published in 1989

Hollywood Hokum   by Ernie Furtado

If hokum can be thought through carefully, this is fine stuff.

83

Across

1 Hit Broadway musical
5 Gogol's "___ Bulba"
10 Gypsies
15 Lesson
16 Coeur d'___
17 Street show
18 Writer Jong
19 "Skoal!" for example
20 Ados
21 Farrah's plumbing problem?
24 Predicament
25 Bishopric
26 Da digit afta two?
27 Actor Christopher
28 Wapiti
31 Make over
34 Most pungent
37 Spanks
39 German Renaissance painter
42 Shelley of "Outrageous Fortune"
43 Attempts
45 Artist Salvador
46 Raga instrument
48 Tidal flood
49 Musical study
51 Oneida Community founder
53 Page
55 Wotan
56 "Tomorrow" singer
57 Neat
58 Severs
60 Ages
61 Sic ___ gloria mundi
64 "Anything ___"
66 Second notes
67 Distaff member, of a sort
68 One tide
71 Likely
73 Companion of odds
75 Memo cancelling "Three's Company"?
81 Tatum's Oscar role
83 Mussel (Fr.)
84 Rake over the ___
85 Peruses
86 Over
87 Vines
88 Rendezvous
89 "Mr. ___ Goes To Town"
90 Congers

Down

1 Heart
2 Kiri Te Kanawa solo
3 Some are brass
4 Butcher
5 Toodle-oo
6 Under, at sea
7 Respond
8 Goose genus
9 Irish ___
10 "___ Miniver"
11 Feed bag contents
12 Mitzi in a high dive?
13 Idols
14 Poetic lines
15 Allen or Tormé
22 Nourish
23 Ducks
28 Kitchen finish
29 "___ Theme," from "Dr. Zhivago"
30 Ted sings Cole Porter?
32 Flashy dresser
33 Speaker
35 To ___ phrase
36 Vocalize
38 Rain from cloudless skies
40 Dodge
41 Word with crop or boot
44 "...look into the ___ of time..." ("Macbeth")
47 Roi's mate
50 Within: Comb. form
52 Tax, once
54 Getting back to even, in sports
59 Center
61 Ovid's "___ of Love"
62 Make
63 Came down in buckets
65 Money
69 Make amends
70 Bluenose
72 Treasure-___
74 Caesar, and others
76 "___ Three Lives"
77 Koppel and Kennedy
78 Salute
79 Seine sights
80 Bks.-to-be
82 Self-help rage

Tagalongs *by Bernice Gordon*

Literary afterthoughts.

Across

1 Unawares
6 Corn or oat follower
10 Old Nick
15 Craft for Hiawatha
16 Assign
18 Soap substitute plant
19 They're in the writer's doghouse
22 Daughter of James II
23 Slender bristle
24 Three, to Pavarotti
25 Wall Street membership
26 Canine visitor to Oz
28 Cut, for one
30 —— mode
33 NCO
35 Cereal grains
36 Tomba's runner
39 Educator's visit to Vermont
43 Wooded
44 Famous penologist
45 Aaron or Williams
46 Dumbo's wing
47 Areas in Eastern churches
48 Kind of band or box
49 Prefix for present
51 Machine for winding yarn
52 Shade of red
55 Playwright's timid cats
58 Asner and Meese
59 Burrows and Vigoda
60 —— it; amen
61 Funnyman Louis
62 "The Green Pastures" character
63 South ——, Indiana
65 Jason's ship
68 Goddess of the dawn
70 Cooper's handiwork: Abbr.
71 Desserts
75 Author from Ohio?
79 Withstand
80 Actor Peter O'——
81 Rose fragrance
82 Cobbled
83 Boris of Bulgaria
84 Gelt

Down

1 Deeds
2 Ruhr road
3 In a little while
4 Celestial body
5 Large green parrot of New Zealand
6 Mealymouthed hypocrite
7 School in North Carolina
8 Wholly
9 Converted factory space
10 —— Paulo, Brazil
11 Entertain
12 Musical kind of poem
13 Robert or Alan
14 Aerie
17 Raised embankments for grapevines
20 Shiny fabric
21 Wasteland tracts
27 Award bestowed in April
29 "Prufrock" creator's monogram
30 Satisfied sighs
31 Actress Myrna
32 Francis and Dahl
34 Blue-gray minerals
35 Ahead
36 Position in life
37 Barbie's friend
38 Bother
40 Make use of
41 One at a christening
42 Lamb Chop's controller
47 Withdrew
48 Legendary kidnap victim
49 In ——; solo
50 Up-to-date
51 Arachnid's creation
52 Great fertility goddess of Asia Minor
53 Ship's curved plank
54 Vane dir.
56 Aviation watchdog agcy.
57 Influence peddler
62 Sinister Peter of films
64 Likewise
65 Copycats
66 Nevada city
67 Caesar's conquest
69 Robert Burns, for one
70 Composer Bartok
72 Roman consul and orator
73 Relative of etc.
74 Vital body fluids
76 Conducted
77 Tyson results
78 Well-known uncle

84

Going On-line   by Cathy Millhauser

Ms. Millhauser admits she isn't a computer expert.

Across

1 Goya subject
5 Horrified inhalations
10 Teasdale and others
15 —— for one's money
16 Fats in pats
17 Short run
18 Major skeletons?
20 Iran, once
21 Simple as ——
22 Buenos ——
23 Stain
24 Urchin
25 Computer complexes
27 Like most cases of computeritis?
29 Dutch South African
30 Hard labor
32 Eye
33 Hardy heroes
35 Present
36 East Lansing inst.
38 Aardvark's ort
39 Pusher's target?
42 British Isle
45 Regret
46 Basketball hoop
47 Narrow inlet
48 Nuptial vow
49 Two hairpin curves
50 Portable computer stand?
54 Rogue
55 Subway opposites
56 Count's English counterpart
57 Humerus sites
58 Child's direction
61 As a prefix, it's plane
62 Lily type
64 Computer shows?
67 Digest
70 Disencumber
71 Ron ——, Tarzan portrayer
72 Take me ——
73 Santa's syllables
75 Like Homer's "Iliad"
77 Pizza before cooking?
79 Presbyters
80 Divert
81 Item for the fence
82 Know-it-alls?
83 Faun
84 "—— Mommy Kissing..."

Down

1 "I Remember ——"
2 Semites
3 Hot data?
4 Hoofer Miller
5 More gruesome
6 Smoke detector, for one
7 School term
8 Edgar Allan, and kin
9 Draft org.
10 Type of whale
11 Part of ETA
12 Losing a lap
13 Kind of magnetism
14 Flour or baking powder
17 Have a feinting spell?
19 The breaks
23 Ott, the homer champ
26 Mayday relative
27 Layer
28 Letters for debtors
31 Assn.
33 Dressed for a birthday?
34 Burden
35 Cannabis
36 "The Ghost and Mrs. ——"
37 Tiff
39 Russian river
40 Small slugs?
41 Spoken
42 Small tollhouse cookie ingredients?
43 Speaker of the first palindrome, supposedly
44 Affirmative actions
51 Iacocca and Cobb
52 Corny part
53 Overstrike, in a way
55 Work unit
57 —— Khan
58 Toots
59 Three-base hit
60 I compound
61 A Carter
62 Window washer, at times
63 TV award
65 Raises
66 "—— Well That Ends Well"
68 Shpeaking like thish, perhapsh
69 Daniel follower
72 —— mater
74 Bias
76 Wax: Comb. form
77 Sol preceders
78 Agnus ——

85

Originally published in 1989

Timing Is Everything *by Louis Sabin*

Momentous? Maybe. Worth your time? Definitely.

Across

1 Hilo hiya
6 Push and shove
11 Computer language
16 Cranial cavity
17 Penthouse of a sort
18 Actress Verdugo
19 From ____; all over
21 Appointments
22 Significant time
23 Maintain
24 Nevertheless
26 "A Chorus Line" song
27 Noted toxophilite
29 "Batman" West
31 Knight's superior
34 Barn inhabitant, perhaps
36 Haddock or pollack
38 Melville's "Billy ____"
39 Lawn sport
42 Robust
44 "____ Buddies," Tom Hanks's sitcom
47 "A Connecticut Yankee..." phenomenon
49 Challenge
51 Succeed
52 Early Ford rival
53 Innisfail
55 Lengths of the pool
57 Make tracks!
58 Mini-marathon
60 Quaker State name
62 39 Down, for example
64 Tarsus
66 Life's beginning, for some
68 Extreme
69 'Bye
71 Immediately
72 Shake up
73 Roughly 1000 B.C.—A.D. 100
76 Time's proverbial companion
78 Poker action
82 Spat
83 Ex-Giant manager
85 Song for two
87 Vex
88 Edenic
91 Cheerleading antics
94 Becker's strength
95 Crow
96 Follow
97 Biblical prophet
98 "Little Orphant Annie" poet
99 Villain's response

Down

1 Profit item
2 Metric unit
3 Tatum ____ McEnroe
4 Chorale effect
5 Nora's pooch
6 Checked out, for a heist
7 Take back
8 Tram filler
9 Like a bantamweight
10 Cygnus star
11 River base
12 Flagon filler
13 Intuition
14 Hole ____
15 Editor's mark
20 Egglike
25 Bill
28 Sites
30 Temper
32 Chafe
33 Reputation
35 Use a chamois
37 Having two parts
39 Diamond Hall-of-Famer
40 Indian, for example
41 Settings for large timepieces
42 Typographic flourish
43 Spencer or Dick
45 Willow rod
46 Verse measure, in England
48 Test
50 Acid rain watchdog gp.
54 Bolero's cousin
56 Zeno taught here
59 Style
61 Easy gait
63 Coagulate
65 Athenian H
67 Play with
70 Once
72 Willie and Joe's vehicle
73 Type of setter
74 Western gala
75 Outer limits
77 Needing cleaning
79 Wash cycle
80 Reason
81 North Sea feeder
84 ____ dancer
86 Very, in Versailles
89 Farewell
90 Meadow
92 Not any, in law
93 Holiday spot

86

Loft Space *by George G. Storey*

A soaring composition.

87

Across

1 Work unit
4 Truman's Secretary of State
11 Physicist Enrico
16 By way of
17 Kind of checkers or lantern
18 Sci-fi/horror film
19 TV sitcom featuring an 18 Across
20 Flood cresting point
22 Skillful
24 Half a dance
25 Juliette Low's org.
26 "____ Girls"
27 West German industrial city
29 Purplish brown
31 Compass dir.
34 In the neighborhood of
36 "Deep in the ____ Texas"
40 Procedure for ending debate
43 Corn or color prefix
45 Native New Zealander
46 Gasoline rating, commonly
48 Matures
50 Damage
51 Neighbor of Ill.
52 Botanist Gray
53 That woman
54 Explosive letters
55 Actor Majors
56 Pronounce carelessly
57 Even with the cup, in golf
60 "*La Vita Nuova*" poet
62 Battering ____
64 Cancels out
65 Author Caldwell
67 Off course
69 Simple sugar
70 Persian chief
71 Postpone, as payment
75 Tango's prerequisite?
78 Chit

80 Teacher's org.
82 Sound in mind
83 Haughty
88 *Uno y uno*
89 "Kate & ____"
90 Radiance
91 Biblical high priest
92 Sobs
93 Uses compressed air to agitate liquid
94 Football's Marino

Down

1 Avoid cleverly
2 Vexes
3 Butchers' hooks
4 ____ *du lieber...*
5 Stylish
6 Like some sales tactics
7 With arms upraised, in ballet
8 Stitch
9 Sioux Indian

10 NBA team
11 ...and yet so ____
12 Shade tree
13 Mideast coin
14 Pool
15 Signs
21 Alleviate
23 Tithe
28 Gram. gender
30 Barracks bed
32 Spade and Malone
33 Time period of note
35 It's been ____ pleasure
36 Luxuriously
37 Nuthatch's relative
38 Word without rhyme
39 Estuaries, in Scotland
40 ____ Harold, Byronic hero
41 One-dimensional
42 Poet Nash and namesakes
44 Hasty

47 "Gone With The Wind" estate
49 Conger catcher
56 Six, in Sonora
58 Old-fashioned expletive
59 19th President
61 Mike Tyson specialty
63 ____-jongg
66 Ruhr refusal
68 Activist Margaret
70 Recap
72 Became dim
73 "____ Gay"
74 Pine extract
75 Melt
76 Artifice
77 Leer at
79 Harem rooms
81 Salt tree
84 Torso area
85 HST's would-be successor
86 IRS foiler of a sort
87 Word of agreement

General Staff — by Jeanette K. Brill

Ah, but which staff?

88

Across

1 Anagram of pleat
6 Layers
12 Crete dweller
18 Heart chambers
19 Wrath
20 Lacking competence
21 Good marksman
23 Fistfights
24 Husing or Kennedy
25 Raged
26 Cause for overtime
27 Pismire
28 Rug or code
30 Respected pollster
31 Kind of lamp
32 Ascend
33 Swiss cabin
35 Anatolia
37 Cached
40 Halts
42 Haul
43 "Stormy Weather" composer
44 Banks or Kovacs
46 Soft drinks
50 _____ into; attacks
51 Kayo counter
54 Eatery
56 '40s govt. agcy.
57 Ice mass
59 ABA members
60 Sentimentality
61 Outstanding
64 Stay in the pot
65 Dirt
66 An Astaire
67 Recoiled
69 Solo
70 Randy's skating partner
72 Successful
74 Reckless feats
75 Steward
79 Be of consequence
81 Sobeit
82 City lines
83 Capital of old Ethiopia
84 Kind of school
88 Numbers runner, in brief?
89 Rage
90 Brutal
92 Before, poetically
93 Cheese ingredient
95 Steinbeck novel
97 Showily adorned
98 Rouse
99 Della, the singer
100 Oozed
101 Thawed
102 Discourage

Down

1 Parma staple
2 Clear sky
3 Commerce
4 Ozone
5 Seats of sorts
6 Tutor
7 Famed American Olympian, and kin
8 Sleeping car accommodation
9 Change
10 _____ off; angry
11 LaGuardia abbr.
12 "Gypsy" or "Hair"
13 Arrow poison
14 Hentoff or Turner
15 Get
16 Cuban-born ballerina Alicia _____
17 Western homesteader
22 Fine violin, familiarly
26 In threes: Pref.
29 Land measures
31 Baseball statistics
32 Hardship
34 Layer
35 Breathing difficulty
36 Protective secretion
37 "..._____ tuffet..."
38 Camera support
39 Fatty ester
41 Ice hockey great
45 Diminutive ending
47 "The Blue _____"
48 Rub with oil
49 Evening wraps
51 Old car
52 Goes astray
53 Gets to the bottom of
55 Yes, admiral!
57 Attest
58 Uniform cloth
62 Rocker John
63 So far
65 Drink noisily
68 Of the home
69 Consumed
71 Imagined
73 Having divisions
74 Purloin
75 Groups of computer instructions
76 Electrical measure
77 _____ d'Arc
78 Like Father William
80 Slaved away
83 _____ beaucoup
85 Sublease
86 Rub out
87 Pianist Nero
89 Entertain
90 Ulna or tibia
91 Hog fat
94 Siesta
95 Thrice daily, USP style
96 Stipend

Originally published in 1989

Thrillers   *by S.E. Wilkinson*

It's nail-biting time.

89

Across

1 Ruth, to fans
5 Peel
10 Kind of tale
14 "Sing —— green willow" (refrain in "Othello")
15 Uncle's issue
16 Territory
17 Hitchcock film of 1954
19 Caught on
20 Guitarist Eric
21 Get into
22 Wall St. concern
24 Ballot marks
25 Hitchcock film of 1972
27 Did a do
29 Miner's find
30 Light ——
31 Support
36 Restraint
37 Bro's sib
38 Free of doubt
39 Nonsense
42 Holiday, in Naples
43 Bills
44 Scuppernongs
45 Hitchcock film of 1960
48 South-of-the-border Mrs.
49 Ending for quart or miss
50 Yeah
51 One liner that didn't go over?
54 Lyric work
55 Hitchcock film of 1939
58 Up and ——!
59 Ditto
60 Pass
61 Singer Bennett
62 Goodman
63 On a single occasion

Down

1 Gin mill
2 Stout relative
3 Hitchcock film of 1929
4 Justice Warren
5 Took a shot
6 Shades
7 Make over
8 Hitchcock film of 1953
9 Sunday seat
10 Spoken for
11 Lucie or Desi
12 Skittish
13 Green scene
18 Floor polisher
21 Funnyman Jay
22 Bandanna
23 "Bobby Shaftoe's gone ——"
26 Torn or tear
28 Tie up
29 Obscures
32 I could —— hand here!
33 Hitchcock film of 1941
34 Worker's collective
35 Letter's paper
37 Hitchcock film of 1937
40 Cut into
41 Encouraging word
42 Mitterrand's monetary unit
44 Unrefined
45 Finish start
46 Luster
47 Scrumptious
48 Blemish
50 —— the crack of dawn
52 "—— Old Cowhand"
53 "Othello" villain
55 Poke
56 "Cosby Show" network
57 Comedian Louis ——

Feathered Friends *by Barbara Lunder Gillis*

They're gathered together for a special reason.

90

Across

1 Falling short
7 Maxims
11 Legends
16 Beast
17 Dismay
18 Pitiful
20 Book size
21 Recover
22 Fleet
23 Folk singer Pete
24 Gait
25 Glanced sidelong
26 Lamb
28 Awards
31 TV's Arthur
34 Bags
36 ___ Fox
37 Chores
42 Opposed, in combinations
44 Portico
46 Bosc fruit
48 Liana
49 Alternate
51 Half of CCCIV
53 Turned
55 Southern constellation
56 Alan or Cheryl
57 Honest man
58 Cask
59 Lady with the Lamp
65 Swiss river
66 Hardwood
67 "Pal ___"
68 Neither's follower
69 Patron
71 Hebrew prophet
72 Handy joints
76 Prong
77 Snoopy
79 Complications
81 High spot
82 Cons
84 Distance measure
86 White or Blue river
88 Twisted
89 Smoother
91 Design
93 Far Eastern temple

97 Drove
100 Rainbows
104 Ignoring ethics
105 South America's continental divide
106 Nook
107 Political activity
108 Hammer heads
109 Austrian composer
110 Dressed to the ___
111 Formerly
112 Sprouts

Down

1 Asian country
2 Story start
3 Place
4 Concept
5 Some buttons?
6 "Sunset Boulevard" star
7 Mast
8 Poise
9 "Mr. Miniver"

10 Crafty
11 Delay
12 Check
13 Sport
14 Culture medium
15 Aspect
17 Carney or Linkletter
19 Bounder
27 Feign
29 Ruby or Sandra
30 Mountain in Turkey
31 ___-relief
32 Compass dir.
33 Dined
35 Plinth
38 Actress Gardner
39 Alaska town
40 Genuflect
41 Marsh plant
43 Danube feeder
45 Loewe's partner
47 "Mork"
50 Zones
52 Dialect
54 Drift
59 Goes hungry

60 Rabbit
61 Maine college town
62 Car trim
63 Green tea
64 Clasp
70 Fresh
73 Stitch
74 Sailor
75 Firmament
78 Sloth or envy
80 Party food
83 Calm
85 Rusts
87 Winter cap feature
90 Glens
92 Recess
93 Cushion
94 Last word
95 Asian desert
96 Algerian port
98 Fender bender result
99 Before tee
101 ...fa, ___, ti, do
102 Always
103 Sun. speeches
105 Mimic

Originally published in 1989

Whatcha Doin'? *by Bert Rosenfield*

Alternate etymologies to consider.

Across

1 Midwest iron range
7 Apia native
13 One tea
18 Primitive computer
19 Right for tillage
20 1984 Olympic slalom champ
21 Fruit crush residue
22 What the shot-putting chef did?
24 UK stoolie
25 Common foreign coin
26 Age
27 Canon parts
28 What actor Jack's boss wouldn't do?
30 Windflower
32 Southwest lizard
33 Pay-TV letters
34 Senate count
37 ____ up; monopolize
38 Tenant
40 What cowardly wrestlers do?
44 Off the ____; immediately
47 Device evoking pity
49 Metal-casting hole
50 Yield from 1 Across
51 Deftness, for one
54 "____ virumque cano"
56 Wings and ells
58 New Rochelle college
59 What reducing clinics try to do?
62 Undiluted
63 Appeared in lights
65 NASCAR champ Yarborough
66 Fresh
67 Rabbit breed
68 ____ ease; edgy
71 Indian foreman: Var.
73 Antiquity
74 What aerial typesetters do?
76 "I 'gin to be ____ of the sun" ("Macbeth")
80 Luftwaffe nemesis: Abbr.
82 Pitch source
83 Howzat again?
84 Lush
85 Closes permanently
89 What sawmill barbers do?
93 Elliptical rock mass
94 Half of MMCII
96 Villainous sound
97 Actual
98 What social censors do?
101 "Silence ____ as eternity" (Sir Walter Scott)
103 Fashion's Oscar de la ____
104 Kind of pot
105 Presley's "I ____ Bad"
106 Burning issue?
107 Humperdinck hero
108 Help

Down

1 Cartographer's doing
2 Bowling ball material
3 Key fruits
4 Without ____; fancy-free
5 What Dakota corn growers have to do?
6 Final ending, UK style
7 Up to here
8 Stood
9 Kind of order
10 Dictionary abbr.
11 Out of the weather
12 Character actress Volz
13 "I ____ Camera"
14 Veiled dancer
15 What container detectives do?
16 Rosalind's forest
17 ____ di voce; bel canto techniques
23 Diego or Remo
25 Paid player
28 Joy or sorrow ending
29 Not on ____; nohow
31 City NNE of Düsseldorf
35 Stamps of approval
36 Vs.
39 Asparagus unit
40 Traditional dumb one
41 Quantico insignia
42 More incensed
43 Some sisters
45 Municipal zones
46 Waspish
48 ____ ever; seldom
51 Usher's turf
52 Yucca-like lily
53 What mythical photographers do?
55 Where mutts aren't welcome: Abbr.
57 Lake emptying into the Arctic Ocean
59 Anchorite's abode
60 El ____, Texas
61 Name of 5 Norwegian kings
64 Jazz licks
66 What pinto observers did?
69 Classified adv. word
70 La-la leader
72 A small smear
75 Vanda and cattleya
77 Tel Aviv native
78 Like an atheist
79 Alts.
81 The unresting Fury
83 Engine strength units, for short
85 See 77 Down
86 First calculus book author
87 Chylak or Conlan, e.g.
88 Spatter
90 Lord paramount
91 Lake ____, formerly Zuider Zee
92 Yellow fever mosquito
95 Marie Wilson's role
99 Jayhawker st.
100 252 gallons of wine
101 "____ body meets..."
102 Kettle's insulter

91

Switch Positions *by Thomas W. Schier*

A two-way title.

92

Across

1 ____ Dinh Diem, first president, Republic of Vietnam
4 Misgiving
8 Dieter's target
12 Garden tiller
16 Dance
17 Melville novel
18 Jamie of "M*A*S*H"
19 Vera's leader?
20 On that date
21 No way!
24 Tooth-like part
26 Togetherness
27 Quaker's pronoun
28 ____ foot; speedy
31 "Do unto ____..."
33 Cried like the whiffenpoof
34 Pitcher's statistics
39 Don ____ de la Vega
40 Hopeless situation
42 Diving equipment
43 Simpleton
44 Solicitation
45 Sharif of "Dr. Zhivago" fame
47 Overwhelming: Abbr.
48 Dir. from Pitts. to D.C.
49 "____ after me..."
51 Blood givers
53 Historical time frames
55 Pine away
58 Bungling performance
59 Removal from office
62 Head garland
64 Govt. bureau
67 Alt.
68 Mil. program
71 Goodbye, Gabriella
72 Coll. deg.
73 He played Lou Grant
75 Peanuts
77 Hammer parts
78 Sketch again
80 Sneers at
81 Denver Broncos' color
82 Serve
84 Garrison
85 ____-million chance
89 Consults again
94 Park sign
97 Bid
98 Interest factor
99 Theatrical award
100 Irish Gaelic
101 Wood sorrels
102 Suit to ____
103 Zees' neighbors
104 Mild oath
105 A Kennedy

Down

1 Flair
2 Behave recklessly
3 Active
4 Glassblower's rods: Var.
5 Mine (Fr.)
6 "Just say ____ drugs!"
7 Race recklessly
8 Poor grades
9 Put forward
10 Win in ____; overwhelm
11 Cinderella's canine friend and Judge Roy Bean's pet bear
12 Linden and Holbrook
13 Medley
14 Long time
15 Coral locale
16 "I've ____ it!"
22 E natural
23 Clear intervals
25 Dynamic beginner
29 Architect Saarinen
30 Red-coated cheese
31 Cross purposes
32 Uncles in Seville
33 Exposed
35 C&W's Roy
36 Writer's faux pas
37 Lift for Klammer
38 Without
40 Shoot the bull
41 Hippie's haven
44 Romero or Chavez
46 "Balcony scene" suitor
49 ____ Shamra, Syria
50 Done ____ turn
52 Fee-foe partner
54 Habitual traveller
56 Awry
57 Skating classification
59 Heartfelt
60 Or ____
61 *Bûche de Noël* shape
63 Court figures: Abbr.
65 Aftertaste
66 Box
69 Sheer nonsense
70 James of "Wholly Moses"
72 Christmas rose
74 Part of NPR
76 Market town
77 Coll. figure
79 Separate
81 Beginning
83 Remained passive
85 Soup vegetable
86 Heroic achievement
87 Gala
88 Dueler's sword
90 Singer Vikki
91 Thessaly peak
92 Audition
93 Grads-to-be
95 Go quickly
96 Some MIT grads

The Late Show *by William A. Smith*

Check your listings.

Across

1 Pitches a tent
6 ____ off the old block
10 Pertaining to heat
17 Conceive
19 ____ Sound, Florida
20 Shaded walk
21 Sleeve style
22 Seed covering
23 Gave birth to two at once
24 1953: boxer tracks down murderers
27 Songlike
28 Duck hunter's hideouts
29 Coleman and Cooper
31 Tilts
34 Largest asteroid
35 Mix salad
39 Bowfin
40 Always
43 Wash. traveler's luggage letters
44 Dickens's scheming clerk
45 Coll. mil. program
46 Made of stone, as a marker
48 Paucity
50 Chief Hindu god
52 Wood dressing tool
53 Hype
54 Diego or Remo
55 Philippine island
57 "____ Ruled the World"
58 Protein derivative
62 Skirt opening
63 Home of the Cowboys
67 Triumvir Marc, and namesakes
68 Bridge holding
70 Apostle Paul's companion
71 Wild hog
72 Manilow's "____ a Miracle"
74 Cádiz cat
75 Former tennis star Nastase
76 Pallid
77 Rice wines
79 Accrue
82 Horse fodder grass
83 ____ your seat belt!
85 Cheat; gyp
89 1950: Grable wants to adopt a child
94 Fine cigars
96 Gist
97 "A fireside is a great ____" (Leigh Hunt)
98 Teems
99 Preminger
100 Saturday matinee fare, once
101 High-level discussions
102 Storied crimebuster
103 Carter and Gwyn

Down

1 Flyer: Abbr.
2 One of Esau's wives
3 Watt or buck leader
4 1942: Colbert runs off to Florida (with "The")
5 Sugar or flour
6 Swiss follower
7 Israeli dances
8 Footnote abbr.
9 Animal hide
10 Manx or Persian
11 1954: treasury officer helps con artist
12 Lion dens
13 Universally, in combos
14 Nevada city
15 March time
16 Herring barrel
18 At last, to Yvonne
25 Start
26 Harvard's is famous
30 Tire reincarnation?
31 Elem. 6
32 Roman counterpart to Eros
33 Hayworth or Moreno
34 1953: Elroy Hirsch plays himself
35 1931: Arliss can't stay retired
36 Wine: Comb. form
37 Amish, for example
38 WWI German admiral
41 Young beef
42 Firstborn
46 1940: precocious kid aids family
47 Eye part
49 Parlor piece
51 Primary
56 Coup d'____
58 Sun lotion chem.
59 Son of Seth
60 Chief Memphis deity
61 To be (Sp.)
64 "Don't Bring ____"
65 Related
66 1956's "The Bad ____"
69 Dead body, of old
73 Take off the cream
78 Older form of a word
80 Values of a people
81 Extend, in a way
82 Sesame plant
83 Soho apartments
84 Cars
85 Roughen from cold
86 Lima bean, in Lima
87 Actor Novello
88 First king of Israel
90 ____ noir
91 Colorado ski resort
92 Relative of etc.
93 Dick Van Patten's "Mama" role
95 Draft org.

93

Medalists In Action *by Dorothea E. Shipp*

"I'd rather be a poor winner than any kind of loser."—George S. Kaufman

Across

1 Length x width
5 Welcoming words to Don Ho
11 Tire
14 Actress Vaccaro
16 Go over with a rag
17 Muslim's faith
20 Feverishly chasing Sebastian Coe?
23 Moderately slow, to Previn
24 Three, in combinations
25 Tiger shark's tagalongs
26 Alfonso's queen
28 Elcar of "MacGyver"
30 Ravi Shankar's music
31 Lost to Ernesto Canto, perhaps?
39 Go-between
40 ___ firma
41 Stat for Thigpen
42 Pinpoint
44 Actress Merkel
45 Earlier: Pref.
46 Tourist's reading material
49 Rome, Venice, etc.
50 Finally!
53 Practice
55 Blue jay's treat
57 Tiny pest
59 Scallopini meat
61 Actress Sheedy
62 Entertainer Tucker
64 Three-lined stanza
66 Play start
68 Gallery offering
69 Madrid Mrs.
71 Jenny
72 Like houseplants
75 Shinto "mecca"
76 "I Remember Mama" mama, ___ Hansen
78 Fish net
79 Copy Carl Lewis?
84 Favorites
85 What ___ is new?
86 Golfer's challenge
87 Arrayed
89 Judge's expertise
92 Handcuff
98 Face trouble like Bruce Baumgartner?
101 Madrid-Burgos *dirección*
102 Old Hebrew coin
103 Workout clothes
104 Call-up org.
105 Absolute ruler
106 Bastes

Down

1 ___ for one's money
2 Tear
3 Sicilian resort
4 Tennis call
5 "The Altar"
6 Riga resident
7 North Sea feeder
8 Cigar case
9 Cleo's finish
10 Writer Laurence
11 Anna's kingdom
12 Oregon port
13 More than one
14 Bikini part
15 Chipped in
18 In ___; furious
19 Butte's relative
21 Actress Rowlands
22 Library habitué
27 Get going
29 APB datum
31 Plug
32 Fee; process: Suff.
33 Easygoing
34 Posing difficulty
35 Singer James
36 Landlord's find
37 ___ hygiene
38 TV horse
43 Name of many streets
45 After-school org.
46 Army personnel
47 Everyone
48 Work at (a trade)
51 Zoroastrian scripture
52 Start a cruise
54 Terrier
55 Rwy. terminal
56 Former Mideast org.
58 Give ___ try
60 Swimmer's unit
63 A.D.C.
65 Mystery writer John Dickson ___
67 Price
70 Cobble
73 Pen: Abbr.
74 Billy ___ Williams
75 Won't take "no" for an answer
76 Ed.'s input
77 Designer's studio
79 Prefix for active or rocket
80 Speaks
81 First in line
82 Ornamental braid
83 Listens to
84 Hock
88 AAA suggestions
90 Andreanof island
91 Reporter's question
93 "___ the hour" (Burns)
94 Busy as ___
95 Fight, in a way
96 Permits
97 Dorothy's aunt, and others
99 What's the reason?
100 Hgt.

94

Originally published in 1989

Gemology 101 *by Elizabeth Arthur*

A jewel of a composition.

95

Across

1 Commencement
6 Fake jewelry
11 Stock quantities
17 Rich boy, in "Nancy" comics
18 Colorado ski resort
19 Pipe
20 Oahu landmark
22 Like a tame horse
23 Part of i.e.
24 Shade of green
25 Covers a hawk's head
27 Law or saw follower
28 "Oliver!" director
30 Incline
31 Of course!
32 Prayer ending
33 With 9 Down, summer drink
35 Stupefied
37 Accident-____
38 Office workers
41 Drive insane, of old
43 Half Mork's "good-bye"
44 Willy ____, salesman
45 Peggy Lee favorite
46 Cone of ____, "Get Smart" device
49 "Car 54, Where ____ You?"
50 Deserve
51 Top-notch
52 Strain
53 Bib. division
54 Oahu landmark
56 Viper
57 Author Levin
58 Pro ____
59 Christmastides
60 "Quincy" costar
61 Tall cocktail
63 Garden bloomer
64 Recedes
66 Moms' mates
67 Climber's need
68 Whipped cream dessert
69 M-16, for instance
71 NYC divisions
72 Thomas or Horace
73 Melville novel
74 Natural tanning agent
75 "____ a man who wasn't there"
77 Name for an old dog
81 Spoil
82 Lyric poem
84 Gluts
86 Whitney
87 Service yard
89 Charlie Chan film of 1945
92 Western squatters
93 Alpine region: Var.
94 Singer Gormé
95 Playful swimmers
96 Consumers
97 Pink table wines

Down

1 ____ of the Garter
2 Kind of pollution
3 Roofing material
4 Main street in "Peyton Place"
5 Wrench or hammer
6 Like some expense accounts
7 Pallid
8 Blow a wad
9 See 33 Across
10 Finishes
11 Loam and marl
12 Ranch workers: Abbr.
13 East Central Oklahoma State University site
14 Nevada range
15 Actress Brennan
16 "Tristram Shandy" author
19 Coherent beliefs
21 Classroom jottings
26 Looked at
29 Actress Merrill
32 "Rule Britannia" composer
34 Kind of game
35 February stones
36 Card game for two
37 Less vivid
38 Indo-European
39 Bullfighter
40 1985 mystery-adventure film, with "The"
41 Yogi with a mask
42 "The ____ that men do..."
43 Chihuahua children
45 Accomplishments
46 Serious
47 Social classes
48 Sensational news story
50 Intends
51 "Let's Fall in Love" composer
54 Fall preceder
55 Motor
62 *"Symphonie espagnole"* composer
63 Tune
64 Took the prize
65 Em, to Dorothy
67 Walden, for one
68 Paired
69 Sharp Italian cheese
70 Turkish hospice
71 ____ up; cheers
72 Gold and silver
74 Some servicewomen
75 Rhône feeder
76 Main course of study
78 Studies
79 Dinsmore, of fiction
80 Golly!
82 Pitcher
83 Words from Caesar
85 Nostradamus, for one
88 Had a bite
90 "On ____ Blindness" (Milton)
91 Muscle: Comb. form

Originally published in 1989

Seat of Power *by Roger H. Courtney*

Humbling words.

Across

1 Of things Vatican
6 Vanishes
11 A-E connection
14 Without a specific key
16 Moon feature
17 Classify
20 Gratify
21 Hard red wheat
22 Tip the ____
23 Quote, part 1
26 Type of dog
27 "The Red"
28 Descartes
29 Attacks the icebox
31 Tobacco quantities
35 Univ. degree
37 Sports activities
39 Quote, part 2
40 In ____; in position
41 One Maverick
42 Crossworddom sloths
44 Concept: Pref.
45 East Indian cedar
47 Quote, part 3
50 Dancer Shearer
52 Moves in a dodging
   manner
54 Prefix for classic or
   colonial
55 Rancher's wear
58 Rapped, of old
60 "A Doll's House"
   author
62 Asst.
63 Fireplace feature
66 ____ of Freedom
69 Kind of pudding
71 Resourceful
73 Effortlessness
77 '88 Olympics tennis
   gold medalist Shriver
78 Confabs, for short
80 Pass catchers
81 Quote, part 4
82 Annul, as an
   amendment
84 Sault ____ Marie
85 Quote, part 5
86 Entertainer Rivera
88 Dwarf cattle of South
   America
91 Smell ____; be
   suspicious
93 SRO presentation
94 End of quote
101 Beard of grain
103 Norwegian composer
104 Mistakes, to a redactor
105 Bring to attention
   again
106 Like some cereal
107 Honeybunch
108 Hereditary letters
109 Moby Dick
110 Makes simultaneous
   with

Down

1 Infant's meals
2 Hun king
3 Keats or Yeats
4 Anecdotal collections
5 Whips
6 Accolade for 53
   Down?
7 Delineate
8 Fudd or Gantry
9 French pupil
10 More peaceful
11 Amer. youth org.
12 Frictional events?
13 Great fear
15 Anagram for Erle
17 Onager
18 Despisement
19 Cook's meas.
24 More unctuous
25 Make the facts known
30 Petal perfume: Var.
31 Greek letter
32 Cached or stashed
33 ____ of Reason
34 Trounce
36 Failure
38 Major ending
40 A.k.a. "Star Wars"
41 UK component
43 Old dirk
46 ____ as the hills
48 First Chinese dynasty
49 Time without end
51 Absorption: Comb.
   form
53 Author of quote
55 Summer hrs. in St.
   Louis
56 Multitude
57 Phantasm
59 Qty.
61 Foolish complaint
64 Zenith
65 Floating on water
67 Large sea ducks
68 Sot's affliction,
   sometimes
70 "____ a man who
   wasn't there"
72 Law object
74 "What Kind of Fool
   ____?"
75 Mineo of films
76 Photog. technique
79 Scotland's main port
83 Clobber
85 Emporia
86 Burn
87 Word with gun or
   hand
89 Pentateuch
90 Bryant or Loos
92 Retired for the night
95 007's Fleming
96 ____-and-toe
97 TV-dinner table
98 Mountain lake
99 Auricular
100 West and Murray
102 Baden-Baden, for one

96

Blueprints   *by Bernice Gordon*

Edifice complexes.

Across

1 Is indebted to
5 Skidded
9 Record
13 Conrad of "Diff'rent Strokes"
17 Lane's colleague
18 Mata ___
19 Additions
20 Aware of
21 Separation center
22 Freeman Gosden's role
23 Word of woe
24 Matures
25 Jack Lemmon film, "The ___"
27 Retreat
29 Before
30 Bulk
32 Delhi nursemaid
33 Manicurist's item
36 Unpleasantly moist
37 Tune an organ
41 Spanish coin
42 Put into a capsule
45 Confounded
46 Actor Peter and kin
49 Bar legally
51 Squealed
52 Matches improperly
54 Cartoonist Gene of "Flirting Flora"
55 Board game
56 Fundamental basis
59 Shop shaper
63 Indian of South America
64 Dick and Tom
69 Garfield's pal
70 Bounds off
72 Shoe parts
73 Bishops' headwear
76 Chooses
78 Famed dynasty
79 Lively, in music
81 Steak choice
82 Adjust the clock
83 Bakery worker
84 "There ___ joy in Mudville..." (Thayer)
85 Dawn goddess
86 Famous Doric temple
90 Quad quarters
95 Cruising
96 NFL beasts
97 Cap-___; from head to foot
98 Selves
99 Call up
100 Coup d' ___
101 Signs of summer
102 A Johnson
103 "Kiss Me, ___"
104 Hideaways
105 Mlle. of Madrid
106 Costly

Down

1 Gumbo ingredient
2 Ooze, in a way
3 Sicily commune
4 Attic, often
5 Discredit
6 Metallic fabric
7 Hawaii's ___ Triathlon
8 Expanse
9 Lions and Tigers
10 Other, in combos
11 Two-dimensional
12 Put to the test
13 Scullers' place
14 Cherub (Fr.)
15 Journey, in old Rome
16 Like some wine
26 Stab
28 Except for
31 Manhattan sights
33 Ancient country
34 Symphony director Riccardo
35 Winged figure in art
36 Arid regions
38 "___ Help" (Billy Swan's hit)
39 Dollar fraction
40 Advantage
43 Depots: Abbr.
44 Wrongful acts
47 Phoebe Cates's miniseries
48 DDE's command
50 Pledge
53 Sidewinder
55 Lapdogs
57 Writer Ludwig
58 Negative prefix
59 Glen Gray's Casa ___ Orchestra
60 Tennis score
61 Squirrel monkey's cousin
62 Famed Russian art museum
65 Settle on government land
66 New Haven students
67 M. Coty
68 Army off.
71 Skeletons in the closet
74 For one
75 Directed
77 Cavalryman
80 Busy-looking
82 *Reine*'s hubby
84 MIT and Cal. Tech.
85 Old name for Homs, Syria
86 Leave the car
87 China, Korea, and so on
88 Ripped
89 Arabian gulf
91 Run amok
92 Blunderbore
93 Roster
94 North Sea feeder

97

Originally published in 1989

Outward Bound *by Norma Steinberg*

If you're optimistic, you know which way to look.

98

Across

1 Eyre's creator
7 Belle or Bart
12 Problem
16 Chartered
17 Craft for Uncas
18 —— Scotia
19 Honest
21 —— impasse; stymied in negotiations
22 Courts
23 Food container
24 Noshed
25 Short shot
26 —— and far between
27 Singer/actress Carter
29 Normal result
30 Brought forth
34 Behaves
36 Ingress
38 Ruled
39 Baleful; urgent
40 Comedian Jay ——
41 English gun
42 Baking ——
43 Touch lovingly
45 —— de cologne
46 Turned over
48 Kook
50 Arena
53 Nanny's charges
54 West Point mascot
55 Distance measurement
56 Frank Herbert fantasy
57 Town twice captured and lost by the Crusaders
58 Amherst Inst.
60 Deal with
61 "A Bridge ——"
62 Prefix with skid or stop
63 Sleep like ——
65 Salt pillar's mate?
66 Pother
68 —— to a customer
69 Marker
70 Big rig
74 '75 Wimbledon champ
75 Funnyman
78 —— soup yet?
79 Garner or Flynn
80 Regal fur
81 Salespeople
82 Impertinent
83 Shadow's place

Down

1 Sometimes furrowed feature
2 Nevada city
3 Atop
4 Ultimate numbers
5 —— up; prepare to drive
6 Drew out
7 Read a bar code
8 Sunbathe
9 Musical direction
10 Some are scenic
11 Disgust
12 —— up; buy immediately
13 Below expectations
14 Archetype
15 Role for Lancaster
20 Fido's foot
26 T-Man
28 Sidelong glance
30 Word in an ultimatum
31 Former tennis star Gerulitas
32 Power player's game
33 Author Kesey
34 Adjutant
35 Start
37 Compass reading
39 Jerk
40 Young men
42 Secure
43 Yield
44 Early wonder drug
47 Eat grandly
49 —— up; rip
51 Possessive pronoun
52 Joy Adamson's cat
54 Chinese leader
56 Feature of a well-read book
57 Doodle
58 Word on a picket sign
59 Frothy dessert
60 '80s rebel
61 "Rug"
64 Comes in second
65 Grant or Gehrig
67 Gels
69 Stands —— by; spectates
70 "You can fool —— of the people..."
71 Two-time Academy Award winner Jannings
72 Short skirt
73 —— tea
76 Digits: Abbr.
77 Weep

General Store *by Helen Hunter Lampe*

A hodgepodge of puns, slang, homonyms, and other fun.

Across

1 Philosophic bear?
5 Do we get 'em when we sit?
10 Fit to be ____, like a mature waterdrop?
14 What the best report card has, customarily?
15 Climbers and creepers
16 Bout, for Tyson, often
18 ____ rib tickled Eve
19 Airs
20 Insipid
21 Emeritus: Abbr.
22 Consumer
24 Jungfrau, for one
26 Do a voice-over
27 Less cloudy
29 Terrier type
31 Greek Ys
32 Superman's archenemy, ____ Luthor
33 The apostle fired off an ____
35 Roamer
38 Role
39 Queen of ____ (Cleopatra in a negative mood?)
43 Rower dropped bauxite and cinnabar overboard so he'd have both ____ in the water
44 Pretentious
45 Rubber snake had a bouncing baby ____
46 ____ Lanka
47 Had debts like Keats, perhaps?
48 Flag
49 Bambi, once
50 Sequel title starter
51 Barrier for Becker
52 Ban
53 Whiskey grain
54 Blow a ____
55 Bogus
57 Character
58 Inexperienced
59 Length
61 Before: Pref.
62 Ad: Small apartment for ____
65 Tree-graft site
66 ____ Slew, the racehorse
70 "Born in the ____"

71 ____ burner; horse
72 Fellow
73 Assist
74 African republic
76 Potato bug's sousaphone?
79 Called
81 In a ____; quickly
82 Musical composition
83 Poem of lament
84 Chief exec.
85 Bring back to splendor
86 Pizza payment

Down

1 The way some people sing in the mountains!
2 Lecture
3 Excellent sports instant
4 Unflappable
5 Britons have a blood bank and a ____ pool
6 Assert
7 ____ money; acupuncture payment?
8 Jell
9 Themes
10 Travel folder: ____ tease
11 Charged particle
12 Pairs
13 Boredom
14 Skippy on "Family Ties"
17 Society gals
23 Gender
25 Disappointment
28 Oy!
29 Nimble
30 ____ and caboodle; everything
31 Prisoners escaped by a slip of the ____
33 Food
34 Slender
35 Not a soul
36 Command
37 Butchers' conventions?
38 ____ fixe; menu amount
40 Publish
41 Got up
42 White sale grouping

44 Painted Desert state
45 Shakespeare
48 Enthusiastically participating
49 Front, in combinations
53 Cell
54 Worry
56 Stern
57 Rotter
58 Anchor
60 Liquor: ____ sauce?
61 Schoolyard missile
62 Junkyard sign: ____ in peace
63 Preempt
64 Lowest point
66 Kate, for one
67 Trainer
68 Loyal
69 Rotate
71 Fiver change
72 Give up
75 Expert
77 Salt Lake City athlete
78 Hot cross ____
80 Boxer with feet of Clay?

99

Haven's Gate   by Walter Co... ell

There's safe passage here.

100

Across

1 Agreement
5 Sweet wine
9 Inclined
14 Ocean liner: Abbr.
17 Culture medium
18 Dairy case item
19 Varnish resin
20 Cravat
21 A Barrett
22 Catcher's glove
23 Corn breads
24 Em's precedents
25 Convey
27 Cry of discovery
28 Hard wood
30 Latin jazz
31 Start for Nevada or Leone
33 Attend closely
34 Cargo space: Abbr.
36 QED part
37 Play
38 Roundup's followup
40 Librarian's command
41 Billiards shot
42 Harbor
44 Seaman's "hail"
46 Wrath
50 Selects
51 Cash or croup ending
53 Soup ingredient
55 Tomahawk, for instance
56 Fate
57 Confess
59 Alerts
60 CD predecessors
61 Galena or bauxite
62 Short section attached to a blouse's waistband
64 Absence of: Pref.
65 Blackthorn
66 Commuter's handhold
68 Mediterranean island
69 Intend
71 Fourth estate
73 "Stark" or "Enterprise," e.g.
76 Inclined
77 Modern aerodrome
80 Arrow poison
81 ____-tac-toe
82 Of the eye
83 Kitty of "Gunsmoke"
85 Bottle resident
89 Old three-stringed instrument
90 Matterhorn, for one
91 Sofa
93 City of Japan
94 Greetings!
96 Royal name of Norway
97 Oast
98 Cambridge univ.
99 Church officer
100 The end
101 Frog genus
102 Compass dir.
103 Clever
104 Domino or Waller
105 Golfing gadgets

Down

1 Portions
2 Greek marketplace
3 Erie or Suez
4 Forwards on a different carrier
5 Ceremony
6 Mixtures
7 Considers a legal case again
8 Moves unsteadily
9 Gun sound
10 Oahu greeting
11 Game of chance
12 Uncle, to Jock
13 Firings
14 "Let him ____ the music he hears..." (Thoreau)
15 Helm
16 Take umbrage at
26 Artillery burst
29 Colorado resort
32 Indy driver Bobby
33 Fleur-de-____
35 Scoff at
37 Short outing
38 Behave
39 Desirable cat
41 Single-celled animal
42 Arias
43 Violent storm
45 Cut
47 Gasoline measure
48 Send abroad
49 Correct a clock
52 Small brooks
54 Slam
57 Nears
58 Three-man vessel
63 Hawaii's ____ Loa
65 Cape Canaveral, for one
67 Delicious or Rome
70 Rule
72 Miscue
74 Elaborate farewell
75 Missouri city
77 Punchbowls
78 Flora migration
79 Like a straw
80 Significance
83 To go, in Paris
84 ____-garde
86 Brilliant stars
87 "Goodnight, ____"
88 Lab heaters
90 "M*A*S*H" star
92 Poetic twilights
95 Shade tree

Role Models   *by Manny Miller*

Sixteen, to be exact, counting 68 Across.
Get your popcorn and soft drink now.

Across

1 Combat detachment
7 Sally Kirkland
11 Ernest Borgnine
16 On land
17 Simpleton
18 Mark Lester
20 Yul Brynner and Deborah Kerr
22 Was equal to
24 Triumphant exclamation
25 Fasten using a strap
26 Seating for two or more
28 Thickness
29 Med. gp.
30 Carpenter's need
32 Operated
33 Spare
34 Whinny
37 Bluefish
40 Rich cake
41 Laugh loudly
43 Outstanding
44 Entertains
45 Trips
48 Household member
49 Luise Rainer
50 Govt. gp. of days gone by
51 Health clubs
53 Arnold Schwarzenegger
58 Reindeer herder
60 Ingrid Bergman
62 Old Ireland
63 Paul Newman
65 ___ Nostra
67 Actress Ullmann
68 Skippy
69 Assam or oswego
71 Cloudlike gases
73 Foxhunts
76 Upright stone slab
78 Hindu garment
79 Loathed
80 Frees
82 Persuades
85 Tsp. and tbs.
86 Monk's title
87 Son of Seth
89 Teacher's gp.
90 Eleventh century date, Roman style
91 Cowboy meets
94 Important crop
96 ___ *gratia artis*
97 ___ up; livening
99 Julie Andrews
102 Hopi's home
103 Fever and chills
104 Social gathering
105 Villain's look
106 Rex or Donna
107 Range animals

Down

1 Afghan
2 "Ain't That ___"
3 William Bendix
4 Korean GI
5 First: Abbr.
6 Communist name of fame
7 Tapering off
8 Negative prefix
9 Droops
10 Rose lover?
11 Pestle partner
12 Unfamiliar
13 Tear
14 Fed. corp. created in 1933
15 Puppies, at times
19 Tell
21 Mardi ___
23 Units of force
27 Old weight allowance
31 Cooking ingredient
33 Pass time idly
35 Malabar Coast district
36 Witches
38 Partridge roosts?
39 City in Italy
40 James A. Baker, for one
42 Meals
44 Other names
45 Electrical unit
46 Brilliantly colored food fish
47 ___ Clara
49 Hoagie ingredient
52 Mineo of films
54 Govt. dept.
55 George Arliss
56 Opera feature
57 Granular snow
59 Stages
61 Vigorous contest
64 Secondhand
66 Goat hair garments
70 Opposite of aweather
72 Coffee vessel
73 Wallace Beery
74 Laurence Olivier
75 Clothes
76 A few
77 Irked
80 Ivor Novello
81 TV melodrama
83 Klemperer of "Hogan's Heroes"
84 Talks impudently
86 Receiver
88 Toward the glacier
91 Ready to eat
92 Name for a caliph
93 Medicinal herb
95 Taint
98 Cowboy Maynard
100 Regret
101 Dessert choice

101

The Short Form *by Bert Rosenfield*

This might be a bit taxing until you make some deductions.

102

Across

1 Least embellished
7 Muscle-car dial: Abbr.
11 They're found near the flutes
16 Bird with an upcurved bill
17 Height: Pref.
18 Old hat
19 "To die; to sleep; ——" ("Hamlet")
20 Kansas
22 Whopper
24 In ——; fundamentally
25 Nautical ropes
26 Soup container
27 Followers
29 —— acid; fungicide
31 "Show Boat" song
34 Do a double take
37 Competed against Louganis
38 Poached egg foundation
40 Eppie's benefactor
41 Tartan design
43 Marvin and Bernard of TV
45 All-purpose truck
46 Canto or Paese
49 Exigency
51 *Rouge et Jaune, par exemple*
52 Former Dodger infielder Ron
53 Antiqua or nova
54 "As You Like It" forest
56 —— for; ambushes
58 Occasional TV specials
60 Doughnut-shaped
62 Litmus reddener
66 Actor Nick from Nebraska
67 Edith Piaf rendition
69 Old serf
73 Wife, in Berlin
74 Defunct Mideast acronym
75 Mineral find
77 Mountainous prefix
79 —— flow
81 Faultless fictive female
84 Old Roman officer
86 Expiate
87 One and ——
88 Crow ——; recanters
89 The Pentateuch
90 Entertainer Martha
91 Depose

Down

1 —— Johnson, World Series originator
2 Guacamole component
3 Michael or Alexis
4 Nobel Prize subj.
5 Harem
6 Playground sights
7 —— Mahal
8 Word with tooth or belly
9 Unrefined
10 In what way
11 Harvest goddess
12 More bemused
13 Anthem start
14 Alberto Azzo was the first
15 —— daylight; gets out of the red
21 Plop leader
23 Zealous
26 One of Fred's dance partners
28 Owl-pussycat destination
30 Strident
32 Cook and book endings
33 England-Wales river
35 Whale
36 It beats the deuce
39 Wigtown wear
40 Gershwin standard
42 Mom's sibs, for instance
44 Item in *la bibliotheque*
46 One dance locale
47 Switch follower
48 OAS member
50 Capt. Miller or Sgt. Yemana
55 ——-pros; legal discontinuance
57 Org. founded in 1889
59 Marathoner's asset
61 Luftwaffe's UK nemesis
63 American poet Cullen
64 Celebrated dancer Duncan
65 "—— Bingle"
68 Type of horse or goat
70 Help!
71 Cuisse, gorget, and so on
72 Soprano Mitchell
75 Blind unit
76 Blast or derm starter
78 Whence the Concorde rises
80 Makes a move
82 OT book
83 One network logo
85 Q-U joiners

Originally published in 1989

Colorful Slanguage *by Lois Sidway*

Ms. Sidway takes special care with a common theme.

103

Across

1 Tom Joad, and others
6 Sot
11 Miss Kitty's fella
15 African tribe
16 Papal vestment
17 "____ *nous le déluge*" (old French proverb)
19 Ready for use
20 Delighted
22 DDE's field of command
23 Alpine air
25 Linden or Holbrook
26 Vulcan's workshop
27 Takeover target's defensive ploy
29 Nothing ____! (Simple!)
30 In
33 Noun-forming ending
34 Get the suds out
35 Poet Clement
36 Try
38 Glib
39 Moralists
41 School subject
45 WKRP's Nessman
46 Dapper fellow?
47 Expert
48 Grog base
49 ____ set
52 Moonshine
55 Tune
56 Accused's need
57 Some are sour
58 Keen
61 Thing, to Nero
62 Slugabeds
63 Wrongful act
64 Dead to rights
67 Sector
68 ____ *on parle français*
69 Earth goddess
70 Small portion
73 Mayor Koch admits being one
76 Mikhail's missus
78 ____ goose; gannet
79 Ring up
80 Graceland name
81 Martha of TV and films
82 Tabulations, in short
83 Keaton of films

Down

1 Orchestral tuning fork
2 German philosopher
3 Happily concerned with
4 Airline abbreviation
5 Gents many cuts above the rest
6 ____ point; succinct
7 Heavenly hunter
8 Lumberman's boot
9 Indiana city
10 Mended a poor tiling job
11 Crazy
12 Eating can spoil it
13 Mythical merman
14 Garrison's forte
18 Aquarium member
21 Pipe joint
24 Middling mark
27 Dukakis beat him in '88
28 Blob
30 Stroll
31 One Chan
32 Give shelter to
34 Dust collector
36 Ivan or Peter
37 Poetic time of day
38 Story line
40 Pervasive quality
41 Seed coat
42 Insensate person
43 Straightedge
44 Untidy
47 Key word?
50 Remove, as trash
51 An O'Neill
52 Cleanse
53 Made well-liked
54 Shape
56 Arrayed
58 Attempts
59 Great fear
60 Small hollow
61 Goes over the highlights
62 Chemical suffix
64 Tease
65 Airline employee
66 Nostrils
70 Sutherland, for one
71 "It's ____ to Tell a Lie"
72 Vile
74 Compass dir.
75 Tibetan gazelle
77 ____ Hakim, Ado Annie's fella

Mule That Over! *by Wilson McBeath*

The judge's decision is final.

104

Across

1 Snooped
6 Bundle
10 Garden product
16 Noisy
17 Kind of collar
18 Lyric poems
19 TNT, loosely
20 Spoils
21 Stair posts
22 **Adage, Part I**
25 Actress Patricia
26 Pool hall choice
31 Canopy
35 Chop
36 Jackson or Bancroft
37 Endured
38 State of mind
40 Beguile
42 Bois de Boulogne, for one
43 Remove from office
44 Matured
45 **Adage: Part II**
48 Pulley wheels
50 Roof edge
51 Docile
54 Christmas pie eater
55 Summer or boot
56 Doled out
57 Shake ——!
58 Possessed
59 Not egotistic
60 Cattle breed
63 Advance
65 **Adage: Part III**

71 Turn against
75 Snoods
76 Clementine's father's occupation
77 Delphi denizen
78 Canadian Indian
79 Atlanta University
80 Cover, nautically
81 Orient
82 Tears

Down

1 Yemen's capital
2 Formally precise
3 Greek letter
4 Merit
5 Overwhelmed
6 Ms. Abzug
7 Bikini, for one
8 Diving bird
9 Came in
10 Dogma
11 Horse or light
12 Hay store

13 Hoosier humorist
14 —— Aviv
15 Predecessor of CIA
23 Cash follower
24 Pledge
27 Gifted
28 Overwhelm
29 Wave (Fr.)
30 Exigency
31 Kitchen abbreviation
32 Greek letter
33 Wizard
34 **End of adage**
35 Impetuous one
38 Kaffeeklatsch containers
39 Chemical suffix
40 Thin coin
41 Above: Pref.
43 Humdinger
44 Invitation initials
46 St.'s relative
47 "—— a Pirate King" (Gilbert and Sullivan)

48 Pahlavi, for one
49 Golfer's objective
52 Quincy, etc.
53 Summer clock setting in S.Car.
55 Rhythm
56 Type of chemical compound
58 Regal initials
59 Andy Gump's spouse
61 Yvette's daughter
62 Frequently
63 Revolutionary War general
64 Thing of value
66 Zeus's sister/wife
67 Quiet actor
68 —— the secret
69 Square one
70 Prohibition instigators
71 Hold up
72 Pitcher's stat
73 Brewery container
74 Fall mo.

Out On A Limb *by Norma Steinberg*

That's where you'll have to go to find these answers.

105

Across

1 Tales
6 Spin
12 Charge!
18 Leonine group
19 Funicello's costar
20 Rose of ____
21 Links great
23 Wrap of a sort
24 Ms. Russell
25 Amenities
26 Concluded
28 "____ now, brown cow..."
29 ____ meet
31 Pulver, e.g.
32 "The ____ of the Cave Bear"
33 Frayed
34 Slack
36 Hillock
38 Took off
39 Exceeds the limit
42 Collegiate women, once
43 Blemish
44 "...it ____ for thee" (Donne)
45 Kind of eel
46 ____ water
49 Carl's celeb son
50 Utrillo contemporary
51 Like Savalas
52 Ms. Lupino
53 GI's address
54 Insensitive
56 Container of sorts
57 Moisture
58 Dairy case item
59 In toto
60 Up-to-date
61 Looks up to
63 Bifurcates
64 Hoofed animal
66 No ifs, ____, or buts
67 In a bad mood
68 Strong
69 Pinnacle
70 Box
71 Departed
72 Hee-haw
73 Quarter or dime
74 Christmas, e.g.
75 Min. fractions
79 LAX info
80 Thomas or Horace
81 In twos
84 FDR brainstorm
85 Like Howdy Doody, perhaps
87 Give in
90 Bundle of energy
91 Tied
92 ____ Arabia
93 Evening in a salon
94 Vapors
95 Word processor's goofs

Down

1 Marina sights
2 Mohican missile
3 Tokyo thoroughfare
4 Uproar
5 Being
6 Plunder
7 Racetracks
8 Like some tales
9 Charity
10 ____ the mark
11 Signs up
12 Colorado ski town
13 Valhalla resident
14 Cure leather
15 Paris landmark
16 Sidekick
17 Recognized
22 Frock
27 Ms. Harper, to friends
30 Pare
32 Buffalo Bill ____
33 Used to be
35 Some are personal
36 Country on the 38th parallel
37 Baseball mitt oil
38 Comes to earth
39 Fellini's "La ____"
40 Exhausted
41 Pasta form
42 Apartment for sale
43 Mr. Loman
45 Manners
46 Sends
47 Nimble
48 Cowboys' longtime coach
50 Toms and bucks
51 Pitchers' errors
54 Crowd
55 Sip slowly
62 "____ Merry Oldsmobile"
63 Kukla's friend
64 "____ Men" (DeVito film)
65 Go-betweens: Abbr.
67 Ripple
68 Brouhaha
69 Water-carved valley
70 Talk into
71 ____ apart
72 Fancy ladies
73 Craft for Uncas
74 Trekker
76 Become
77 Set of beliefs
78 Bombay wraps
80 Eager student's classroom call
81 Ambition
82 Twinge
83 Clean
86 Patriotic assn.
88 World Series league: Abbr.
89 Uh-uh

Originally published in 1989

Sex Changes *by Ronnie K. Allen*

Literary confusion.

Across

1 Feeds the kitty
6 Prefix with dollar or glyph
11 Essence
15 Religion emphasizing unity
16 Soaps up
18 Racecar driver Bobby
20 Open
21 Anger
22 First of the *año*
23 ____ Vegas
24 Oh, to be, in Paris!
26 Winter weather
28 One Little Woman
29 "____ Is Your Life"
31 Dolly's greeting
33 Bell-____
35 Arias of Costa Rica
37 *Mens* ____ *in corpore sano*
39 Political comedian Sahl
40 Like many bathrooms
42 Buttonlike flower
45 Exclamations
47 Medieval interjection
49 Mr. Washington
50 Sudsy
51 Fish dam
53 Of greater size: Abbr.
54 Correspondent Elie
56 Court event
57 Cartesian connection
58 Coup
60 Yellow pigment
62 13 x 9 shape
64 H.H. Munro
65 Eccentric
67 Rational
69 Pot-au-____
70 Ginger cookie
71 More faithful
72 Sound of disgust
73 *Uno, due,* ____
74 Deco or nouveau
75 Hawthorne heroine
77 Cut prices drastically
79 Top-notch
81 Freudian controls
83 Finished
85 Impedes

88 Cake topper
90 Help a felon
92 Out ____ limb
93 Respect
96 Have to
98 Cheer
99 Prepared for wallpaper
101 Try
103 ____ *curiae*
105 Purloined
106 Underground passages
107 Newsy environmental concern
108 Zealous
109 Well dressed
110 Play part

Down

1 Like ____ from the blue
2 Southwest Indian
3 Dostoevski's siblings
4 Corn on the cob
5 Location

6 Jury lists
7 And so forth: Abbr.
8 Donizetti offspring
9 Tenant's payment
10 Phrase of approximation
11 Magician's word
12 Singer Janis
13 Edward Streeter's parent
14 Sultan's privilege
16 Coins in the fountain
17 Yugoslavian
19 Captain's diaries
25 Chekhov's siblings
27 Spider
30 ____-fi
32 Drink up, cat style
34 Mason's tool
36 Kelp and spirogyra
38 Fondness, in Firenze
41 John or Jane
43 Poker openers
44 German grandmother
46 Hancock, obviously
47 Hygienist's instruction

48 Galápagos denizen
52 Elephant bachelor
55 Water lily
59 Summit
61 Minoan island
63 Playwright Brendan
66 Function: Suff.
68 Hung. neighbor
76 Fabled bird
78 Follower of Wm. Miller
80 Had requisites
82 In an uncomplicated way
84 "Amen" character
85 Little Joe's brother
86 Loos woman?
87 RBI or ERA
89 Streisand film
91 "To ____ own self..."
94 Vingt-____ (blackjack)
95 Sicilian volcano
97 Prepares for feathers?
100 Inventor Whitney
102 Encountered
104 Big burger

By The Numbers *by Elizabeth Arthur*

But not necessarily routine.

107

Across

1 Baffling question
6 Vestiges
12 Casper, for one
17 Of use
18 Finery
20 Kind of eclipse
21 Sight, hearing, smell, taste, and touch
23 "Martha" or "Louise"
24 Kayo count
25 The March of ___
26 Part of GBS
28 Silent signal
29 *Esposas,* in brief
31 Tosspot
32 Clotho, Lachesis, and Atropos
34 Evergreen tree
35 Don
37 Quagmire
38 Roost harvest
39 Footnote specialists
42 Artistic discernments
43 Words from Scrooge
44 Sadat
45 Chile export to Britain
46 Like proverbial milk
48 Notice
49 Fifth-largest planet
50 Unity
52 ___ *wiedersehen*
53 Overjoyed
55 Gumshoe
57 Bell ringers
59 Twig-and-mud homes
60 Arrest; collar
61 Singer Della
62 Runs the motor in place
63 Feather
64 Rwy. terminals
65 Insertion mark
66 Smoothed
67 Surprised expressions
68 Put on (a show)
70 Rank's partner
71 In ___; peevish
72 ___ Antipas
73 Eye protection
74 Compete
78 Last year's jrs.
79 Jump
80 Top ratings
82 Dawber's sitcom, "My Sister ___"
83 Snicker
85 Poker choice
89 Ham it up
90 Everlasting

91 Insult
92 More recent
93 Anticipates, in a way
94 Actress Valentine

Down

1 Holes out
2 Tom Tryon's "The ___"
3 Venetian red
4 Pixie
5 Tim of "Frank's Place"
6 Vibration
7 Turned the clock back
8 Matures
9 Soup container
10 Urban trains
11 Oaxaca naps
12 Incandescence
13 Marching syllable
14 Single performance
15 Lamour garments
16 Professions
19 Fire residues
22 Passport endorsements
27 Nincompoop
30 Work out
32 The ___; exclusive social set
33 Commedia dell'___
34 Norman Vincent ___
36 Make a boo-boo
37 Slogan
39 Home, to Juanita
40 Computer fodder
41 Second line of a child's stanza
42 "Little ___," from "Annie"
43 Twining stem
45 Mother-of-pearl
46 Agitated states
47 Corrals
49 Chemistry suffixes
50 Assault
51 Fishing net
53 *Corrida* cheers
54 Removed, in publishing
56 Dressed
58 Slightest
60 Forty-___
62 Stage villain
63 Buddy
64 Diana Ross backup singer
65 Covers a floor
66 Partisan
67 Expedite
68 Andress film
69 Toy with
70 Some exams
73 Not widespread
75 "___ Is Born"
76 Bring about
77 Lower Saxony seaport
79 Lecher's look
80 Green Gables girl
81 Mt. Rushmore's state
84 Summer, in Arles
86 Fido's doc
87 Palindromic preposition
88 Commerce agcy.

Ands Up! *by Louis Baron*

Connections you should be able to make without difficulty.

Across

1 Some 72 Across attenders
6 Big Apple neighborhood
10 Pueblo Shoshonean
14 Shake a ___!
17 Part of Stein's line
18 Aesir VIP
19 Israel's Abba
20 Cretan E
21 Red Riding Hood alternative
24 "Honor ___ Father"
25 Pull up ___ and sit down
26 Seine feeder
27 Seething
29 Actress Virginia
30 Georgetown's country
33 Mrs. Reagan
34 Baked-blackbirds' number
39 What's the ___!
42 Cad
43 Ending for pay
44 Beach top
47 Out of practice
49 Nay neutralizer
51 Newspaper monicker
52 Melee
53 Curtain raiser
54 Chief architect of Florence's Duomo
56 Past deadline
57 1987 TV fantasy-romance series
62 Beatles' film
63 Consorts of rajahs
64 Site of Illinois Benedictine College
66 Lili has two
67 Auspices
68 Ending for law or saw
71 "Holberg Suite" composer
72 After-school org.
73 Old hand
74 Soft drink
76 A bit of work
77 Vanity and Times?
83 Intrigue
86 Clean slate need
87 Ham's brother
91 Soap or horse
92 Slowpoke's opposite
94 "Tender is the Night" heroine
96 ___ overboard!
97 Possible bonebreakers
101 Ornamental vase

108

102 "Pure Reason" philosopher
103 Graf ___
104 Actor Jeremy
105 Pig's digs
106 Dovekies
107 Sherpa's critter
108 Dogie

Down

1 Israeli left-wing party
2 Palm variety
3 Like camphorless closets
4 "...arms against ___ troubles..."
5 Sonora Indian
6 Seth, to Eve
7 Kind of ball
8 Paid killer
9 Available
10 Axed
11 Clarinet's kin
12 Crony
13 Newborn
14 Spill the beans
15 Moral standard
16 With merriment
22 Disagree
23 QED's midriff
28 Kind of window
31 A-bomb Nobelist
32 New Haven campus
35 "___ Beautiful Doll"
36 Value
37 Top group
38 Mogul
39 William Tell's milieu
40 Region for baskers
41 "Great Expectations" heroine
44 Golf club
45 Sidewinder
46 Briny affirmative
48 Catches
50 A de Mille
51 Hotsy-___
52 Knack
55 Carp's cousin
58 Famed Bernini fountain
59 Short-barrelled rifle
60 Actress Louise
61 "Enigma Variations" composer
62 Wise
65 Part of *ab ovo*
69 Gentlemen: Abbr.
70 Womanizer
75 Fixes rips
77 Wide's partner
78 Chilkoot Pass locale
79 Smooch
80 Fashionably formal
81 Poncho: Var.
82 Accompany
83 Mardi Gras god
84 Divorced
85 Berle's associate
88 Ennoble
89 Mrs. Sakharov, ___ Bonner
90 Like Junior's room
92 Skater's hangout
93 Riot and Mann
95 "And that's the way ___" (Cronkite)
98 T, as in Timon
99 Tennis prop
100 Agnus ___

Shell Game *by Douglas Behrend*

Mr. Behrend's catch of the day.

109

Across

1 Hodgepodge, briefly
5 High card
8 Elec. unit
11 Urge forward
16 Concerning
17 Savings and ___
19 Never, in Nuremberg
20 Actor Nick
21 Nittany or paper
22 Disconcert
24 Runs in the Hambletonian
25 Bandleader for senior snails?
27 Georgetown's players
28 Mortician's vehicles
29 Objective
30 Yen fraction
31 ___ Scott decision
32 Upper House member
34 Max ___ Sydow
37 Comic actor Jack
40 Exist
41 Legendary lady of the Wild Wet?
43 Rely on
45 Patriotic org.
47 Idealist
48 Prefix for coat or fog
49 Family member
51 ___ de vie
52 Jack of "Hawaii Five-O"
53 Shellfish's wake-up call?
58 Give ___ for one's money
60 Writer Anaïs
61 Roadhouse
62 Out of practice
65 Ennui
67 Children's game
69 Budget cutters
70 Where body-building bivalves gather?
74 Bird of Arabian myth
76 Mineo or Maglie
77 Revered one: Abbr.
78 Dagwood's bride
79 Flightless birds
81 ___-relief
82 Home for 21 Across
83 The very last of
86 Baby's discomfort
89 Underwater marauders?
92 Sandy islet
93 Ban
94 Take ___ from me...
95 Produce a show
96 Beast of burden
97 Take sustenance
98 Pueblo ceremonial structure
99 Dwellings
100 Observe
101 Farmer's bus.
102 Actor Roscoe

Down

1 Shopping center
2 NBAer Thomas
3 Vermont resort
4 He's TV's "Fatman"
5 Several-time Indy winner
6 Admits as true
7 Lets up
8 Rabbit ears
9 Pond creator of a sort
10 Quick glance
11 Salinger's "The Catcher ___"
12 Dolt
13 Clever ruse
14 Songstress James
15 Minus
18 Unused
23 How some Chicagoans commute
26 Unstable; inconsistent
30 Phrase of agreement
32 Seafood choice
33 Kind of wave
34 Scrams
35 Unique thing
36 Campus outcast
37 Oil additive
38 Mine find
39 Prevail in the profanity department
42 Envious, in Paris
44 The Rolling ___
46 Church corner
50 Me, to Yvette
51 Novelist Ferber
54 Hillocks
55 Uncertain state
56 ___ go; busy
57 Stoker's stalker
58 Defensive weapons: Abbr.
59 Easy victory
63 Chorus syllable
64 Fashionable monogram
66 Fiascos
68 Lube man's task
71 Back a candidate
72 Glandular
73 Bind fast
75 Careless one
80 Singer/songwriter Neil
81 Stale ideas
83 Shinbone
84 Shout starting 67 Across
85 See 11 Across
86 Country singer Johnny
87 Palindromic emperor
88 Rich soil
89 Some IRS foilers
90 Secreted
91 Health farms

Parish the Thought! *by William Canine*

Saluting the Pelican State.

Across

1 Evangelist's command
5 Baden-Baden and others
9 USN ranks
13 Pause
17 Thomas ___ Edison
18 Stroll
19 Easter entrees
20 Faulkner's "As ___ Dying"
21 Joe Isuzu, for one
22 Bayou denizen
24 Noise from 22 Across
25 Gypsy
27 Epigraph
28 Queeg's vessel
29 Reception room
30 Flash flood
31 Irene and Finley Peter
32 Move on the edge
35 Trombonist Jack, interpreter of the blues
37 Rainbow
40 Out of the wind
41 Floodgate
42 The Crescent City's state
45 *Niña*'s aunt
46 "___ Rheingold"
49 Price of "Family Ties"
50 Libelant
54 Actor Eddie
56 More unusual
58 Jeremiads
60 Match race runner-up
61 Rarely
63 Wyoming city
65 Baseball team
66 Hallux
67 Misery
69 Shrove Tuesday doings
71 Keir of "2001"
75 Check
76 Big curve
77 Ragtime derivative
80 Cypress growths
82 San Diego athletes
83 Cookies
85 Freshman at The Point
89 Places
90 Pitiless, ironically
91 Bayou boats
93 Salver
94 Creole specialty
96 Raison d'___
97 Greenback
98 Uttered
99 Tan
100 Thrum
101 Overcome
102 Destructive force
103 "One small ___ for a man..." (Armstrong)
104 Location

Down

1 Scotches
2 Stowe character
3 Benefit
4 Symphonic movements
5 Cygnet
6 Wan
7 "...and ___ for one" (Musketeers' pledge)
8 Be stingy
9 Fixed property
10 French painter (1684-1721)
11 Melville title
12 Russia or Estonia, e.g.
13 Hair ornament
14 Sir Galahad's mother
15 Swiss resort commune
16 Youngsters
23 Toggenburgs
26 Singer Paul and family
28 Panacea
30 Type of pattern
31 Ancient Romania
33 Rhea Silvia, mother of Romulus and Remus
34 Show a response
36 Skedaddle!
37 Well-nigh
38 Trucker's competition
39 Clabber
43 Finished off a cake
44 Essence
46 Tennessee's streetcar
47 Superdome and Kingdome
48 Emphasis
51 Patriotic org.
52 Cheese
53 Observes
55 Signal from Big Ben
57 Tampa Bay's soccer team
59 Lorelei, for one
62 Grimaces
64 Actress Adams
68 Letter shape
70 Hopeless
72 Vincent Price's "The ___ on Earth," 1964
73 Exalt
74 Turkish city
77 Famed defender
78 Think
79 Worked in radiology
81 Snoozes
82 City on the Ganges
84 Howard and Ernie
86 Devour
87 Smallish equine
88 Put forth
90 Poet Teasdale
91 Cow barn
92 Coll. educ. org.
94 Responsibility
95 Perform

110

Originally published in 1989

Comic Relief *by Sidney L. Robbins*

...in the form of an original couplet.

111

Across

1 Emanations
6 Worry
10 Golden —— Bridge
14 Bias
15 Irrational, in a way
17 Beloved puppet
18 Ms. Loos
19 Furious
20 Ms. Bailey
21 **Part 1 of verse**
24 Hooter
25 Soft metal
26 Rogue
30 Nicholas, for one
32 Vatican figure
36 Figurine
37 The stuff beams are made of
39 Man of La Mancha
40 **Part 2 of verse**
43 Groups of species
44 Military helper
45 Those folks
47 Achieve
51 **Part 3 of verse**
57 Fragile
58 TV dinner supports
59 Positive
60 Take care of
61 Bridge seat
62 Toward the back of the boat
64 Auto input
65 Use a straw
66 **End of verse**
75 Coolant
76 Weird
77 Like some seals
79 Ball beauty
80 Use chemicals to thaw
81 Finished the dishes
82 Unemployed
83 1956's "The Bad ——"
84 Transmits

Down

1 Botanist Gray
2 Arm bone
3 Kind of road
4 Opponent
5 Nonmoving machine part
6 Needless trimming
7 Unusual
8 Israel's Abba ——
9 Broz, to most people
10 Colorado River's —— Canyon
11 O, woe!
12 Become weary
13 Slippery one
16 Pertaining to teeth
17 Ready for business
22 Clock-changing hour
23 Knight's title
26 Sticker
27 Wedding words
28 Moo-moo mama
29 —— carte
30 Links mound
31 Guard
32 Write
33 In ——; solo
34 —— *favor*, please
35 Time period of note
37 Not irreg.
38 "—— not to reason why..." (Tennyson)
39 Truck
41 Brad
42 Clamor
43 Firm up
46 "For —— a jolly good..."
47 Far from fore
48 Half of *sei*
49 Flail
50 Succor
52 Convened
53 Fast plane, briefly
54 Shade
55 Miss the mark
56 Lair
58 Examined
61 Had been
62 Be under the weather
63 Races
64 Not here
65 Charger
66 Raised
67 Scream
68 Lawn pest
69 Exclamations of wonder
70 Pennsylvania city
71 Pleasant
72 Filly, in the future
73 Dublin's locale
74 Require
75 Anti-racketeering org.
78 Med. degree

Out Front   *by Walter Covell*

Mr. Covell's early warning system is working.   Hope yours is, too.

Across

1 Straw bundle
6 Assn.
9 Retired
13 School gp.
16 Zaire, once
17 Relax
19 Anticipated
21 Brief entr'acte
23 Promontory
24 Vinland explorer
25 Operatic air
27 Medicinal plant
28 Square-rigger's canvas
32 Quake sites
36 Anabaptist sect
37 Peachy treats
39 Plum variety
41 Vex
42 Pronto, in the O.R.
43 Conjunction
46 Chemical suffix
47 Pop-goers
50 Spiny anteater
52 Kind of jockey
54 Added up
56 Tautened
57 Sesame
59 Organic compound prefix
60 Flying agcy.
62 "Flying Down to ___"
63 Trust
66 Pays back
69 U-joint
72 Jury leader
74 Got rid of
76 Coll. deg.
77 Ave. crossers
78 Small nail
80 Scottish explorer
81 Grape disease
83 Spiny shrub
86 Litter laggers
87 Prevents
90 Drafted recruit
92 Winning serves
93 Birthright seller
95 Ed.'s convenience
96 Thin moon
100 Type of exercise
105 Chromosome end
106 Hamlet, for one
107 Handles

112

108 New World gp.
109 Red and Yellow
110 Rooter
111 Long for

Down

1 High school subj.
2 Judge's title: Abbr.
3 Inside, in combos
4 Eternal
5 Demonstrate; predict
6 Ethylene, for one
7 Actress Ryan of "Amen"
8 Mideast Strip
9 Business dealings
10 Scare word
11 It's human to do it
12 Billy ___ Williams
13 Noted clergyman
14 Purport
15 Llama's milieu
18 Predict
20 Bed boards

22 Farrow
26 Symbols of precise pronunciation: Abbr.
28 Lost brilliance
29 Near Easterner
30 Poets
31 Fishing spear
33 Quote
34 Legislate
35 Lower
38 Produces
40 Profit
43 Like activated carbon
44 Windsock dir.
45 Family member
48 "Perfect," per 73 Down
49 Nonreligious
51 What's ___ for me?
53 Killer: Suff.
55 Angry states
58 West Indian dances
61 "Much ___ About Nothing"
63 Meas. for 110 Across
64 Spoil

65 Seer's card
67 Mentioned earlier
68 NCO
70 Sharp
71 In and of itself
73 Shuttle gp.
75 Mast-to-bow rope
79 Erases
82 Swiss city
83 Painting base
84 OPEC units
85 Sycophants
87 Ipso ___
88 Plant sheath
89 Projection room units
91 New Guinea city
94 Colorado Springs Acad.
97 Length units, for short
98 Shoe width
99 1930s legis.
101 ___ tear; binging
102 "Rose ___ rose..." (Stein)
103 Box or freight follower
104 D.C. figure

Scrub Team   *by Jean Davison*

Ms. Davison must have constructed this one on a Monday.

Across

1 Door hinge site
5 Con game
9 Don't you ___!
13 Plush
17 In the past
18 Waikiki's island
19 DeMille production
20 Wimbledon's Arthur
21 Helen of Troy's mom
22 Property encumbrance
23 ___ avail
24 LBJ revelation
25 Fool
27 Roberts and Carson
29 Safire interest
30 Hang out to dry?
33 Actress Hartman
34 Enthusiastic about
35 "Annie" pres.
36 Dark secrets?
41 WWII enlister
43 Van Ark's role
46 Important time
47 Points a finger at
49 "Where the Boys ___"
50 ___-de-France
51 Kitchen name-callers?
53 Address for a knight
54 Stern
56 ___ different tune; changed stories
58 Following
60 Reb letters
62 ___ longa...
63 An Avenger
64 Shade
65 "Stormy Weather" singer
67 Pulver's rank: Abbr.
69 Fairy-tale heavy
70 Wed. kin
71 Eur. country
73 Root crop
76 Make public
77 Easy and Main, for short
78 Robert Stack role
80 Where 36 Across gets broadcast?
82 Vanity
83 Archbishop Desmond
85 Curtis or Rosewall
86 Ends up okay?
93 Dirt mover, commonly
94 College kid's homecoming present?
95 Watergate, to Woodward
97 Muslim state

98 Douglas of "The Fall Guy"
99 Faction
101 Ripped
102 Joker
103 PM period
104 Other, in Lima
105 Mediterranean volcano
106 Service club
107 Garage sale tag words
108 Broadway light
109 Stains

Down

1 Shock
2 Head off
3 Radio, television, and so on
4 Shelf holder
5 Impresario Hurok
6 Illinois city
7 "We're having___ wave..."
8 1987 Harvey Korman film

9 Emulate Columbo
10 Handsome young men
11 Get the soap out
12 System or sphere leader
13 Quarterback, often
14 Brando doorstop?
15 Catches flies
16 On this spot
26 Former British colony
28 TV's Marilu
29 Get nude
31 Baby powders
32 Off a ways
36 Shows
37 Resolve a pressing problem?
38 Disconcerts
39 Jack Frost's work
40 Tend the sick
42 Kin of 73 Across
43 Half a salad dressing
44 North African country
45 Conductors
48 Dead or Red

52 Jack of "Barney Miller"
55 Omni, for one
57 From ___ Z
59 Put through the ___
61 Music's Adam
66 Texas city
68 Wheel rod
72 Early autos
74 Attacks suddenly
75 Acts like 105 Across
79 Singer Enzo
81 Legislated
82 Changes
84 Traffic maneuvers
86 Peachy shade
87 Arkansas range
88 Norwegian kings
89 Stale
90 Pert. to water: Pref.
91 Like Santa, at times
92 Diva Marilyn
93 Casino "bones"
96 Veggie twins?
98 Meadow cry
100 Thousands of years

113

Falling Stars *by Barbara Lunder Gillis*

A one-way trip.

114

Across

1 Cost-of-living meas.
4 Cheery word
7 Recedes
11 Feat
15 Comments from Bossy
16 Mature
17 Christmas song
18 Above
19 1949 Steve Allen film compendium
22 Commodity
23 Disregard
24 ...out of a sow's ___
25 Comic strip menace
27 JFK posting
28 Disadvantage's site
33 Misplaces
34 ___ hand; assist
37 Salary
38 Havoc
40 Wasted
45 Study of light: Abbr.
48 Legal noun
49 Fished for morays
50 One tide
52 Handsome Greek
55 Double curves
57 Certain ester
59 Ethical
60 Some disco discs
61 Coveted award
62 Declaimed
64 Harass
66 Ill-use
67 Sediment
68 Unanimous
70 Japanese poetry form
72 Ember
73 Commodore's toast?
76 Chemical compound
78 Lupino of film fame
79 Migrant Sooners
82 The Gem State
85 Sad
90 ___-Magnon
91 Commit a no-no at bridge
93 Temp. scale
94 Porter
97 Teen's woe
98 Sad
103 Labor
104 Smell ___; be suspicious
105 Fear-respect mix
106 Gourd fruit
107 Watches
108 21st-century residence?
109 Fight
110 AARP members

Down

1 Ranch worker
2 Corn ___
3 Woe ___!
4 Batter
5 Have ___ at; attempt
6 "He done ___ wrong..."
7 Chou ___
8 Lodger's meals
9 "___ Hur"
10 Winter get-about
11 Unfortunate
12 Dale or Linda
13 Weird
14 Attire
15 Three-card ___
19 Battle of honor
20 TV actor Byrnes
21 Why not?
26 Actor Wallach
29 Chooses
30 Attention-getting shout
31 American humorist
32 New York canal
35 Shabby
36 Shortly
39 Reverse
41 Denials
42 Rooted firmly
43 Singer Della
44 Hirt and Haig
46 Truce
47 Casual goodbyes
51 Lively
52 Minor prophet
53 "Andrea ___"
54 Some tests
56 Ohio politician
58 Seek counsel from
63 Pedestal part
64 Curtsy
65 Robert Conrad's third TV series (1971)
66 Farrow
69 As ___ to (biographer's credit)
71 Triumphant shouts
74 ___ *et ubique*; here and everywhere
75 Noisy spasms
77 Strong ale
80 A Muse
81 Next year's jr.
82 Angry
83 Lure
84 Broadway hit
86 Man-___; battleship
87 Desires
88 Brit. hosp. coverage
89 *Uno, due,* ___
92 Cracker cheese
95 Napoleon, et al.
96 Activist
99 Man-mouse connection
100 Capture
101 Deuce
102 Bewitch

Originally published in 1989

Important People *by Bernice Gordon*

Generically speaking.

Across

1 Chest material
6 City destroyed by fire and brimstone
11 Examples
16 Dutch Antilles island
17 Of a clan
19 Piece for solo instrument
20 Frosts
21 Diocese manager
23 Common Atlanta place-name
25 Egg on
26 Bankbook abbr.
27 Being
28 Greek vowels
29 Sleigh
30 Hideout
31 Abide
33 Bog
34 Bristles
35 Lock up or in
38 Houdini specialty
40 Delaware Senator
41 Glanced sidelong
43 Clumsy person
44 Swab
45 Like prints from fastest film
48 Dull
50 Cordage fiber
54 Deeds
55 Final notice, in brief
56 Campus mil. program
57 Ready for the plucking
58 Actress Meg
59 Raggedy Andy, for one
60 ____ expectancy; presumed inheritances
62 Some people
63 ____ Marie Saint
65 County Kerry seaport
66 Insect stages
69 Rascals
72 That is, to Nero
73 Kovacs
74 Musical Getz
75 Furnish
77 Mother of Castor and Pollux
78 Host a tea party
79 Kind of gin
80 Notion
84 Sugary suffix
85 Pal, in the old west
86 Exhaustion
88 For whom nothing is good enough
92 Med. subjs.
93 Marx's collaborator
94 Hans Christian Andersen's birthplace
95 Actress/writer Taylor
96 Vermont ski resort
97 Pressed forward
98 Rabbit and Fox

Down

1 ____ diem; live for the day
2 Lake Indians
3 Musketeer author
4 Lettered one
5 Heedless
6 Take unawares
7 Trials and tribulations
8 March collection
9 Sash for Madame Butterfly
10 Irish Sea island
11 Emotional bond
12 Alicia of "Falcon Crest"
13 Glut
14 British schoolboy
15 1964 Literature Nobelist
18 Traditional precious stone
19 Bambi's dad
22 Loudness unit
24 Placekicker's prop
29 Fantastic hope
30 Was ahead
32 St. Paul's architect
33 Atlas asset
34 Taste
35 "The Kingdom" composer
36 Portia's quality
37 Blessed woman
39 Roundup follow-up
40 American lynx
42 Electron tubes
44 Helm or Dillon
46 Dark
47 Part of RSVP
49 South African tennis star Fairbank
50 Bacon bringer
51 Bridal path
52 "____ Like Us"
53 Belief
61 Threesome
62 Actress Busch
64 ____ Cliburn
66 Kind of participle
67 Experience
68 Singer Zadora
69 Work space
70 Fur-trimmed cloak
71 Expressed derision
73 Weds on the run
74 Clarify
76 Billy ____ Williams
78 Lumberjack's boots
79 English rock-jazz singer
81 Groton Revolutionary agitator
82 Chemical compound
83 Ninnies
85 Soccer name of fame
87 Very attractive
89 Not many
90 James Russell Lowell's "Commemoration ____"
91 Beatty or Sparks

115

D-day Secrets   by Elizabeth T. Holcomb

Researching early 1944.

Across

1 —— Beach
6 Ans. evoker
10 Irritate
15 Polytheist
16 Useful, in Ouistreham
18 Virile redundancy
19 Peculiarity
20 Ancient city of Asia Minor
21 Soon to take office, in combinations
22 Establish securely
24 Place to find a legend
26 Masher's expression
27 Dee flat's neighbor?
28 South Korean GI
29 Harbor towed to Normandy
31 Full of juicy details
34 "Sylvan historian," to Keats
35 Allied equipment producing false radar readings
38 Platitude
41 "—— Ben Adhem," Leigh Hunt poem
42 NYC airport letters
43 Date for D-day readiness
45 —— de guerre
46 God of oath fame
48 Stubborn animal
49 RR mail place
50 Official code name for D-day invasion
52 Millennia
53 Seagull hangout
54 Confidant
55 Deception about D-day site
58 Churchill's few, in brief
59 Alongside
60 Popularized code name for D-day invasion

64 Detailed account: Abbr.
65 Determine the sum
68 Wine valley
69 Hit the pedal
70 Large beetle
72 Encomium
74 Watch rim
76 Vacant
77 Beckett's awaited one
78 Bakery by-product
79 Potassium nitrate
80 Kind of theatre
81 Computer sound
82 Curate's land

Down

1 Kind of nerve
2 River of WWI fame
3 Tiny type
4 Rock musical
5 Avenger of unrequited love

6 Phantom invaders of Calais
7 D-day beach
8 Ice, to Rommel
9 Ready for urban renewal
10 Guevara
11 Greek
12 Moslem commander
13 Stunning defeat
14 Dictionary unit
17 Biblical twin
23 Raid the fridge
25 More than one
30 South Dakota county
31 Bearded antelope
32 "Picnic" playwright
33 Kind of bean
35 School reformer
36 Melancholy woodwinds
37 Bubbling vigor
38 D-day map exercise
39 Turkey's neighbor
40 Downcast one

44 North, in Bayeux
46 Legal
47 —— the books
48 Othello, for one
51 Béarnaise sauce herb
52 Decline
53 Impose
56 Palm-leaf mat
57 Gypsy Rose Lee's "The —— Murders"
59 Versatile modifier
60 Europe's second-largest lake
61 Knight's asset
62 Lyric poem
63 Singer McEntire
65 Lessen
66 Swan star
67 Farm implement name of fame
70 Delicately embellished
71 Deep blue
73 Between zeta and theta
75 Actress Caldwell

Mantel Thoughts   *by Joy L. Wouk*

Warming trend predicted.

Across

1 Prattle
5 Artillery need
9 Hairdo
13 Network
16 Opera's Ponselle
17 Do an usher's job
18 Farmer's machine
19 Corrida cheers
21 Bret Harte's "The ____"
25 Boundary marker
26 Tint
27 Bridge positions
28 Gp. for Mehta
31 Entice
32 Cpl.'s boss
33 James Baldwin work
38 Simple Simon's yen
41 Place for a shoe
42 "I love," to Cato
43 Puts in order
45 USNA grad.
46 Near to
48 Some parkways
50 Caudal appendage
52 Chambered, as a shell
54 Held and Moffo
56 Santa's entry
57 Avoid meeting
61 Like a paddlefish
63 Blood fluids
64 Supplant
67 Wide: Comb. form
70 Belfry denizen
71 Melting-pot land
72 Recent: Comb. form
73 Insect stage
74 Some records: Abbr.
75 Jack London work
81 Out of use: Abbr.
82 Of an age
83 Kind of chop
84 Atoll material
87 ____ up; evaluated
89 *Ad ____ per aspera*
93 Song from "Roberta"
98 Social no-no: Var.
99 Heap
100 Lairs
101 Cathedral part
102 Sleep-researcher's letters
103 Wallet stuffers
104 Some are fine
105 Allows

Down

1 Some relatives: Abbr.
2 Boor
3 Nora Charles's dog
4 Retreat somewhat
5 Onager
6 Encountered
7 Neither fem. nor neut.
8 Actor Peter
9 Bring to the material world, as at a séance
10 Small blossom
11 Seoul's country: Abbr.
12 Be indebted
13 "Hawaii Five-O" arch-criminal
14 "Wheel of Fortune" guesses?
15 Defeated
20 Ave. crossers
22 Gas: Comb. form
23 Continual change
24 Put into proper adjustment again
29 Bird's crop
30 Half: Pref.
32 Small salmonlike fish
33 Greek letter
34 Cheng-chou's province
35 Red dye
36 Tallied
37 Tooth filling
38 Pod veggie
39 Neither Dem. nor Rep.
40 Road curve
44 ____ *los días*; every day, in Cuba
47 Ethiopia's ____ Selassie
48 Taut
49 Scandinavian strait
51 Intense beam
53 Mrs., in Metz
55 Write carelessly
56 Lucid
58 Fix a computer program
59 Diagram with bars, curves, or broken lines
60 ____ home; dine in
62 Fungus sac
64 Mineo of films
65 Ref's assoc.
66 Foot: Zool.
68 Actual
69 Cellist Ma
73 Wallet leather
76 Shelter
77 Flags
78 Hitlerite
79 Actress Jackson
80 Prevaricator
81 Caulking material
84 Iowa hrs.
85 General Bradley
86 Judge's garment
88 Color changer
90 Sort
91 Remainder
92 Enzyme suffixes
94 D.C. publishing agcy.
95 Richard Strauss's "____ *Heldenleben*"
96 Can. province
97 "____ Enterprise," "Star Trek" vessel

117

Binary Stars   *by Manny Miller*

Ones and zeros are the heroes.

Across

1 Former
6 Bowler's target
11 Rascals
17 Divans
18 Skulls
20 Rest
21 Catcalls of a sort
22 Rodgers-Hart '30s hit
24 Gumbo component
25 Teen's woe
26 Overdramatize
27 Hebrew letter
28 Make lace
29 1000: Pref.
30 Luigi's lang.
31 In the altogether
32 Selassie
34 Devastate
35 Sitting room
37 Anne of ____
39 Inside info
40 Full of: Suff.
41 Identifier
42 Secure tightly
43 Spanning
47 Baseball's Slaughter
48 Gorge
49 Aware of
50 Lord's Prayer start
51 ____ yong; Chinese omelet
52 English-French series of conflicts
54 Berliner, e.g.
55 Disapproving cluck
56 Painter's needs
57 Pertaining to birth
58 Nimbus
59 Attached directly to the stem, as a leaf
61 Fall flower
62 One on the run
63 "Ulalume" writer
64 Go away!
65 Heavenly bodies
66 New York lake
69 Reel
70 ____ Alegre, Brazil
71 Buddhist priest
72 Take ____ from me...
73 Between walk and run
74 Zero
77 Egyptian cobra
78 Solution strength
80 Overlay top surface
81 Loafer
82 Whence Ali Baba, Aladdin, etc.

118

85 Lasso
86 Harness ring
87 Comtemptuous grimaces
88 Choir voices
89 Ancient Turkish city, now Urfa
90 Meander
91 Dinsmore

Down

1 Occurring only a single time
2 ____ chance; gambled
3 A record
4 ____ Hari
5 Peer or seer ending
6 Winter stalactite
7 University of Maine campus locale
8 Horse's gait
9 Chemical suffix
10 The Gay ____
11 Numerical fact
12 Procession: Suff.
13 Fict. name lead-in
14 Of the mind
15 Rogue
16 In any case
19 Hindu self
23 Impresario Hurok
25 Suffers
29 West German port
30 Getting the better position artfully
31 ____ Rabbit
33 Bird class
34 Excite
35 Relating to the mails
36 John Jacob ____
37 Chin features
38 Like a lamb
39 Sleds and sledges
42 Gunwale pin
43 Sadat
44 Western headwear
45 Used epees
46 Miscues
48 In rings
49 Bone, in combinations
52 21, in binary notation
53 Play stoolie
58 New Orleans trumpeter
60 Humane gp.
61 Medicine chest items
62 Comedic Sahl
65 New Zealand "crop"
66 River to the Missouri
67 Fastened with rope
68 Electrical unit
69 British guns
70 Affectedly proper
72 Unified
73 Tropical freshwater fish
75 12:50
76 Real estate instrument
78 Stocking parts
79 Particle
80 1988 Oscar actress
81 Window support
83 Uncle Sam's collection agcy.
84 Receive
85 "Norma ____"

Am. Lit. 112   by Joy L. Wouk

This salute to American authors has only 112 words, well below the typical total.

119

Across

1 Gangs
6 Alexander ___ Bell
12 Cast off
18 Curb
19 Site
20 Captivate
21 Spry
22 Sicilian code of silence
23 Regard highly
24 *Ici on ___ français*
25 American financial editor
26 Fear
27 To be, e.g.
29 Narrow strip of land
31 Room in Rosa's house
34 ___ nous
36 Candy wrapping
40 Walks noisily
42 Under a fiduciary's control
45 A Gardner
46 Wading bird
47 Word in title of work by 9 Down
48 Another word, same title
49 Not acquired
51 Son of Seth
53 "The Sun Also ___"
54 Silent actress Lee
55 Implore
56 Saroyan hero
58 In the least
61 Soft mineral
63 Indicated
67 Metallic fabrics
68 Rare baseball game
71 Desert illusion
72 Any minute now
73 Shakespearean hero
75 O'Neill's "The ___ Cometh"
76 Azure
78 Offshore ridges
80 Coin of little value
81 Columnist James and family
84 Italian sauce
86 Appointed meeting
88 Sell to consumers
90 French sculptor Auguste
94 Vitiate
95 Handsome young man
96 "Norma" or "Martha"
97 One who sets things straight
98 Seat of Comanche County, Oklahoma
99 Office notes
100 Deportments, of old
101 Having mixed snow and rain
102 Impression

Down

1 Applaud
2 Latvian port
3 Eastern bigwig
4 He wrote "To a Waterfowl"
5 Dutch genre painter
6 Blood protein
7 Fanciful
8 Maple genus
9 Antislavery novelist
10 Chorus members
11 Intended
12 Let in again
13 "Student body right," in football
14 Natty Bumppo's creator
15 Blood condition: Suff.
16 String
17 *Due, ___, quattro*
28 Of a joyful celebration
30 Alts.
31 Scrutinize
32 Menlo Park name
33 Spoils
35 Gene letters
37 Killer whales
38 "*Winnie ___ Pu*"
39 Wine sediment
41 Pauline's adventures
43 Circus feature
44 Numero ___
48 Celestial
50 Lang. subj.
52 Unhappy
55 Splash of color
57 Negligent
58 Word of woe
59 Gas container
60 Taiwan Strait island
62 Very old: Abbr.
64 Domesticated
65 "The French Connection" role model
66 Impression
69 Brooklyn or Bronx ending
70 Work by 14 Down
73 Collects
74 Of age: Abbr.
77 Tenant
79 Arson, for instance
82 Some exams
83 Himalayan country
85 Step heavily: Var.
86 Distant: Pref.
87 Stats for Andre Dawson
89 Der ___, Adenauer
91 Actress Moore
92 Press
93 Boss Tweed's nemesis
94 Hammarskjöld

Originally published in 1989

Obviously! by Arthur W. Palmer

Is it flummery or not? You be the judge.

120

Across

1 Certain anesthetic
6 Breed of cat
12 Tooth problem
17 Incensed
18 Feature of some apartments
20 Take the stump
21 Uninterested VIP?
23 Tortellini, for one
24 Neighbor of Scot.
25 Wide awake
26 Actress Evans
28 Ralph Rackstraw, for one
29 Chicago landmark
31 Officeholders
32 Locale of Mt. Ida
34 A ____ able
35 Capital of *Italia*
37 ____ the devil; told the truth
38 Catskills: Abbr.
39 Suave
42 Stock unit
43 Antagonists
44 Ticket data
45 Rhône tributary
46 Central axis
48 Staff of authority
49 Sebastian or John
50 Lawyer's or doctor's sign
52 "Raiders of the Lost ____"
53 Sign at a quiet condo?
55 Tennis match fraction
57 *El toro*'s nemesis
59 Arabian chiefs
60 Tennessee senator
61 Cassanova, for one
62 Declivity
63 Steppe
64 Moderate
65 Large pill
66 Fell into folds
67 Tried's partner
68 High flier
70 "It might have ____" (Whittier)
71 Injury
72 Beneath
73 Rickles or Johnson
74 Baby's word
78 Actress Arden
79 Third Reich salute
80 Light wood
82 Word of cheer
83 Kid
85 Crow's result?
89 Fall bloomer
90 Intensify
91 Winged
92 Courser
93 Los Angeles pro
94 "M*A*S*H" character

Down

1 Defamatory statement
2 Maine town
3 Freight
4 Broke fast
5 Mother of Helen
6 Greek goddess
7 Approaches
8 Fortitude
9 Bruin ice great
10 Aries
11 College environment
12 Nitwit
13 Age
14 Mill worker's cleanser?
15 Reaches
16 Aches
19 Related to mother
22 Weather, poetically
27 Took up the baton
30 Chatter
32 Wandering minstrel turned university official?
33 Like a June day, to Lowell
34 "Love ____ the Ruins"
36 Switch settings
37 ____ the rapids
39 Service inst.
40 Supply new weapons
41 Support a poet?
42 Sword
43 Locate
45 Taste
46 ____ up; support
47 One of many popes
49 Zip, for one
50 Declines
51 Strange
53 Cathedral part
54 Love, in Lyons
56 Cultivate
58 Pole carving
60 Endocrine, for one
62 Carrying a grudge
63 Grand ____, "Evangeline" setting
64 Most intrepid
65 Eroded area
66 Thick
67 Eta's followers
68 Take to court
69 In reserve
70 More venturesome
73 "Shall We ____?"
75 Winning
76 Statements
77 More fitting
79 Group
80 Thrill
81 At some distance
84 Notice
86 "The Man ____ Came to Dinner"
87 Certain sack
88 Neighbor of Ala.

Originally published in 1989

Do Something! *by Peter Swift*

Don't just talk about it!

121

Across

1 "Not with ___ but a whimper" (Eliot)
6 Envelop
10 Actress Britt
13 Ruthian blast
14 Michelangelo creation
15 ___ Khan
16 Overwhelmed with work
18 Diarist Anaïs ___
19 Become bloated
20 Get ___; manage
22 Islet
23 Titanic's undoing
26 Mr. Marner
29 Talks angrily
30 Pindar's forte
31 Quarrel
32 *Avril* follower
35 Survive a troubled time
38 Forty winks
39 French painter
40 Over the ___; halfway to a goal
41 Agamemnon's father
42 Deuce takers
43 Fallacious argument
45 Monk
46 Outpouring
47 Narcissists
51 Stovepipe
52 Under any circumstances
56 Domino pip
57 So much, in music
58 Principle
59 Debussy's "La ___"
60 Dumbarton ___ (Georgetown mansion of 1944 meetings)
61 Lauder of lipsticks

Down

1 Sighs
2 Close tie
3 Mine, to Jacques
4 Television staple
5 Garbo and namesakes
6 Reeds and double reeds
7 River through Louisiana
8 Broke bread
9 Allegories
10 Landed estate
11 Maturation
12 Yin and ___
14 Word play
17 "L.A. Law" player Susan
21 Band leader Brown
24 ___ in on; takes advantage of
25 Writer Gardner and others
26 Planted
27 Concept
28 Entrechat, for one
29 Certain noncoms
31 Painter Rousseau
32 Grimace
33 ___ ants
34 Urchins
36 Up to now
37 Flogs
41 Quick to learn
42 Sibelius's "*Valse ___*"
43 Orbiter's locale
44 Tom Mix movie, for instance
45 Favoring
46 Pretense
48 Glop
49 Hair dye
50 Old dagger
53 Motorists' org.
54 Sepia
55 Hot time on the Left Bank

The Old College Try   *by Bert Rosenfield*

The theme is in the definitions, but that doesn't lessen the fun.

Across

1 PRATT
6 Nominally
11 Figures of speech
18 Tilting
19 Of a ____; consistent
20 Embattled 1979 cinema couple
21 Permeate
22 GEORGIA
24 ____ Strait, Arctic channel
25 Slanted back
27 Junket ingredient
28 *Logeuse*'s collection
30 Hall of Fame pitcher Rixey
33 Violinist Mischa
36 Port ____, Trappist cheese
37 TEXAS
40 Chic's partner on Broadway
41 South American turtle
43 Woody Allen's "____ Days"
44 On the summit
45 Yemeni capital
46 GI refill item
48 1954 Wilder film comedy
50 RICE
55 "Shazam!" Captain
56 Outer, in anatomy
57 Rodgers-Hart hit waltz
59 Medicinal plant
63 BROWN
69 Quits
71 Film critic Pauline
72 ____ Islands, former name for Pacific group
73 Tree trunk
74 Groucho's tattooed lady of song
77 Avow anew
80 Bulldog booster
81 Rapunzel's pride
83 Actor Martin
84 Camporee abodes
87 8-pt. type size
88 Follows the cookbook
89 Taxonomic categories
92 Its big star is Betelgeuse
94 Taxi
97 PACE
101 ____ at the office
103 Worshipful
104 Goddess of peace
105 Neck regions
106 Atomistic
107 Fraught
108 Activists

Down

1 Base umpire's ruling
2 Miss Rubens of the silents
3 Granted manumission
4 Baton Rouge campus letters
5 Breastbone
6 Pig in ____
7 Little guy: Var.
8 River of the Carolinas
9 Lendl pointmaker
10 Garden whistler
11 ____-Ball, boardwalk game
12 Mashie, for one
13 WW1 river of contention
14 Spur
15 WAGNER theme
16 North or south ender
17 Sarasota, from Clearwater
23 Charlatan
26 '30s pitcher Russ Van ____
29 1500-pound antelope
31 Word of mouth
32 Ben Crenshaw's org.
34 Song in "A Night at the Opera"
35 Kathmandu's country
36 Actress Thompson
37 Upholstery fabric
38 Ice, in Berlin
39 Itinerant
41 Phiz
42 Sour
44 Bus station info.
47 Berle, to pals
49 Snide comment
51 Affirmative votes
52 Cabalistic
53 Soprano Frances from New Zealand
54 Intermission meeting-places
58 Meadow mouse
59 Conditional wager
60 First fiction Pulitzer winner
61 DUKE
62 B-F fill-in
64 Edict
65 Loom bar
66 Arboreal vista
67 Vacillating
68 And still
70 Fire: Comb. form
75 Blackball
76 Mideast rep.
78 Anent
79 Kind of example
82 Conjured up
85 One-third of dodeca
86 Three-time Masters champ
88 Manatee
90 Met soprano Berger
91 Levantine weight unit
93 M. Coty
95 State with confidence
96 Miss Myerson
97 First name for 86 Down
98 Tokyo, previously
99 Wire measure
100 Ex-coach Parseghian
102 D.C. watchdog gp.

122

Legend *by A.J. Santora*

She once claimed she only said, "I want to be *let* alone."

Across

1 Cesar's family
8 Stiller and ___
13 Penniless
18 Nepal cloudbuster
19 Poe name
20 Riprap
21 Flamboyance
22 Having regrets
23 On ___; streaking
24 **Start of quote by James Wong Howe**
27 KO org.
30 Oven
31 Punishment
32 Ax handles
34 Kind of relief
37 Does exterminating
38 ___ minute; soon
41 **Part 2 of quote**
44 Rink
45 Stravinsky
46 Nebraska county
47 **Part 3 of quote**
50 Scholars
52 Greek cross
53 Cordage fiber
54 Discounted
57 Recoiled
60 Bodanzky of the Met
63 Sort
65 Contestant
69 **Part 4 of quote**
74 Switch tag-on
75 Give the heave-ho
76 Cry of delight
77 **Subject of the quote**
79 Nolan Ryan, once
80 Engrossed
81 Girl sib
82 Bikini is one
83 Helps do wrong
85 Mealy
88 Baseball's Gardner
89 **End of quote**
96 Tête-___
97 Kin of Ionic
98 Put in solitary
102 A quart has two
103 Skip syllables
104 Banded
105 Eight grouping
106 Had surf 'n' turf
107 Speeds up

Down

1 Agent: Abbr.
2 Eggs
3 Not quite half of us
4 Times of note
5 Picked over?
6 Dressy Tessie
7 Frets
8 Space stop?
9 Hebrew month
10 Et ___
11 Placement; position
12 American fortified wine
13 "Academic Festival" overture composer
14 Pave again
15 Error of omission
16 South Seas parrots
17 Raison d'___
25 Facing Clemens, maybe
26 Poet W.H. ___
27 Yahoo!
28 African tribe
29 Gently flowing river
33 Benefit of ___
35 Bonn cry
36 Variety bit
37 Do a makeshift repair
39 French Christmas
40 British anthem writer
42 Explosives
43 Sub ___
45 ___ seeing you again!
48 Pensacola, e.g.
49 Force
51 About
55 Mild
56 "Xanadu" mus. gp.
58 Torn
59 Time ___ half
60 Big banger
61 Madlyn of "Executive Suite"
62 Will
64 Spigoted casks
66 Pointer
67 Worthy
68 Kit contents
70 Reluctant
71 Unsymmetrical
72 ___ Lanka
73 Moralizer
78 Janet and Mitzi
80 Another audition
84 Actress Davis
86 Mischievous
87 Seed covering
89 Soap, in combos
90 Of the ear
91 ___ me tangere
92 Smile some
93 Secrete
94 Served a winner
95 Skirt feature
99 Gorilla
100 Finger count
101 Ames and Asner

123

Still A Legend *by A.J. Santora*

She's worth two entries.

124

Across

1 High roller
8 Irritates
13 Good-bye, Yanqui
18 Greed
19 Gangbuster Ness
20 Mario of song
21 *Semper* ____
22 Small crown
23 Cast steel
24 **Start of a Ken Tynan quote**
27 Make ____ in one
30 African laugher
31 Lacking
32 Shannon and Webb
33 Win easily
34 "...is still ____..."
36 Wild West?
37 Today I ____ man
38 Hem in
40 Very, in Versailles
44 Slangy pistol
46 Toward the abdomen
48 Off. phone
49 Caress
51 Utah lilies
52 Mohawk craft
54 **Middle of quote**
58 Passport picture
59 Grab
60 North
61 Liberian native
62 Cher and Streep
65 Zhivago's love
66 Mrs. Stengel
68 Pastries
69 High trump
70 Marker
71 Bihar capital
73 NFL players
74 Speck
75 On land

78 "Mack The Knife" singer
80 ____ over; studies
81 **End of quote**
85 Math books
86 Utopian
87 Missile
91 Apply chrism
92 Lowing singers
93 Queued up
94 Predicts
95 Car of the '20s
96 Island east of Borneo

Down

1 Space
2 One of Mickey's exes
3 Deface
4 Fights
5 Nimble
6 SA land
7 Infirmary of a sort
8 Wise up
9 E.T. was one
10 Sturdy vine
11 Noyes's poem, "The ____ of Misrule"
12 Earn the ink
13 Trues the wheels: Var.
14 Most moist and chilly
15 ____ We Trust
16 Fresh air
17 Over-satisfied
25 "Falcon Crest" star
26 Oneness
27 For the record
28 Encouraged
29 Turps ingredient
33 Craven bird
34 Do ____ burn
35 Hall-of-Fame racehorse, inducted 1967
38 Wins easily
39 Tidal flows
41 Make-over expert
42 Clear
43 Areas on ships
45 Sniff
47 Popular wear

50 Tool set
52 Single cartoon frame
53 Indigo
55 Italic tongue
56 Opah's tank pal
57 NBAer Malone
62 When the scholar arrives?
63 Wraps, in 71 Across
64 ____ indicators
67 Missionary
72 Comes up
73 Verbose
74 Team spirit
75 Make ____ at; try
76 ____ evil
77 Snake-bit
78 Frock
79 Humble
80 Lotus part
82 Mock
83 Huxtable and Rehan
84 Anathema
88 Drop a fishline
89 Washington bill
90 Home tel.

Originally published in 1989

Boxquote   *by William A. Smith*

In this puzzle a quotation starts at 28 Across and runs clockwise around a rectangular track in the grid.

Across

1 More learned
6 L.A.'s state
11 ____ rasa
17 Dancing Castle
18 "That's ____" (Martin hit)
19 Lined with durable, fragrant wood
20 Small
21 Swift
22 Italian herb
23 Automated bkg.
24 Heads, in France
25 Grand ____ Opry
26 Cut
27 Sweet girl of song
28 **Part 1 of Boxquote attributed to Henry Ward Beecher**
31 Can. province
32 Dirty old man
34 Sludge
36 "____ of God"
38 Mona ____
39 Celerity
43 Islam branch
46 Takes a chance
48 Off one's rocker
50 Knobby items
51 Possessed
52 "Three cheers for the ____ and blue!"
53 Pretty ____ picture
54 Ms. Burstyn
57 Backs
58 1, 2, 3, etc.
59 Study aid
61 Large, extinct bird
62 British carbines
64 Soon, old-style
65 Gee, ____, eye
67 ____ nova
68 Typeface enhancement
69 Low line
71 More healthy
73 Salesman's quest
75 Hire a lawyer
78 Take revenge on
81 **Boxquote, part 3**
85 Name, to Pierre
87 Lower-priced spread
89 Fleur-de-____
90 He hit 61 in '61
91 Countertenor
92 Nebraska's capital
94 Mash thoroughly
95 Exhaust
96 Highwayman
97 Chemical compound
98 Between then and now
99 Subway car features
100 Works in the garden
101 West Point student

Down

1 Dries
2 Angry
3 Small sofa
4 Doorways: Abbr.
5 Orchestra leader Alvino
6 Charged along
7 Strad's cousin
8 Wolf, at times
9 From Dublin
10 Served
11 Brewer from Toledo
12 Summer cooler
13 Works at the supermarket
14 Heavenly prefix
15 Revolutionary leader
16 Assume
19 Liquid from the right tap
24 In the past
25 Singles
28 **End of the boxquote**
29 Egyptian goddess
30 **Boxquote, part 2**
33 Flogging implement
35 Per
37 Sahara region
38 Digital watch type: Abbr.
40 Polishes
41 Wyoming river and range
42 Macedonian capital
43 Emulates Witt
44 Hesitant
45 More in order
47 Operated
49 McMahon and Sullivan
52 Hairdo detail
55 Waterfall (Scot.)
56 Fail to keep up
57 Period
60 Medley
61 Wrongly: Pref.
63 Part of a war film's title
65 Org.
66 Cross-country runners
70 Music, drama, dance, and more
72 Light Horse Harry and Robert E.
74 Street and Reese
76 Away from the shore
77 Spot
78 Challenges Nancy Lopez
79 Nobel author, 1948
80 General sense
82 Entertain
83 Author Bret
84 Cornered
86 Claude ____, French artist
88 Eight, in combinations
91 Operatic solo
93 Anti: Abbr.
94 Church bench
95 Mil. decoration

125

Originally published in 1989

Patently Punny *by Jeanne Wilson*

A collection of forehead-slappers.

Across

1 E. Power Biggs's forte
6 Sitarist Shankar
10 Hip joint?
13 Eng. part
17 Seine tributary
18 Bakery specialist
19 Parseghian
20 "___ no evil..."
21 Related to mother
22 Greek letter
23 Ladies' wear grouping
25 Desire the ornate at any cost?
28 Actor Stu and kin
29 Dissenting relative?
30 Vestment
31 ___ dixit
33 This is only ___
34 From Scandinavia
37 Stiff collar staple
39 Give a nod
42 Ulster, for one
44 Adriatic gulf
48 Scram!
49 "___ and Sympathy"
51 Stocking run start
53 Amelioration
54 Wendell Willkie work
57 Soho streetcar
59 Cutter's cousin
60 Spring mo.
61 Magellan as second banana?
64 Akkadian god
65 Allen of old Vermont
67 Dynamics preceder
68 Now living
71 Rotating cutter
73 ___ homo
75 Chinese chess
76 Broadcasting initials
77 Rita Hayworth, née ___
79 Attention getter
81 Responded to a villain
83 Fixed a hem
85 Big man in mimicry
87 Sheriff's squad
90 Condition of sale
92 Haggard novel
93 Earring support
97 "___ now to my setting" ("King Henry VII")
99 Watchcrows?
102 Georgia town
104 Lively, in mus.
105 Lace again
106 Jason's ship
107 Poisonous snake
108 Trevi fountain find
109 Goddess of peace
110 "Mine eyes have ___..."
111 Shelter
112 Sorbonne summers
113 Grant portrayer

Down

1 The end
2 Babbled; prattled; chattered...
3 Pol's payola
4 ___ de Saint-Exupéry
5 ___-do-well
6 Risqué
7 Biting
8 Presidential turndown
9 Mesopotamian
10 Most wan
11 Jackie's second
12 Hamlet, for one
13 Copy sociable Soho termites?
14 Peregrine's penthouse
15 Claude of "Casablanca"
16 French seaport
24 Fields and Allen
26 Exchanges
27 Young whippersnapper
32 Ingest
35 Aware of
36 Bill of TV
38 Sch. basics
39 Past
40 Famous Frank
41 Douglas or Foster
43 City visited by St. Paul
45 Oklahomans
46 Beat badly
47 Napoleon, e.g.
50 Calgary's prov.
52 Spunky
55 Gift-preparation bee?
56 Tedious, to a Scot
58 Long skirt
62 Place of peace and quiet
63 First-___; premiere patron
65 Common abbr.
66 Simplicity
69 Sully
70 Little fellow
72 Compass dir.
74 Conger
78 "Three Men ___ Horse"
80 Fail to discharge
82 Clouseau
84 Get away
86 Aquinas
87 Arizona Indians
88 Busy airport
89 Non-com nickname
91 Low spot of land
94 Of a certain grain
95 Where pickles swim
96 Arabian prince: Var.
98 65 Down's cousin
100 Tizzy
101 Sills's solo
103 Mao ___-tung

126

Wishy-Washy *by Bert Rosenfield*

A bold composition. Would you believe confident? Would you settle for a weasel-worded hodgepodge?

127

Across

1 Thymus, for instance
6 Bundle of arrows
11 Waikiki wear
14 Honorific for Falstaff
17 TV component
18 Diamondbacks, for example
20 Rochester, from Buffalo
21 Tentative Youmans musical
23 Part of RCMP
24 Hobbies: Abbr.
25 ____ a time
26 Esoteric
28 South Bend campus monogram
29 Journey, to Juvenal
30 Curve or wave type
31 Rounded hairdo
32 Ran the ____; dazzled, more or less
36 "The ____," Redford-Newman enterprise
37 Summer sign
38 "When I Was ____" ("HMS Pinafore")
39 *Tres* ____
40 No. 1 at sea
43 TV tube image area
46 Realtor's sign
49 Stress, perhaps
50 To the ____; nearly all the way
52 Yacht race segment
53 "Peter Pan" nursemaid
54 William Webster's org.
55 Gas: Pref.
56 Stem for hops
57 Aussie big bird
58 At the ____; just in time, or thereabouts
62 Israeli burp guns
63 Cracker
65 Tragus
67 Budget item
68 Civil wrong
69 Ancient Irish capital
70 Razorbill
72 Missed by ____
74 Not very quick to anger
80 Hoosier or Carrier
81 Bus station info.
82 Provokes to wrath
83 Drop a pop
84 Asia Minor
86 Pocket billiards champ Jimmy
88 Tale of derring-do
89 Skedaddle!
90 Limit of endurance (pretty close, anyway)
93 Old French coin
94 ILGWU-approved
95 With a jump, in ballet
96 Malone of "Cheers"
97 Match the bet
98 ____ down; softens
99 Keyboard jockey

Down

1 At the table, in Vegas
2 Angolan capital
3 Innermost shrine
4 His ____; the boss
5 Stag's mate
6 Pitting device
7 Dyne or doxy opening
8 ____ Berger; soprano from Dresden
9 "Like ____ without a tail" ("Macbeth")
10 Rooter
11 Prayer recital
12 ____ *nous*
13 Medium's phrase
14 Make complete (approximately)
15 Trainee of a sort
16 Gridiron defensive call
19 Well-rounded sentence
22 "____ all the tea in China"
27 Clotho and colleagues
29 Follower: Suff.
30 Sometimes icy look
33 Extreme
34 Diff. calculus, for one
35 Drained the radiator
36 Bluegrass celeb
39 1899 belligerent
40 Astaire props
41 Buddhist tantric treatise
42 "Or else" word (well, almost)
44 Organic compound
45 Pronto, in the OR
46 Jacques, for one
47 Kerensky's successor
48 Disgorge
51 France, long ago
54 Coin often called red
56 Eloquent opponent of George III
58 Flag
59 Oodles
60 Mata ____
61 Mouthward
64 Landlord's sign
66 Least exciting
69 Monster: Pref.
71 Brown truck initials
72 Saws
73 Comedian Corbett ____
74 Alice's upstairs neighbor
75 Philippic
76 Obliterates
77 Stand tall, Dobbin!
78 Worker ant
79 Bureau unit
81 Idaho's Coeur d'____
85 The joke's ____
86 Lombardy province
87 Actor Mowbray
88 Obedience-class command
91 Big-boom letters
92 Atl. streaker

Dilemma   *by Sidney L. Robbins*

Except for 1 Across, every clue defines two words.   Decide which word goes in each of the identical halves of the grid.   The solution is unique!

Across

1 Debris
9 Once around/ Actor Marvin
10 Prefix for surgeon or transmitter/ Specks
11 So be it/ Traditional divorce site
12 Flame fatale?/ Not so much
13 Wild fight/ Tight
14 Tart/ Collection
15 Paris university/ Entrusts
21 Running track/ Words of comprehension
22 Snare/ Give food
23 Send payment/ Not long
24 Limb/ Pub pour
25 Dance for two/ Rubbish
26 Caustic stuff/ Stinger
28 Drains strength/ Gait
31 Played smithy/ Time periods
33 Pants/ Permitting
36 Fracas/ Kind of child
37 Otherwise/ Ferber
38 Blow/ European river
39 Miss Kett of the comics/ Fuzz
41 Aged/ Catch

128

44 Show contempt/ Recorded
46 Paste/ Kind of beer
47 Time long past/ Grafted, on a shield
48 Napoleonic locale/ Frisky
49 Three feet/ Plant starter

Down

1 Apartment/ Mgt.-union arbitration gp.
2 Metallic fabric/ Bambi, for one
3 Not shut/ Napoleonic victory site
4 Plenty, poetically/ Soft metals
5 Sophie Tucker's song/ Who cares!
6 Upon/ Goes to court
7 Early performance/ Arms warehouse
8 More than a plurality/ Tennis name of fame
15 Separate/ Sacred box
16 Govt. job-safety watchdogs/ Done with
17 Sign gas/ Avatar of Vishnu
18 Heavenly ——/ Twill weave
19 Seize/ TV's Carter

20 Rims/ Haste
27 Sailor's tale/ Ages
28 Eerie/ Clerics
29 Voice/ Solo
30 Not rich/ Nile queen
32 Sword part/ Fix over
34 Indian/ Select
35 Meshed/ Used emery board
40 Had been/ Four: Comb. form
42 Building addition/ Chop
43 Vat/ Beetle
44 Pig pad/ Oolong
45 Spanish queen/ Edgar Allan ——

Originally published in 1989

Patriotic Interlock   *by James E. Hinish, Jr.*

Recalling the challenge in Fremantle.

129

Across

1 Actress Rowlands
5 Untested
8 Canal Zone country
14 —— Clayton Powell
15 *J'aime*, to Juvenal
16 Type type
17 Get up
18 —— *avion*; by air
19 Petroleum hydrocarbon
20 Sports headliner, Feb. 4, 1987
23 Laid up
24 Lizard: Comb. form
25 Imp
28 Medici capital
31 Eight: Pref.
32 "—— *mio*"
34 Perfect
36 Realm of 20 Across
37 Object of Coronado's quest
38 Burden
39 Athlete Heiden
40 Father, in combinations
42 Cong. subgp.
43 Beyond uncouth
45 Unravel
47 —— Vecchio
48 Actress Joanne
49 20 Across, for one
56 Cactus: Var.
57 Where cows browse
58 Matty or Felipe of baseball
59 Recorded history
60 "Exodus" hero
61 Clan
62 Emulates Brian Boitano
63 A George Burns role
64 Stage direction

Down

1 Needlefish
2 Revise
3 Houston-based org.
4 20 Across, in 1987
5 Ligurian seaport
6 To ——; unanimously
7 20 Across, possibly
8 "The —— of Dorian Gray"
9 Pied-——; temporary lodging
10 What 20 Across represents
11 Run ——; do penance in gym class
12 Not yours
13 Top cards
21 Org. that kidnapped Patty Hearst
22 Deck hand
25 Cellar selection
26 Bitter
27 Word with way or well
29 Some lenses
30 Maternally related
33 In order that
35 Shangri-la's analogue
40 Lacking a fastener
41 Card game
44 Roll merrily along
46 Pay dirt
49 Workout places
50 American, in 55 Down
51 Talking bird
52 Dynamic prefix?
53 Holly
54 —— arteriosi; ventricle artery exits
55 Home of "Kookaburra III": Abbr.

72 Pickup   *by Roger H. Courtney*

No special theme, here. Just good, solid puzzling with interesting words.

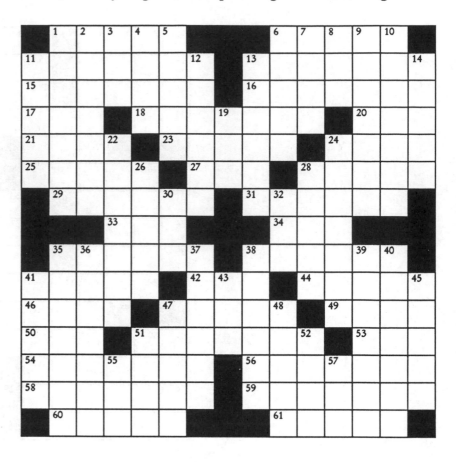

130

Across

1 Scottish chemist/physicist
6 Flinched
11 Six-sided object
13 Evened the score
15 "What's ___?" asked Juliet
16 Brahms's favorite
17 Old sailor's drink
18 Like the universe
20 Antonio or Juan
21 Prune, in a way
23 Tour of duty
24 Nice noggin?
25 French lawmaking body
27 "I do not ___ for any crown..." (Louisa May Alcott)
28 Tidal floods
29 Putrefies
31 Make a special point of
33 Albeit, shortly
34 Layer
35 Repugnant
38 Impede
41 Old-womanish
42 She sheep
44 Traffic jam
46 Take a shower
47 Reach the top
49 Zhivago's love
50 A mean Amin
51 Grim TV miniseries
53 Anatomical vessel
54 Decked out (dial.)
56 Inexperienced
58 Singer's adjunct?
59 Like many sages
60 Film swashbuckler Flynn
61 Fern stem

Down

1 Stripped of forestland
2 Survey
3 Languid
4 Hey, daddy-o, the party's been ___
5 Wins by a landslide
6 Crouched position
7 Popcorn nuisance
8 Adjectival ending
9 Chalkboard sweepers
10 Candidates' discussions
11 Charters
12 ___ a pin
13 Moves sinuously
14 Units of force
19 "___ the season..."
22 Perceptible by touch
24 Hammer obliquely
26 Ski resort
28 George of the Royals
30 "Are ___ Lonesome Tonight?"
32 Much-used article
35 Because challenged
36 Dowsing rod expert
37 Part company
38 Ponder the past
39 Serve again
40 Jimmy, "the Nose"
41 Give ___; exhilarate
43 Trojan or 1812
45 Wallop
47 "...the ___ of the Crowd"
48 Those who make do
51 Actor Ray
52 In ___; racked by rote
55 Needlefish
57 HST's successor

Originally published in 1989

Cooperstown Caper? *by Sidney L. Robbins*

Mr. Robbins keeps rolling them out.

Across

1 Musical symbols
6 —— to riches
10 Business expansion
14 Tidal rush
15 Beige
16 Taj Mahal site
17 Look anywhere for resources
20 Appear
21 A Barrymore
22 Smallest
23 Kind of friend
25 Construction site tray
26 Kind of grin
27 Bawl
29 Baden-Baden, for one
32 Portico
34 Autumn
35 Digital adjunct
36 Popular dance tune
39 Enjoy the glow
40 Household critters
41 Entry fee, of a sort
42 Troop lander
43 Charges
44 Familial one, familiarly
45 Novelty
46 Style; layout
49 Crosswords' favorite flower?
52 Actor Muni
54 Nebraska's governor Kay, and family
56 Fun's benchmark?
59 Münchhausen
60 Body of knowledge
61 Feel
62 Abounding in certain shade trees
63 Sibs of 44 Across
64 Coll. clubs

Down

1 Luck, in Dublin
2 Spikes
3 Plumed bird
4 Outline
5 Aug. follower
6 Attempt again
7 Dull pain
8 Did thrive
9 "Das Boot" feature, in brief
10 Peeled
11 Monster
12 Mineral rocks
13 Beer ingredient
18 Whirlpool
19 Mil. fugitive
24 Sinai citizen
25 Big heap
27 Unattractive aspects
28 Flagon fillers
29 Taboo for some dieters
30 Food fish
31 —— mode
32 Oceans
33 Essay
34 Priceless?
35 Front-of-the-plane passenger
36 Cask: Abbr.
37 Copied
38 Two of a kind
43 Passage
44 Unaccompanied
45 Harbor vessel
46 Is furious
47 Stadium
48 Appointment of a sort
49 Ready, willing, and ——
50 Go to sea
51 Trolley
52 Like a churchmouse
53 Hairdo
55 Pilot's headings: Abbr.
57 Att.'s first deg.
58 Research grant agcy.

131

Manhunt by Lois Sidway

He's hiding among several of these entries.

Across

132

1 Beam maker
6 Entertainment choice
11 Pole
14 Maine campus town
15 Not hidden
16 Crude metal
17 You can spot him in this stage show
19 Tart apple, familiarly
20 Caught sight of
21 Exam
22 Supped
23 Game of assembling a plastic critter
25 Presently
26 Mayberry boy
29 Nail biter
32 Put on
33 Discomfort
35 Special tec
36 Forfeiture
38 Gymnast Retton
41 "Coffee, Tea, ____?"
42 Ship's officer, commonly
43 A little bit of work
44 Dumas hero
47 D–I link

48 "Desire Under the ____"
49 Signs up for
52 "I ____ Camera"
53 Tater
55 Held up
59 Director Howard
60 He's keeping a cartoon couple together
62 An acct. draws it
63 Established practice
64 Liqueur flavoring
65 Mag. VIPs
66 "John Brown's Body" poet
67 Casts an evil eye

Down

1 Hoop spot
2 War god

3 TV fare, for short
4 Lure
5 Logger's contest
6 Philip Wylie's target
7 People stand for it
8 Superficial appearance
9 Writer Murdoch
10 State, to de Gaulle
11 He's helping develop a literary form
12 Speechifier
13 Respectable
18 Conductor de Waart of the Minnesota Orchestra
24 Taunt
25 Wrong
26 Funny-peculiar
27 "The Bells" author
28 These stoolies couldn't do without him

30 Hereditary factors: Abbr.
31 Story
33 Big cat
34 Shake ____; hurry
37 Some are fine
38 ____ Blanc
39 Assn.
40 Groan of disgust
42 Dressing
44 Honeypot
45 Candy nut
46 "What, me worry?" name
47 Old mystic
50 Antiquity, of yore
51 Indian ruler
53 Ticket end
54 Model
56 Cereal for kids
57 Gaelic
58 Tints
61 Bottom-line amount

Movie Marathon *by Peter Swift*

Six great films in one great interlock.

133

Across

1 Hootchy-kootchy or two-step
6 Flabbergasts
10 Won the serve without contest
14 Vast amount
15 It's sometimes held in sandwich shops
16 Grand slam, in cards
17 1932 Oscar-winning film
19 Jacques' *femme* friend
20 Parlor furniture
21 More surly
23 Coy
25 Use radar
26 Supplicant
30 ___ Altos, California
32 Potter's clay
35 Pace
36 Camporee resident
38 Weed
39 1954 Oscar-winning film
42 Baseball's Mel
43 Lode modifier
44 Give off
45 He put the words in Watson's mouth
47 Orch. choice
48 Dog's bane
49 Adversaries
51 Make over
53 Prosper
56 More chichi
61 Marine creatures
62 1944 Oscar-winning film
64 Fashion magazine
65 Zola character
66 Stem
67 On one's ___; alert
68 Distort
69 Theater awards

Down

1 Trails persistently
2 Plot
3 Straight
4 Jargon
5 Make beloved
6 Latin I word
7 Paul Lukas's 1943 Oscar-winning film
8 Ogling type
9 Alone, to Augustus
10 Archetype
11 1978 film that earned Oscars for Voight and Fonda
12 Writer Wiesel
13 Natty Bumppo's prey
18 "And I Love ___"
22 Fashion accessory
24 Superbowl shoe features
26 "...And to all ___ night" (Moore)
27 ___ Domingo
28 Ginger Rogers's 1940 Oscar film
29 Ordinal ending
31 Addison's partner
33 Old land of Asia Minor
34 Some Baltic people
36 Brace
37 Go astray
40 Arabian dignitary: Var.
41 Kinsman, in brief
46 ___ up; botches
48 Magazine's general appearance
50 Omens
52 Hammarskjöld
53 Worry
54 French composer
55 Overcharge
57 Beginner
58 Heads, ___,...
59 Kind of chair
60 Deli choices
63 Slangy denial

Associations *by Manny Miller*

Signs of recognition.

Across

134

1 Entrance
5 Youth org.
8 ID for an angel
12 Really pale
13 Explorer La ___
15 Spoken
16 ID for Robert T. Ironside
18 ID for a hostess
19 Custodian
20 Letter carriers' IDs
22 Culture medium
24 ID for Capone
25 ID for Joplin
28 IDs for wool cutters
32 Build
33 Dole's Department under Bush
36 Cry from the cote
37 Flame fatale?
38 Sofa
39 Plot-free hit musical
40 ___ was saying...
41 Thin-shelled nut
42 Large bulrushes
43 "Downtown" singer Clark
45 ID for Sammy Davis, Jr.

47 Sausage meat
49 Galena and bauxite
50 IDs for painters
54 Go to bed
58 N ___ Nancy
59 IDs for Borrah Minevitch and Larry Adler
61 Critic Rex
62 Series of steps
63 Supermarket carrier
64 Soaks up some rays
65 Faster-than-sound plane: Abbr.
66 Leg joint

Down

1 Stare stupidly
2 Tennis's Arthur
3 Biblical pronoun
4 ID for Rooster

Cogburn or Moshe Dayan
5 Exclamation of comtempt
6 Steffi Graf's grand ___
7 Assumed name
8 Man, in Mexico
9 Space
10 Tolled
11 In addition
13 Beat it!
14 Explorer Leif
17 On the up and up
21 Funnyman Bert
23 Memento
25 Chart anew
26 Stood
27 Understand?
29 Have ___; live it up
30 Film-board member
31 Impudent

34 Actress Gardner
35 ID for a minstrel
38 Scarcities
39 ID for Minnesota Fats
41 Secret plan
42 In the middle, to 48 Down
44 Defeats, surprisingly enough
46 Boo-boo
48 English poet (1795–1821)
50 ___ and parcel
51 Cruising
52 Property claim
53 Mex. matrons
55 "___ See Clearly Now"
56 Unusual
57 Italian noble family name
60 Cambridge univ.

Originally published in 1989

Duchy Denizens   *by Ernie Furtado*

"'A noble theme!' the tyro cried,"—Carolyn Wells

135

Across

1 Mimicked
5 Fellow
9 "My ___" (1930 song)
14 Farm structure
15 Assistant
16 Bishop's headdress
17 DUKE of the comics
19 DUKE, the actress
20 Establishes a connection
21 Currencies
22 "___ *Misérables*"
23 West Indian nut
24 Ices
28 "The King ___"
29 "___ ramblin' wreck..."
32 "Dr. Zhivago" character
33 Essays
35 THE IRON DUKE
38 Least in need of dieting
39 Comfort
40 Induction gp.
41 Pub missile
42 Destiny
44 Descartes

45 Sy Oliver's 1941 hit, "___, Indeed!"
46 Francis ___ Sinatra
49 Italian gulf port
53 DUKE of films
54 THE DUKE of films
56 Pointless
57 Siouan
58 Honest
59 Belief
60 Cat's-paw
61 Dry

Down

1 "___, and ye shall receive..."
2 Dock
3 Magazine for parisiennes
4 Raggedy Andy, or Ken

5 Social groups
6 Pelts
7 Fusses
8 "___ O' My Heart"
9 Discourteous
10 Rigg or Ross
11 Major chaser?
12 Bohemian
13 Coins for a Romanian fountain?
18 George Bush's alma mater
21 Of a musical form
23 Genuflected
24 Backboard, to 26 Down
25 Pranks
26 Gilmore of the NBA
27 Sammy of song
28 "There's no music in ___" (John Ruskin)
29 Muslim faith

30 '80s Attorney General
31 Till now
33 "...___ well it were done quickly," says Macbeth
34 British verb endings
36 Riptide
37 Cheerful
42 Corn unit
43 "___ Mommy Kissing Santa Claus"
44 *Roi*'s mate
45 Yokel
46 Mine entrance
47 Sole
48 Cereal fiber
49 In ___; wholly
50 Temple
51 Use a keyboard
52 Unique person
54 Not a ___ or tittle
55 Compass dir.

Club Ties *by William Canine*

Batter up!

Across

1 To-do
5 TV alien
8 Gradient
12 Cradle
15 Geometrical points
16 Tormé or Tillis
17 Concept
18 Hail, to Caesar
19 Concluded
20 Bar or late leader
21 Vatican official
23 —— of Lebanon
25 Don't raise the bridge—— the water!
27 Sonata part
28 Shipworm
30 Taste and smell
31 Noisy yard bird
34 Junk
37 Becomes void
38 Claim
39 Runner
42 CPA
43 Yellow vehicle
45 Trawl
46 Red coin?
48 Spathe
50 His fastball, to Nolan Ryan
52 His batting, to Wade Boggs
53 Adam's third son
54 Noun ending
55 Workout joint
57 Sister
58 Garland
59 "...first —— I see tonight..."
60 Zealous
62 Amazon rodent
64 Hangbirds
65 Tabby's pick-me-up
68 Disburse
70 Loos or O'Day
71 Signal flare
73 Natural process
77 Seamen
79 Undergarment
81 Tied up
82 Hall-of-Famer Traynor
83 Hickory, for one
84 Cereal spike
85 Incarnation of Vishnu
86 Venerable
87 Broadcast
88 K.C. clock setting
89 Persuade

Down

1 Make fancy wallpaper
2 "I —— a Parade"
3 —— a test; scored 100
4 Corsairs
5 "What Kind of Fool ——?"
6 Singer —— Gore
7 Baseball's Curt ——
8 Fenway's Jim
9 Jewish month
10 Debussy's sea
11 Chaplains
12 Notice of a sort
13 Sidestep
14 Apollo's birthplace
22 "Rhinoceros" playwright
24 Forswear
26 Big news in October
29 Tabula ——
30 Warbled
31 Tattles
32 Bay tree
33 Announce the latest scores
35 Cork's locale
36 Triple plays and perfect games
40 Grain
41 Playable for Serkin
44 African language family
47 Pavilions
49 Dry wine
51 Sing like Bobby McFerrin
52 Meal
54 Fable writer: Var.
56 Whittle
61 Handbills
63 Fafner and Fasalt
64 "Falstaff" and "Macbeth"
65 South American plain
66 "For want of ——..."
67 Bushed
69 Three-masted ship
71 —— agent; unsigned ballplayer
72 Secondhand
74 Lendl of tennis fame
75 Verne character
76 Chew at
78 Rather than, in poesy
80 Linkletter

136

Bemused *by Walter Covell*

They're all here.

137

Across

1 Tire type
6 With it
9 Monastic VIP
14 Charge with gas
15 Put out of commission
16 MUSE
17 Lucifer, for one
19 Shiny fabric
20 Memorable Belgian singer
21 Word of denial
22 Neighbor of Leb.
24 Luck
25 "___ old cowhand..."
27 Iroquoian language
29 Seer's card
32 All over
36 Untidy piles
37 Kind of sch.
38 Slightly ahead
40 Fergie's sister-in-law
41 "Star Trek" speed factor
43 ___-pros
45 Actor Erwin
46 Neptune, of Irish myth
47 Treat with phenol
49 Geog. region
50 Sundial numeral
51 Exiled Amin
52 Castle defense
53 Ceramics
54 Decorate
56 Now's partner
58 Hoys
59 Salisbury Plain structure

62 Intelligence tester
63 *La Marseillaise* marchers
64 Österreich's capital
66 Supply an overhead "wall"
69 Set
70 "Planes, Trains, and Automobiles" character
71 African land
75 Caesar's tongue
77 MUSE
80 Daughter of Themis
81 Flag
82 MUSE
83 Kind of orange
84 J. Davis's country
85 Highway stopover

Down

1 Bring up
2 A Gardner
3 MUSE

4 Consumed
5 Keystone state: Abbr.
6 Crone
7 Offensive view
8 MUSE
9 Loser to DDE
10 Fern
11 Ebb
12 Elevator man
13 Great amounts
14 Place for a B-1
15 Rd. Table personage
18 Top-drawer
23 Uncooked
26 Ararat, St. Helens, etc.
27 MUSE
28 Entire
29 MUSE
30 Vergil translations
31 Grew luxuriantly
33 Part of speech
34 Color again
35 MUSE
39 Least adulterated

41 Large amount
42 School subject
44 Jeweler's wt.
47 "Julius Caesar" plotter
48 Yearn
53 Small brown and buff European songbird
55 Undulating
57 Ward politicos
58 Mariner's dir.
60 Work unit
61 Some of Bo-Peep's charges
65 Pelvic bone
66 MUSE
67 Corncrib contents
68 Willow
70 Foot medic degs.
72 Sharpen
73 Seed covering
74 Juno, for one
76 Society page word
78 Inlet
79 ___-Magnon

Southern Lights *by Betty Tuck*

Though she lives in New York, Ms. Tuck turns her attention here to another part of the country.

Across

1 Persiflage expert Dick
7 Bergman role
11 Restaurant list
15 National Military Park in Tennessee
16 Armstrong's photos
19 Piranha
20 Tara, for example
21 Atlanta belle
23 Nat. police org.
25 Trotsky
26 Pose
27 Sch. org.
30 Actor Alfred
32 Songwriter Carole Bayer ——
35 Newark suburb
37 Diana's love
39 "Blue Tango" composer Anderson
41 Classic Western
42 New York lake
44 Cyclotron target
46 Pass catchers
47 Southern epiphyte
51 Both: Pref.
54 Lawn pest
55 —— word; equivocation
59 Miniskirt designer
61 Electrician, often
64 Violin craftsman
65 Total agreement
67 Old Turkish coin
69 Author Hunter
70 Be under the weather
71 Ballet step
73 Change for a fiver
75 Beer's relative
76 Ernie Ford adjective
80 "Waiting for the ——"
83 European finch
86 Jack Benny's perennial age
87 Eastern Church member
88 Unit of loudness
89 Crossworddom's favorite poems?
90 Bible book

138

Down

1 Govt. agcy. concerned with public employees
2 Gotcha!
3 Dare to name her?
4 Newsman Abel
5 River of Siberia
6 Where —— smoke...
7 Encroach
8 Girl of song
9 Castile cake
10 Lindbergh, Boleyn, and others
11 School topic
12 Finial
13 Modern, in combinations
14 Amer. seamen
17 Refinish furniture
18 "—— Flower"
22 Hockey score
23 Dud
24 Folksinger Ives
27 Scheme
28 —— to; favor
29 Affirmatives asea
31 Alarms
33 Schoolroom needs
34 "Goodbye, Columbus" author
36 One and ——
38 Chill in the air
40 —— Kippur
43 Boulder, for one
45 Loft
48 Right away!
49 Nastase
50 Red or Yellow
51 Blue-green
52 Actor Paul
53 —— out; depart harm's way
56 Southern port
57 Relative of etc.
58 Queue
60 Sail ——; go left
62 Heroic poems
63 Eclectic School painter
66 Spruce
68 Do a puzzle editor's job, perhaps
72 Office worker
74 Washington team, familiarly
76 Wax
77 Strong-scented
78 Hawaii state bird
79 What's —— for me?
80 Privileges: Abbr.
81 So that's it!
82 Coal bunker
84 One *saison*
85 Threefold: Comb. form

Originally published in 1989

Diploma Mill *by Ronnie K. Allen*

"...behold a map of my collegiate life."—Wordsworth

Across

1 Camp David conferee
6 "Falcon Crest" star
11 Blueprints
16 Wear away
17 It's ——! See you then!
18 God of Islam
19 Nouveau ——
20 Proverbial haste product
21 Mikhail's spouse
22 Destiny
23 Author Loos
24 Look-alike
25 Stendhal character
27 Verso's counterpart
29 Former Ugandan dictator Amin
30 Subscribe again
32 Squabble
35 What the winner often takes
37 Stop
39 Jimmy's predecessor
41 Country singer Patsy
43 Beatty-Keaton film
45 Patriotic horseman
47 —— trough; gutter, in northern America
48 Solidify
49 Poetic adverb
51 Israel's Abba
52 Concealed shooter
54 *Nom de* dog
56 Bowie's last stand
57 —— with; equal to
59 Wall section

61 Crow's call
62 Ice Age sight
64 Poor quality publication
66 Hosp. dosage
68 Over
70 Bay, for one
72 Copter airfoils
75 Newton of the apple
77 Designer Cassini
79 Love, Italian style
80 Politician's soapbox
81 Once —— time...
82 Undecided's position?
83 —— and goes
84 Pithy
85 "Don't —— on me"
86 Goodnight girl
87 Ford fiasco

Down

1 Peasant
2 Costa Rican leader
3 With 55 Down, Stanley's remark
4 Stick
5 Golfer's gadget
6 Wimbledon's surface
7 Oil-fire fighter Red ——
8 Learned
9 Fasten
10 Bishopric
11 Hindu dress
12 "A man, a ——, a canal..."
13 Men about town
14 Checked out, before a heist
15 Lambchop's creator
23 Sheltered
24 General Lee
26 Noun suffix
28 Harbor helper
31 Goods
33 "We —— the World"
34 "Bolero" composer
35 Graff's displays

36 A plain, in Spain
38 '80s magazine
40 Soap opera
42 Everest's locale
44 Pop
46 Rubáiyát rhymer
48 Thalia *et alia*
50 Baptismal basin
53 Ecol. bureau
55 See 3 Down
56 King, of comedy
58 —— Tin Tin
60 Skater Heiden
63 Manuscript polisher
65 On an incline
66 Skilled occupation
67 One with potential
69 *Fraus*
71 Past, present, or future
73 Killer whale
74 Papyrus
76 Basilica projection
78 Celt or Scot
80 ——-fi
81 Salt Lake athlete

139

Originally published in 1989

Spooner-fed *by Barbara Barry-Johnson*

Lips of the stung.

140

Across

1 Awkward
7 Neil Simon character
12 Stan-Ollie foul-up, always blamed on Stan
16 Connect
17 Richard's first veep
18 Division class word
19 Director's command
20 Kin becomes cover-up expert
22 —— tank
23 Glut
24 Despicable one
25 Chancy city?
27 Ruler re 47 Across
29 Ring opponents in Spain
30 Cloudburst becomes migraine
34 Remainder
35 Overcharge
36 True-life story
37 Off the market
39 Palette partner
41 Like a satellite dish
44 Method: Abbr.
47 Houston's pride
49 Stylized Japanese theater
50 England, Latin style
52 Range risers: Abbr.
53 Having knowledge
56 Strange
57 One course
58 Flee
60 Ubangi tributary
61 Hammer genre
64 Nectar eater becomes mooching mob
68 "The Subject Was ——"
70 See 73 Across
71 Arafat, for one
72 Musical group of specific number
73 With 70 Across, USSR feature
75 Lariat
79 Snooze becomes tattletale crones
82 Nonproductive
83 Plus others: Abbr.
84 Adolescent least likely
85 At an angle
86 Trust
87 Deck occupants
88 Evaluate

Down

1 Supporter: Suff.
2 "Solidarity" name
3 Mate starter
4 Lancaster role becomes top yard man
5 Furnace tender
6 Hankering
7 Bones
8 Burp like baby
9 Movie house
10 This for its own sake
11 Round starter
12 State awkwardly
13 Kit and caboodle
14 Pool people?
15 Hurting the most
21 Adherent of: Suff.
23 —— boom
26 Pen point
28 Leaner locale
30 Irreverent fête
31 Ovens
32 Loan shark's aides
33 PBS series
35 Take-in or let-out place
38 Horne of jazz
40 Corporate icon
42 —— on your life!
43 Hot stuff
44 More shrewd
45 Give in
46 Having all one's marbles
48 Ignore
51 Bait takers become stickum tabs
54 "Bloom County" critter
55 Panama zone
57 Endearingly
59 Owner's lieut.
61 Boastful type
62 Find
63 Like a 33 Down
65 Less pleasant
66 Noticeable
67 Pester
69 Porcine palace
74 Serpents
76 Skin aid
77 Goes one better
78 Overwhelms
80 Airwaves watchdog agcy.
81 IRS foiler of a sort
82 Airlines regulating gp.

Originally published in 1989

Like It Says *by Norma Steinberg*

Following directions.

141

Across

1 Rosemary or basil
5 "Classic Concentration" objective
10 Nottingham's river
15 On —— with
16 Hi in Hilo
17 —— to form
19 Hip
20 Chile export
21 Sort of
22 CAPE
25 Drill sergeant's counting word
26 Adolescent
27 Printer's purchase
28 Edith Sitwell, for one
29 Yon's opposite
32 Like summer tea
34 Succotash ingredients
35 Single
36 Lingerie items
37 Rope plant
38 Cozy home
39 Word with out and sharp
40 Lynn's sister
43 Response: Abbr.
44 TUO
46 Drone
47 Reversal
49 Comedian Martin
50 Galileo's birthplace
51 Gaelic
52 Chamberlain
53 Polonius hides behind it, only to be killed by Hamlet
54 "Quo ——?"
56 Physically attractive
57 Decorates oneself
58 Perry's creator
59 Canine warning
60 Cut

61 Part of Washington's signature
62 TASHER
67 Ms. Lansbury
69 Indian, for one
70 Mideast country
72 City renamed in 1975
73 Facade
74 Adjutant
75 Key middle name
76 Earthy, like some blues music
77 Burden

Down

1 Hem and ——
2 De Mille's kind of movie
3 Ill-considered
4 Rest
5 "Away in a ——..."
6 E.T. was one
7 Dorothy's dog

8 Paul Prudhomme, for one
9 Mythological hags
10 Halloween option
11 Descartes
12 A Gabor
13 PRIME HASH
14 Shock
18 Sorts
23 Prerequisite
24 "—— so to bed" (Pepys)
28 Coin to stop on?
29 Maui dances
30 Silly
31 COLGI
32 Work on laundry
33 AKEC
34 It follows Mardi Gras
36 1987 newsmaker
37 Schlepp
39 Publishing name
40 Electrical measure
41 Actress Sarandon
42 Gather

44 Soviet news agency
45 According to procedure
48 Runny cheese
50 Like certain hearings and motions
52 Exercise to counter a meal
53 Operatic showstopper
54 Nevada city, for short
55 Stadia
56 To and ——
57 More than enough
59 Lou or Lee
60 Lower leg
62 Absorb
63 Wedding gown color
64 Broadway light
65 Andrew sisters, for instance
66 Actress Thompson
68 Conceit
71 Formal abbr. at the end of a proof

Bridge Game   by Kenneth Haxton

"Patience, and shuffle the cards."—Miguel de Cervantes

Across

1 Widespread fright
6 Misbehave, as a candidate?
11 Footless creatures
16 Riled up
17 Tolstoy titular antithesis
18 Cuttlefish secretion
19 Observes everything
22 French pronoun
23 Perfect, for example
24 Recruit
25 Expire
27 Risk something in Reno
28 Subtraction word
29 "___ Street Blues"
30 Cranial adornment for Picasso
32 Actress who originated role of Martha in "Who's Afraid of Virginia Woolf?"

142

35 100 square meters
36 Woody's kid
40 Water (Sp.)
41 Indonesian island
43 Kind of court
46 New Zealand authority figure
49 Walks like Mae West
50 In raiment
51 One more than *zwei*
52 Come from
53 Discovery word
54 Be affected by a stimulus
55 Suiting choice
58 Professional charges
60 Home, to Jaime
64 Curling target
65 Highwayman, to Ben Jonson
69 Jelly fruit
71 Ship seepage collector
72 Gehrig
73 Stings
76 Soviet native
77 20th-century American poet Paul ___

78 Palindromic dogma
79 Asian people
80 Bowler's button
81 Like unginned cotton

Down

1 Grable was one
2 Gladiator's milieu
3 Church longitudinal areas
4 Israel or labor follower
5 Sure
6 Rob Reiner's film, "This Is ___ Tap"
7 Not exactly neat
8 Assuage
9 Top card in subject game
10 Prosecutor, after presenting case
11 Nora Charles's dog
12 Pauline's problem

13 Say what you think
14 Indulges at Monte Carlo
15 Japanese potables
20 Emulate Shakespeare's infant
21 Skill (It.)
26 Put away one's sword
27 Spelling or quilting event
30 Egg bun
31 Record
32 Toque and cloche
33 Turkish honorees: Var.
34 Household poet Edgar
35 The Eiger, for one
37 Most embarrassed
38 "The Glass Menagerie" heroine
39 Mexican civilization
41 Help the merchant
42 Forenoon hrs.
43 ___ standstill; stuck
44 Master's next deg.
45 Shish kebab necessity
47 Battering and buck
48 Neighbor of Ga.

53 "___ cannot wither her" ("Antony and Cleopatra")
54 Performs surgery
56 Miss Kett of the comics
57 Elementary-school text
58 Catfish cut
59 "The ___ of Night"
60 Mafioso types
61 Talking effusively
62 Jazzy Latin music
63 "That Old Black Magic" composer
65 All-time bestseller
66 "A Night at the Opera" song
67 Interfered
68 Inevitable nickname for someone named Rhodes
70 Followers: Suff.
71 A famous bunny
74 "A Chorus Line" showstopper
75 Arikara

Mr. Roberts *by Randolph Ross*

Bob—bob—bobbing along.

143

Across

1 License
8 London's river
14 Be the boss
15 Question at a masquerade
18 Ol' Blue Eyes
19 Carriers
20 The 15th
21 Radio transmission
23 Red or Dead
24 Funny Bobs
29 Compass pt.
30 Hall of Fame QB Bobby
31 Undisciplined; malicious
35 Prepare baby food
37 Ladies of Spain, in short
40 Pre-metamorphosis young
41 "Smooth Operator" singer
43 Spats
45 Traffic sound
46 Baseball Bobs
50 Soviet body of water
51 Not spicy
52 ___ vera
53 Start the feast
55 Pedestal part
57 Become lovable
61 Observes Yom Kippur
63 Bring out
65 Teacher's grad. deg.
66 Political Roberts
70 Charged particle
73 Like a naughty child
74 Swing around the mast
75 British officer
78 Catch in the web
81 Responds positively to a wish
82 Took turns
83 French town of race fame
84 Play producers

Down

1 Trigonometry ratios
2 Clear
3 Certain magazine subscriber
4 Refuse
5 Ending for special or dent
6 "___ shure" (Valley agreement)
7 Full of froth
8 Five books of Moses
9 Sanctify
10 "Exodus" hero
11 One restroom sign
12 Potato features
13 Tender
15 Acting Roberts
16 Cut of beef
17 Springsteen "birthplace"
22 Fleming and others
25 "America's Most Wanted" datum
26 By chance
27 Buddy
28 Permitted
32 Shoe preserver
33 Last word in a transmission
34 Siesta
36 ___ as a bat
38 Extend
39 Divan
42 Oklahoma city
44 Opt
46 Toughness
47 Shakespearean villain
48 Sen. Heflin's state
49 Wallflower
50 Dentist's org.
54 Prefix for lith or phyte
56 Vegas numbers
58 Take after
59 One who guarantees
60 Supplements the garden
62 Got to second base the hard way
64 Poe's family
67 Gives off
68 Simians
69 Hit ___; interrupt progress
70 PC maker
71 Kind of exam
72 Goddess of sneakers?
76 Ruby or diamond, for example
77 Simile words
79 "Ask ___ what your country..." (Kennedy)
80 Penn. or Union: Abbr.

Double Doings *by Jeanette K. Brill*

Presenting one way to double your pleasure.

Across

1 Some men at the Met
6 Gear
9 Hold a boat steady to windward
14 Old West watering hole
15 Andalusian affirmative
16 Exhausted
17 African fly
18 Washington city
20 Sixth sense: Abbr.
21 Killer whale
23 British nobleman
24 ___ Amin
25 Shed tears
27 Rent
29 More precipitous
31 Ermine
33 Shoshonean Indians
35 Helper: Abbr.
36 George or Thurgood
39 Metal worker
42 Aiding digestion
44 Bender
46 Tan shade
47 Mil. gp.
48 Baseball's Slaughter
50 Redact
52 Summer mo.
53 Mimic
55 Audacity
57 Prima ballerina
59 Wall Street rush
61 It's "up the river"
63 County in Missouri or Nebraska
65 Cheer for
66 Art style
70 High spirits
73 Stole
75 Even
76 Chess pieces
77 Down-under bird: Var.

144

79 Perennial plant
81 "Cakes and ___" (Maugham work)
82 West German spa
85 Gay '90s dance
87 Happening
88 Ping-___
89 Venomous snakes
90 Spawning areas
91 Fast plane, briefly
92 "Gypsy" composer

Down

1 Hound
2 City of northwest Syria
3 Toper
4 Middling
5 Not active
6 Inlet
7 Capri, for one
8 Certain "monsters"
9 Anarchistic
10 Stevedore's org.
11 With words omitted
12 Diacritical mark
13 Walking ___; delighted
14 Fumes
15 Dark-complected: Var.
19 Department of Greece
22 Steamed semolina, meat, and vegetables, North African style
26 Pack firmly
28 Trim
30 Salinger miss
32 London gallery
34 Wild plum
37 ___ in the new
38 Guiding principle
40 Factual
41 Embrace
42 "___ Doc" Duvalier
43 Impartial
45 Tree or monkey

47 A pause that refreshes
49 Mix together
51 Secret Chinese society
54 Public disturbance
56 Flake makeup
58 "___ a Kick Out of You"
60 Customers
62 Matador's risk
64 Burial chamber
67 Nicotinic acid
68 Tell
69 Barbara and Anthony
70 Smoldering coal
71 Depart
72 Some tides
74 Selects
78 Ginseng family plants
80 Skirt feature
83 Conclude
84 Tolkien creature
86 Opposing vote

City Slickers *by James Hinish, Jr.*

Assembled by a slick puzzlewright.

145

Across

1 Kathleen Windsor heroine
6 Laddies' lids
10 Underwear monogram
13 Zoo section
14 Kohoutek's discovery
15 Dutch painter Jan van der ___ Delft
16 They deal with lots of Canadians!
18 Normandy river
19 Imprint, in a way
20 Show contempt
21 Metro or Indiana ending
22 "Jacques ___ Is Alive..."
23 Repairmen in 56 Down?
26 Mosquito genus
28 Those with clout
29 Cyrano's love
30 Agate or elite
32 Angkor ___
33 "Nautilus" captain
35 Qoph's follower
36 Mideastern PR specialist?
38 GI's address
40 Florida religious leader?
43 Colony builder
44 Peruvian physiotherapist?
46 Utah senator Jake
48 Strong ___ ox
49 Work unit
50 Where *la Chine* is
51 Of amino-benzene
53 Three ___ match
55 Cold spells
59 Another Florida religious leader?
61 Norwegian king
62 Pond scum
63 ___ superiority; snob's attitude
65 London art gallery
66 Coward of the stage
67 New England chiseler?
70 Fido's warnings
71 Caravan stopover
72 His ___ worse than his bite
73 CIA's predecessor
74 The ___ the limit!
75 Oil-yielding legumes

Down

1 ___ *santé!*
2 Chopped finely
3 Somerset soccer player?
4 Fluff
5 Sandwich choices
6 Family emblems
7 Love, in Livorno
8 Debussy's "La ___"
9 Blvds.
10 German nose tackle?
11 Did he cometh by gondola?
12 Garb
13 Microorganism: Var.
14 Browning poem
15 "The ___ Sixpence"
17 Sandy's mistress
21 ___ Britannica
24 Climber's conquests
25 Skis recklessly
27 Org. meths.
31 Effect by stages
32 Boer or Crimean
34 Neighbor of Man.
35 Alitalia executives?
36 ___ Harbor, Maine
37 Author Nin
38 Heart of Dixie: Abbr.
39 Italian seamen?
41 ___ *beaucoup*
42 Nose shape
45 Orwell characters
47 Nevada official?
50 Hammerin' Hank
52 Tall tale
53 Ear inflammation
54 Wolfe and namesakes
56 "Seward's Folly"
57 Local dialect
58 Explorer Hedin, and others
59 Tropical fruit
60 Impudent
64 Cal. pages
67 Derek and Diddley
68 Strong wood
69 Beijing name

Prized Possessions *by Arthur W. Palmer*

Unusual collectibles. Must have been some garage sale.

146

Across

1 Wave precursor
6 Vaporous atmosphere
12 Ne ___ ultra
16 Benefit
17 Partial
18 "Too ___ the Phalarope"
19 Actor's crowbar
21 Saharan
22 Vane reading
23 Lake in the Panama Canal
24 Advance obliquely
25 Pop
28 ___ sanctum
29 Oil container: Abbr.
32 Chipper
33 Make effervescent
35 Chose
37 One of several Phoenician kings
38 Tach letters
41 Hero
42 Bridge seat
43 Anagram for "solo"
44 Iowa commune
45 See 9 Down
47 Goofed
48 Word on the wall
49 Adams of "Tattoo"
50 Live
51 Feb. clock setting, on the Atlantic seaboard
52 Chinese gangs
53 "Now he ___ to the ages" (Stanton, upon Lincoln's death)
54 Walk briskly
56 Face
57 Understand
58 Task

60 Addison's partner
62 Riveter of song
63 Munster county
65 Hoover's org.
68 Maj. ref. works
69 Singer's gem
73 Another's poison
74 Paternal kinsman
75 Banks, for one
76 Brontë heroine
77 Proven
78 Lessened

Down

1 Staff of authority
2 The Terrible
3 Batting practice area
4 ___ Tin Tin
5 Designer Cassini
6 Cut the ___; succeed
7 Harm
8 "___ Romance"; Fields-Kern song
9 Fictional detective, with 45 Across

10 Demure, in England
11 Budget or unit follower
12 Bleat
13 Author's clique
14 Practical
15 Ceremonial dinner
20 Pomeranian, at times
24 "Anna and the King of ___"
26 River nymph
27 Concise
29 "___ Mucho"; '40s song hit
30 Censures
31 Pianist's award
32 Zeno's bailiwick
34 Informer
36 Motion picture, briefly
37 Acts as boss
39 Toast
40 Like Swift's proposal
43 Words of approximation

45 "Footprints on the ___ of time" (Longfellow)
46 Seattle's Sound
47 Wriggly
49 Miss Piggy's pronoun
50 Assigns
52 Apple or pear
53 Did a climbing maneuver
55 "Valse ___"
56 Erase
58 ___ de cacao
59 "...how a bear likes ___" (Pooh)
61 Fame
64 Foil's companion
65 Rooters
66 Cheese choice
67 "___ Three Lives"
69 Masterson
70 "The ___ of Reason"
71 Officeholders
72 Significant time period

Weeding Out *by Donna J. Stone*

This quippy crossword incorporates every letter of the alphabet.

Across

1 Imminent
5 Kind of party
11 Lummox
15 City founded by King Harald III in 1050
16 Like some dogs
17 Overhead
18 **Start of quote** from Edith Zittler
21 Guarneri's master
22 Superman's lunch?
23 Flat-backed fiddle
24 Outlaw
25 Part of a Yale cheer
27 Ahead of "place"
28 Donovan's agcy.
31 Deposit
33 Cow
34 Dropped out of sight
35 "____ in Calico" (Tex Beneke hit of the '40s)
36 Primogenitary
38 Coat color
40 Kilt's kin
41 Olympian's weapon
43 Suffix
44 Immobile class
45 **Part 2 of quote**
50 Contrived
51 SAT's big brother
52 Gander
53 "Climb ____ Mountain"
54 "Boss" Tweed's nemesis
56 Mingo's portrayer
60 At one, in Worms
61 Rouen rooster
62 Social
64 Church area
65 Get-up-and-go
66 Dracula's cover
67 Second to none
69 Veto
70 Picnic disaster
72 Dum Dum dress
73 Problem solvers
75 **End of quote**
78 Went by wain
79 Grownup grub
80 Yard fractions
81 Out of range
82 Ate, at West Point
83 Govt. agents

Down

1 Big cheese
2 Fictional cetologist
3 Made out
4 Bit
5 Baby kisser
6 Carelessly
7 Multi-faceted one?
8 Opera's Lucine
9 Bread spread
10 Cool close
11 Depression
12 Sergeant Snorkel's bulldog
13 Darwin, for one
14 Ant.
19 Loon lips?
20 Classical mythopoet
26 Fit for Flicka
27 Like some toys
29 ____ Domingo
30 Make like Brier Rose
32 "Georgy Girl" group
34 Trip to the Kaaba: Var.
35 He's at home in Nome
37 Pointed
39 Thar features
40 Did something
42 Holiday spirit?
45 Second hand movement
46 Flick
47 Heat-resistant
48 Date site
49 Trickles
55 Suffers from polydipsia
57 Sirenian
58 On the street
59 Misogynists, among others
61 Rooks
63 Songbird
66 Band member
67 Loses color
68 Appendage
71 Opera written for the opening of the Suez Canal
72 Old dirk
74 Shine
75 Blue Eagle agcy.
76 DOD device
77 Cherry or cranberry

147

Simply Loverly *by Joy L. Wouk*

"All love is sweet."—Percy Bysshe Shelley

148

Across

1 Dir. from Paris to Orléans
4 Doctor Joe Gannon, ___ Everett
8 Misanthrope
13 *Comique* actor Jacques
14 Hand holders
16 Worship
17 Ancient Egypt's chief deity
18 Take away
19 Wash cycle
20 Thomas Wolfe work
23 Immature
24 Aunt, pop, etc.
25 Dos Passos work
26 AC or DC supply
28 Makes a fool out of
30 Knock
33 These, to Henri
36 Press
38 East or west ending
39 Theater part
40 Bandleader Shaw
42 Airline watchdog bur.
44 Unbeliever
46 Shirley MacLaine film, 1983
49 Staff for Victoria
50 Mos. and mos.
51 Residence
52 Siouans
53 Perverse
55 Originate
57 Gloomy
58 LA clock setting
59 Franck or Romero
61 Fasten (Scot.)
63 Bad: Pref.
64 Like Willie Winkie
66 Cold symptom
70 "Yes, ___," 1937 Broadway comedy
75 Seine feeder
76 Alfred de ___, Jr., producer of 70 Across
77 Kind of dollar
78 Beethoven's *Für ___*
79 Ashore
80 Fusses
81 Excessive
82 "Breathless" actor Richard
83 ___ Plaines

Down

1 Islands north of Tonga
2 Bar accessory
3 Oyster enemy
4 Kadiddlehopper
5 Stat for Mark McGwire
6 Sworn
7 Lower currency's worth
8 Annoy
9 Donizetti heroine
10 Chinese secret society
11 Gaelic
12 Whirl
13 Soft mineral
14 Agronomist
15 Pulpit speech: Abbr.
21 Most sacred
22 Chaperone, in Chantada
27 Strongboxes
29 Church figures
30 Western shows
31 Chairman's concern
32 Beat repeatedly and heavily
33 American condiment
34 Puts up
35 Sinclair Lewis's "Main ___"
37 Scottish negative
39 Tree branch
41 Mischievous ones
43 More than none
45 Contriving evidence
47 "1984" author
48 AMA members
54 Agape
56 Followed
59 Rush wildly
60 Treat; entertain
62 Use the guillotine
63 Minister's home
65 Mystery award
67 Chopin piece
68 Mere nothings
69 God of passion
70 Mothers of mlles.
71 Yellow Sea feeder
72 Faucet problem
73 Workers' gp.
74 "Masque of Alfred" composer

General Store *by Clare T. Smith*

A random sampling from our Mountain State puzzlewright.

Across

1 Fashions
6 Adult insect
11 Scorch
15 "Martha" or "Norma"
16 Casaba
17 Fad
18 Aboveboard
19 Foreordained
22 Chemical ending
23 Bring out
25 Arthur and Solomon
26 Transmitted
28 "Exodus" hero
29 Smart
31 Jeer
33 Freshwater fish
34 Put off
38 Nevada resort
39 Demure
41 WW II command
42 Cher film
43 Veto
44 Comparative ending
45 Like sushi
46 Clobbers
47 Iguana, for one
49 Young mischief-makers
50 —— was saying...
51 Michael Keaton's "Mr. ——"
52 Aurora
53 Leg joint
54 Equal: Comb. form
55 Insight
57 Oven
58 General purport
60 Earth's nearest star
61 Mexican gift wrapping?
63 Groom
65 Sprout
66 "The Longest ——"

68 Thorny plant
70 Sudden effort
72 Prefix with pod or color
73 Michigan city
76 Foreign
78 Hurting
79 Vast
80 Lodge member
81 Stuns
82 Cone-bearing tree
83 Gives up on fourth down

Down

1 Double agents
2 Unwrapped
3 Retrogression
4 Time period
5 Bargain hunter's delight
6 Mixed with something extraneous

7 Thanks, in the Thousand Islands
8 Toward shelter
9 Deity
10 Billfold foldover
11 Wince
12 Dangle
13 Reacts to stress, perhaps
14 Scarlet
20 Enjoy a winter sport
21 Kindling
24 Wall decoration
27 Ringlet
29 Downcast
30 Santa Fe and Oregon
32 Printing fluid
33 Refined
35 Enzymatically controlled chemical change
36 Day's march, military style
37 Theater seating

39 Syrup source
40 Plumber's joint
42 Billiards shot
43 Distract
46 Fishing need
47 Fabled bird
48 Charged particle
49 Develop a mosaic
51 Impaired
53 Relatives
56 Sun. follower
57 Fools
59 Conjectures
61 Ship's clerk
62 Detain
64 Make a goof
65 Move slightly
67 Eats
68 Forehead feature
69 Unusual
70 Larry of the NBA
71 Pack tightly
73 Youth org.
74 In the manner of
75 Chum
77 Comedian Costello

149

Ubiquitous *by William Canine*

No flubdub, this. Don't stub your toe.

150

Across

1 Record
5 Riffraff
9 Not more
13 Townspeople
15 Mortify
16 Wings
17 Typecast?
18 Exclamation of approval, to Kilroy, perhaps
20 "... —— any drop to drink" (Coleridge)
21 Run into the ground
23 Music hall
24 Prospector's outfit
26 Vaulted recess
28 Caucasus native
29 Sarajevo citizen
31 Modern hotel feature
35 Govt. branch
37 Puddle ducks
39 Sign of a hit: Abbr.
40 Show up
43 In reserve
44 Ventilate
45 PGA member
46 "Showboat" composer
48 Dress
50 Opponent for DDE
51 With it
52 Oscar winner Rainer
54 Strength
56 Dessert
57 African people
58 Dressing gown
59 Cactus wren's milieu
61 Monastery head
63 Headstrong
67 Tokyo legislature
69 Exultation
71 Highlander's garment
74 Narrow, as a country road
76 Gear tooth
77 Ogle
79 Snub
81 City south of Moscow
82 1956 Mathis hit
83 Mine gallery
84 Soccer star
85 Bible book
86 Boulder Dam's lake

Down

1 Contributors
2 Unlucky pioneer flier
3 Tyrrhenian Sea isl.
4 Popular café item
5 Theatrical family members
6 Republica de —— Verde
7 Shadow
8 —— culpa
9 Scot singer Sir Harry ——
10 Hamburg's river
11 "Elephant Boy"
12 Furrow
13 Pig Latin, for instance
14 Proofreader's word
15 Quiver
19 Throngs
22 Hindmost
25 "Adam ——"
27 Sicilian port
30 Neutral shade
32 Newton
33 Milton's "Regent of the Sun"
34 Samuel or Wayne
36 Archbishop
38 Nabokov title
40 Garden pest
41 Vincent of film
42 XVI Gregorys
43 Louise of "My Friend Flicka"
47 Seek office
49 Chicle product
53 Sentence parts
55 Inoculants
57 "The —— Came C.O.D."
58 Singer McEntire
60 Fit to eat
62 Massive
64 Adriatic seaport
65 Made a point
66 German philosopher
68 Bracer
70 What's —— for me?
71 Support
72 Decoy
73 Genesis name
75 Beehive or anthill
78 Sandhurst inst.
80 Dir. from Phila. to NYC

Small Change *by Norma Steinberg*

...but what a difference that change makes!

151

Across

1 Component of a slugger's statistics
6 Written untruth
11 Radiate
15 Actor Christopher ____
16 Bloodhound's clues
17 Warning to baby
18 Black bird
19 Communist luminary?
22 Actor Vigoda
23 Chuck ____
25 Leaves
26 Tale
28 Neighbor of Ind.
29 Finger or number
31 Dreary
33 Cal. column
34 Robert Allen Zimmerman, a.k.a. Bob ____
38 Antiquity
39 Hanky of a sort
41 ____ had my way...
42 Aide, in brief
43 TV's Caesar
44 ...ar, ____, tee,...
45 Writer Anaïs ____
46 Ballet exercise
47 Kabob sticks
49 Only
50 Winner's take, sometimes
51 ____ the piper
52 Break bread
53 Come in second
54 Coolidge, for short
55 Hair-setting gadget
57 Military takeover
58 Herb
60 It's "good" for an astronaut
61 Steam rooms
63 "Harold and Maude" director
65 Prefix meaning "wrong"
66 Double
68 Lark
70 Carl of "Cosmos"
72 Commit perjury
73 Composer of rag?
76 Double-jointed
78 A grand ol' name
79 Rigg or Ross
80 Mister in Madrid
81 Super (Ger.)
82 Oust
83 Seeing red

Down

1 Display
2 Dunker of sorts
3 Opera Boffo star?
4 Blvd.'s relative
5 Sawbucks
6 Solitary
7 Perfect
8 Make ____ on
9 North or south ending
10 WW II craft
11 Being
12 The lion's share
13 Printer's purchases
14 Yo-yo or rubber ball
20 Normal: Abbr.
21 Rusty compounds
24 Use a stopwatch
27 Old West "necktie"
29 Half of *cuatro*
30 Newspaper advertising section
32 Remnant
33 Wednesday
35 Chemist/singles bar operator?
36 Blazing
37 "...in the pot, ____ days old"
39 Reason for overtime
40 Destroyer's letters
42 Islamic supreme being
43 High-flying research project
46 Agreement
47 ____ Paulo, Brazil
48 Sympathetic organ
49 Pitcher's place
51 Like some conditions
53 Gehrig or Grant
56 Actress Myrna ____
57 *Mi* ____ *es su...*
59 Sufferer for a cause
61 Meaningful motion
62 Tar
64 Wise to
65 Election bellwether?
67 Chary
68 Picket line crosser
69 Read closely
70 Word with stick and happy
71 43 Down agcy.
73 Dallas inst.
74 Keatsian output
75 "Variety" shorthand
77 Pentagon VIP

Them's Fightin' Words *by Martha J. DeWitt*

Well, sez you!

Across

1 Bud
6 Due
11 Peace-seeking Anwar
16 Mightily
17 Refute
18 Lissome
19 See 38 Across
21 Robin's roosts
22 Cheese choice
23 Function
24 Matched pair
26 Charpoy
27 Chicken of the future
28 Caustic stuff
29 Fanfaronade
32 Closely packed
34 Tacloban's island
35 Columnist Bombeck
38 Fractious
41 Chinchilla's habitat
42 Spoil
45 Tip over
46 Entrances
48 Boise's county
49 One with another point of view
51 Nancy Astor, _____ Langhorne
52 Persian governors
54 Piece of _____; cinch
55 Let it stand
56 Fed the kitty
57 Envisage
59 Lounge
60 Entertain
62 Duds
66 Auto graveyard, usually
68 Director's direction
70 Draw on

71 Mayday relative
73 Oohs and _____
74 "Dust shalt thou _____" (Genesis 3:14)
75 Lawn pest
76 At _____ for words
78 See 38 Across
82 Textile fabric
83 Practical
84 Eyed
85 Put _____ to; cease
86 Describing an otary
87 Fun and pun endings

Down

1 Gossiped
2 Issue forth
3 Bad-mouth
4 Eight furlongs
5 Blackbird
6 Unpleasingly plump
7 "The Way We _____"
8 Isère island

9 Writer Anaïs
10 Reaches with effort
11 Fe or Ana
12 Get on
13 See 38 Across
14 Palo _____
15 Tryout
20 M. de Maupassant
25 Actress Arden
28 "The Lip"
29 See 38 Across
30 Ham on _____
31 Fender-bender result
33 Demure
34 Perjuries
36 Free-for-all
37 Resource
39 Supporting actor Homeier
40 D'Urberville girl
41 Van Gogh's forte
42 Fundamental
43 Hersey's fictional town
44 See 38 Across
46 Small dog, for short

47 Change for a fiver
49 Old moneybags?
50 First family of Virginia
53 Depend
55 Symph., perhaps
57 Skin
58 Newt
60 Rowan
61 Masjid
63 Peter, the Irish-born actor
64 Magician, at times
65 Goes too fast
67 Ameliorated
68 Gave a hoot
69 Shoshonean
71 Poet Teasdale
72 Pearl Buck heroine
74 _____ Stanley Gardner
75 Mil. rank
77 Impiety
79 Southwestern lizard
80 Tire filler
81 _____ Angeles

152

Dance Form *by Bernice Gordon*

"...one must also be able to dance with the pen."—Nietzsche

153

Across

1 Church area
6 Hadj's destination
11 Seven-year occurrence
15 Greene of the screen
16 Relieve
17 Christmas berry
19 "Top Hat" star
21 Confuse
22 Extremely cold
23 Language for the masses
24 Gave consolation to
26 New York's —— River
28 Tendencies
30 Conquerors of Rome
31 River to the Rhône
33 Eye part
35 "The ——" (1964 Reagan film)
38 Rajah's mate: Var.
39 Plain-weave fabric
42 Sister to 19 Across, and namesakes
43 Party poopers
44 Toper
45 Up
46 —— off; reduce gradually
47 Speed
48 Form
49 Used a beeper
50 English county
51 "—— Blue?"
52 Van Gogh's residence
53 Gravel-voiced folks
54 Musical Garner
56 Todo
57 Berate
58 Vista
60 Eat graciously
64 Most old-hat
66 Marble
68 —— pros (legal maneuver)
69 Moslem holy book
70 "The Turning Point" dancer
73 —— ear and out the other
74 —— once; suddenly
75 Peace goddess
76 Intentions
77 Brings up
78 Challenges

Down

1 Burt Bacharach song
2 Spanish dramatist Frederico García ——
3 Playing cards
4 Connecting word
5 In earnest
6 Is important
7 Comedienne Boosler
8 Walker or Eastwood
9 Auto
10 Words of approval
11 Go ——; ignore help
12 Up ——; modern
13 "Singin' in the Rain" dancer
14 Burrows
18 Sparks of film
20 Cavalry weapons
25 Blunderbore, and others
27 Cultivated the fields
29 Intimidated
32 Witnessed
34 Special person
35 Destiny
36 Form of expression
37 "An American In Paris" dancer
38 What experts know?
40 Put on record
41 Pound and Frost
43 Lox bases
44 Not true
46 Like a basketball player
47 Fire fighter's need
49 Incites
50 Hebrew letter
52 Dahl and Francis
53 Big meals
55 "Topper" star Young
56 Hungarian
57 Riverbed item
59 "Cheers" waitress
61 Old-time printer's roller
62 Nary a soul
63 The shoemaker's little friends
64 Race Tamara McKinney
65 Slopes lift
67 Arthurian lady
71 "Cakes and ——"
72 One of the Gershwins

Be Counted! *by Sidney L. Robbins*

Say what you think!

154

Across

1 PD alerts
5 Kettle and Barker
8 *Avril* follower
11 Whip
15 Mild expletive
16 Perform
17 Hand holder
18 Preminger
19 Matador's pase
21 Did again
23 **Astute observation, part 1**
25 Oozes
26 Chem. or psy.
27 Town near Padua
28 Conversational stopgaps
29 Restore it
30 Prim and proper
34 Pieces
36 Beam
39 Bagel topper
40 Agree
43 Hard to hold
44 Copter leader
45 **Observation, part 2**
49 Leave out
50 Tangle
51 Taoism founder
52 Salt Lake City athlete
53 Purloin
55 Aug. follower
56 Renter
58 River into the Firth of Clyde
60 Follower: Suff.
63 Shoe size
65 North or south ending
66 Sheathing
68 **End of observation**
72 The art of effective speaking
73 Vote dry
74 Top drawer
75 NYC line
76 Greek letter
77 Cattle
78 Says vows
79 Singer Sayer
80 Russia, e.g.
81 Founds: Abbr.

Down

1 Consult
2 Choose
3 Small units of pressure
4 How to conquer?
5 Hotel employee
6 Confronts
7 Bearing
8 Damages
9 Mountain ridge
10 Deadlock
11 Full up
12 Member of the Near Island group
13 —— off; measure, in a way
14 Brick carrier
20 Greek letters
22 Come in
24 Champ
29 Hold back
31 Chain for 12 Down, e.g.
32 "For Whom the Bell ——"
33 Banish
34 Superlatively good
35 Altar promise
37 Landed
38 With: Pref.
40 Run —— of; aggravate
41 Napoleonic nobleman
42 Shouts
43 Sicilian landmark
44 Ape an owl
46 Make do
47 —— Canyon, on the Colorado River
48 Talk too much
53 "...—— evil..."
54 Vine's shoot
55 Fourteen-line poems
57 Says with authority
59 Says passionately
60 Eye woe
61 Lodger
62 High flyers
64 Burning
66 Mel, the Giant
67 —— up; become speechless
68 Brogan
69 Care for
70 Eight, in combos
71 Decade fraction
72 Untried

Sound Stage *by Roger H. Courtney*

One hundred words and fifty black squares, making a balance of sight and sound.

Across

1 Mike Tyson, for instance
6 TV's Winfrey
11 Scintilla
16 Vowel run
17 Disgrace
18 Age beer
19 Kitchen tool
20 Antisocial one
21 Fiber plant
22 "All About ____"
23 Airs
26 Neckline shape
27 Certain house value
29 Switch settings
30 Fragrant compounds
32 One type is eared
34 Funny lady Martha
35 In order
38 Pilot's word
42 Action word for the ILA
46 Motel offerings
48 Phone leader
49 Turn-of-the-century French artist
50 Maladroit
51 WW II craft
52 Gyrates
53 Be charitable
54 Coma
56 "____ Were the Days"
57 Reflection of a sort
58 Playing card
60 Sugary endings
61 Sch. sports org.
63 Comparative word
65 Child's marker
68 Arrow's launch vehicle
71 Mrs. Marcos
75 "Stir" time
76 Right to write?
79 Swiss river
80 "There Is Nothing Like ____"
82 Weasel's relative
83 Austria's western boundary
85 Electrician, often
86 "Over ____"
87 Magna ____
88 Lenya
89 Torrid zone?
90 This car was a bust

Down

1 Prank
2 Elevate
3 Buenos ____
4 One Stooge
5 Prince's color
6 Norway's capital
7 Graph starter
8 Arrested
9 Church closures
10 It's opposite to 86 Across
11 Dull, like tired eyes
12 Fall behind
13 ____ at the office
14 At no time
15 Weyerhaeuser harvest
24 Big wheel?
25 Center of government
28 "I Hear ____"
31 Bell's transmitter
33 Guitarist Paul
34 Genetic ltrs.
35 Insubstantial
36 Kind of column
37 "Whatsoever he ____ shall prosper" (Ps. 1:3)
39 Wise lawgiver
40 Apices
41 Bar
43 Exchange premiums
44 "____ Macabre"
45 Double curves
47 Sault ____ Marie
49 Summer time: Abbr.
54 Sargasso or Bering
55 Balderdash!
58 Pueblo of New Mexico
59 "The ____ Man"
62 Be consistent
64 Punish with a fine
65 Move like baby
66 Broadcast medium
67 Isolated
68 South Africa leader
69 Chose
70 "____ the Boys Are"
72 Leo's pads
73 "Divine Comedy" writer
74 It's been ____ pleasure...
77 Butterfly's cousin
78 Galena and bauxite
81 Encountered
84 Owned

155

Yesterdays *by Arnold Moss*

Radio remembrances.

156

Across

1 Señoras
6 Orient
10 Wrinkle
16 Von Stroheim of films
17 Mine, in Montmartre
18 English novelist James
19 Goose genus
20 Door slam, for example
22 Like thin paper
24 Allen or McQueen
25 Eleventh-century date
26 Lang. of Isr.
27 Highlands slope
29 Bridge's Culbertson
30 Gaff or boom
31 H.S. hotshots
33 Eyeball covering
35 Made off with
36 ——-leaf cluster
38 Rubber bands
40 Walloped, in the Bible
42 Homily: Abbr.
43 Stat. for Hershiser
44 Tipsy comment
47 "He that —— warning shall deliver his soul" (Ezek. 33:5)
49 Med. workers
51 Mistaken
53 What Ado Annie *could* say
54 Cask
56 WW II area
58 Gives up, at poker
59 Basin brightener
61 Gloomy
62 Ruby Dee's husband
65 Malodorous
67 Debussey's "*La* ——"
69 —— of thumb
70 —— *appétit!*
71 Self-images
73 Former Portuguese possession
75 Jackie's second husband
76 "*La* —— *Vita*"
78 Cooling devices
80 Famed jazz pianist of the '40s and '50s
83 Israeli VIP
84 Endless, to Keats
85 Mongibello, to most of us
86 Pianist Watts
87 Slept, British style
88 Marine entertainer?
89 "...the land whereon thou ——..." (Gen. 28:13)

Down

1 "—— in Venice"
2 —— Army of golf
3 Eve Arden role
4 Know-it-alls
5 Bush
6 Radio's Goody and Jane
7 ——, *amas, amat*
8 ——-chef; kitchen lieutenant
9 Some artists
10 Actor Chase
11 Abundant
12 Pixie
13 Previn direction
14 —— Security
15 Complete
21 Accuse, in Aberdeen
23 Conversational stopgaps
28 Aunt —— of "Oklahoma!"
30 Beale and Bourbon: Abbr.
32 Oversupply
34 Word in a Wilde title
35 Wraps
37 Ma or Pa of film
39 Vex
40 Pen
41 Actress Busch
44 "Incomparable" '40s radio songstress
45 Neither Rep. nor Dem.
46 Meas. system
48 Partner of cry
50 Cubic meter
52 Gad about
55 A seaport of *Italia*
57 Oddball
59 Co., French style
60 Male relatives, British style
62 Emulated Bryan
63 Be —— write!
64 Playground equipment
66 Little person of film
68 Dancer Ginger
70 Acknowledged applause
72 Flower part
74 Black-ink item
76 Force unit
77 6 Across, in Ponce
79 Blessed, in Bordeaux
81 AMA members
82 "Three Men —— Horse"

All to the Good *by Peter Swift*

"Good words are worth much, and cost little."—George Herbert

157

Across

1 Did office work
6 Harmonica ace Larry
11 Gobs
15 Designer Simpson
16 Food preservative
17 Glossy black enamel
18 Literary category
19 Eccentric
20 City on the Missouri
21 Prosper
24 And others, briefly
25 With 17 Down, singer-pianist
26 French pronoun
27 Talks impudently
30 Writer Deighton
31 ___ off; drive
32 ___ in the back; betrays
36 Edit
41 Vases
43 Growing outward
45 Caustic
47 Prosper
51 ___ tartare
52 Sudden outpouring
53 Cut
54 Respect
57 Treats for wild birds
59 ___ with it; wise up
60 CSA soldier
62 Haulers
64 A musical Stone
67 Summoned to court
69 Beneficiary
70 Prosper
75 Masher
76 Ryan or Tatum
77 ___ by; comply with
79 ___ Noster
80 Actress Cilento
81 Bottle imp
82 Insult
83 Car
84 Ruhr valley city

Down

1 Aficionado
2 Graven image
3 Son of Jacob
4 Sorbonne students
5 Cancels
6 Cooking
7 Sedate
8 Supple
9 Join up
10 Appear again
11 Lustrous fabric
12 Moonfishes
13 Western resort lake
14 Hidden obstacles
17 See 25 Across
22 Hotfoot it
23 Musical sound
27 Rain checks
28 Ventilate
29 Becomes aware of; recognizes
33 Pismire
34 Scrooge's expressions
35 Passage
37 "___ Kapital"
38 Woeful cries in Kiel
39 Cower
40 Smaller
42 Card game for three
44 Brother of Jacob
46 Govt. agencies
48 Mamie's man
49 Western Amerind
50 Cleared
55 Writer Ambler
56 Systems
58 Crops cut for fodder
61 Cap
63 Extended families
64 Swill
65 ___ tender
66 Black Sea port
67 Singer Vikki
68 Angst
69 Soprano Traubel
71 Obscure
72 Divine power, in Oceania
73 Fivers
74 Entertainer Adams
78 Time of day, to Keats

Chain Gang *by Barbara Barry-Johnson*

The chain starting at 1 Down includes a rock singer, a trumpeter, an actor, two religious figures, a sitcom actor, and a '60s singer.

158

Across

1 Roy's honey
5 Pub pastime
10 Shrewdness
16 Conceits
17 Revolutionary path
18 Rounded roof
19 Partiality
20 Chief followers
21 Braggart
22 To-go choice, w/ mayo
23 Green or black beverage
24 Opera villain
26 Bottle top
27 **Second link of chain**
31 Reason to seek AA
32 —— nova
33 Poly ender
35 Spotted
38 Full of sauce
40 Soul
44 Spring period
45 Stocking content, for bad kids
47 Designated "X"
49 Principal return: Abbr.
50 **Fourth link of chain**
52 —— française
53 Moved in 4/4 time
55 Renders
56 Eagerly expectant
57 Take off
58 A certain smile
60 Working stiff
61 Alan of "The In-Laws"
63 Composer Erik
66 FDR's veep
69 **Sixth link of chain**
74 Antioch locale
76 Scorch
77 Coll. measure
78 ——, O, U
79 Signs of spring
81 Lively dance
83 NCO
84 Gather
85 Novelist Zola
86 Of the ear
87 Highest suit
88 Light lunch
89 Legend

Down

1 **Start of chain**
2 Limber
3 Unwilling
4 Ending formerly used to designate a woman
in a "man's job"
5 Indulgent parents
6 Fineries
7 Sac. fly statistic
8 Knee's neighbor
9 Bamboo ——
10 Greet intrusively
11 Contemptible one
12 —— my word!
13 Dealt with overgrowth
14 Choose
15 Stool pigeons, in London
23 Trampled
25 Shrug, for example
28 Help a hood
29 Fuji's land
30 **Third link of chain**
34 Life's "building blocks": Abbr.
35 Sleazeball
36 —— code
37 Opening, familiarly
39 Suppress
41 Adult insect
42 Casaba
43 Words of wisdom
45 "The Hustler" prop
46 Conservative
48 Seagoing fly-boy depot: Abbr.
50 **Fifth link of chain**
51 Sculpture focus, often
54 Books looker: Abbr.
56 Field
59 Hires
60 1981 Wilhelmina Fernandez role
62 Hershey favorites
64 Luanda's country
65 Went one better
66 Cargo containers
67 Submissive ones
68 Princess's put-on
70 Emotional event
71 Really unpleasant
72 Quite all right
73 **End of chain**
75 Poet of old Rome
80 12/24 or 12/31 time
82 Diamond ——
83 He's a turkey!

Franchises Available *by Norma Steinberg*

What a country!

159

Across

1 Phone
7 Having a rhythmic flow
13 Spigot
16 Stir
17 Gum arabic
18 The second Mrs. Sinatra
19 Vincent's rheostats?
21 Hither's counterpart
22 Athlete Kyle ____
23 It might be sordid
24 Actress Shire
26 Yes, Captain!
27 Mass. coastline
28 Nontraveler
31 Animal
35 More refined
36 Idle
37 Lyric poetry
39 Rock concert musts, familiarly
42 Drum along the Mohawk
45 Needy
46 "...____ told by an idiot..." (Shakespeare)
47 Pitcher's stat
48 James's containers
51 Coq ____
52 Ms. Gillette
54 Sonora coin
55 ____-camp
57 Ms. Lisa?
58 ____ novel
59 Paycheck deduction: Abbr.
60 Fairylike
62 Faced
66 Rotates
69 Uh-uh!
70 Jamaican export
72 Gladiator's milieu
73 Collect wages
75 Welles's citizen
76 Opp. of max.
77 Deborah's fix-it-alls?
82 Vegas transaction
83 *Ecole* attenders
84 Papas and Dunne
85 CIA forerunner
86 Remove
87 Formal

Down

1 Director of note
2 Dry gulch
3 Hang around
4 Ex "Time" head
5 Function
6 Chest muscle, familiarly
7 Mars landscape features, to some
8 Deeds
9 Villain Vader
10 Prefix for sphere or system
11 Zilch
12 Winery employee
13 Elizabeth's custom clothes?
14 Skirt
15 Mindoro's neighbor
20 Of sight
25 Without missing ____
27 Soul
29 "Porgy and Bess," for instance
30 Orch. output
32 Obtain
33 Fragrance
34 Daily event of variable time
38 Karate school
40 Trudge
41 Dry
42 Side
43 Whether ____
44 Marjorie's parties?
45 cummings's construction
46 Cold ____
49 Backbone
50 Inclement
53 Claw
56 Pop
58 Kin of a batt.
59 Coin for Pierre
61 Cut into shavings
63 Upheaval
64 Works out
65 Liquid measurements
66 Stallone hero
67 New York Indians
68 Wait table
71 Like Oscar Madison's room
74 Iowa city
75 On bended ____
78 Actor Wallach
79 Gun the motor
80 Stayed undercover
81 Part of ETA

Easy Listening   by Joy L. Wouk

"Music is Love in search of a word."—Sidney Lanier

160

Across

1 Work on the lawn
4 Duke lab topic
7 About 14.7 psi
10 Signals to
15 Grand ____ Opry
16 Pool hall item
17 Peruvian Mrs.
18 River past Verona
19 Pod element
20 Napierian notions: Abbr.
21 Average
22 A bummer of a car
23 Cather work, with "The"
27 ____ Khan
28 Mountain crest
29 Actress Veronica
33 Long running musical, "A ____"
37 Lathered
39 "You can lead a ____ water..."
40 Yellowish-brown cattle
41 Pulpy fruit
42 Granular igneous rocks
46 1973 film about two baseball players
53 Bernstein and Nimoy
54 Hawk parrot
55 Grammatical modifiers
58 More cantankerous: Var.
62 Stay
63 Victor Borge's specialty
66 B ____ boy
67 Corpulent
69 Beverage served hot or cold
70 Hersey novel
75 Eye color
79 ____ glance; casually
80 Press for payment
81 Red-carpet: Abbr.
82 Greek market
83 Cardinal number
84 Funny Philips
85 Seine sight
86 Entrances
87 Append
88 Spring mo.
89 Lair

Down

1 Swabs
2 Bread spread
3 Separate
4 Short pastoral poem
5 Not likely to fade as a result of light
6 Nuisance
7 Henry James's novelette, "The ____ Papers"
8 Kerry county seat
9 Corday's victim
10 Pitcher's failure
11 Humorist George
12 Vigor's companion
13 Self esteem
14 D.C. figure
24 Needlefish
25 "Bali ____"
26 Bowling lane buttons
29 Riata
30 Simian
31 Riddle explanation
32 Asner and Begley
33 Bait fish
34 Madagascar native
35 Algerian port
36 Coat cloths
38 City on the Oka
40 Poisonous weed
43 Mrs. Cantor
44 Hockey great
45 Tiller's attachment: Abbr.
47 Collect grain
48 Actress Garr
49 Buzz around
50 Tory opponent
51 Stead
52 Seaworthy
55 Southern constellation
56 ____ Moines
57 Monogram at Lexington
59 Bridge bidder's choice
60 One Roosevelt
61 Highway
63 Struck with missiles
64 Christmas or Easter
65 Pershing's gp.
68 Holy woman
70 Word of woe
71 Concert halls
72 Eager
73 Shade of green
74 Ready for business
75 Possessed
76 Past
77 Menagerie
78 Flub

Originally published in 1989

Shaping Up *by Bert Rosenfield*

Another fine construction by puzzle architect Rosenfield.

161

Across

1 Soviet nonperson, nowadays
7 Film, to "Variety"
10 CA, formerly
15 Ratatouille ingredient
16 Negotiations delay
18 Middle East combining form
19 Lessened
20 —— sense of the word
21 Word from the ghost of Claudius
22 Construct a doily
23 —— *amis;* my friends
25 Sand and glass
27 It's common to March and April
28 "—— Rhythm"
30 "Zoo ——"; old TV series
32 Moscow landmark
33 New York City landmark
36 Work units
38 Storefront signs
39 Michael Jordan's org.
40 Author-editor Tarbell
43 Device for Dennis Conner
47 Trap-building arachnid
49 Relative of "alas"
50 East-west Mass. hwy.
52 Without club soda or ice
53 Boston landmark
57 Escamillo and El Cordobés
61 Main and Elm, e.g.
62 Rock chisel
63 Painter Veronese
64 Turkish chieftain
65 American financier and bon vivant
69 Mae West 1928 play
72 Not ——; nohow
74 Canal called "Clinton's Ditch"
75 Out of ——; forthwith
76 Double "tetra"
77 Tic-Toe connection

80 "—— Alone" (1924 Berlin ballad)
81 Basketball Hall-of-Famer Baylor
83 Delineate
85 Pregame ritual
87 Coeur d'—— Lake, Idaho
88 For heaven's ——!
89 Snake idolater
90 Went for broke
91 Q-U filler
92 Unsnapped the leash

Down

1 Atmospherics
2 Trinidad's neighbor
3 Explosive containing TNT
4 It intersects long.
5 Gossip-column twosome
6 Collection point
7 —— phenomena: ESP, telepathy, etc.
8 Clique

9 Cretan capital
10 William Webster's org.
11 Intensities
12 English jazz singer Cleo
13 "—— Your Love Tonight" (Presley '59 hit)
14 Unswerving
17 Pittsburgh landmark
24 Feistiness
26 Sarajevo residents
29 Lincoln or Sumner
31 Tact, for example
34 "I Hate ——" (song from "Kiss Me, Kate")
35 Nile green
37 Opening
40 Starter for graphic or logic
41 Exorbitant
42 Crafts' partners
43 Wisconsin Indians
44 Illumination unit
45 Brats and urchins
46 Say again: Abbr.
48 City 340 miles northeast of Bombay

51 Small hill, in South Africa
54 Kind of roll
55 Lout
56 Hoedowns
58 Singer John of "The Pajama Game"
59 Bus. acct. abbr.
60 Churchly vestment
64 Old name for italic type
65 Some rattlers
66 The Chevalier d'Herblay
67 Attenuate
68 Reacted to a hotfoot
69 Oahu landmark
70 "—— Rookh" (Thomas Moore poem)
71 Swedish actress Stevens
73 Rose oil
78 MP's prey
79 Crime syndicate biggie
82 Dime novel pioneer Buntline
84 —— up; in a tizzy
86 P-shaped Greek letter

Writer's Block?   *by Donna J. Stone*

J. Terry Bechtol's question to secret agents.

Across

1 Plant
5 "___ on the Hudson"
11 Tall ship's features
16 Disoriented
17 Revelation
18 Restive
19 **Start of quandary**
22 Foreign
23 Used up
24 Informed
25 ___ Shamra, Syrian Bronze Age site
26 Had fun at the mall
28 Cedar Rapids campus
29 "Cars" vocalist Ben
32 Particular
34 Rout finale
35 Use a microwave?
36 It can be very tacky
37 Tahini base
39 Wattle and ___; construction technique
41 Like autumn weather
42 Make much of
44 ___ bonne heure (well and good)
45 "Big" star
46 **Middle of quandary**
49 Expiate
51 Smash letters
52 Self starter
53 Turns away from
54 Substandard contraction
56 Crow's toes?
60 Tennis star Mandlikova
61 Sault ___ Marie
62 Codswallop!
64 Ever's partner
65 UK division
66 Kasbah cap
67 Prolific diarist
69 Corday's confidant?
70 Unlikely
72 Smell ___
73 Urdu or Sinhalese
75 **End of quandary**
79 Prepared to propose
80 Filmdom's Signoret
81 Hook's hand
82 Huck Finn in girl's dress: ___ Williams
83 Emulate Hamlet, in a way
84 Vaticinator

Down

1 "Route 66" star
2 Pinpoint
3 Sinclair and Meriwether
4 Teddy trim
5 Blades
6 Priestley concern
7 Served the stew
8 Di Luna or Dracula
9 Bony beginning
10 Early
11 "Now We Are Six" author
12 Periodic Table datum: Abbr.
13 Guidance
14 Common article
15 Thesaurus detail: Abbr.
20 Ques. reply
21 Belt holder
27 Christian art theme
28 Poolside area
30 Zwieback
31 Mouthpieces
33 Ms. Caccione
35 South African
36 Breakfast mixture
38 Grimaces
40 "Titus Andronicus" villain
41 Ms. Rivera
43 Mock
46 Rug rat
47 Ontario's neighbor
48 Like Jerry Lewis's professor
49 Wimbledon's Arthur
50 Comparative word
55 Dorr's crime
57 Where to stop?
58 Life of the party?
59 Scornful sound
61 Highway rig
63 Leaning toward
66 Dominant, to Dorati
67 Flower
68 ___ vous plaît
71 Girl who gets what she wants
72 Tel ___, Israel
74 Nitti's nemesis
75 Endorses
76 ___ voce poco fa (Rossini aria)
77 Cryptic bur.
78 "Hive Gotta Be Me" creature

162

Animal Movies *by Robert A. Sefick*

Who's zoo at the cinema.

163

Across

1 Go out with
5 Emerged
10 Eastern monk
14 Hemmed in
15 Injustices
16 Iowa church society
18 Red as ___
19 Disney pet?
21 Kind of deal
22 Tempests
24 Read my ___!
   (Bush campaign
   slogan)
25 Take a little
26 Propagated
28 Founded: Abbr.
29 Break fast
30 Social events
31 Emissaries
34 Theater section
36 Brightened the day
38 NYC bldg.
40 Get cozy
44 "___ Mockingbird"
46 Wing
48 Spare; distinct
49 Raw material
50 Some war protesters
53 ___ minute; soon
54 Antelope
57 Gym cushion
58 Needs help
61 Like home brew
63 Brown or Paul
65 Raucous
66 Radio's Molly
68 Morning-after
   emotion
70 Grease
73 Whitney

75 Chaney
76 Nelson
79 'Hoptimism
80 Diamond cut
81 Scandinavian
   literary collection
83 Where the grass is
   green
84 Grizzly fragrance?
87 Edge
89 Log
90 Pets
91 Despoils, in a way
92 Miami's county
93 Fomenter
94 Itches

Down

1 Exclude
2 Woolly flick?
3 Kicker's device
4 Comics old-timer
   Kett
5 Limiting phrase
6 Rickles, usually

7 Rink's famous
   Bobby
8 Charismatic word
9 Observation
10 Turns
11 Elec. measurement
12 Principal state?
13 Hall or Orphan
14 Mrs. Bush, to
   friends
17 Slitherers
20 Sinclair
23 Extremely accurate
27 Ethnic grocery
30 Defeat
32 Take shape
33 Wand
35 Earth: Pref.
36 Some do this to
   conquer
37 ___ Castle
39 Ex ring champ
41 "The ___" (film
   about a hungry
   jungle cat?)
42 Gives, to some

43 Expurgate
45 Aspire
47 Set the pace
51 Sidekick
52 Go along with
55 Rebozo
56 Made of: Suff.
59 ___ favor; please
60 The good life
62 Forest primeval
   makeup
64 Chooses
67 ___-eyed
69 Like some maidens
70 Ear area
71 Flip
72 ___ hasty retreat
74 Dancing Castle
77 Makes progress
78 Imitates a
   chatterbox
80 ___ Marquette
82 With efficiency
85 Carmine
86 Publishers' org.
88 Pitcher Preacher

Animal House *by Manny Miller*

Another interpretation of the same theme.

Across

1 Wild rush
8 Like a chimp
13 Garden nuisance
18 One who transfers property
19 Oscar de la ___
20 Mick Jagger or Keith Richards
21 Candid
23 NCO's nickname
24 Man or Pines
25 Condemn
26 Extract
28 Lawn
29 All right, informally
30 Sheep's shelter
31 Believer
32 NBA team
33 Of the nostrils
35 Free from noise
37 Unearth
39 Party line
41 U.S. Grant foe
43 Wounds a matador
46 Originates
49 Puts to flight
51 Family designation
53 Anagram for sear
54 Relatives of hedgehogs
55 Common lawbreaker
56 Opposed to pos.
57 Champion choreographer
58 Kasparov's game
60 Work unit
61 K2's higher-up
63 Partner of starlit
64 Press by persuasion
65 Old Greek city
66 Kind of book
67 Beasts of burden
68 Day in spring
69 Plant fluid
71 Deserve
73 *Hiver* opposites
75 Western land formations
77 Stitcher
81 Saratoga attractions
83 Dodge
85 Christmas poem starter
87 Outer: Pref.
88 XXVI, quadrupled
89 Muscat citizen
90 Endowment beneficiary
91 "Thin Man" pooch
92 "___ Kick Out Of You"

164

94 Illegal blows, in boxing
97 Dismisses
98 Bound set of maps
99 Component
100 Map detail
101 Plants
102 Is antipathetic toward

Down

1 Allowance
2 Polar bear country
3 Grain grinder
4 Lap dog
5 Bird with bladelike bill
6 Venice conveyance
7 Cereal disease
8 European flowering plant
9 ___ diem
10 Old school-desk containers
11 Lifeless
12 Nineteenth president
13 Helper: Abbr.
14 Sch. org.
15 Shrewd bargainers
16 Metal bar
17 Acts
22 Some digits
27 Ship: Abbr.
30 The ___ meow
31 Regimens
32 Not anybody
34 Dogmas
36 More allegiant
38 Folklore giants
40 Expansions
42 Perfume
44 Develop
45 Worsted fabrics
46 North American Indian
47 Claire of films
48 Zealous workers
50 Chihuahua cheer
52 ___ daisy
54 Greatest degree
57 Whodunit or romance
58 Squiggle in a series
59 ___ polloi
62 Tumults
63 Computer gadget
64 Annapolis inst.
66 Trustworthy
67 Counterpart of Mars
70 Come forth
72 In general
74 Rel. inst.
76 Proofreader's word
78 Interlocks
79 Scope
80 Main course choices
81 Fiction form, familiarly
82 ___ a poke
84 Iberian length units
86 Applied cloths
89 Hops dryer
90 Snake's sound
91 Summit
93 Golf bag item
95 Sinful
96 Part of the court scene

Originally published in 1989

Ladies' Day *by Elizabeth Arthur*

Names from then and now.

Across

1 Humiliates
7 Of an inscribed pillar
13 Kind of hit
18 Split pea, for instance
19 Statesman/orator of old Rome
20 Hustle or bustle
21 First female trans-Atlantic flier
23 Inventor Howe
24 A or T
25 Buck or stink ending
26 Magnani and Lollobrigida
28 Every twelve months: Abbr.
30 Tennis's Chris
31 Prepare for a physical exam
35 Anne Sullivan's pupil
41 1941 Bogart film, "High ___"
42 "...to thine own ___ be true"
43 Despoil, of old
44 Like "The Love Boat"
46 One ___ time, please
49 Made a hole in one
50 Spoke interminably
51 Dull routine
52 Gentle quality
54 Saline solution?
56 Harbors
57 VCR fodder
61 Chums
62 Body conditioning, in Yoga
67 Ancient strongbox
68 "For ___ a Jolly Good Fellow"
69 Unlettered
71 Discover
73 Nice summers?
74 Collect Social Security
75 Greek-American soprano
79 Actress Smith
80 Musical tags
81 Explorer Vasco da ___
83 Eligible one
87 Offer at a price
89 Suprise victory
94 Song belter Merman
95 Charles's spouse
98 Olfactory sense
99 Outer garments
100 Graf's forte
101 "The Velvet Fog"
102 Sudden showers
103 AKC statistics

Down

1 ___ dunk
2 Blood: Comb. form
3 Like good wine
4 Stubborn beast
5 "Wuthering Heights" author
6 Word with horse or cow
7 Frightening
8 Beginner: Var.
9 Reverberate
10 Meadow
11 Prosper
12 Scandalous
13 Umbrella, perhaps
14 West African country
15 Largest continent
16 Baseball's Musial
17 Pianist Dame Myra ___
22 Spitchcock
27 Noah's vessel
29 Scan
30 Leprechaun
31 Employer
32 Kind of palm
33 Control
34 Thereabouts
35 Makes warm
36 Model McPherson
37 In shape
38 Alençon, for one
39 Pre-holiday times
40 Riverfront Stadium team
42 Makes a hit
45 Like a wet hen
46 Bikini and Eniwetok
47 Ankles
48 Qty.
53 Cosmetics name
55 Old English letter
56 Turns ashen
57 Storm preceder
58 Bailiwick
59 Battle memento
60 Garb for Indira Gandhi
61 Pocket bread
63 Commedia dell' ___
64 Peace, in Paris
65 Abruzzi town
66 Understands
70 Piccadilly trolley
72 Aircraft enclosure
73 They loop the Loop in Chicago
76 Mil. rank
77 Takes on
78 Spank
81 Daly's TV partner
82 Hirt and Haig
83 Better than better
84 Air: Pref.
85 "Mask" star
86 Tiller
87 In a ___; miffed
88 ___ homo!
90 Conifer
91 Reasonable
92 Author Bagnold
93 USSR's news agcy.
96 ___ minute; soon
97 Seminary deg.

165

Originally published in 1989

Testimonies *by Roger H. Courtney*

From the Good Book.

Across

1 Dresser
6 Cruise accountants
13 Transfer
18 With expediency
19 Embellishing shoulder pad
20 Muse of poetry
21 Antony and Chagall
22 Bible book, with "The"
24 Personal letter from St. Paul
26 Peter and Paul: Abbr.
27 Far and ____
28 Old French coins
29 Leader for sent or tend
30 Magazine fillers
33 Religious observances
36 Railroad bridge
38 Comic commentator Mort
39 Jai ____
40 Like Yale's walls
42 Rosemary, for one
44 Actress Farrow
45 Milan moolah
46 Mammy Yokum's creator
47 Chew one's ____; ponder
48 On the lookout
50 Anagram for "else"
51 Besets
53 Rio ____
54 Distant: Pref.
56 Aussie leaper
57 Polite term of address
58 Subway coins
61 Examination
63 One sch.
67 Patrol boat
68 Funny Caesar
69 Lady of Spain
70 Winning
71 Understanding
72 Construction area
74 Kind of light
75 Tangy
76 Units of work
78 Stole cattle
80 One with lofty ambitions?
82 Arid
84 TV control
85 Stand by
86 *Joie de vivre*
87 Marble
88 Liturgical melody
92 Chronicles, in the Douay Bible
96 Actress Ruth ____
97 "Oh, give me ____..."
98 Use a scalpel
99 Restored
100 Muslim judges
101 Have exclusive use of
102 Some NCOs

Down

1 Interstate entry
2 Brilliant fish
3 Italian seaport
4 "Vanity of vanities, all is vanity" book
5 Cut surgically
6 Coins for Cantinflas
7 Once ____ a time...
8 Also-____
9 Like some doughnuts
10 Sneaks off to wed
11 Kayo counters
12 Main, Sesame, etc.
13 Supermarket counters
14 Eats away at
15 Cinematographers
16 From ____ Z
17 Actor Chaney
23 Title holder
25 "Cats" and "Annie"
29 Got ready
30 "____ Three Lives"
31 Baseball's hot corner
32 Roof tile material
33 A season
34 Author Wiesel
35 Berne's river
36 Asparagus parts
37 "____ Spake Zarathustra"
41 Flower holder
43 Theda of film
47 Less distinct
49 Book of five poems
52 Super ending?
53 Citizen addressed by a Bible book
55 Genesis name
57 ____-war; frigate bird
58 Snaps a picture
59 ____ barrel; in trouble
60 Ruler of Judea in 4 B.C.
61 Crusted goodies
62 Realtor's word
64 Prevaricator
65 Beige shade
66 Shea Stadium group
68 Type of gun
73 Ayatollah's follower
74 Farmers, at times
77 13 Down selection
79 London's river
81 Kumquat or tangelo
83 Chest sounds
85 Abates
87 Place: Comb. form
88 Barrack beds
89 In charge: Abbr.
90 Cafe au ____
91 Some are loose
92 Video arcade "man"
93 Triumphal cry
94 Parental nickname
95 Burnsian turndown

166

Originally published in 1989

Hmmm... *by Ronnie K. Allen*

Restating an old proverb for our time with a twist and a bite.

167

Across

1 Lawyer's org.
4 Jazzy phrase
8 Blunder
12 Niger's neighbor
16 Yuppie cheese
18 Stravinsky
19 Traditional knowledge
20 Claudius's home
21 **Start of axiom**
24 "____ La Douce"
25 Rose Parade entry
26 Goose insulation
27 Biblical muscleman
29 Pipe wood
31 Crew tool
32 Cable
33 Sailor's affirmative
34 **Part 2 of axiom**
42 Indonesian island
44 Hip homes
45 Saunter
46 Spill the beans
47 Ways ____
49 Transported
50 Latvian capital
51 Bois de Boulogne, for one
52 Ashen
53 December decor
54 Source of axiom
60 "...no way to treat ____"
61 Dessert wine
62 Phone prefix
63 ____ au lait
64 Numskull
65 Forbearing
69 Front of a cycle?
70 An Age
72 Italian lake
73 Corner
74 **Part 3 of axiom**
78 Prohibition
79 Bridge expert Sharif
80 New World gp.
81 Alex Haley work
83 Robin Hood, in fact
86 One-time presidential candidate
88 "____ is human..."
90 Not a cc
91 **End of axiom**
96 Green Gables girl
97 Enthusiastic
98 Ethereal
99 Hawaiian island
100 Tailless amphibian
101 *Buona* ____
102 Tailless cat
103 Science center

Down

1 Honest president
2 Libber's fire fuel
3 Landing strip
4 "Educating ____"
5 "____ Rhythm"
6 In favor of
7 Working week's ends
8 Aviated
9 Mortgage, for one
10 Subject for Keats
11 Doctor's manner
12 Russian peninsula
13 ____ d'oeuvres
14 Bullets, etc.
15 College official
17 That *femme*
22 Times past
23 Organize
28 Its mascot is a mule
29 Ali *au rhum*?
30 Tatum's dad
31 Auto pioneer
32 Word in Greeley's advice
35 Separate
36 Dressing variety
37 Eggs with a pedigree
38 Goof
39 Whale food
40 Two under par
41 Remains
43 Get in the way
48 Street of the rich
49 Cavalry sword: Var.
50 Actor Redford
52 Drive
53 Oft-quoted patriot
54 ____ *alea est*
55 Rooster replacement
56 "The Godfather" group
57 Once ____ time...
58 Tree-dwelling
67 Trim
68 Column next to ones
70 Big rig
71 ...no lady, ____ my wife!
72 Pitt, Earl of ____
75 Rented a room
76 Wrong, to 1 Across
77 ____ Scott decision
82 Church calendar
83 Vessel
84 Florentine river
85 One of Pinta's partners
86 '60s musical
87 "M*A*S*H" star
88 Mountain lake
89 Black
92 Adam's rib
93 Psalm adverb
94 Cry of discovery
95 Copy a cassette

Seventeen Times Three   *by Walter Covell*

Low overall word count and three long words combine for an excellent challenge.

168

Across

1 Old Spanish kingdom
7 Fern at first
12 Impose a fine
18 Administration
19 Heavy with water vapor
20 A contemporary Cesar
21 Delusion's companions
22 Type type
23 Worthless writings
24 Did alchemy, maybe
27 Commemorative slabs
28 Bermuda, e.g.
29 Napoleonic marshal
31 Adopt
34 "I ___ Know What Time It Was"
37 Sicilian sight
38 Kingdom
39 Triturates
41 Noted wise guy
42 Freshwater fishes
43 Old Roman "Neil Simon"
45 Cubic meters
46 Switch positions
47 Donning sword and buckler
48 Pronoun oft misused
49 Addiction of William F. Buckley, Jr.
55 A memorable Mischa
56 California county
57 Spasm
59 Tulip tree
62 Corporal punishments
64 Murder: Suff.
65 *Élève*'s milieu
66 Dicker
67 Barbecuer's gear
68 Brazilian border river
69 Rose, and others
70 Takes an eye for an eye
72 Dine
73 ___ soda
74 Nests aloft
76 Cézanne or Matisse
83 Tall ship crew member
84 Permitted
85 Served soup
87 Shoe part
88 Strophe, at times
89 Ancient
90 Fretted
91 Moore's TV boss
92 Suit materials

Down

1 ___ *longa, vita...*
2 Torn
3 Culture medium
4 Fire opals
5 Peritoneal fold
6 Headlands
7 Biblical land
8 Consensus
9 Gloss over
10 Hayworth
11 Former British prime minister
12 Grandma Moses, for one
13 Aesopian lesson
14 Send forth
15 Contrite one
16 Belief
17 Dawn goddess
25 Rubber tree
26 Preserves in Poole
30 Asian oxen
31 Therefore
32 Connery and O'Casey
33 Analyze, in English class
34 Jingles
35 Bus. abbr.
36 HST follower
37 Varnish resin
39 Valise
40 Film director Clair
41 Make amends
43 More factual
44 Levantine VIP
45 Cormorants
47 Waters
48 House addition
50 Pierre's room
51 Seed covering
52 Bowling aisle
53 Apian defense
54 Gnatlike fly
58 Tax
59 Pod partners
60 Junk mail recipient
61 Dolphin
62 Kind of sailboat
63 Mature
64 Reflect
66 Tiller
67 Between twelve and twenty
69 Yoked
70 Onassis, to friends
71 Chamber music instruments
73 Deacon's scarf
74 Digression
75 Organic compound
77 Street sign
78 Pretext
79 Tears
80 Bus. study
81 Work long and hard
82 Video broadcast
83 Rel.
86 Dental deg.

Originally published in 1989

Rooked Again! *by Dorothea E. Shipp*

Flights of fancy, executed by an expert from Virginia.

Across

1 TV announcer Don
6 Copied a coot
10 Pant
15 Old marketplaces
17 Bad thoughts
19 ____ now; previously
20 Icarus's avian cousins?
22 Gold or silver
23 Was acquainted with
24 Each
25 Soft topper
27 Prefix for form or cycle
28 ____ Tomé
29 ____ spumante
30 Indian ape
32 Devils
34 Buchwald
35 Minus
36 Chips in
37 Royal angling bird?
42 Coat with plaster
44 ____ midnight; beating curfew
45 Ku ____ Klan
46 Mal de ____
47 Lingerie grouping
50 The Boy King
51 Armor
52 ____-sized
53 Univs.
55 Verdigris: Var.
57 Avian imitators
59 Hire a new crew
60 Glacial ridge
61 Rats!
62 Author Ayn
64 Had a bite
65 Office fixture
66 Time immemorial
67 Cheek: Comb. form
68 Way or code
69 Err
71 Shore bird with a new golf club?
73 Iowa town
75 Leftward, at sea
77 Ex-coach Parseghian
78 Throws about
79 Good news on B'way
80 Grocery store needs
82 Part of RSVP
85 Ancient
86 Wager
88 Indian village
90 Inner Hebrides island
91 Silents actress Pola
93 Avian *siffleur*?
96 Curl one's lip
97 Vergil's hero
98 Moon goddess
99 Roman chariot
100 Agnes, Jeanne, etc.
101 Pools

Down

1 Hikers' gear
2 One rocket
3 Copland work
4 Sketch
5 Primitive propeller
6 Bird of movement?
7 Eye cosmetics
8 Med. test
9 "Go ____, young man"
10 Avian that doesn't know the words?
11 Chemical ending
12 Harmonize
13 Provisions
14 "The Name Game" singer Shirley
16 Nazi symbol
17 DVI doubled
18 Cause wonderment
21 Likely
26 Like the horizon
29 Fido's formulation
31 Quaking forest plant
33 Forever, in poetry
34 Representative: Abbr.
35 Barker of Tarzan fame
37 High-flying birds?
38 Toughened
39 Character
40 Stumbled
41 Faddish gadgets
43 Gallery event
46 "O Sole ____"
48 Eritrea's capital
49 New York Island
51 Derisive avian?
52 Favoring
54 Tattletale
56 Fire boss
58 Writer L. ____ Hubbard
63 Nine-sided figures
67 "The A Team" player
68 Word of discovery
70 MS tagalong
71 Carping birds?
72 Some dads, namewise: Abbr.
73 Steve and Woody
74 Biters
76 Sedum
78 Common or horse
80 Cooper's wares: Abbr.
81 Pasha or Baba
82 Johnny Appleseed, for one
83 Silly
84 Country roads
87 "____ the night before..."
89 Airport info.
90 Capri, for one
92 Female ruff
94 All ____ up; excited
95 Jewel

169

Double Duty *by Louis Sabin*

An expert New Jersey cruciverbalist offers names you know, in surprising ways.

170

Across

1 Ringlet
6 Links norms
10 Burst inward
17 Penthouses
19 "___ a Song..."
20 Landis and King
21 Sad song
22 Location
23 Fancy
24 Vikki and Darleen at the auto museum?
27 Soap box?
28 ___ hat
29 Kind of band or show
31 Homeric opus
34 Genetic material: Abbr.
36 Compass dir.
37 How to address a lady
41 Actress Diana
42 Swell
44 Emulate Hines
47 Palindromic preposition
48 Opinion
49 Asian observance
51 Hair-raisers
52 First-grade subject
55 Dogie call
57 Frankie and Cleo
58 Thomas in Berlin?
61 Get by
64 Challenge Clemens
65 Mediterranean vessel
69 Catapults
71 Fabric
73 Swabby
74 Tokyo, once
75 Defeat
77 Hollows
79 Gymnast Korbut
80 Pitcher
81 Guy's companion
83 Sidekick
84 Teaching tool
85 Spenser's "The ___ Queene"
88 Encountered again
90 Region of NE Spain
94 Kay sings for Judy?
99 Strands

101 Salad protein
102 WW II builder
103 Displays
104 Cut texts
105 Tyson aide
106 Most exacting
107 Strike
108 Winter runners: Var.

Down

1 Soft mineral
2 Tangible
3 Bombeck
4 San Luis snoozes
5 Perceived, in a way
6 Sacristy basin
7 Inter ___
8 Rocket type
9 "Tristram Shandy" author
10 Rocks at the bar
11 Republic near Italy
12 Dress up
13 Theater section
14 Norwegian monarch
15 Brighton sand hill
16 Villa d'___
18 Motivate
25 Make a fuss
26 Enraptured
30 Protein source
31 Conceit
32 Lady's man
33 Vexed
35 Termite's foe
37 Gyrene
38 By-and-by
39 Ranch segment
40 Base food
42 Dives
43 Lowered
45 Jai alai missiles
46 Hose holder
48 Ancient actor
50 Sigma follower
53 Artist
54 Collar
56 Maj. ocean
59 Interdiction
60 Fink

61 Oliver's request
62 Freshly
63 Church area
66 Singer Carter
67 Sidle
68 Winner's reception
70 Professor, perhaps
72 Get-up-and-go
76 Julie Christie role
78 Recite
79 Alice Springs region
82 In the book
84 Meets with again
85 Skywalker's power
86 Sweetens the pot
87 Chopin work
89 Young woman
90 Yemen port
91 Dijon dream
92 Europe's neighbor
93 Chap
95 Indigo
96 Flute's neighbor
97 M. Lacoste
98 Buntline and Beatty
100 Fast Atl. crosser

Originally published in 1989

Zippy Greetings *by Elizabeth T. Holcomb*

As part of her greeting, Ms. Holcomb sent actual postmarks.

Across

1 Burst of activity
6 Politicians William and Robert
11 Olympic uniform initials
14 Loft a baseball
17 Comet heads
18 Setter or terrier
19 Offspring: Comb. form
20 Very early
21 String or sing ___
22 Kenyan pastoral people
23 Mineo of films
24 Quick to understand
25 Shell hurler
27 49862
30 Tarzan
32 Muse of comedy
33 Word curtailment
36 Become known
38 Whimper
42 Fungi growth, in Britain
43 Quartet member
45 Superlative ending
47 Asian language
48 Official doings
49 Conclusion
51 French department
53 Frankfort campus letters
54 Mil. unit
55 Overhang
57 Canadian National Park site
58 Actress Meryl
61 Mason capacity
63 Bulgarian capital
66 Large number
68 Durocher
69 Second sight: Abbr.
72 Vacuum opposite
74 Reform-movement leader
76 Vaudeville singer Bayes
78 Narrow inlet
79 Mountain pool
81 Boxer's best punch
82 Green Mountain name
83 Days of ___
85 Blush
87 Unwholesome
89 Ornamental panel
91 Comic writer
93 99705
96 Plant migration
100 Occupation
101 Star's rep.
102 European siskin
104 City in Kweichow, China
105 Hail, in Mass
106 Cheer unit
107 Boadicea's people
108 Turn inside out
109 Out-of-the-___
110 Function
111 Public fund
112 Stuns

Down

1 Confidence game
2 Kind of shirt
3 Cupid
4 47579
5 Large-footed Aussie bird
6 Dickensian child
7 Birchlike tree
8 Herring catchers
9 Peter or Nicholas
10 Moslem sect
11 Hog the spotlight
12 Perfectly joined
13 Stevenson
14 Used a natatorium
15 Soldier's cap
16 However
26 Kind of theater, in brief
28 Sheriff's district, in Britain
29 Illusionists' org.
31 Corn
33 Today I ___ man
34 Pit
35 Inning tallies
37 Grimace
39 Oxbridge prep school
40 Street urchin
41 Would as ___; gladly
44 80538
46 Forbidden, to some
49 Nav. rank
50 Indian sovereignty
52 23887
56 Soon, to a poet
59 Strained
60 Kind of talk
62 Opponent
63 Still kicking
64 Miscellany
65 Carolina cape
67 Came out of a trance
70 Manhattan art center
71 Malay boat: Var.
73 Will-o'-the-wisp
75 Spiced wine
77 Test resp.
80 "___ Wild Wind" (De Mille '42 film)
82 Demanded
84 Be human?
86 Of river-mouth regions: Var.
88 Group: Suff.
90 Japanese seaport
92 Actor Claude
93 Pop star?
94 Comply with
95 Apiece
97 Mideast canal
98 Concerning
99 Poses
100 Tooth holder
103 Son of a louse

171

Living Proof *by Elizabeth Arthur*

A favorite theme, excellently executed.

Across

1 Succotash beans
6 Nematode's chemoreceptor
12 Not express
17 Wipe out
18 Inner-ear part
20 Rust
21 Balderdash!
23 Essence
24 '30s actress Dvorak
25 Catchers' gear
26 Receives visitors
28 Gymnast's move
29 Whiskey choices
31 ____ Vegas
32 Bill add-on
34 ____ over; study
35 Kind of order
37 Spanish coin
38 Heavy-fisted blow
39 Cycles' kin
42 Made over
43 D.C. leader
44 "*Deutschland über* ____"
45 Belonging to one of Jacob's wives
46 Runs amok
48 Disparaging remark
49 Cringe
50 What sailors develop
52 Tic-____-toe
53 Egg deliverer
55 Black gold
57 Hit the road!: Dial.
59 Lassos
60 Book or folk follower
61 "Little Orphan ____"
62 Tendon
63 Comes in last
64 Official proceedings
65 Baseball's "Big Poison"
66 Breaks 65 mph
67 Dull pain
68 Objects
70 Perukes
71 Jewish rite
72 Sways
73 "Peck's ____ Boy"
74 Road repair warning
78 ____ room
79 Fur source
80 Walkway
82 Japanese sash
83 Jack ____, double-take artist
85 Killer instinct
89 Representative
90 SO₄ compound
91 Herb of the carrot family
92 Fender bender results
93 Dinnerware
94 Tied up

Down

1 "Merry Widow" composer
2 O. Henry specialty
3 Famous WW I battlefield
4 Apuleius's "The Golden ____"
5 Appear
6 Kind of acid
7 Castles' surroundings
8 Hundredths: Abbr.
9 LBJ's veep
10 ____-de-France
11 Criticized
12 Spare
13 Famed defenseman
14 Ruin
15 Esteems
16 Frog, for instance
19 Plus-side item
22 Replenishes
27 George's usual lyricist
30 Steak on the hoof
32 False clues
33 Egyptian goddess
34 La ____, Indiana
36 Commercials
37 The dove symbolizes it
39 Double feature on a schooner
40 Spanish cooking pots
41 Prepare a fowl meal?
42 French annuity
43 Many: Comb. form
45 Hosiery thread
46 Subscribe again
47 Hunter and Fleming
49 African gully
50 Great!
51 Begat
53 Writer Ferber
54 Nickname for Doctor McCoy
56 Not so much
58 Plays poker
60 Loamy deposit
62 Declined
63 Camper's fuel: Abbr.
64 Farmland
65 Tepee's cousin: Var.
66 Move crabwise
67 Overseas
68 Three, in combos
69 Sharpens
70 Gets clean
73 Please (Ger.)
75 Reasoning
76 Unpleasingly plump
77 Played electrician
79 Shea team
80 ...to buy ____ pig
81 Relative of etc.
84 Bankbook abbr.
86 Building wing
87 Two ____ kind
88 One ____ million

172

Originally published in 1989

Place Settings by M.R.

Everything in its place.

173

Across

1 Showed concern
6 "Camille" author
11 Roles
16 Fernando's friend
17 Region of east-central Europe
19 Docket doing
20 Valedictorian's place
22 Big bird
23 Palindromic preposition
24 ___ the bill; paid
25 Pre-revolution ruler
27 Coal scuttle
28 City on the Truckee
30 "Moon ___ Miami"
31 Fast-fading phone feature
32 Alps, Rockies, etc.
33 Old hat
35 Government official, in Canada
37 School papers
39 Soave or claret
40 Abalone
42 Julius or Sid
43 Heels
44 Enjoyed appreciatively
46 Chagrin
47 Adoring
48 Revealing photo?
49 Sphere or system starter
50 Hollywood's Hayworth
51 Wholesaler
53 Sandpaper stuff
54 UK–Can. separator
55 Carry on
56 Historical periods
57 Minoan's island
58 Go to ___; deteriorate
60 Seeks alms
61 Wailed
62 Blazing
63 Pod packings
64 Grand ___, Michigan
65 Smaller than tiny
67 Chief Scandinavian god
68 Fusses
70 Lacrosse teams
71 Yemen Arab Republic capital
72 Adages
76 Atlas abbr.
77 Mata ___
78 Skedaddles
80 Fraternity letter
81 Heston's 1971 film, "The ___ Man"
83 Hell, perhaps
86 Deserve
87 Looked into
88 Rag
89 NAACP and NCAA
90 ___ up; clinched
91 Commits miner fraud?

Down

1 Bring the food
2 Love, Italian style
3 Mature
4 Cause of "I" strain
5 Remove
6 Counted calories
7 One result of stress
8 Canasta play
9 Pretty ___ picture
10 Vatican visit highlight
11 Wing: Comb. form
12 Ex-coach Parseghian
13 Ecclesiastical title
14 Claw
15 Pungs
17 Hard nudges
18 Very, to Verdi
21 Horn blower
26 Loser
29 "Potemkin" mutiny port
31 Uproars
32 Office note
34 Asian nurse
35 Where to find anvil and stirrup
36 "Iliad" locale
37 "Bewitched" baby
38 Fix what's in the doggie bag
39 Magician's prop
41 Says
42 Jeweler's weight
43 Zip or area
44 Mardi ___
45 Played gramps
47 Eden fruit
48 Dec. holiday
51 Purplish red
52 Bits of work
53 Rye and wheat
55 Had on
57 Manage
59 Molds
60 Some are workers
61 Bovary or Butterfly
63 Wings
64 Gerald, Jimmy, ___
66 Some Slavs
67 Got cozy
68 Bakery enticement
69 Parking meter fodder, once
71 Range
73 Dismay: Var.
74 Bridge forerunner
75 Locations
77 Bowlers
78 Pack away
79 Concordes, etc.
82 Card game for two
84 Foot part
85 Black or Yellow

Sizing Things Up *by William Lutwiniak*

"I think no virtue goes with size."—Ralph Waldo Emerson

Across

1 Saudi
5 Reverberate
9 Like a pilgarlic
13 Type style: Abbr.
17 '30s actress Damita
18 Four roods
19 Out of the gale
20 Colorado feeder
21 On a roll
24 Golden Rule word
25 Gaston's god
26 Judge
27 Coloring item
29 Actor Finney
32 One schoolchild
33 Halloween trickster
34 Lanark landowner
35 Has a hankering
36 Certain pigeons
39 Saturnalia
40 Certain bass
42 Actress Farrow
43 NCO
44 Areca or areng
45 Pipe bends
46 Plays parts
47 Takeover
49 Collations
51 Reynolds and Lancaster
52 Does not
53 Twoscore
54 Much-heard
55 Slithered
56 Charon's craft
57 In black and white
59 Hoohas
60 "Winnie ____ Pu"
61 Transaction
62 DOD VIP
63 Capitol VIP
64 Midnight to dawn
67 Chastity's mother
68 Tenets
70 Previously
71 Sends off
72 Winter apples
73 Dele not
74 Go pell-mell
75 Manhattan Transfer hit
77 Detected
78 ____-war
79 Held up

174

80 Gradually
86 Niche object
87 Check manuscripts
88 Arrange
89 "____ a Male War Bride"
90 Staff: Abbr.
91 Illustrator Gustave
92 Mineral baths
93 Lackwit

Down

1 Math subj.
2 Ramon's river
3 Actress MacGraw
4 Bookmaker's plant
5 Actress Debra ____
6 Beige
7 "You ____ There"
8 In front
9 Holey roll
10 Reuner
11 Author Deighton
12 Writes at length
13 Part of a Tennessee Williams title
14 "A Christmas Carol" role
15 Chorister
16 Laudanum, today
22 Encircle
23 Laconic
28 Actress Roman
29 At ____; confused
30 Daunting task
31 Wheeler-dealer
32 Invader of a kind
33 Moves freight
35 Cavett's school
36 Rashness
37 "The Old Curiosity Shop" girl
38 Impudence
40 ____ Porsena
41 Substantive
44 Golf stroke
46 Family female
48 ____ up; fastens
49 Edible mushroom
50 Goof up

51 Wicket topper
53 Topples
54 Lingerie grouping
55 Harp
56 Some condominiums
57 Wolf type
58 Scandinavian
60 Made go
61 Air handler
64 Teamster unit
65 Convention site
66 Unity
67 Neck artery
69 Defrauds
71 He played Pasteur
73 *Otto* preceder
74 Ceases
75 Radarscope item
76 Sprint
77 Swizzle
78 Dame Hess
81 Court vow
82 Jazz style
83 Pair
84 Drink like Tabby
85 Canton follower

Originally published in 1989

In So Many Words *by Manny Miller*

Taking the long way around.

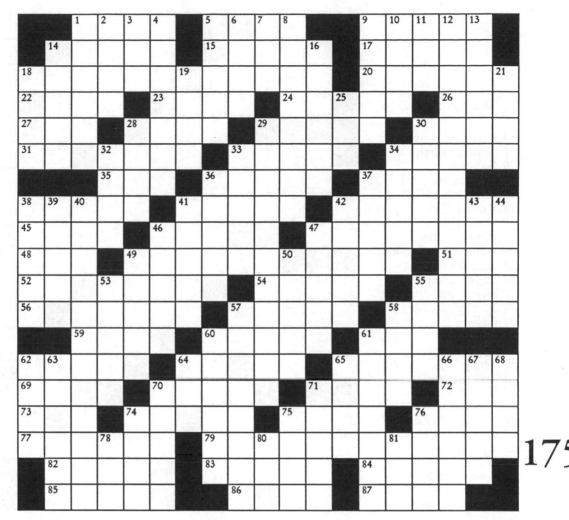

175

Across

1 Grey or McCrea
5 Electrical unit
9 Swamp swimmer, for short
14 Permission to be absent
15 Up and ____
17 ____ at the office
18 Recklessly
20 Soft caps
22 Aardvark's meals
23 Follow
24 Leg joints
26 Fish delicacy
27 Vocal or local ending
28 ____ and woolly
29 Charlie Chan portrayer
30 Supermarket aid
31 To a great extent
33 Levels
34 ____ Arenas, Chile
35 Public notices
36 Top
37 Like worn tires
38 Steals
41 County carnivals
42 Range
45 Concerning
46 Around
47 Likely
48 Wait and ____
49 Informal
51 Fulcrum piece
52 Twelve-year-olds
54 Earthenware
55 Tel ____, Israel
56 Dirty
57 Celestial body
58 Locale
59 Giraffe feature
60 Musical comedy
61 Knight's title
62 Core group
64 One on the run
65 Fulton and Vaughn
69 Curves
70 Craze

71 Wraps
72 Corrode
73 Wire measure
74 Spud
75 Detailed program
76 Eye amorously
77 Written in verse
79 Repeatedly
82 Pan-fry
83 Wading bird
84 Rock scratch
85 Satellite's path
86 Bar for draft animals
87 Foreboding

Down

1 Professional fool
2 Feed bag filling
3 London's Le Gallienne
4 Soup stuff
5 Cogent; sound
6 Old Greek coin
7 Old card game
8 Like some elephants

9 Scoffed
10 Lifetimes
11 Sailor
12 Besides
13 Cutting reply
14 Tenor Mario
16 Occupant
18 Lose strength
19 Actor James
21 ____ precedent
25 Printing measures
28 Unites
29 Several times
30 Mea ____
32 Amount taken in
33 Soap villain Kane
34 Namby follower
36 Concerns
37 Increase
38 Speaks childishly
39 Sluggish
40 Unencumbered
41 Wicked one
42 Skill; knack
43 Murdered
44 Hold office

46 Brook
47 Martinique volcano
49 Barrier
50 Protest
53 Stadium areas
55 Land measure
57 Rapidity of action
58 Relatives
60 Comic strip canine
61 Unnamed person
62 Tent area
63 Musical passage
64 Got to know
65 Sorrel or bay
66 Get back
67 "Rocky" player Shire
68 Submachine gun
70 Cut gem surface
71 Eubie or Amanda
74 South American monkey
75 Make coffee
76 Fairy tale principal
78 Old, slow boat
80 Pasture plaint
81 U. of pressure

Originally published in 1989

Just Desserts *by Walter Covell*

Eat, drink, and be merry, for tomorrow we diet.

Across

1 Computer input
5 Muscle twitch
10 GP's org.
13 Grande, for one
16 Some exams
18 Author Bret
19 Game fish
21 Fruited dessert
24 Addison's collaborator
25 ____ precedent
26 Equine creatures
27 Diving bell inventor
29 Smithy's item
31 Café au ____
34 Kennel cry
37 Drain
38 Yearn
42 Dairy dessert
44 Eccentric one
46 Priest of Troy
48 "____ and Old Lace"
50 Reception dessert
52 Actress Arthur
53 Erode
55 Footed the bill
56 Diminutive endings
57 Annual desserts
61 Assail
64 Coconut fiber
65 *Juillet et Août*
66 Decimal point
69 Fruit desserts
72 Toward the sunrise
75 Impartial
76 Kristofferson of film
78 Frozen dessert
79 Lairs
80 Former South
Vietnam rebel org.
82 Eve's youngest
84 Glasgow girl
85 Fine thread
87 Art ____
89 Infinitesimal
93 War god
96 Neglected regions
100 Baked dessert
104 Fretted
105 Packing box
106 Manicurist's concerns
107 Printing measures
108 Weather vane dir.
109 Royal house of Henry
VIII

176

110 Gram or vision starter

Down

1 ____ Passos
2 College course
3 Pastry dessert
4 Wings
5 Ally of "Short
Circuit"
6 Equality
7 LAX notices
8 Eye irritation
9 Partying Perle
10 From ____ Z
11 Confectionary dessert
12 Soviet cooperative
13 Lion's vocalization
14 ____ dinka do
15 Carbohydrate endings
17 Add sugar
20 Toxic chem.
22 Coll. deg.
23 Brinker
28 Dry, winewise

30 Substantiate
31 Attract
32 Handle
33 Mamie's spouse
35 Ordinance
36 Dessert makers
38 Auditor's concerns, in
brief
39 Paint layer
40 Misrepresent
41 Hydrocarbon endings
42 Boxer's move
43 Row
45 June 6, 1944
47 Curved molding
49 Derisive hoots
51 Gaming cubes
54 Quaker's pronoun
57 Girds
58 Roman passage
59 Tom, ____, and Harry
60 Ferocious parrots
61 Alexander's group
62 Fencer's handful
63 Twirled
66 Society teens

67 Cinnabar and hematite
68 Explosive letters
70 Medicinal plants
71 German pronoun
73 Wise Biblical king
74 Refrain syllable
77 Norm: Abbr.
81 Musical symbol
83 Assistant
85 Social standouts
86 Upright
88 President's mil. title
89 Land measure
90 At that time
91 Galoot's exclamation
92 AT&T competitor
94 Grayish yellow
95 Food fish
97 Gravy container
98 Migrant worker
99 Window ledge
101 Summer drink
102 Robert ____ of
"Quincy"
103 Ending for Canton or
Japan

Originally published in 1989

Planter's Punch Lines *by Wilson McBeath*

Mr. McBeath has sown some wild seeds for your pleasure.

Across

1 Singer Reese
6 Worn
12 Lupino and Tarbell
16 Inventor Howe
17 "The Big ____" (1980 war film)
18 Bird's delicacy
19 Like Kate, if Allie punched her?
23 End for fabric or domestic
24 Top rating, sometimes
25 French planes
26 Fateful time
28 Cato's 151
29 Cookie
31 Pitcher's stat
32 Friendliness
35 Mimicked
37 Symbol of the good life
38 Bovary and Samms
39 Marten's cousins
42 Of the Arctic
43 Concept
44 Donald the dealer
45 Plebe
46 Capital of Somme
48 Diminutive suffix
49 Duffer's dream
50 Integuments
52 State
54 Peach stone
55 "Magister Ludi" writer
57 Moola
58 Bakery product
59 Compass pt.
60 Trenchermen
62 Put to service
63 Asiatic palm
64 Court events
66 Swindle
68 Of nil face value, as some stocks
69 Chip in chips
70 Bellamy or Edwards
71 Lucky numbers
72 Saddle girth
74 Seeger and Rose
75 Main church part
76 Confused
78 Impresario Hurok
79 Dear (Ger.)
83 Formerly called
84 Indian princess
85 Pattern junctures
87 FDR brainstorm
88 Old horses
90 Poultry house contents?
94 Seaweed
95 Riata
96 Craggy abode
97 Being (Lat.)
98 Moves furtively
99 Computer memory measure

Down

1 Obligations
2 Scott's "Lady of the Lake"
3 Climbing vine
4 Fond du ____, WI
5 Interrogates
6 Singer Payne
7 Communists
8 Classifieds
9 "____ Send Me"
10 One who stores fodder
11 Fatal
12 This ____ fine how-do-you-do!
13 Amsterdam smoker's need?
14 Asia Minor region
15 Decorticates
20 Rapiers
21 Home playground
22 Recent: Pref.
27 From Göteborg
30 Assassinated Stockholm prime minister
32 Arranged
33 Overjoyed
34 Freshwater duck
36 Kind of talk
37 Scepter
39 Dance elements
40 Musician
41 Dairyman's concern?
42 Decode, grammatically
43 Reflection
45 Forms in a foundry
46 Divert
47 Mariana island
49 Norman Vincent ____
51 Unpolished
53 Time periods
55 Shrub of Scotland
56 Worker ant
61 Like shoes
63 New
65 Comprehensive: Abbr.
67 Good times
68 Neighbor of Ida.
70 Of an eye part
71 Game ragout
72 Where Hannibal defeated Rome
73 Archetypes
74 Juries
75 Webster
77 Exclamation of disgust
78 Religious groups
80 Like radon or neon
81 Tennessee ____ Ford
82 Headquarters
85 Huron's st.
86 Wound cover
89 Org. for some GM workers
91 Jackie's second
92 Author Anaïs
93 West, for one

177

Boxquote   by William A. Smith

This puzzle features a line from Goethe running clockwise in the grid
starting at 36 Across.

Across

1 Kind of gas
5 Judge's bench
9 Domesticate
13 Hit
17 Sweet spire
18 Quechuan
19 Indigo dyestuff
20 Swingin' Horne
21 Hell
23 Forces to prison
25 Extol
26 "Alas," to Hans
28 Shoelace tip: Var.
29 Insect: Comb. form
30 "___ a Match"
34 "Common Sense"
   author
35 Golf starting places
36 **Start of Boxquote**
38 Necessitude
39 Perlman of "Cheers"
40 Salami cutters
42 Like acetic acid
46 Leningrad's river
47 Couch potato's gadget
50 Floating bridge
   pontoon
51 Starch source
54 Snake or lizard
56 New York county
57 Move furtively
59 Caused trouble
60 Fashion choice
62 Offer at a price
63 Yiddish gossips
64 Length measures:
   Abbr.
65 Actress Redgrave
67 Viennese
69 Lanes
72 Morse Code units
73 Carry on
76 **Boxquote, part 3**
78 SSS rookies
82 Wall hanging
84 Strove toward
85 **Boxquote source**
86 Jewelled headpieces
88 Yoko ___
89 "___ bomb"
   (anti-nuke battle cry)
90 Discover
93 Office fastener
96 Look intently
97 Wheel shaft
98 Hot spot
99 Heavenly instrument
100 Certain linemen
101 Sets
102 Posted
103 Bone: Comb. form

Down

1 Shoulder covering
2 Forever, to Shelley
3 Charge with gas
4 Broadcasts
5 Use the teeth
6 Cuckoo-family bird
7 Sgt., e.g.
8 False story
9 Durham native
10 Anecdotal collection
11 CCCXXXIV tripled
12 Fitzgerald
13 Catch phrases
14 Ear of corn, to Botha
15 Coal tar derivative
16 Sipped
22 Doctrine
24 Van Winkle, for one
27 Bees' chasers?
30 Girl's name meaning
   "goddess"
31 Centers
32 Supreme Norse god
33 More pleasant
36 **End of boxquote**
37 **Boxquote, part 2**
39 ___ available; at hand
41 Two-edged swords
42 Like one
   meteorologist's device
43 Newspaper articles
44 Simon or Armstrong
45 Asian beasts
47 Band of color, in
   zoology
48 Free of dirt
49 Beatty film
50 Danish physicist
52 Regret
53 ___ podrida
55 Wife of "The Captain"
58 Rube Goldberg affair
61 "___ Gay" (famed
   B-29)
66 Makes like a shrew
68 Dupin's pseudonym
69 Porters
70 Declares under oath
71 Leg bone
73 Algonquian thread:
   Var.
74 Up
75 Enriched, as by
   presence
77 Conditions of battle
   fatigue, strine style
78 Cattle farm
79 Single-edged sword:
   Var.
80 Popular pullover
81 Siberian plain
83 Patriotic org.
85 1955 film, "The ___
   Horizons"
87 Kind of party
89 Inclined
91 Lizzie Borden's alleged
   tool
92 Not well
94 Hail, to Caesar
95 Stir

178

Originally published in 1989

Five by Nineteen *by Yvonne R. Helms*

Interlocking long entries always results in fine puzzling.

Across

1 Wood strips
6 Loudly, like Simba
11 Kind of wave
16 Flynn of film
17 Rising above the water
19 Action locale
20 Southeastern U.S. turtle
23 Annapolis insignia
24 Carried on
25 Operatic Estes
26 Devoured
27 Annoyance
29 ____ diem
30 Element used in metallurgy
31 Fastener
32 Estrada's series
34 Grimaces
35 Gym pad
36 Croce's "bad" Brown
37 Quickness
38 Skin
40 Trigonometry ratios
41 Jazz style
42 Most conspicuous
44 Food fishes
45 Aussie creature
47 Breathing sound
48 Sgt., e.g.
49 Blatant nationalist
53 Confine
54 Exigency
55 Burn
56 Oven
57 Inheritances
59 Word in a society column
60 Holds sway
61 Hindu wraps
62 Prison guard, in B films
65 Conclusion
66 Recline
67 Birds larger than geese
68 1969 Hitchcock film
69 Put ____ on it!
71 ____ over; raves
72 Bowler's target
73 Magic lantern
76 French possessive

77 Throw
78 Smoothes
80 Confucian's "path"
81 Backlash against eggheads
85 Tour of duty
86 Coat features
87 On the rampage
88 Bobby ____
89 Charger
90 Musical sounds

Down

1 ____ to; preceded
2 Originate
3 Of a visionary philosophy
4 Alike: Comb. form
5 Snaillike
6 Dark orange-yellow
7 Scan
8 Tolkien monster
9 Tries to date
10 Pensioner

11 Mountain pool
12 IRS foiler of a sort
13 Division into sections
14 Santa ____
15 Like many city streets
17 Rims
18 Salesroom pitches
21 Soho diaper
22 Reagan
28 Beat
30 Derek and Diddley
31 Poet
33 Kayo counts
34 Sap source
35 Donnybrook
36 Elsa, for one
37 Keep
38 "La ____ Vita"
39 Self-disciplined states
40 Range
41 Portends
42 River craft
43 Civil wrongs
45 Where Namath wore braces
46 Printed commercials

47 Extend a subscription
50 Free
51 Yearns
52 Of a part of speech
58 Waterless
60 Cleave
62 Turns
63 Small cloak
64 Hosp. workers
65 Buffet centerpiece
67 Lanky one's nickname
68 Hues
69 Pull together
70 In a slow manner, to Mehta
71 Marsh
72 ____ off; measured
74 Billiards shot
75 Apples and pears
77 Success stories
78 Golfer Ballesteros, to pals
79 Experienced seaman
82 Squid's defense
83 Appomattox figure
84 Old card game

179

In Vogue *by Bernice Gordon*

After a fashion.

180

Across

1 Winter sports locale
5 "___ Lap"
9 Stare openmouthed
13 Rooster's crest
17 Tuneful air
18 Thread
19 Makes angry
20 Soviet range
21 Filmdom's Sharif
22 Vulcan's workshop
23 Frolic
24 Set right
25 Summer topper
27 Levis
29 Sit for Wyeth
30 Cows
32 Parent, for one: Abbr.
33 Feel the heat
36 "...___ I saw Elba"
37 Rowboat metal pin
41 Bit parts
42 Jump
46 Jejune
47 Charity
48 Seabirds
49 Made use of
51 Beauty's friend
53 Part of a play
54 Made an assertion
55 Method of skiing
58 Moderately slow, to
   Muti
61 Intention
62 Type size
67 Punish severely
68 Virginia, for one
69 Frenzied
70 Athletic contest
71 Grape disease
73 People conquered by
   the Romans
75 Kind of drum
77 To a ___; as one
78 Got serious
79 Sandy's sound
81 ___ facto
83 Former TV emcee
84 Ulsters
88 Dress trimming
93 Burst of laughter
94 Western state
95 Unit of wood
96 Impression
97 Frost
98 "Rosanna" musicians
99 St. crossers
100 Bills
101 Baseball's Slaughter
102 Small barracuda
103 Make over
104 Once, once

Down

1 Crooked
2 Succotash bean
3 Have in mind
4 Like some gowns
5 Delights
6 Over here
7 Moffo of opera
8 Lariat
9 Sir William, and kin
10 Soviet body of water
11 Brazil's neighbor
12 Ridge of coarse gravel
13 Coat fabric
14 Olive genus
15 Author of "The Magic
   Mountain"
16 Invitations
26 Marquand sleuth
28 Fast flyer
31 Leather boots
33 Mark of healing
34 Corduroy rib
35 Samms of "Dynasty"
38 Shield part
39 Spoke an untruth
40 Byrnes, the actor
42 Bolivia's capital
43 Meter preceder
44 Italian measures
45 Tied
48 British Order
50 Field
52 Comparison word
54 Wane
56 Refer ending
57 Tibetan gazelles
58 Southern constellation
59 High time
60 Rodeo wear
63 Smock frock
64 African potentate: Var.
65 Voice quality
66 ___ out; made do
67 Dinner check
68 Album entry
72 Do like
73 Disparaging
   characterization
74 Down with (Fr.)
76 Grampus
78 Restrained from
80 Dan ___, retired
   NFL great
82 Jazzy Peterson
84 Fictional villain
85 Hollow
86 Lincoln of the silents
87 On the peak
89 Used a shuttle
90 Czech river
91 Involved schemes
92 Political cartoonist

Originally published in 1989

On a Role   by William Canine

Notable portrayals.

181

Across

1 One step
5 Merman role
10 USAir posting
14 Pennies: Abbr.
17 Biblical kingdom
18 Countertenors
19 ____ way; never
20 With it
21 Richard Burton role
23 Atmosphere
24 Surface measure
25 Dramatist George
26 Negative
27 Opposed to
28 Other (Sp.)
29 Sediment
31 Errol Flynn role
34 Jolt
35 St. Patrick's land
36 Corrupt
37 Sioux
40 Timber wolf
42 Ubangi tributary
43 Brunchtime choice
44 Andress role
46 Tree seed
48 Spanish women
49 Taunt
50 Superficial
54 "____ Clear Day..."
55 Injure
56 Halftime group
57 MacGraw
58 Great ____, Utah
61 Porter
62 ____ one's ways; stubborn
64 Golf name of fame
65 To the point
66 Expand
67 Wotan
69 Spring
71 Revised
72 Tomorrow, in Tampico
74 Writer Harte
77 Tasseled topper
78 Charles Laughton role
80 Lots
83 Just
84 Spy
85 Spoiled
87 Active
89 Le ____ soleil
90 Fountain
91 Peter O'Toole role
93 Owing
94 Sask. neighbor
95 Dunne
96 Noddy
97 Pope's title: Abbr.
98 Borneo native: Var.
99 A-wandering
100 Listen to

Down

1 Furtive look
2 Enlarged
3 Cringe
4 Paul Muni role
5 Fairy queen
6 North Carolina college
7 Moe Howard role
8 Stagger
9 Fire residue
10 Chinese river
11 Pat O'Brien role
12 Caruso
13 ____ favor; help
14 Property
15 Mundane
16 Javelin
22 Denies
27 Ligurian Sea feeder
28 Belgian port
30 Cat fight
32 Houston pro
33 Driving maneuver
37 Dullards
38 Iowa town
39 Atatürk
41 Igneous rock
44 Calm
45 Haw's partner
47 Human ending
49 Robert DeNiro role
51 ____ home; dine in
52 Jet set
53 Longed for
55 Witch
56 Gillespie's jazz
59 In a sparse way
60 Hawaiian porch
61 Blue Grotto isle
62 Motorcycle adjunct
63 Bette Davis role
66 Crossword clues: Abbr.
67 Menacing
68 Played around
70 Fit
73 To wit
75 First king of the English
76 Former German coin: Var.
78 Verbs and adverbs
79 Desolate
81 Gift recipient
82 Ecuador's monetary unit
86 Wynter or Andrews
88 Look after
90 Tablet
91 "My Country, ____ of thee..."
92 Thames tributary

Radio Days *by Roger H. Courtney*

Remembrances of things past.

Across

1 Old saw
6 Picnic shelters
13 Circuit; scope
18 Sink
19 Bowling ball material
20 Pamphleteer Thomas
21 Writer _____ Rogers St. Johns
22 George and Gracie
24 Leech, perhaps
26 Aliens: Abbr.
27 100 dinars
28 WWII Greek resistance force
29 *Avril, _____, juin*
30 Tenon's companion
33 Pinnacles
36 Arrests
38 Times without end
39 Master Brinker
40 Stadium sounds
42 Genealogy abbr.
44 Crooner Cole
45 Cain's brother
46 Kind of test
47 Central
48 Metric unit in Montreal
50 Stun
51 Flight deck person
53 Ground corn flour
54 Like Steven?
56 Neither's partner
57 Diving bird
58 Baked-potato topping
61 "_____ Babe," Sonny & Cher hit
63 Verve
67 Coty and Descartes
68 Onager
69 "Terrible" ruler
70 Italian painter
71 Op _____
72 Danny DeVito sitcom
74 Modify
75 Flour container
76 "Thanatopsis," for one
78 Snuggles
80 Troop camps
82 Fills with anger
84 Kin of atmo
85 Branding _____
86 A code
87 Lyricist Gershwin
88 Segmented
92 The All-American Boy
96 Aviator-politician Balbo
97 "Bonanza," for one
98 Because challenged
99 Perverse card game
100 Demotes
101 Chimes hammer
102 Drag through the mud

182

Down

1 "I'm _____ boy," said Costello
2 Miami's county
3 Confused
4 "Great" personality
5 Make possible
6 McEntire and others
7 Border on
8 Afr. kingdom
9 Tempers
10 Condense: Var.
11 Taxonomic suffixes
12 D.C. figure
13 Fifteen-two and _____; cribbage score
14 Chemical compound
15 A _____ one shot; very high odds
16 Chemical ending
17 Number for Bo Derek
23 Refuse
25 Early radio show
29 Ovolo and torus
30 The talking horse
31 Traffic tie-up
32 Lauder of cosmetics
33 Roe source
34 Sun-block chem.
35 Don Juan's mother
36 Cut
37 Mine entrance
41 College subj.
43 TV ad award
47 _____ Snerd
49 "Twilight Zone," old radio style
52 Old card game
53 Six-_____; projectile-throwing guns
55 Give legally
57 Provide temporarily
58 _____ myrtle
59 Wading bird
60 Cooperates
61 Wife of Osiris
62 Actor Montand
64 Jump
65 Common suffix
66 Ends for refuse and sput
68 Hews
73 Lend _____; listen
74 Lombardy patriot
77 Grocery
79 Type of sauce
81 Cambers
83 Transmission parts
85 Actress Stevens
87 "Say It _____ So"
88 Concerning
89 Account
90 First name in scat
91 Entryway
92 Patient one
93 Non-pro alliance
94 Nov., Dec., etc.
95 Mature acorn

Once Is Not Enough *by Robert A. Sefick*

Enjoy! Enjoy!

183

Across

1 Scene set
4 Break the bonds
10 Knocking noise
17 Porcine parent
18 ____ gold
19 Came from (a source)
21 "____ time..." (Story opener for John-John?)
23 Tree ornament
24 Hauls again
25 They buy anything
27 Parisian's world
28 Upsets
29 Big whip
31 Range rope
33 Crystal gazer's asset: Abbr.
34 Believers
36 Soviet co-op
38 Hill dweller
40 One Ford
41 "I thought ____ pussycat!"
42 Like the old school
46 ____ as Rockefeller
48 Alpine river
50 Voice of "Lonely Boy"
51 Wield the axe
53 Previously
54 Kind of pay
55 Lombardy's metropolis
56 All shook up
58 Old youngsters
59 Office directive
60 Byron heroine
61 French dance: Var.
62 One-liner
63 Pot top
64 It was Christiania
65 Semi-desert tableland
66 Hunting trip
68 Letterer's aid
70 Ablush
72 Some chinos
75 Cumberland, for one
76 ____ firma
77 ____ Gardens
78 Current measure: Abbr.
81 Where to grab knaves
83 Melville book
85 ____ girl!
86 The pit's bottom
88 Proportion
90 Posy tosser
92 Horace Mann
94 Suddenly, to JoJo?
96 TV, at times
97 Runyonesque racehorse
98 Middle: Abbr.
99 Made a fist
100 Lays down the law
101 Kind of curve

Down

1 In the saddle
2 Flincher
3 Old song for Duran Duran?
4 German's name for the Ohre
5 Card party seats
6 Thicket
7 Scene
8 First woman, in Greek myth
9 Biblical bad trader
10 Annul
11 Mile's equivalent?
12 Sunbathe
13 Delicate flower
14 Tex-Mex snack
15 Make up
16 Cares for
20 Heavy, man
22 Currant syrup
26 Cheerful
30 Precipitous
32 With it
35 Mother ____
37 Quick look, for Humbert Humbert?
39 Bent
41 Man or box leader
42 Iron, naturally
43 "You ____" (Shirley Maclaine's motto?)
44 Giraffe's kin
45 Leonine
47 NYC subway
49 Chicago transits
51 Angel toppers
52 Cast out
54 Most rigorous
55 Giant: Comb. form
57 Beside
58 Price holder
59 Brit. fliers
61 Set
62 Riant
65 Palm
66 Grand ____
67 Pan or rave
69 Complex composition
71 Overanxious one
73 Bugs
74 They look and look
76 Watered
77 Type of pin
78 Dazzles
79 Computer communication device
80 Lip-purser
82 Back up
84 One tribe
87 Check
89 Shakespearean villain
91 AAA suggestions
93 ____-tac-toe
95 Was in the vanguard

Pun Fun by Jeanne Wilson

More paronomasia from Pennsylvania.

184

Across

1 "___ Entertain You"
6 Entertainer Moreno
10 Dance, for example
13 Matlock matter
17 Lukewarm
18 QED part
19 Harbor cities
21 Hornlike
22 Cupola topper
23 Insect appendages
24 "Delta Queen" trip?
27 Saxony river
28 Jacob's big brother
29 "___: A Roman Space Odyssey"?
30 Assn.
32 ___ favor; please
34 Pass catchers
36 Like a conga line
40 Pasture parent
42 Young socialites
44 Ripens
46 Kind of club
47 Deft
49 Garage happening
51 Ordinal suffixes
53 S.A. country
54 Eye part
56 Pinochle honors
58 Track tipster's forte
60 Weekend pass result?
63 Hairy
66 Comic swamp critter
67 Dazed state
71 Idaho county
72 Shade trees
74 Enthralled
76 "You're ___, Alice!"
77 Smirky type
79 Puppy's cry
81 "Wizard of Oz" actor
83 Poet Burns, for one
84 Leon Uris novel
86 Scheherazade specialty
88 Meadow
89 Frankfort campus letters
90 Sleep cycle: Abbr.
92 Mrs. Nick Charles
94 Lorry, yankee style
97 Nursery window ritual?
102 Like some sales
103 Raison d'___
104 Scottish hills
106 Lamp fuel
107 Fancy flounder?
108 Right-hand page
109 Icon
110 Mom's mate
111 *Very* French
112 Play host

Down

1 Jean-___ Godard of film
2 Genesis name
3 Dished a southern dish?
4 The world, in Paris
5 Needle cases
6 Run of bad luck
7 Persia, these days
8 *La plume de ma* ___
9 Military command
10 Sober ___
11 Nevada gambling town
12 John McEnroe's wife
13 Submarine's ___ tower
14 "God Save the King" composer
15 Corset part
16 Chin chaser?
20 Hairdressers give them
25 Famed anthropologist
26 Turner
30 General Bradley
31 Fad
33 Ease up
35 Brief brawl
37 Asian range
38 Composer Jerome
39 Thug
41 Walter ___ Disney
43 Nod off
45 Not tall
48 Follow
50 Biblical witch's home
52 Above
55 In a fitting way
57 Actor George
59 Russian rulers
61 Pay
62 Fossil resin
63 Possesses, old style
64 Distinct, in combos
65 Incline
68 Nolte's talent?
69 Lovebird talk
70 "___, *Bruté?*"
73 Star-___ Banner
75 "I Talk to ___" (Lerner song)
78 Freckle protector
80 "The Time Machine" tribe
82 Like a day in June?
85 Nothings, arithmetically
87 Hemingway
91 Dug for ore
93 Thespian
95 Shadow
96 Hearts
97 1956's "The Bad ___"
98 Edible root
99 Zola novel
100 Writer Gardner
101 Abominable snowman
102 Enjoy the slopes
105 Jeff or Beau, to Lloyd

Initial Impressions *by Bert Rosenfield*

Don't overlook the miniature stairstep entry at 47 Down.

Across

1 Rum-soaked cake
5 Mouth tops
10 Simple sugars
14 Patricia Neal film
17 Not right now
18 Getting there
20 Sue ___ Langdon
21 F.
23 Doctrine
24 South Alaskan peninsula
25 Small whale
26 Rail support
27 Sector
28 Parnu native: Abbr.
30 Rifle ammo meas.
32 Memorandum books
35 Klee's contemporary
37 Easter entree
39 C.
42 Curtain and fund
44 Jaguar's cousin
45 Fungal spore sacs
46 1920 Čapek play
48 Apron string
49 ___ part; dissemble
53 Jiggery ___; monkey business
55 Bony prefix
58 Dead ducks
60 "We ___ amused" (Victoria)
61 See 47 Down
63 Extract
64 Marilu of "Taxi"
65 Santa Anita margin
66 "___ Real" (Williams play)
67 Pelion's neighbor
68 Boss of a shield
71 WWII arena
73 Thicke of comedy
74 Pro golfer Mark
76 Blandish
78 S.
83 Shell requisite
84 Tee preceder
85 Rams and Chiefs
86 ___-Magnon
88 "Cheers" barfly
90 Jai ___
91 Comfort's companion
94 Certain artillery shells, briefly
96 "Plaza ___"
99 Pigeon variety
100 D.
104 Milan or Nepal ending
105 Sherlock Holmes's retirement hobby
106 First home of the Olympics
107 Weber's ___ *Freischutz*
108 ___ Didrikson
109 British diplomat Howard and namesakes
110 Marginal notation

Down

1 Luxuriate
2 Ending for utter
3 T.
4 Anagram for Satan
5 WWII fliers
6 Cole Porter's regretful miss
7 California sea mammal
8 Causing worry
9 Newspaper logo
10 Ahab's father (1 Kings)
11 Kamchatkan, for one
12 Photog. blowup
13 Opp. of unorthodox
14 Cornrow, for example
15 Oust from office
16 Strip down a ship
19 Becker-Lendl divider
22 Contribution of a sort
27 Old: Abbr.
29 S
31 ___ volente
33 M.
34 Jan. hrs. in "The Hub"
35 Plains brave
36 The scratching birds
38 Lansing campus monogram
40 Some Mozart serenades
41 Alejandro of films
43 Reddish-brown pigment
47 With 61 Across and 62 Down, E.
49 ___ *mundi*; world vital forces
50 B.
51 Experimental tests, of old
52 Just ___ throw away; nearby
54 Lobster coral
56 Lady of the casa
57 "Sold out" sign
59 Boff ending
62 See 47 Down
69 Indian honorific
70 Relative of "phooey"
72 Four halves
74 Goose, to Yvette
75 Kind of weld
77 Irregular
78 Put on solids
79 Maltreat
80 Near miss, in horseshoes
81 XIV, quadrupled
82 Political pamphlets
87 Caulking material
89 Took charge
92 Early film director
93 Actress Joanne
95 Dry
97 Linden tree
98 Gaelic
100 Boxer's probe
101 Leon Henderson's org.
102 Chic's "Hellzapoppin" partner
103 Onetime Moroccan capital

185

Take a Bough *by Joy L. Wouk*

"A circulating library in a town is as an evergreen tree of diabolical knowledge."—Mrs. Malaprop

Across

1 Thanksgiving vegetables
5 ___ Blanc
9 See previous clue
12 "Desire Under the ___"
16 Discharge
17 Cruising
18 Risk
20 Small bottle
21 Cautious
22 Staff symbol
23 Candid
24 Israel's Eban
25 Robin Hood's milieu
28 Judge
29 German article
30 Horizontal line
31 Actor Tom and family
33 Change
36 Nice season
37 Earlier, in combos
38 Is suitable (to)
41 Free ticket
48 Small hill-dweller
49 Stadium sounds
51 Actress Claire
52 Large net
53 North Carolina's capital
56 Get power from
57 Grahame's children's classic
63 Tell
64 Of a church room
65 City on the Tigris River
66 Poet's contraction
67 Building additions
69 Hell, to Sherman
72 Respighi's "The ___"
76 Respects
78 Slice
79 Conjunction
81 "Weird Al" Yankovic parody
82 Tree in the ficus family
86 Cup (Fr.)
88 Debussy's "La ___"
89 An Adams
90 Sinclair Lewis novel
96 Best or Ferber
97 Periods
98 Dancer Montez
99 Limned
100 Agglomeration
101 Beget
102 George Orwell's college

186

103 Monster
104 Layers
105 "Spring ahead" initials
106 Moist
107 Othello, for one

Down

1 Evergreen trees
2 Asian nurse
3 Bog
4 Ingredient of synthetic rubber
5 Georgia city
6 Scandinavian capital
7 Betsy Ross requirement
8 Fancy fabric
9 Worship
10 Boutonniere site
11 Title for Reagan: Abbr.
12 Elude
13 Defamatory statement
14 Female name meaning "lovable"
15 Noisy impacts
19 Intestinal: Comb. form
26 More spacious
27 Baker's need
32 Marten relative
33 Lawyer's org.
34 Almost half of us
35 Superlative ending
37 Princess's irritant
39 French river
40 Food fish
42 "The ___ of the Iguana"
43 Belong
44 Sailboat's stabilizer
45 Beach resort
46 Enough, formerly
47 Desires
50 Splinter
54 January in Lima
55 "___ Now Or Never"
56 Completes
57 Snare
58 Half: Pref.
59 Verve
60 Goods
61 Mississippi source
62 Ridge
66 Newt
68 Guide
69 Moist
70 "___ Blue?"
71 Q–U fillers
73 Liquid measures
74 Tall spar
75 Stored (fodder)
77 Nobleman's sphere of influence
80 Lower in rank
82 Tree with three-cornered nuts
83 Confuse
84 Curtain fabric
85 Poet William Butler
86 Despots
87 Valuable thing to have
88 Labor leader George
91 Really dry
92 ___ hot and cold; vacillate
93 Jason's ship
94 Depraved Roman emperor
95 Pitcher

Originally published in 1989

Careful! *by Elizabeth Arthur*

A cautious approach may be warranted here, although there's nothing dangerous lurking about.

187

Across

1 At some distance
5 "I Kid You Not" author
9 Medium-dry, as wine
12 Figure of speech
17 Actress Daniels
18 1953 Caron film
19 ____ annum
20 Felt poorly
21 Dollar fraction
22 Author Ambler
23 Palindromic preposition
24 Puttered around
25 Be careful!
29 Some deer
30 ____-tac-toe
31 Full house letters
32 Not brightly
34 Take care!
41 ____ carte
42 Islam branch: Var.
43 "____ Not Unusual" (Tom Jones hit)
44 Saline drop
45 Winnower
48 Charge
49 Beatrice was his beloved
50 Bills' followers
51 Satan's forte
53 Arabians, for example
54 Be careful!
58 Goads
59 Rose of baseball
60 City on the Oka
61 Freeway cloggers
62 Heel
63 Birthday goodies
67 Slightly unsightly tire
68 Coolidge, to pals
69 Wounded, in the corrida
71 A Gabor
72 Think first!
75 Egypt dam site
77 Norm: Abbr.
78 Tatami, for one
79 Polypeptidic secretion: Abbr.
80 What a careful person uses
87 1988 Olympics site
88 Man-mouse connection
89 Lubricates
90 Pitcher Tiant
92 Of a more advanced age
93 Uncle or aunt: Abbr.
94 ____ of Man
95 ¿Cómo ____ usted?
96 Extols
97 Sault ____ Marie
98 "____ Heart" (Ford-Page 1964 film)
99 Thin stratum

Down

1 Christie's "The ____ Murders"
2 Intuit
3 Anomalous
4 Adapt machinery
5 The masses
6 Yorkshire river
7 Arabic letter
8 Lasagna cheese
9 Oration
10 Mysterious: Var.
11 Wood preservative
12 Make to a special need
13 Harass
14 Spanish stewpot
15 Look through a keyhole
16 Byrnes of "77 Sunset Strip"
26 Anthem writer
27 Like Croesus
28 Extinct wild ox
32 Marx's "____ Kapital"
33 ____ du Diable
34 Anybody
35 Mien
36 Street sign
37 Electrify
38 It may be past, present, or future
39 Eroded
40 Corp. head
42 Planes needing little runway, for short
46 Goods and services in motion
47 Some Egyptians
48 Elegant
49 Measured amounts
51 ____ out; made do
52 Large tub
53 Engaged
54 Namesakes of Israel's first king
55 Private student
56 October birthstones
57 Legends and myths, collectively
58 Forbidden: Var.
62 Sedan entries
63 Before, in combos
64 "A ____ has no sense of the have-beens" (Hardy)
65 Rural elec. corp.
66 Clemente or Simeon
68 Perky and attractive
69 Dog's warning
70 Bonelike
73 Film awards
74 Pierce: Var.
75 Put-on
76 Fence crossings
79 Goose genus
80 Alley Oop's girlfriend
81 Pakistan's language
82 Require
83 Worry
84 Holding device
85 Actress Raines
86 Naldi of films
87 Bengal native
91 Fictional Spade

Computer Illiteracy *by Thomas F. Odom*

1. Reset brain. 2. Enter data. 3. End.

188

Across

1 Sword handle
5 On
11 Ease up
16 Jazzy Fitzgerald
17 Fixes Tex-Mex beans
19 Hatchet rite?
20 Work for the *Tribune*
21 Glue again
22 Noble prefix
23 Little black book?
25 Tiriac of tennis
26 Is Johann awake?
27 West. hem. gp.
28 ___ as a fruitcake
31 Glacial ridge
32 Sticky candy
35 NFL's Otto and PGA's David?
37 Mine entrance
38 Ego
39 Old French coin
40 Certain Asian
43 Collects
45 Mil. fraction
49 Easterners
51 Exude
52 Prolific plant
53 Landlord's income
54 Gift ___ (salesman's asset)
57 Cassandra, for one
60 Join
61 Ark mountain
63 "Give a ___ horse he can ride" (Thomson)
64 Weaponry
66 French philosopher
67 Fox or Rabbit
68 Member of the wedding
72 Vat
73 Opening
75 Related
77 Challenge Carl Lewis
78 Sad story?
82 Silly ___
83 Greek portico
86 Descriptive title
87 Dry, wine-wise
88 One who swears by a computer?
90 Romance, to Burns
91 Fishing fun?
96 Insult artist
97 Adrenaline substitute
99 "___ Around" (Beach Boys hit)
100 Recently
101 ___ shine!
102 Spicy stew
103 Exploits
104 Meanders
105 Pecans

Down

1 Pay attention
2 "M*A*S*H" star
3 Move like a butterfly
4 Modern London gallery?
5 Rich tapestry
6 Honey and spelling
7 Mother-___
8 Ex-coach Parseghian
9 Awakening
10 Long way around
11 Vibes
12 Building blocks
13 Mohammed's wife
14 Ryan's hope?
15 Marry in secret
18 Actress Berger
19 Be gentle with the jalopy
24 Tampa or Botany
29 Cashmere sweater?
30 Mundane article
32 Label
33 Computer language
34 Match
35 Gnats and ants
36 History exhibits
38 ___ Lanka
40 "Mon Oncle" star
41 Premed. course
42 Homophone for "I'll"
44 Trade restriction
46 Ruhr city
47 Watch Shaw play?
48 Orthodontist's deg.
50 Hotel map?
54 Kiln
55 *Haus*keeper
56 Raiment
58 Dipl. building
59 Fine fur
62 Wintergreen fruit
65 Stop light
69 "Welcome" site
70 Make a scene
71 Napoleon's marshal
74 Part of speech: Abbr.
76 Like Ollie North in 1989
78 Talked back
79 Tanker
80 More's paradise
81 Belief in a god
82 One dot on a computer screen
83 Cook with steam
84 Tunnel clouds
85 Make a speech
87 Plants
89 Seafood choice, for some
92 Relative of -trix
93 Yukon pad: Var.
94 Warm up to
95 Greek letters
98 One bill

Originally published in 1989

Group Tour *by Walter Covell*

Quite a collection of collections.

189

Across

1 Wine group
7 Management group
12 Fish group
17 East
18 Stargazer's Muse
19 Island near Bay of Naples
20 Stellar group
22 On the qui vive
23 Inquire
24 Opp. of 17 Across
25 Tin plate
27 Trivial detail
28 Group's mtg.
30 Move aimlessly
33 Grotto
34 Where the "man who wasn't there" was
36 Free from
37 Food supply
39 Social group
42 Leif, to Eric
43 Adar holiday
44 ___ y plata
45 Instability
48 Distinctive theory
51 Entire
53 Limb
54 Unseal, poetically
55 ¿Cómo ___ Vd.?
56 Depart
57 Chapels
59 Haciendas
60 Perry's originator
61 Operated
62 NOW's interest
63 Lesser Antilles group
64 Color
65 Limiters
68 Corrida cheer
69 Garlic section
71 Humorist George
72 Adjusts the ivories again
74 Like the Earth's shape
76 Golf course position
77 Certain joints
78 Shoe group
79 Deserted
82 Encyclopedia groups
86 Power hammer head
87 Sleep like ___
88 Roman bronze
89 Diamond ___
90 "Ghosts" playwright
92 Professional group
98 New York city
99 Iced
100 Prior to
101 Wasps' groups
102 Inward
103 Flour sifter

Down

1 South American shrubs
2 Irregularly indented
3 Sausage groups
4 "___ Misérables"
5 Hill group member
6 Map abbrev.
7 Partridge group
8 Horse's morsel
9 Blackbird
10 Reveled
11 Mother of Perseus
12 Peruse
13 "2001" computer
14 Enrollment policy
15 Reach
16 Pup group
18 Corrupting influence
21 Australasian parrots
26 Maltreat
29 Compass pt.
30 Feeble
31 Unjustifiably stubborn
32 Female red deer
33 Dernier ___
35 Break in hostilities
38 ___ Poetica
39 Wound spirally
40 Stubborn and mean
41 Celestial phenomena
42 Tallow base
43 Vigors
46 Fragrant
47 Actor Lloyd
49 Horse group
50 People in groups
52 City rd.
55 Attention
57 Diamond "bag"
58 Lake or Canal
59 Social group
61 Divulge
63 Religious belief
65 Spoil
66 Come down
67 Hemingway
70 Household god
73 Nav. designation
74 Choice
75 Trinket
76 Water bordered by coral
77 Massage dough
80 Lawn game: Var.
81 Rowed
83 1948 Nobelist
84 Strength of substance in solution: Var.
85 Foxier
87 Cape and Arbor
91 Consume
93 Negative word
94 Neighbor of Ga.
95 Decline
96 Early car
97 Super Bowl org.

Spring Training   *by Louis Sabin*

"Will Fortune never come with both hands full,
But write her fair words still in foulest letters?"—William Shakespeare

190

Across

1 Alcott family
6 Metamorphic rock
12 Desert structures
18 French department
19 Witchcraft
20 Spirit
21 Bull-pen seats?
23 King Arthur's abode
24 Gave confidence
25 Dimensions
27 Fleur-de-____
28 Danube feeder
29 Guitarist Paul
30 Church feature
32 Get up
33 Arctic explorer
35 Cord
36 Mystic letters
37 Get lost!
40 Carry
41 Yearn
42 Map collection
43 "Forty-Second Street" George
44 Teresa and Richard
47 Food fish
48 Jargon
49 Surprised reactions
50 Time frame
51 Grasps
52 Moves from the field?
54 Actress Miner
55 Printer's measures
56 Wit
57 ____ and assigns
58 Make hay?
59 Lament
61 Castro
62 Bad habits
63 Carmichael and Paisley
64 "The Spirit of '76" member
65 Sell
66 Photo finish
68 Spoiled ones
69 Oater actor Tim
70 Roguish
71 Ditches
72 Adult boys
73 Disrelish, plus
77 ____ degree
78 Erelong
79 Tamarisks
81 Poured

83 Berra's remarks?
86 Get in
87 Snub
88 Make up for
89 Method
90 Field dog
91 "And so to bed" writer

Down

1 Clerical headdress
2 Pale
3 Showed over
4 Traffic light site
5 Cuts
6 County's British counterparts
7 "My Native Land" poet
8 Cargo space
9 Altar agreement
10 Grunter
11 Restless, in a way
12 Stupefy

13 Hawk's opposite
14 Anglo-Saxon coin
15 Flingin' "heat" at Clark?
16 Tyke at the Plaza
17 Has a hunch
22 Beat
26 Vex
30 Factory team's switch hitters?
31 Milk measure
32 Ladder step
34 Cricket positions
35 Poll finding
36 Contract issue
37 Slugged
38 Natural gas component
39 Hurlers who crack under pressure?
40 Range identifier
41 Elbows
43 Trumpet call
44 Rotate
45 County Kerry port
46 Most reliable

48 Boggs and Hershiser
49 American dogwood
52 Tea snack
53 Panama pest
58 Population factor
60 Wood strip
61 Decree
62 Actor Bisoglio
64 Movie mule
65 Annual division
66 Some rays
67 Highway
68 Hair-raiser
69 Aide
71 Computer–phone line connector
72 Skier Phil or Steve
74 Fabulist
75 Kind of bopper
76 Slalom lines
78 Golfer Ballesteros
79 Kiltie
80 Hazard for 78 Down
82 A Cambridge univ.
84 "The ____ of Reason"
85 Explosive

Over and Out *by Thomas W. Schier*

Follow directions.

Across

1 Share billing
7 Giant of myth
12 "Out of ____"
18 Keenly insightful
19 ____ ear and...
20 Hudson feeder
21 Is something wrong?
23 Gets beaten
24 Declare
25 Glacier reminders
26 Presidential period
28 Houston–NYC dir.
29 Michael Jordan's org.
31 Fitting
32 Actually
34 "I cannot tell ____"
36 Win ____ nose
37 Thespian's goal
38 Remedial assistant
41 Bean
43 Wine label data
45 "This Bud's ____"
46 Squared stones
48 Fatal conclusion?
49 Caboose
50 Attack
51 Tom Kite's objectives
53 Preserves container
54 Menlo Park inits.
55 Entraps
60 Engl. county
63 Took the gold
64 Darts or jarts
65 "A community is like ____" (Ibsen)
69 Better than
72 Corn portion
73 1980 Eloise Greenfield book
75 Pronto
76 Copy ivy
78 ____ path; make way
79 Calendar page
80 Rushdie condemner's country
81 Pig out
83 Punchless punches
84 Plaintive
86 Jimjams: Abbr.
87 Brown truck letters
88 When lunch hour ends
90 Reddish-brown color
91 Sidekick
93 No friend!
96 River of 12 Across
98 Spying activities
101 Fabrics: Var.
102 Personnel manager
103 Like one admirer
104 Melodic
105 Famed Belgian violinist
106 Abstract

Down

1 Cornfield cries
2 Job-safety agcy.
3 Remain till morning
4 Famous mummy
5 Bewildered
6 Gets better
7 Extra compensation
8 Like helium
9 Playthings
10 *Enero...diciembre*
11 Spays
12 Ghana's capital
13 Thoroughly
14 Mfg. stat
15 Wait a minute!
16 Slot machine input
17 "I'm in" action
22 Rubber stamp
27 Eastern newt
30 Louise Beaver's TV role
32 Pub missile
33 Ankara native
34 Lackaday!
35 Majesty lead-in
36 Jujube
37 Do not promote, once more
39 Mrs. Chaplin
40 Ungracious
42 ____ Hari
44 Gael's land
45 Jamie or Felicia
47 Track
49 Showed all
52 Dancer Miller
53 Muffin topping
56 ____' Pea
57 Farm feature
58 Bowler Anthony
59 Backgammon move
60 Con game
61 "____ be in England..." (Browning)
62 1941 Ameche-Grable film
66 Seeks shelter
67 Concerning
68 Pod partners
70 Enthusiastic about
71 Nightclub fees
72 Israel's airline
74 Emote
76 Like peanut brittle
77 Come, now!
80 "____ Man Answers" ('62 Dee-Darin film)
82 Zitherlike instrument
85 Din
86 White dwarf?
87 Complete
88 Ambience
89 Ski lift
91 Actress Witherspoon
92 File
94 "The ____ Love Belongs to Sombody Else"
95 Superlative endings
97 Recent, in combos
99 Start of a seasonal song
100 Cover with sleet

191

Dilemma   *by Sidney L. Robbins*

Except for 1 Across, every clue defines two words. Decide which word goes in each of the identical halves of the grid. The solution is unique!

192

Across

1 1900–1901
9 Certain Easterner/ Antoinette
10 Pathet ——/ Constrictor
11 Tiff/ Friends
12 Beat beaters?/ Part of speech
13 Floating/ Facilitate
15 Hide/ Part of H.O.M.E.S.
16 Food fish/ Exist
17 Ceremonies/ Falsehood fabricators
18 Having gifts/ Took the wrong way
24 Polish partner/ Allied assn.
25 Encourage/ Guthrie
26 River of Italy/ Ripped
28 Tricycle's big bro/ New Mexico resort
29 Ripens/ Observed
30 Fewer, mistakenly/ School subj.
33 Make leather/ Fury
34 Rhône feeder/ Go over the books
35 City transits/ Permit
36 Sprinkle/ Lawful
38 Unusual/ Plane needing little runway: Abbr.

41 Kiln/ Reminder of a sort
42 Offer/ Enlargement
45 Upon/ "...—— o'clock scholar..."
46 Wordplay author Willard ——/ European capital
47 Sample/ Feeling
48 Former NBA star Thurmond/ Like TV's Columbo

Down

1 Light touch/ Printing measures
2 Lid/ D.C.'s country
3 Wipe out/ Irritated
4 Potassium salt/ Of the nose
5 Rare/ 9:50
6 Submarine/ Botanist's study
7 Awaken/ Rhino's relative
8 Americans/ Firehouse gear
13 Performs/ Merit
14 Cleanser/ Region
19 Broad or Wall/ Closet contents
20 Collar style/ Long time periods
21 Indication/ —— and true
22 Certain lodge member/ Self
23 Bambi's mom/ —— Moines

26 Kind of daisy/ Waggish appendages
27 Actual/ Monster
31 Valuable veins/ Anna's adopted homeland
32 Fr. city/ Eft
34 Coney, for one/ Syrian city
37 Gorbachev/ Painter's paste
39 Funnyman Johnson/ Broz
40 Margarine/ Elbow follower?
42 Hoover, for example/ Fill out
43 Pacino and Martino/ Choose
44 Myrna of films/ Actress Carrie

1

```
C A S H E W   W E A K   T A M
O C T A N E   H A L O   R E O
W H Y B O T H E R T O F I N D
    A S T E R       E P E E
P E O N   E R E C T   A L A S
A L L E G R O   A R M R E S T
T I A R A     A S E A
    F A U L T T H E R E S
      Z E R O     I X I O N
M A C H E T E   S P O I L E R
E C H O   A S T I R   S O D A
A R A N     O N E A T
N O R E W A R D O F F E R E D
I S M   A I D A   A R N O L D
E S S   X R A Y   B O T T L E
```

2

```
C L A D   A L M S   P R I M E
R I C E   N E A T   L A S E R
I A M B   T A P E   A N I S E
B R E A D I N S P A N I S H
    T A C T     B E N
S T E A L   O W E N S   C S A
H E R B A L   A G E   P R O D
I T A L I A N F O R B R E A D
N O S E   C E E   S L E E V E
E N E   S T A R T   U P P E R
    T A I     R A R A
  F R E N C H F O R B R E A D
S O U N D   A L U M   I P S O
A R I S E   R O P E   N E S T
W A N E D   D E E D   G E N E
```

3

```
S L U R P   B A I T E D   P A C E R S
E A S E L   U P S I D E   G R A C E S
T H E H A U N T I N G F E A R T H A T
A R D E N T     S T E E R   A T O M S
    A T T A R     D R O W N S
A M O R   E X E R T   S A G   D A G
G A R S   R E S O R T S   R E J O I N
L O S E R   S O M E O N E   D O G M A
E R O D E S   D E S P O T S   H I E R
T I N   V I E   S O O T H   N E D S
    S I D L E S     P A O L O
A P A C E   S A T I N   R E H E A R
S O M E W H E R E M A Y B E H A P P Y
I R O N E R   E L A T E D   A R I S E
S K I E R S   D E M O N S   R A C E S
```

4

```
T A F T   A S P S   G A S P
O L L A   A U L I C   A C H E
B E A R   D R U S E   S C O T
E X T R A V A G A N T   E V E
    E R A   N E E D L E R
C R E D E N C E   S E R E
R O X   S C A N T   M A R S H
I V A N   E L D E R   M A L E
B E G O T   M E T E S   T U N
    G R A M   D E P O S E R S
S T E A M E R     I R K
W A R   P R E T E N T I O U S
O P A L   G L O V E   F I R E
R I T A   E A G E R   F L I P
D R E W   R Y A N   S Y S T
```

5

```
C A R S   W O R S T   E V I L
A L O T   E R A T O   M E R E
R E G A T T A D A Y   P R O D
T R U L Y   N I G E R I A N
S T E E R   G A N D E R
      A R E N A   M E S A S
H U M A N E   T N T   D A R T
A V E R T E D   T I T A N I A
R E A M   L I D   M A Y D A Y
P A N I C   S E D E R
    S A M P L E   G L A S S
L I T T O R A L   E A R T O
L O C I   L O Y A L T Y D A Y
O P E C   A V E N A   N O V A
W E R E   R E D O S   E R E S
```

11

```
DOWEL EIDOS ■SEPAL
AWARE■DOURO ELATE
YETIS■INKER MAKES
■ENACT ESERINE■
ABR GASES SOT NBA
LILTER■LOG LECHER
FLOE■PALFREY RANK
ADORNER WAR LAME
■BATTLEFIELD■
TRIP IAL ENDLESS
EMEU SONLESS ENTO
REDMAN KIP OLDGOD
ENC GIB NAHUA LPS
ORATING ALPHA
TRAIT HOTEL PONDS
ANTRE AMOLE ENDUE
BASES RENDS RESET
```

12

```
■TEST LIBS VAPID
SHREW AGUE PALATE
PEACE PURL AROUSE
AMSTERDAMFLIMFLAM
TEE DIONE SNIT
AGAS TEN FRA
ASSES SEW TILER
SWARMED SOLD RAND
SACRAMENTOPIMENTO
INRE PEAR SPONGER
SEEDS BID WEEDS
TED HRS PIUS
ARIA TANTE PGA
RUSSIANPERCUSSION
UPHILL HAIL TALON
STEALS ISEE ERODE
TOWNY LESS RATS■
```

13

```
SWISH SCAR OMBRE
MISTO POLES SIREN
ISLAM INLAW STIPE
THETELLTALEHARTE
ELATE LAO ETAL
HARDYS TYRO SETA
ERA SARI SPP NSW
ACRID WINS LAM
THECALLOFTHEWILDE
ETA TODO LOIRE
ASP AZO ISEE DEL
BELA URAL ROSSES
UNAS LIS FAIRE
ACHRISTMASCARRYL
ATALE ORALS TAHOE
NOTED NORSE OPERA
TREYS STET REEKS
```

14

```
ESE OPAH LACK CRT
SPY MIRA OBOE HOR
THELONGVOYAGEHOME
HELIO ODA PULPS
ERIS EXCELS ALLES
REDPONY ALOSTLADY
ATLI YOU
ASSET ECO RENEGE
LOOKHOMEWARDANGEL
ABLEST EVA SWORD
HAS ANTE
DODSWORTH GOLDBUG
ERICA COOPER EASY
APRON LOA PARER
THETIMEOFYOURLIFE
HAL NOON TITO TON
SNY GENS OLES ERE
```

15

```
ALTA ADANA SERF
ALOSS REMAN ISERE
BEGET EXPONENTIAL
UTA ISNT MALE NIB
TARA COR ILL ISLE
INERTIA SEGO
RETONE NNE NATHAN
INHALES STE PAYEE
CUM NEWWAVE PRE
ERICA APE ANDROID
RECOIL ARF SUITES
CLAM SOLUBLE
IPSO MAE LAR ENID
RIO GILL IDEE URE
EQUILATERAL ASSAY
DUNNE EMOTE REEDS
EDGE DINED LESE
```

16

```
S A L A D . . S A A R . P A G E
E L O P E S . S A B L E . I M A N
L O V E R C O M E B A C K T O M E
F E E . R A V I . A R T I C L E .
. S L Y . M E T S . M O T H E R
. E E K . N E W T . R E W
. S T A I R . S E A T . D O T T Y
R A T . S O D . E I R E . O H I O
A R E . S W E E T L O V E . E L K
J E R K . S E L L . D I M . L E E
A E S I R . R I I S . L I M O S
. N O D . A F A R . L U V
. E N D S U P . E V O E . D E R
. M I N A R E T . A N N E . B E E
L O V E S B E E N G O O D T O M E
I T E S . A L L I E . S E R A I L
D E N S . N E L L . N A T T Y
```

17

```
L L A M A S . . C H A . C H A R
A U R I C L E . E R O S . H O M E
S A N D M A N . P U P S . A R E A
S U E . E N D . A M P E R S A N D
. T O W . B E T A S .
B E S O M . W I E L D . P I C L S
A V A L O N . D A Y . W I S H E S
S A N D P I P E R . W A D . E E E
. C D S . N O R . S O N . C A P
C U B . B E T . S A N D P A P E R
P E A R L S . A I R . S E V E R E
A E R I E . S P L I T . T E N S E
. P A I N T . S A M .
Q U I C K S A N D . S E A . E R A
U N D O . T R E E . S A N D B O X
I T E R . L E S S . E N N O B L E
T O A D . E S S . S E N S E S
```

18

```
B L A S E . I P S O . O P U S
E A S E L . E N A C T . S H I R T
I T T A K E S T W O T O T A N G O
G E O M . S P E N T . C A R T E L
E R N . S T I R S . T H R E A D
. E P E E . R E T .
D O U B L E D E C K E R . D A S
A R T O I S . D A R E . T E M P
T A U N T . M E R O S . C H L O E
E R R S . A M O N . H E E H A W
D E N . S I A M E S E T W I N S
. R A M . T A U S .
S Q U A T S . S C A R S . S P A
S P U N K Y . S P A R S . A L A S
C O O P E R A T I V E E F F O R T
A R T I S . S A T E D . A R O S E
T E E N . A G E D . T O P E R
```

19

```
M A N . A F A R . A P P . I M A N
U S E . U R D U . H I E . C O P E
S T A . G O O S E E G G . E R A S
T A R S . G R A B A T . T R A C T
. T Y K E . B R A K E . L E S
A N D R E I . T I A R A .
R E O . S C A L A . L Y R I C A L
E R G S . K L I N E . A D A T E
T O T E . B O W L S . E T E S
E L A N D . N A K E D . D N A S
S I G N O F F . R E C U R . A S E
. A L O O F . C O P P E R
E A R . T E X A N . S K I D
D R E S S . T R E A T S . Q U I P
S N I T . C R O W F O O T . R T E
E I N E . I O U . A L U M . G O P
L E E R . A T T . T A P S . E N E
```

20

```
S H U T . G A S . B A R B . U P S
L O S E . N U T . A G E E . N E T
A S E A . A D O . T A L L . P R O
G E R S H W I N . R A I S E U P
. E A S T E R . T E T E .
O P A R T . R O O S E V E L T S
D O G S T A R . A B E . E V E R Y
E W E . E L E A N O R . E D E N
. C R E A M . E M I R S .
S T A R . P E R S O N A . B A A
S A L E S . E N E . N A T T E R S
W I L D H O R S E S . I O N I A
. S O A P . D I S C O S .
N E W S M E N . S P I N S T E R
A R E . P R E S . T A T . P I K E
S I L . O A S T . E R E . O M E N
H E L . O S T E . R E D . T E S T
```

21

```
C A P R A ■ ■ S A R A ■ ■ D R N O
A L I E N ■ D O R A L ■ C R E E K
S O N N Y ■ A L I N E ■ R A M A R
A N T E ■ S C O T E R ■ A G O R A
■ G O W I T H T H E T I D E ■ ■
■ ■ N O A H ■ ■ ■ S L E D S ■ ■
I M P A L A S ■ E A G L E ■ E T A
S E R R A ■ T A S T E ■ A M O I
S W I M W I T H T H E S T R E A M
U L N A ■ B O O N E ■ E N A T E
E E C ■ A S T R O ■ I N T E N S E
■ R E A D E ■ ■ ■ U B E R ■ ■ ■
■ ■ D O N T M A K E W A V E S
S N E E R ■ R A D A R S ■ A X E D
W O D E N ■ I C O S I ■ O L I V A
I T E M S ■ K O R E A ■ R U L E D
T A N S ■ ■ E N E S ■ ■ T E E N S
```

22

```
G E E S E ■ S U B ■ R A V I N E
L A S E R S ■ E R A ■ O P I N E S
A S T R I N G E N T ■ T E N S E S
S T A B ■ I O N ■ T U T S ■ E D E
S E T ■ A P O ■ C E N E ■ P T S
■ R E S T ■ ■ S H R I N E R ■
■ ■ P A M P E R S ■ ■ W E E P Y
P E R E ■ A E R O ■ ■ S E T T L E
A L E C ■ T R E N T O N ■ E T O N
S L A T E S ■ I O N A ■ N E W S
T A M E S ■ S C R A P E S ■ ■
■ ■ R E G A L L Y ■ L E S S ■
K M S ■ R H E E ■ A S K ■ T E C
R O I ■ C A A N ■ I L L ■ T R I O
A R A R A T ■ D E V I A T I O N S
D E M I S E ■ E T A ■ M A R K E T
S A I N T S ■ R O N ■ L O E S S
```

23

```
G A F F S ■ T A R O T ■ S C A M S
O T A R U ■ A M O U R ■ I O N I C
C O N T R A R I E T Y ■ D I T T O
A N E ■ E G A D ■ L O N E L I E R
R E G A L E ■ D I N E R ■ T S E
T R A C Y ■ E G A N ■ B E T H
■ ■ T I E G A M E S ■ A R E N A
A P R E S V O U S ■ P O L I T I C
N E E D ■ O I L ■ T O P ■ A I N T
D E M I S E S ■ V A R I A N C E S
I N O N U ■ T W I S T A N D
■ T A B U ■ A S K S ■ T E N A M
O R E ■ T R A L A ■ ■ C H R O M E
M O N A L I S A ■ A L I I ■ V P S
A D E L E ■ S P E C I A L T I E S
R E S E T ■ E A T E R ■ L U C R E
S A S S Y ■ T I A R A ■ S T E E D
```

24

```
A D O P T S ■ A S S A Y ■ C A M P
B E W A R E ■ S C O N E ■ O B O E
A F L Y I N T H E O I N T M E N T
C E E S ■ ■ R E N T S ■ A B A T E
A R T ■ C E A S E ■ ■ S L I M E
■ ■ B A L I ■ ■ C A P O N ■ ■
■ A D O G I N T H E M A N G E R
A D E L E S ■ W A R E S ■ ■ S A W
A L L E Y ■ S E R I N ■ A R T I E
A I T ■ ■ L O E S S ■ ■ F R I E N D
■ B A T S I N T H E B E L F R Y ■
■ ■ A M A S S ■ ■ A T E E ■ ■
T A M E R ■ M U S E S ■ ■ E S S
F O C A L ■ S W I S S ■ ■ A T T U
A B U L L I N A C H I N A S H O P
T E T E ■ N A C R E ■ O C T A V E
A D E S ■ S P O O R ■ W H I N E R
```

25

```
■ O P A L ■ T A T A S ■ L E A D S
A N I T A ■ E D I C T ■ A N G I E
N I N E S ■ M A T R I ■ P E A R L
T O T ■ S A P P H I R E S ■ T E L
E N A M E L ■ T E D ■ P E T E R S
■ ■ O N E S ■ ■ ■ P E R U ■ ■
S O L O ■ C A T S E Y E ■ R O B E
A P I N G ■ T H E R M ■ E Q U I V
D E N S E ■ E R A ■ R U S S E
A R E T E ■ A C U T E ■ R O T O R
T A R O ■ D I A M O N D ■ I S N T
■ ■ N A R D ■ ■ L I D S ■ ■ ■
C I N E M A ■ S O C ■ N E E D L E
O L E ■ A M E T H Y S T S ■ O A R
T O P A Z ■ L E A N S ■ ■ O M I T S
E N A T E ■ M E R I T ■ T O L E T
S A L A D ■ S P E C S ■ O N Y X ■
```

26

```
S C A M   V I S I T   A S P
S T O L E   C A N A D A   W O O D
T E N O R   H M S P I N A F O R E
R A V E   L O P E S   G R U N T S
I K E   W A I S T   S I L L
P S Y C H I C   T O B E   F L O
  O R A T E   S O U L S   R O W
S T R U T   S P I N E   S E R E
C U B E S   F I E L D   C H U R N
A B E L   M I D A S   H A D E S
M E L   B A R E R   S H A R I
P S T   L I E S   L E O P A R D
  W I N D   U S E R S   N E O
S T R A N D   E N T E R   T S P S
T H I N K I N G C A P   M E L E E
S E N T   S C O U T S   B A I L S
M G S   H O S T S   A M P S
```

27

```
W A G E S   L I L A C   P L A N S
A D A T E   I N A N E   L E D O N
D E F E R E N T I A L   A M A T I
E L F   A D D E R   L T S   N E D
D E E P   S E N D S   O T I O S E
  U P E N D   H A T I N
P A T R O L S   H I J A C K I N G
A C O R N S   H O R A L   S O U
S E N S E   B O R E R   A L L O T
T R I   P O L E S   C L I E N T
A B C O U L O M B   S H A N T E Y
  U N I T E   L E A S E
C A T T L E   S L E D S   N O P E
O L E   O S S   O R A T E   D O S
A L A M O   S T U N T E D N E S S
L O S E S   T E P E E   G O O S E
S W E D E   S N E R D   E R N E S
```

28

```
D E A F   A M O N G   R I B A L D
R A R A   F E R A L   U V U L A E
E U B I E B L A K E   B E R L I N
A D O R N   L E A R Y   T O R N
M E R   D A B   D S O   R O W D Y
  R O M E O   O N I O N
C A K E W A L K   N A N A   S T S
A R N E   O I L   C R E W E L
C O O K   T W E L F T H   R A N I
H O W S E R   D I E   A M O N
E M S   L I E D   T H E S T I N G
  N I O B E   S E T T O
C O C O A   O P S   E A R   N T H
A R A B   A N O T E   A L O H A
J O P L I N   S Y N C O P A T E D
U N R E S T   E L T O N   I T T O
N O I S E S   D I E G O   R O A N
```

29

```
  R F D   D A M E   M I T T S
P A R E E   G E N A S   I N E R T
I D E A S   E V E N T   B E R I A
P I E R S P L O W M A N   X R A Y
S I S T E R S   A D O   P A D S
  O H N O   E N D O R S E
A V I S   B R I E   F A R M E D
M A L   S C A M P   H O S T I L E
I C E   T U B A   H A L S   L I P
N U R S E R Y   P I C K Y   Q T O
E A S T E R   B A L K   S U E T
  A D A M A N T   P E P E
C R A B   N O T   B I R E T T A
H A L L   T H E A L I E N C O R N
E L L I S   A M B I T   S T A I D
S L A N T   W A L K S   T E S T Y
S Y N G E   K N E E   R T E
```

30

```
P O P L A R   B R A Y   F A B E R
O T I O S E   R O L E   A D L A I
S A N D A L W O O D S   L A U R A
T R U E   A N D A   A S P E N S
S U P   M A R C   F R E T S
  M A G N O L I A S   P P D
A R C A N E   S O T T O   O R L E
M O O N E D   C A E N   R U I N
P U T T S   P A U L S   C A C A O
E T T A   L E S S   D E T E N T
R E O S   A C I T Y   A D E S T E
E R N   S A S S A F R A S
  W O M E N   K I E R   R A T
C O O L E R   L A U D   D O L E
H O O D S   B U T T O N W O O D S
I N D I A   E N L S   H O R N E T
C A S E S   L E E K   L O S E R S
```

31

```
FLOOD MATE  CABLE
LANKA TURIN ONION
OVERWHELMED ATLAS
PARADISE PISTIL
  LET PINK  SILT
PADDED CONGE  NEO
ALOES POT  STAGGER
YAWL SAME  CLASSY
  NEXTTONOTHING
BUTTER CHOY  NANA
INHERIT IMP  SETON
ATE  ARIES OTTERS
SOHO TUNS  ARR
  ASCEND UNDERTOW
COTTA DOWNTOEARTH
LACED LOADS  TRITE
ETHOS ERGO  SEPOY
```

32

```
CAROM SEEDED  AHAB
ADORE ALLIED  PULI
RUMBLETUMBLE OGLE
TEE SLADE  EGGER
  ENERGY  SEERS
AWN AMID RENTER
SEISMIC PEACE MOW
PAMPAS EBRO  MUIR
EVIAN MIRES BUGLE
CENT FORK  CONGAS
TRY TOPAY SALIENT
 PUREED SEND  RDS
ALINE DECENT
REMIT AROAR  EGO
LAIT FENDERBENDER
EDNA ATHENA SEINE
NAYS DELTAS TOTES
```

33

```
SABLE CORE  STABS
IDEAL SLAIN LILAC
LINDY COROT ANISE
LED EASE RAN  EIN
SUSPENDEDSENTENCE
 AXES TENET
 ETTU RDA ADAGES
SNARL SERIAL ERE
CAPITALPUNISHMENT
ATE GORIER OASES
RESALE ODD  ONES
 LINGO LIKE
PERIODOFPROBATION
ARE NAB REAM  RNA
POISE BLOND OVOID
EDNAS LANDS WINCE
RESTS EGGS  LASER
```

34

```
EPACT ASIS  PALATE
RAPHE RENO  EDITED
GREENACRES NESTED
STREET BROWNSTUDY
 STRAIT OATS
TALE INA LONE  PAR
ATE SUE LILT  GIBE
BLACKMARIA SPIRIT
LANAI RIANT TRALA
ONDINE GRAYMATTER
ITEN LAOS LOS  END
DAR HERR BEA  IDES
 GAPE TURNIN
BLUEWHALES ENCASE
EUREKA AMBERLIGHT
ARISEN SPOT  ATREE
DESERT SOYA  YEARS
```

35

```
CALIF SCAB  DOUSE
AOUDAD TOPE  EXPEL
INSOLE IDES  BYLAW
NET LILLE EAU  ANA
 LIFEEXPECTANCY
ACRONYM ACH  DDE
BEING ANATHEMA
ALL SANER RIMOSE
CLEATS ZEN OSSIAN
KIDNAP NORNS  DIT
 AREACODE IRADE
 POI RLO ANNULAR
NOBLESSEOBLIGE
ALE LEO CAMEL  ODE
VIRAL ROUT CITRIC
ATONE ALLO ENIGMA
LENIN NEON  KEYED
```

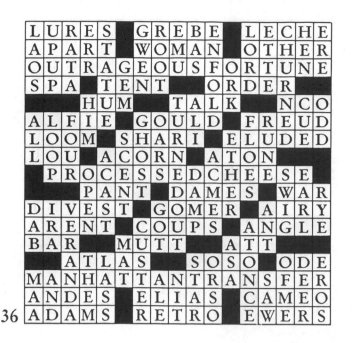

36

L	U	R	E	S		G	R	E	B	E		L	E	C	H	E
A	P	A	R	T		W	O	M	A	N		O	T	H	E	R
O	U	T	R	A	G	E	O	U	S	F	O	R	T	U	N	E
S	P	A		T	E	N	T			O	R	D	E	R		
		H	U	M		T	A	L	K			N	C	O		
A	L	F	I	E		G	O	U	L	D		F	R	E	U	D
L	O	O	M		S	H	A	R	I		E	L	U	D	E	D
L	O	U		A	C	O	R	N		A	T	O	N			
	P	R	O	C	E	S	S	E	D	C	H	E	E	S	E	
	P	A	N	T		D	A	M	E	S		W	A	R		
D	I	V	E	S	T		G	O	M	E	R		A	I	R	Y
A	R	E	N	T		C	O	U	P	S		A	N	G	L	E
B	A	R		M	U	T	T			A	T	T				
	A	T	L	A	S		S	O	S	O		O	D	E		
M	A	N	H	A	T	T	A	N	T	R	A	N	S	F	E	R
A	N	D	E	S		E	L	I	A	S		C	A	M	E	O
A	D	A	M	S		R	E	T	R	O		E	W	E	R	S

37

S	T	O	W		E	S	C	A	R	P		S	C	A	R	C	E
P	I	L	E		A	V	O	I	D	E	R		O	A	T	E	R	S
R	A	D	S		D	A	Y	S	O	F	O	U	R	W	I	V	E	S
I	R	E		R	A	N	A	T		G	N	U	S		E	W	E
G	A	S	B	A	G	S		F	E	E	T	S		C	A	E	N
	T	O	N	E		S	I	L	E	N	I		H	A	L	L	E
C	A	B	O	T		F	A	M	I	L	Y	L	I	E	S
A	L	O	S	S		L	U	B	E	S		S	L	I	M
R	O	O	T		C	U	T	E	R		B	A	L	L	O	O	N
R	O	K		S	A	T	E	D		R	E	N	E	S		O	A	R
	F	I	A	C	R	E	S		G	E	L	D	S		A	N	N	O
	E	S	O	P		E	L	G	A	R		C	I	S	C	O
	P	R	I	V	A	T	E	A	Y	E		A	R	I	E	S
B	I	S	O	N		A	N	N	A	L	S		D	R	E	G
A	N	A	T		S	L	O	A	N		F	R	E	S	H	L	Y
S	S	H		D	I	E	T		B	L	U	E	S		T	I	E
H	E	A	D	O	F	T	H	E	C	R	A	S	S		T	I	E	S
E	R	R	A	N	T		E	L	A	I	N	E	S		I	N	G	E
S	T	A	R	T	S		R	I	N	G	E	D		A	G	E	S

38

A	S	T	R	O		S	N	A	I	L	S		P	A	S	S	E
S	T	R	U	T		P	A	S	S	I	N	G		S	H	O	A	L
S	A	I	N	T	N	I	C	H	O	L	A	S		S	A	U	T	E
A	L	L		O	U	T	R	E		R	U	N	T		T	I	C
Y	E	L	P		B	E	E		B	E	L	I	E		W	H	E	T
			A	R	I	D		D	E	L	E	T	E		A	C	T	S
P	O	R	T	I	A		S	I	T	A	R		S	L	A	Y
A	V	O	I	D		S	T	E	R	N		B	L	U	E	R
L	O	B	O		P	L	A	T	O		T	R	A	N	S	O	M
L	I	E		M	A	I	N	S	T	R	E	A	M	S		L	A	S
	D	R	O	O	L	E	D		H	E	N	C	E		C	I	T	E
	T	R	U	E	R		E	M	M	E	T		P	A	N	I	C
	B	R	A	E		S	L	E	E	T		A	R	R	A	N	T
S	U	E	T		S	P	H	I	N	X		S	L	O	T
H	I	D	E		P	L	E	A	T		O	I	L		E	V	E	S
E	L	F		G	A	E	L		E	R	R	O	L		A	L	E
A	T	O	L	L		A	T	T	O	R	N	E	Y	A	T	L	A	W
V	I	R	E	O		S	E	S	S	I	O	N		P	I	U	T	E
E	N	D	O	W		R	E	S	E	T	S		S	N	E	E	R

39

T	E	E	U	P		M	A	S	C		B	R	A	C	E
T	U	R	T	L	E		A	L	C	O		R	O	L	A	N	D
C	A	R	R	O	T	S		L	E	A	F	L	E	T	T	U	C	E
H	U	N		N	O	T	E		E	L	F	I	S	H		L	O	T
O	T	I	S		R	E	X		L	I	N	T		B	I	D	E
R	E	P	L	Y		R	E	S	P	O	N	D		R	E	F	E	R
E	N	S	U	E	D		C	A	U	P	S		K	I	L	L
	R	Y	E	S		C	R	S		P	A	S	T	O	R	S
R	E	D	P	E	P	P	E	R	S		B	A	R	K		W	A	N
I	T	I	S		L	O	C	A	L	C	O	L	A		A	E	R	O
N	U	L		S	O	R	A		A	L	A	S	K	A	C	R	A	B
G	I	L	B	E	R	T		P	N	A		Y	U	M	A
	P	E	R	E		B	A	E	R	S		M	A	R	S	H	A
C	H	I	E	F		F	O	R	S	A	L	E		R	I	P	O	N
H	E	C	K		D	E	N	S		A	N	S		D	I	M	S
I	L	K		B	A	S	I	N	S		T	A	T	A		N	A	A
C	E	L	E	R	Y	S	T	I	C	K		C	A	B	B	A	G	E
A	N	E	M	I	A		O	P	A	L		T	H	R	I	C	E
A	S	P	E	N		S	S	T	S		S	L	A	S	H

40

G	R	A	S	P		A	M	A	T	I		B	A	C	K	E	R	S
P	O	N	T	I		S	O	P	O	R		A	P	R	I	C	O	T
O	A	T	E	R		A	N	O	D	E		K	E	Y	N	O	T	E
S	R	I	L	A	N	K	A		O	L	D	E	R		G	L	O	W
		E	T	U	I			A	I	D		U	S	E	R	S
A	C	C		E	C	T	O		D	N	A		A	L	T
I	R	A	Q		L	E	O	N	I	D		R	E	N	O	I	R
M	I	N	U	T	E		N	Y	E		D	E	C	A	N	T	E	R
	M	A	O	R	I	S		A	S	W	A	N		S	D	S
R	E	D	D	Y		A	R	C		O	R	E		E	N	A	C	T
M	A	I			T	O	K	Y	O		S	C	R	I	B	E
S	N	A	T	C	H	E	D		E	E	L		O	N	S	I	D	E
	S	N	A	R	E	S		G	A	R	I	S	H		I	R	A	N
	N	E	W		A	E	S		L	E	O	S		D	R	S
A	M	A	Z	E		A	G	O		S	R	O	S
B	A	B	A		A	S	T	R	O		I	S	T	A	N	B	U	L
A	T	O	N	E	R	S		G	A	R	N	I		R	O	O	N	E
S	T	R	I	A	T	E		I	R	I	D	O		E	R	O	D	E
E	S	T	A	T	E	S		A	S	T	O	N		D	E	M	O	S

41

```
IMPS  DENIM  CHE  BOPS
RILL  ENATE  OER  ERAT
ONEARRIVES  UAR  FATA
NEAPTIDE  TART  MOTIF
     SES   ATTHEAGEOF
SOL  SIBS  SLEEVES
OTIS  VENT  SRA  SHE
DISCRETIONBY  DARIUS
SCARE  SPOOR  EPOCHS
  AFT  STRIA  SIT
ELOPER  LIARS  NABOB
BOLERO  LEARNINGTOBE
BYE  PSI  SOLO  EBON
  PLIABLE  SOWS  SEE
INDISCREET    HIS
MOUND  ALOU  USEDTOBE
BONN  ACE  DISCREETLY
ESNE  MER  ENSUE  ROUE
DEED  INS  SARDS  NEED
```

42

```
  APPAL  ASTER  RIALS
ALLURE  NOBLE  OBLATE
SPARROWGRASS  UNITED
PINGS  HUT  ETON  TINA
SNEE  BASIC  RID  NOM
  EDDIE  EASIERTO
    ALUM  RAN  ORALES
SWANLAKE  DUG  BUTANE
COCO  ASPIC  SIS  HET
HOTLIPS  ONE  INSHORT
EDT  NIE  LADDS  URGE
MEWING  DAL  EAGLEEYE
ADOREE  INN  FLOE
  TRONADOR  AWAIT
SSS  NAP  SUSAN  MCIV
ETAT  TRAP  STY  SPICE
POTATO  SITTINGDUCKS
TRALEE  ONALL  BALLET
  KNEAD  NEWEL  SKEET
```

43

```
PIES  PHIS  ISSUS  DCC
LOGO  TORMENTINE  IOU
ENOL  SPOILSPORTLAND
DAMON  INLET  NISANS
  AMOS  HEMIS  PILATE
PANORAMARILLO  NAHAL
AGIN  DEN  LIRA   ENT
REATA  ADOG  GAR  PICO
DECREED  COCODY  OMEN
    ERS   HRH   AWE
ANSA  NONOME  UNITARY
NACL  EGO  EMAR  TIMEO
NRA  SETT  MAL  CADY
ACTSA  EUREKALAMAZOO
SOLONG  MAMET  SILO
  TANANA  PILEI  AGNES
DINGBATONROUGE  AIRE
RST  ASIDESIRED  RANT
YMA  SHEET  DSTS  YNES
```

44

```
LIMP  TALC  MOMS  TATA
AGAR  AMAH  ANEW  OURS
DOYOULIKETHEMAPPLES
DROWSED  ERRS  HIDDEN
   LES  CREE  HILO
CANED  DOIN  KILOGRAM
ALAR  WHODONEIT  ERA
PIN  CHAOS  WEDS  APAL
PANTHER  ILL  ARUBA
  YOURFEETSTOOBIG
MAGOG  LGE  BALANCE
ALOT  LEVI  PEETE  ALA
TEA  LAWISAASS  KNOT
EXTREMES  BRAE  MITTS
  ITER  TUTU  VIN
DAWSON  NISI  PEDDLER
ITAINTNECESSARILYSO
BORN  ERIK  ARID  ERMA
SING  DALY  NILE  DEEM
```

45

```
SAFES  SARAPE  DRAMAS
AMIGO  ADONAI  RIPOST
LONGDIVISION  ANATTO
ELA  ADAGE  KOBE  HEN
PELE  INE  LOOKS  SERE
  MOOT  COBRA  HEROD
ACCENT  PECAN  COMO
LEHUA  SIDON  CONIFER
BLAS  ANNAM  DOVE  PLO
ELM  MICROWAVE  EAT
RAP  LODE  TAMER  BAIT
TRIBUNE  BIGOT  BORNE
  ORIG  DEVON  FALLEN
ANNAS  HELEN  CAGE
COST  MAMAS  LAK  SHAW
HRH  MOTE  AIRES  ISA
EMILIO  SLUMBERPARTY
NAPIER  NINERS  OCEAN
ESSENE  ENURES  TERRE
```

46

```
SANS  POND  AREA    JEW
PLOW  ABOU  DEBT  SOLO
ALIARWILLNOTBE    PHAR
TORRENT  LONIS  JANIS
  TEMPE  ANEAR  MARINE
  ERE  BELIEVEDEVEN
  BIDE  BASS    AMAT
NAB  SOULS  AFRO  IMAS
ITE  ELMO  WIRY  TRASH
STRAND  NOONE  WHENHE
ALIST  HERO  SHOE  ICE
NEAT  VASE  CHEER  LAP
  RAIL  CLEM  AMAN
AESOPSFABLES  API
CRANIA  TREAT  MISDO
ARNAS  STERN  SISTERS
DIEU  SPEAKSTHETRUTH
INST  ERST  ERIN  ACHE
AGT  MYTH  RAMS  LEOS
```

47

```
FILS  AMIGOS  OME  MEL
ARAL  ROBERT  COMPASS
LALALUCILLE  STIRRED
ANADEM  STOLA  ELEM
  PEA  PEPELEMOKO
RCA  RADAR  SRO  EREV
ERLE  LAMED  ONONDAGA
NAOS  ARENA  NIRO
ENOSIS  BEDE  ACROBAT
WIZEN  GAGARIN  AVENA
SOANDSO  EIER  ADOBES
  IOTA  SNARL  LEMS
RARAAVIS  MOTTO  ODIE
OMIT  NAL  WEDGE  ACT
COCOCHANEL  TAN
  KNEE  AMASS  MONICA
CILIATE  MIMIBENZELL
CLEARUP  ONETOA  ALOE
SOS  API  NEWEST  CSTS
```

48

```
  ZOLA  RELICS  OMAHA
MORAL  AMOTHER  LABOR
ADAMANDEVEINAMERIKA
SIT  REINE  NINA  DUB
TAOS  COD  GROAN  HEMS
  CRUSTS  CHER  DUO
  LEA  CROSS  ATTACK
DOCKER  HOST  ATE  RAN
ERRED  MINT  ADO  SOLE
FAIRYTALESOFDRACULA
INNS  END  TARS  BASED
EGG  ETE  COSO  BORERS
DEEPER  PALES  RUE
  IRA  ARES  FUTURE
OPTS  PAINT  ELI  PELT
BOO  OMRI  ASONE  EVE
EDWARDIIVERSUSRELEE
SINGE  SNAKIER  APERS
EASED  GLEANS  LIDS
```

49

```
GOA  ITAL  GOLDA  EBON
ACR  TARA  INION  XERO
SEA  ABUT  LAURAKEENE
JAMESONEILL  GERBIL
ENESCO  REEL  POETESS
TIARA  BART  SIGN
SANO  SAL  TBONE  TAPA
  GRIS  BEAU  SEABED
ASA  HASTE  NSA  LHASA
BARRYMORE  JEFFERSON
BYGUM  SUP  OSRIC  ESO
ANADEM  SETS  ANTA
SOLE  INTRO  CID  SIMA
  ACUS  GOAD  APRON
ALGIERS  DEBS  SLEAVE
KOODOO  OTISSKINNER
EDWINBOOTH  ALEG  IDO
LENO  ENATE  BATH  AMI
ASST  SATYR  ABET  NED
```

50

```
SAHARA    MMDL  BASLE
STERILE  MEARA  ASHEN
PEACOAT  ADIEU  SPIED
  EDH  MOIRA  INSTEPS
  LEMONSOLE  CHIN
TRITE  SLO  REHAN  ARM
BUNYAN  ENDURING  LEE
SEEP  OKS  APIN  TESS
  INDI  STAG  AORTA
LACTIC  ABS  PILOTS
DINAH  KENO  ADIT
IDOL  UNDO  ODE  SWAM
ADD  IMPOSTER  SHYING
LYE  TESLA  MIA  OWNER
  SALT  TOEOFFROG
  HEELTAP  VENAL  OLA
JINNI  ILLER  TITTERS
EVITA  ROARS  EPISTLE
REDAN  STET  SAYSOS
```

51

```
GRIST    PTAS   ASWAN
SUNLIT  LEADON  SHONE
AEROBE  ORIOLE  PEREZ
 ROBERTCONRADVEIDT
   TIO  TEN  INK
CASCA RAGE IAN SALT
ELTONJOHNDENVER LEA
IDEA ASEA REA ISLET
LAPS PENT ASS STAKE
  THE        AKA
MEDEA SPY HART TASK
AWARD ARE OLEO UCLA
GEL JAMESDEANMARTIN
ISIS MET EDEN BEEPS
  AWE ENC EGO
 JAMESCRAIGSTEVENS
KABUL TIMBER LEVITE
INLET STEERS DIETED
PEELS ERLE TRAMS
```

52

```
 ABLE RHOMB   APERS
STRAP AESIR PLANET
THEHARDESTOFALLTHE
REAR HOLA MIRES IRK
AND EENS TANTE ERNO
DEBATE OSTIA AREEL
 ARTSTOSPEAKOFIS
ATSEA ARM LEVIN
SAKI ONEILL NER DRI
ICECAP MUSIC REPEAL
NOT MEN MUTANT HERE
 TINEA MNO WIRED
 BECAUSEMUSICHAS
ALENE TSARS HALTER
FIDO GRITS TRIM ALE
TAP WHOSO SHIM PLIE
 NOMEANINGTOSPEAKOF
ASIANS ELYSE BRETS
STOLA SIXES BARS
```

53

```
SENDA ABEAT FETAS
OCEAN GILDA PIANOS
FOURTEENFORTONIGHT
ANTI XED NOR OURS
  NOT ATIP ALMON
THEGROUNDISOURTABLE
ROX ALLOW DIET LLD
INION ETAS ESTA ESS
BELUGA URN NERD
EYES BOPFABLES ECCE
  THAW IOU TAMERS
DOT ISLE LOLA DOLES
ORO KEEN LAINE EDE
BIGGERTHANABREADBOX
LEERS SURE HRE
ANTE SIT TAR NAPE
 THETALKSHOWMURDERS
 SENATE TEHEE ARRET
 RENEW ORMER HOOPS
```

54

```
 SILT ALTAR RGS JOB
RADIO MARTI ERA EGO
THETOWEROFBABEL SEW
SLAT INDIA BATISTES
  EAT KUNA ENE
 MARYHADALITTLELAMB
MER RENI THEO ELIE
TOM RENO STENCILS
SWISH SALEP LATEST
 STOUTHEARTEDMEN
ATTICS SPOOK EDICT
DRINKSUP SKIM SOU
DICK GRAM ENID TAX
SPEEDTHEGOINGGUEST
 REO LARS UNA
DIASPORA EAGRE RAYE
ROB THEWILDWILDWEST
OWL HOD SLOES VIREO
PAY STS HORNE IGOR
```

55

```
AMOR ABBE WORD RAIL
LAVA SIAM ABIE ENDO
FRENCHDRESSING GILA
 INCHES TINT REARED
 HEN MINT FERRIS
LOCO DOC FIELDS
ERA SWISSCHEESE HMO
SENATORS ROAR CLOD
 ADORE CATTY COULD
ENDURE AVE CHILDS
VOILE APPAL SHALL
ERAT MART GLISSADE
RAN SPANISHRICE BOW
 SOLONG EAT SYNE
 CUPOLA CLAM ASP
TONITE LAID ACTION
ITSA CHINESECHECKER
MEET AURA ETRE ERIE
ESTE TEAL TOED SAND
```

56

57

58

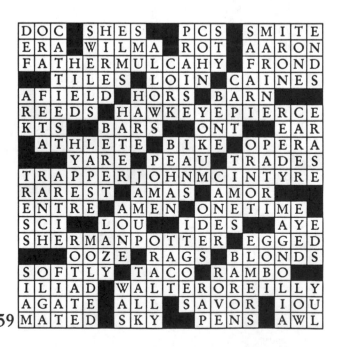

59

60

61

```
PASTA  GRATED   WAR
AGNEW  REGALES  ABEL
GREENWICHTIME   WADES
EEE  SANTA   UVEA  RAH
SERB  IDO  YPRES  SIRE
     LASS   SERENE  EDNA
PALEST  VILER    ERIS
AMISS  MANLY   LAPIN
POTS  PALEO   RAGINGS
ANT   SNOWWHITE   HOE
 GLACIER  ROSES  GOOD
  EXIST  DIVER  ALONG
  ABLE   SAVES  BRIDGE
FROE  LEADER   BRED
LAYS  ALTAR  ARI  EMPS
EBB  EPIC   ABASH  ARA
WILDS  THEBLACKARROW
 CURS  EERIEST  LEASE
  EYE   LANCES  TOTED
```

62

```
CALMED  CHAIR   CADS
ARIOSO  HARDUP  ODETS
FIRSTTHINGIDO   NOFAT
ELATE  ACK   DICK  ERA
SSS  SSH   SILO  SACK
  WHENIWAKEUPINTHE
LENIENT  AMIR   IDO
ABASED  OXEN  LEEWAY
DOTED  RUER  OARS  REM
LAIR  MORNINGIS  MAMA
ETO  PAWS  CIRC  CORAL
 SNEERS  MAZE  SAVANT
  LAC  MONA  PESETAS
 BREATHEONAMIRROR
ROAN  ELMO   SUE   FEE
ALS  ERLE   GOD  SALAS
SLIMY  ANDHOPEITFOGS
SEEME  STEREO  CAROLE
 DRED   SNERD  ERODES
```

63

```
PAPAS  BARDIC   INCAS
ATALE  ELAINE  AVIATE
NORTHOLINIAN   PELLET
ILK  RATED   TESS  CAT
CLAN  SEN  AMUSE  LIME
  APER   INERT  CAUSE
CESTUS  ODDLY  BALM
ONTAP  EVERT  MARABOU
BALL  CEASE  RITE  OHM
AMO  BILLTWRIGHT  NAP
LOU  EVES   NICHE  BARI
TRILLED  RELET  TATAR
 SALT   ROGER  TALESE
RADII  DAVID   THUS
AVID  LEVEE  DOR  ALEF
TEN  RUNE   SORES  OAR
TRACER  NALKNOWLEDGE
ASLOPE  AVOIDS  ADELE
NESTS   LADDIE  POSER
```

64

```
SNUGASABUGINARUG
TOTALEGOSINESONE
ATTULEERURNSTIDE
REELGONEALESHIES
ERRSOUTSLOREETRE
WITHDRAWLASTWEEK
ABIESSPAERATOMAN
TENDCOPSVANERIRE
EVERHELPENDSLONE
RIPEIRESREDODUST
SLIPLACESWABTIER
SETADORNDRYSURGE
ELDERREDRIDERAGO
AMORETEEALIENTER
TOTONAPSBEERSERB
```

65

```
S N A P   E R G S     M A C R O
R E M O   N O I L     O P H I R
S T O W   C U R E     C H I M E
    H I E R O G L Y P H I C S
        R I D E     L A D
    S A L V E   S E A     T I P
A L B E E   T A C T   C O R A
B O U S T R O P H E D O N I C
L E S S   O L I O   A N I S E
E S E   O L D   W I T C H
        L O S     S A L E
    C R Y P T A N A L Y S I S
M A U D E   W A L L   T O L D
A L L I N   L I V E   E T U I
P L E A S   S L O T   D A M P
```

66

```
R E A G A N     C A N     P A C
E R R A T A   C U R T     O R A
O L I V E R N O R T H     I E S
S E L L     E N T   S I N C E
      E C L A T S     D D A Y
E C O   H A R R Y   T E E
F I R   A R E A   C O A X E D
T A R   S U R F E R S   T I E
S O I R E E   U R I S   E R A
    N E D   G N O M E   R E F
H A H A   A D D E R S
O C A L A   W I E   E D I T
R A T   C L A N D E S T I N E
A S C   H A I G   S H U N T S
E T H   Y O N   S E P A L S
```

67

```
A B C S   P A N D A   A D I M
L O O S   A T E A M   N O V A
D Y L A N T H O M A S G R A Y
A D E   E T O N   T R A N S
    E R O S   G A R Y
C A R T O N   S O L O   A D O
A L E C   D A M O N   M A C
M I C H E L E L E E G R A N T
U N A   S A F E R   E T T A
S E P   T H O S   D A N I E L
      C A R E   R A V E
H E C H T   C O M O   E E R
O Z Z I E N E L S O N E D D Y
L I A M   S P A I N   D I N A
M O R E   W A Y N E   S T A N
```

68

```
M A K O   C A S T   C A S H
A M O R   A L L A H   O L I O
N O B E L P E A C E P R I Z E
E Y E   U P O N   N A N T E S
      I R A S   F A T E
W I E S E L   S A K H A R O V
A R C E D   P E K E S   O B I
Y A L E   C R I E D   A P E X
U T A   I R O N S   M E E S E
P E T E R O S E   G O O D E N
      V A S E   L O O N
C R O O N S   A I T S   A V A
R O O K I E O F T H E Y E A R
A D Z E   S H A H S   E R I E
W E E D   T O R E   P O L A
```

69

```
S C A R F   T H I N   M A E S
C A M E O   R O D E   A B B A
O S I E R   I M A B A D B O Y
W E D   B I T E   E D E N S
      D A T E   C O R E
S A L A D S   B A D I N A G E
C R I M E   H O R D E   S O V
R E N E   M A L L S   D I R E
U N E   C E N T S   B A D E N
B A D L A N D S   C A R E S S
      O P U S   M A D E
P R I O R   B A N G   A P T
B A D M I N T O N   E R R O R
A L L E   B A N D   R A I S E
S E E D   A N D Y   S T A T E
```

70

```
F J O R D   S P A R   A C T S
D O V E R   E T T E   R O O T
R E E D Y   M A S T I C A T E
      R A D I I   E E N   T A P
H O B N O B   W A S S A I L S
A T O   C E D E   T E E
S T A   K A Y A K   T R A S H
T E R N   M E T E R   O N T O
O R D I E   S H E A F   C R Y
      L S U   E L M O   H A L
P O L E S T A R   B E C O M E
E T A   E A T   M O L A R
S H I P S H A P E   E R A S E
T E N O   A L E E   S A G A N
O R E S   N E W T   S T E W S
```

71

```
M A S K S   P R E P   A S H E
A L O O P   S O T O   L I A M
C A U S E   A B C D E F G H I
E S P   C E L T   D I N A R
      J K L M   E P E E
A N N A L S   W R E N   A P B
B E A M E   K E R R S   M A E
B A T S   A E I O U   M I T E
E R E   S N A R L   R O G E T
S S S   O T T S   C O L O R S
      P R E S   C O D E
O S S I E   T A P E   W P A
N O P Q R S T U V   N I X O N
E S A U   A O N E   T R Y S T
R O T E   O W E S   S I Z E S
```

72

```
C U S T E R   N O R T H   B L U E
A S H I N E   O R A L E   R E N D
G E O R G E G O R D O N M E A D E
E D S E L   I S I S   O L D E N
      I S L E S   A I R   S R S
R A D I S H   A R D E N
A B R A H A M L I N C O L N
B A I L   R I A N T   S W A M P
A S P   P I C K E T T   B O R
T E S L A   E E R I E   B O L E
      A B N E R D O U B L E D A Y
      G R O W S   E I D E R S
B B B   A B E   C R A T E
E R R E D   I R A N   B A S E S
R O U T E T O G E T T Y S B U R G
I O T A   R E L E E   A T B E S T
A M E S   A D U L L   M E E S E S
```

73

```
G O R D O N   S O U T H   G R A Y
A M E R C E   A R R A U   R A B I
G E N E R A L R O B E R T E L E E
S N I D E   V I N I   E W E L L
      A V I S O   A R N   S E D
A G O U T I   A G E N A
J E F F E R S O N D A V I S
O N T O   G E L E E   S T A M P
U R E   A E D I L E S   S O O
R E N A L   A G I S T   O H R E
      G E O R G E E P I C K E T T
      E V A D E   L A S S E S
A P B   A R S   R U L E R
P O R E D   N E N E   F E S T A
R O U T E T O A P P O M A T T O X
I N I T   A U D I O   A R R I V E
L A N E   G R A N T   S E E R E D
```

74

```
P A S H A   L A M A S   B E G I N
A R L E N   A G I L E   A T O N E
N E E R D O W E L L S   G O L D A
T A P   O R E S   U T E S   D I P
  S T A V E S   V E T   M B A S
      M E L   L O I T E R E R
A B L E R   S O R A   R E S I D E
G R O S   S T A R   A N T A C I D
N I L   S H E M   F R A S   K A I
E N L A C E S   T E A L   C E N T
S K Y L A B   M A S T   N O R A S
      G A D A B O U T   S O T
E T A S   N O S   T O T E M S
P E G   O G R E   A O N E   A T A
O R G A N   S L A C K S P I N E D
C R E T E   C L I M E   A C T E D
H A R E S   H E L E N   D E A R S
```

75

```
L O O T S   H A S P   B E F I T
A C C R A   A L T A   P A L A C E
M E T I C U L O U S   A R I S E N
A L O P   N E E D S   I N A T
S O P   S T Y   I N N S   I D A
  T I T H E   S C O U T   A D E N
      H E S I T A N T   O R I B I
G A T E   T R I M   P U T O U T
A C H   D E E R   F A R R   U N A
M O O R E D   A R L O   A S K S
B R U T E   D E T A I L E D
I N G E   C O M E T   I D E A S
A S H   C O M B   A F T   L A B
      T R A P   A B A C I   E L L A
B E F O R E   S O L I C I T O U S
E X U L T S   S L I D   R O U T E
D E L L S   Y E A S   A N T E S
```

76

SCARF · LANDS · PUPAS
ELGAR · ASYET · ENOLA
PORTERHOUSE · THROW
ANI · EARN · IND · UTES
LENAPE · EAR · WARMS
· ROSS · REGATTA ·
WADER · ILK · ERE · NBA
EDENTATE · INVESTED
NAPA · RUE · ATE · AERO
CROSSBAR · MISPLAYS
HER · AIT · HAL · OVULE
· TENTERS · EIRE ·
LANGE · ETC · STREWN
PITT · RCA · HAIL · RIO
EMIRS · APPORTIONED
OBOES · SERIN · EDILE
NONET · ADORE · REEDS

77

WEBB · PLOY · DOG · CAM
ALAI · LORE · ELEVATE
LANGUAGES · BANANAS
STD · LIES · MINERALS
HELMETS · LTD · ILLY
EONS · HAL · SOO
APAST · COMES · SUPRA
RODS · GAPE · TUSSLED
OLE · PENINSULA · AIR
MARCELS · DUDE · RYNE
ARSON · TREES · SEISM
LSD · ADS · APIN
DEAL · RUG · BRIDGES
ANTELOPE · CURE · CRY
MORGANS · COMEDIANS
ALIENEE · ALPS · WRIT
SAP · EST · TEST · ODES

78

AFTER · FIERCE · GAGES
CRONY · ENLARGE · AMUSE
HIREEDUCATION · MOIST
EAT · SUDAN · IAMA · SET
DREG · CAN · GESTE · GENE
REAL · HITTER · RACE
REGENT · RIMES · TUNE
EARED · FARMS · CREED
EVEN · ALGAE · SHIELDS
FEE · FLEEMARKETS · OTO
SCALDED · BOISE · PLAN
ELIOT · PROPS · SOLVE
SMIT · PRAMS · IRISES
STOA · SPOOKY · TRIS
TANS · TEASE · BRA · EROS
ARK · NARC · BOONE · ICH
PTERO · THEMANWITHAHO
LEYTE · HEROINE · TATER
EDSEL · DACTYL · AWARE

79

ACT · COS · ADA · MASK
BIRD · HIRER · PATIENCE
ATOM · MAORI · SULLIVAN
FRUITS · NICHE · AIRILY
TIPTOP · OAHU · RSA · LEA
NEREID · LAM · ETCH
ISNO · ROLL · ELSA
PAP · HAW · ADROIT · LOPS
ADENOF · RID · ASH · MCII
THEYEOMENOFTHEGUARD
MEWL · ROT · YEH · SETTEE
OREO · EDIBLE · JON · EDS
SEEN · EERY · CRUD
STAR · ACE · SCIONS
SSH · EON · VANS · ENDEAR
WHALER · HORDE · REGINA
IOLANTHE · TANTE · EGGS
SAVOYARD · ELDER · SHEP
STES · SHY · LST · SRS

80

BRACE · LOGE · SHOAL
RETAR · ASONG · PANDA
AVARS · NIECE · IDEAS
YULETIDES · RIN · ANE
SELF · CUR · LODESTAR
RIIS · SONATA
DEFENCE · AVIS · TARA
UNREAL · STEM · MELON
ANA · NEUT · IOWA · OWE
LUISE · NEON · ARENAS
SILO · TIRE · PRESENT
STOVER · ASST
SCROOGES · ENA · EVAS
NAE · OAR · SNOWFLAKE
ASSET · SCARP · ALLIN
REEVE · ERROL · MEETS
ESTER · OILY · ESTEE

81

PATON · RETRO · IMET
ADELA · AROOM · SATIE
CANES · TAMOSHANTER
EGG · ABASED · OBTUSE
REAR · ETE · SORER
LEOTARD · SALAMI
HALFWIT · IKILL · ODD
AROUND · ELEE · AGREE
RING · ESQUIRE · ETAL
USHER · AUER · LANATE
MEA · EATIN · EMPIRES
STEAMY · TAXICAB
DWARF · SER · LOAM
LARIAT · ANIMAL · AGO
STOCKINGCAP · ACRID
DANTE · RIANT · LADLE
PASS · ANASS · ANSEL

82

```
■ A C R E S ■ S A M ■ A L L A
A T H E N A ■ I L O ■ S O U R
S T O N E D ■ C A T A P U L T
I N W A R D S ■ R E S I D U E
■ ■ M O L E C U L A R ■ ■ ■ ■
P A C E ■ E D A M ■ R A T E D
I N A ■ B R A Y ■ U T I L E
P E R D U ■ N E Z ■ L E T I N
E A T O N ■ ■ N O N E ■ A D S
T R A G I ■ I N R E ■ S N E E
■ ■ G O O S E B U M P ■ ■ ■
E X P E N D S ■ A R E A R U G
B E A R S O U T ■ O D D E S T
O R L E ■ R E O ■ N E E D E D
N O E L ■ S S E ■ S A S E S
```

83

```
■ C A T S ■ T A R A S ■ M O T H S
M O R A L ■ A L E N E ■ R A R E E
E R I C A ■ T O A S T ■ S T I R S
L E A K Y F A W C E T T ■ S P O T
■ ■ S E E ■ T R E E ■ ■ L E E
E L K ■ R E D O ■ R A C I E S T
T A N S ■ D U R E R ■ L O N G
T R I E S ■ D A L I ■ S I T A R
E A G R E ■ E T U D E ■ N O Y E S
■ S H E E T ■ O D I N ■ A N N I E
■ T I D Y ■ R E N D S ■ E O N S
T R A N S I T ■ G O E S ■ R E S
H E N ■ N E A P ■ ■ A P T
E N D S ■ G E T R I T T E R H I M
A D D I E ■ M O U L E ■ C O A L S
R E A D S ■ E N D E D ■ I V I E S
T R Y S T ■ D E E D S ■ E E L S
```

84

```
A B A C K ■ M E A L ■ S A T A N
C A N O E ■ A L L O T ■ A M O L E
T H O M A S W O L F E H O U N D S
A N N E ■ A W N ■ T R E ■ S E A T
■ T O T O ■ ■ ■ R A T E ■
A L A ■ S E R G ■ O A T S ■ S K I
H O R A C E M A N N C H E S T E R
S Y L V A N ■ L A W E S ■ H A N K
■ E A R ■ B E M A S ■ H A T
O M N I ■ C O N E R ■ C E R I S E
N O E L C O W A R D L Y L I O N S
E D S ■ A B E S ■ S O B E ■ N Y E
■ L A W D ■ ■ B E N D ■
A R G O ■ E O S ■ B B L ■ I C E S
P E A R L B U C K E Y E S T A T E
E N U R E ■ T O O L E ■ A T T A R
S O L E D ■ T S A R ■ M O O L A
```

85

```
M A J A ■ G A S P S ■ S A R A S
A R U N ■ O L E O S ■ S P R I N T
M A I N F R A M E S ■ P E R S I A
A B C ■ A I R E S ■ M A R ■ I M P
■ S Y S T E M S ■ T E R M I N A L
■ B O E R ■ T O I L ■ O G L E
B O Y S ■ ■ H E R E ■ M S U
A N T ■ U S E R G R O U P ■ M A N
R U E ■ R I M ■ ■ R I A ■ I D O
E S S ■ A P P L E C A R T ■ C A D
■ E L S ■ E A R L ■ A R M S
S T I R ■ A E R O ■ S E G O
P R O G R A M S ■ S T O M A C H
R I D ■ E L Y ■ A S I A M ■ H O S
E P I C A L ■ F L O P P Y D I S K
E L D E R S ■ A M U S E ■ E P E E
S E E R S ■ S A T Y R ■ I S A W
```

86

```
A L O H A ■ C R O W D ■ B A S I C
S I N U S ■ A E R I E ■ E L E N A
S T E M T O S T E R N ■ D E C O R
E R A ■ A V E R ■ Y E T ■ O N E
T E L L ■ A D A M ■ B A R O N E T
■ O W L ■ C O D ■ B U D D
B O C C I ■ S T O U T ■ B O S O M
E C L I P S E ■ D A R E ■ R I S E
R E O ■ E I R E ■ L A P S ■ G I T
R A C E ■ P I T T ■ C A T C H E R
A N K L E ■ F O R T Y ■ O U T R E
■ T A T A ■ N O W ■ J A R ■
I R O N A G E ■ T I D E ■ D R A W
R O W ■ O T T ■ D U E T ■ I R E
I D E A L ■ H A N D S P R I N G S
S E R V E ■ E X U L T ■ E N S U E
H O S E A ■ R I L E Y ■ S N E E R
```

87

```
E R G ■ A C H E S O N ■ F E R M I
V I A ■ C H I N E S E ■ A L I E N
A L F ■ H I G H W A T E R M A R K
D E F T ■ C H A ■ G S A ■ L E S
E S S E N ■ P U C E ■ S S E
■ N E A R T O ■ H E A R T O F
C L O T U R E ■ T R I ■ M A O R I
H I G H T E S T ■ A G E S ■ M A R
I N D ■ A S A ■ S H E ■ T N T
L E E ■ S L U R ■ H O L E H I G H
D A N T E ■ R A M ■ N E G A T E S
E R S K I N E ■ A S T R A Y
■ O S E ■ S H A H ■ D E F E R
T W O ■ I O U ■ N E A ■ S A N E
H I G H A N D M I G H T Y ■ D O S
A L L I E ■ A U R E O L E ■ E L I
W E E P S ■ S P A R G E S ■ D A N
```

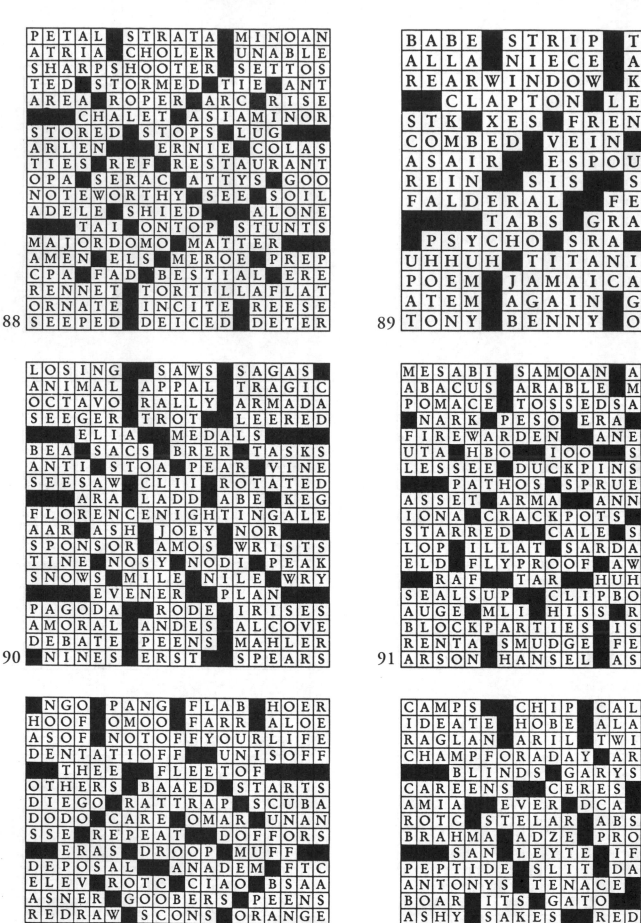

88

P E T A L	S T R A T A	M I N O A N
A T R I A	C H O L E R	U N A B L E
S H A R P S H O O T E R	S E T T O S
T E D	S T O R M E D	T I E	A N T
A R E A	R O P E R	A R C	R I S E
C H A L E T	A S I A M I N O R
S T O R E D	S T O P S	L U G
A R L E N	E R N I E	C O L A S
T I E S	R E F	R E S T A U R A N T
O P A	S E R A C	A T T Y S	G O O
N O T E W O R T H Y	S E E	S O I L
A D E L E	S H I E D	A L O N E
T A I	O N T O P	S T U N T S
M A J O R D O M O	M A T T E R
A M E N	E L S	M E R O E	P R E P
C P A	F A D	B E S T I A L	E R E
R E N N E T	T O R T I L L A F L A T
O R N A T E	I N C I T E	R E E S E
S E E P E D	D E I C E D	D E T E R

89

B A B E	S T R I P	T A L L
A L L A	N I E C E	A R E A
R E A R W I N D O W	K N E W
C L A P T O N	L E A R N
S T K	X E S	F R E N Z Y
C O M B E D	V E I N
A S A I R	E S P O U S A L
R E I N	S I S	S U R E
F A L D E R A L	F E S T A
T A B S	G R A P E S
P S Y C H O	S R A	I L E
U H H U H	T I T A N I C
P O E M	J A M A I C A I N N
A T E M	A G A I N	G O B Y
T O N Y	B E N N Y	O N C E

90

L O S I N G	S A W S	S A G A S
A N I M A L	A P P A L	T R A G I C
O C T A V O	R A L L Y	A R M A D A
S E E G E R	T R O T	L E E R E D
E L I A	M E D A L S
B E A	S A C S	B R E R	T A S K S
A N T I	S T O A	P E A R	V I N E
S E E S A W	C L I I	R O T A T E D
A R A	L A D D	A B E	K E G
F L O R E N C E N I G H T I N G A L E
A A R	A S H	J O E Y	N O R
S P O N S O R	A M O S	W R I S T S
T I N E	N O S Y	N O D I	P E A K
S N O W S	M I L E	N I L E	W R Y
E V E N E R	P L A N
P A G O D A	R O D E	I R I S E S
A M O R A L	A N D E S	A L C O V E
D E B A T E	P E E N S	M A H L E R
N I N E S	E R S T	S P E A R S

91

M E S A B I	S A M O A N	A S S A M
A B A C U S	A R A B L E	M A H R E
P O M A C E	T O S S E D S A L A D S
N A R K	P E S O	E R A	O D E S
F I R E W A R D E N	A N E M O N E
U T A	H B O	1 0 0	S E W
L E S S E E	D U C K P I N S	B A T
P A T H O S	S P R U E	O R E
A S S E T	A R M A	A N N E X E S
I O N A	C R A C K P O T S	N E A T
S T A R R E D	C A L E	S A S S Y
L O P	I L L A T	S A R D A R
E L D	F L Y P R O O F	A W E I G H
R A F	T A R	H U H	S O T
S E A L S U P	C L I P B O A R D S
A U G E	M L I	H I S S	R E A L
B L O C K P A R T I E S	I S D E E P
R E N T A	S M U D G E	F E E L S O
A R S O N	H A N S E L	A S S I S T

92

N G O	P A N G	F L A B	H O E R
H O O F	O M O O	F A R R	A L O E
A S O F	N O T O F F Y O U R L I F E
D E N T A T I O F F	U N I S O F F
T H E E	F L E E T O F
O T H E R S	B A A E D	S T A R T S
D I E G O	R A T T R A P	S C U B A
D O D O	C A R E	O M A R	U N A N
S S E	R E P E A T	D O F F O R S
E R A S	D R O O P	M U F F
D E P O S A L	A N A D E M	F T C
E L E V	R O T C	C I A O	B S A A
A S N E R	G O O B E R S	P E E N S
R E D R A W	S C O N S	O R A N G E
D I S H O U T	F O R T
O F F E I N A	R E C O F F F E R S
K E E P O N T H E G R A S S	O N E R
R A T E	O B I E	E R S E	O C A S
A T E E	W Y E S	D R A T	T E D

93

C A M P S	C H I P	C A L O R I C
I D E A T E	H O B E	A L A M E D A
R A G L A N	A R I L	T W I N N E D
C H A M P F O R A D A Y	A R I O S E
B L I N D S	G A R Y S
C A R E E N S	C E R E S	T O S S
A M I A	E V E R	D C A	H E E P
R O T C	S T E L A R	A B S E N C E
B R A H M A	A D Z E	P R O M O T E
S A N	L E Y T E	I F I
P E P T I D E	S L I T	D A L L A S
A N T O N Y S	T E N A C E	L U K E
B O A R	I T S	G A T O	I L I E
A S H Y	S A K E S	R E D O U N D
B A R I T	F A S T E N
C H I S E L	M Y B L U E H E A V E N
H A V A N A S	M E A T	O P I A T E
A B O U N D S	O T T O	S E R I A L
P A R L E Y S	N E S S	N E L L S

94

```
AREA   ALOHAS  SAP
BRENDA REDUST  ISLAM
RUNNINGATEMPERATURE
ANDANTE TRI REMORAS
     ENA  DANA  RAGA
WALKEDACROOKEDMILE
AGENT  TERRA   ERA
DENOTE UNA   PRE MAP
 ITAL  ATLAST  DRILL
SUET MITE  VEAL  ALLY
TANYA  TERCET  ACTI
ART  SRA  ASS  POTTED
  ISE  MARTA   SEINE
RUNTHESTRAIGHTRACE
PETS  ELSE   LIE
ATTIRED  LAW  MANACLE
WRESTLEWITHAPROBLEM
NORTE  SHEKEL  SWEATS
  SSS  TYRANT   SEWS
```

95

```
ONSET  PASTE   SHARES
ROLLO  ASPEN  CONDUIT
DIAMONDHEAD   RIDABLE
EST  LODEN  SEELS  YER
REED  TEND  YES   AMEN
     ICED  AWED  PRONE
STENOS  BEMAD  NANU
LOMAN  FEVER  SILENCE
ARE  MERIT  AONE  TAX
VER  PEARLHARBOR  ASP
IRA  RATA  YULES   ITO
COLLINS  ASTER  WANES
  DADS  PITON  MOUSSE
RIFLE  BORS   MANN
OMOO  SUN  IMET  TREY
MAR  EPODE  SATES  ELI
AREAWAY  THEJADEMASK
NESTERS  TIROL  EYDIE
OTTERS   USERS  ROSES
```

96

```
PAPAL   FLEES    BCD
ATONAL  RILLE  ASSORT
PLEASE  EMMER  SCALES
SITSHEONNEVERSO  LAP
    ERIC  RENE  RAIDS
CHAWS  LHD  EVENTS
HIGH  SITU  BRET  AIS
IDEO  DEODAR  ATHRONE
   MOIRA  SIDLES  NEO
CHAPS   SMOTE  IBSEN
DEP  MANTEL  MEDAL
TAPIOCA  ADROIT  EASE
PAM  MTGS  ENDS  AMAN
  REPEAL  STE  STILL
CHITA  NATA   ARAT
HIT  SITSONHISBOTTOM
ARISTA  GRIEG  ERRATA
REOPEN  OATEN  DEARIE
DNA    WHALE   SYNCS
```

97

```
OWES  SLID  TAPE  BAIN
KENT  HARI  ELLS  ONTO
RENO  AMOS  ALAS  AGES
APARTMENT  MONASTERY
   ERE  MASS   AYAH
EMERY  DANK  REVOICE
DURO  ENCYST  DEUCED
OTOOLES  ESTOP  SANG
MISMATES  CARR  PENTE
    CORNERSTONE
LATHE  TAMA  SMOTHERS
ODIE  SKIPS  INSOLES
MITRES  ELECTS  MING
ANIMATO  RARE  RESET
   ICER  ISNO  EOS
PARTHENON  DORMITORY
ASEA  RAMS  APIE  EGOS
RING  ETAT  LEOS  ARTE
KATE  DENS  SRTA  DEAR
```

98

```
BRONTE  STARR   SNAG
RENTED  CANOE   NOVA
ONTHEUPANDUP   ATAN
WOOS  CAN  ATE   PUTT
   FEW  NELL   PAR
EVOKED  ACTS  ENTRY
LINED  DIRE  LENO
STEN  SODA  CARESS
EAU  UPENDED   NUT
 SPHERE  KIDS  MULE
  MILE  DUNE  JAFFA
UMASS  COPE  TOOFAR
NON  ALOG   LOT
FUSS  ONE  IOU  SEMI
ASHE  STANDUPCOMIC
ISIT  ERROL  ERMINE
REPS  SASSY  EYELID
```

99

```
YOGA  LAPSE   TIDE
MORES  IVIES  ROUND
ADAMS  VENTS  INANE
RET  USER  ALP   DUB
CLEARER  SKYE  PSIS
   LEX  EPISTLE
NOMAD  PART  DENIAL
ORES  ARTY  BOA  SRI
ODE  IRIS  FAWN  SON
NET  NIX  CORN  FUSE
ERSATZ  CARD  GREEN
   FOOTAGE  PRE
RUNT  NODE  SEATTLE
USA  OAT  CHAP  AID
SUDAN  TUBER  NAMED
TRICE  ETUDE  ELEGY
PRES   RENEW  LIRE
```

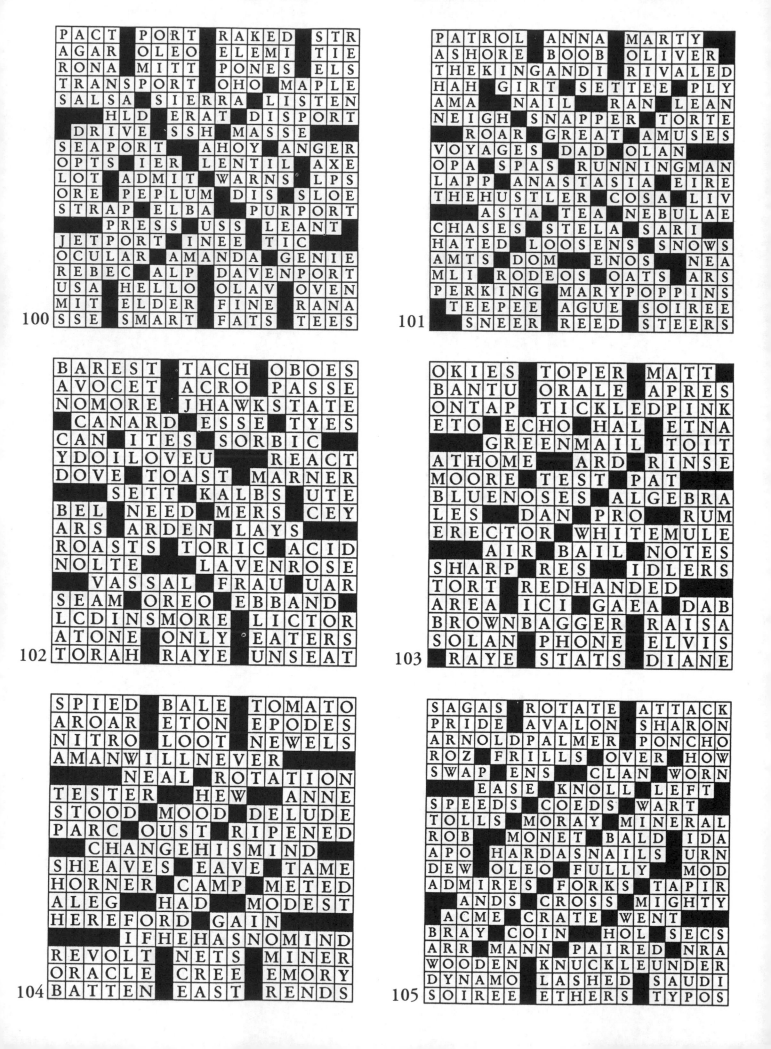

100

```
P A C T   P O R T   R A K E D   S T R
A G A R   O L E O   E L E M I   T I E
R O N A   M I T T   P O N E S   E L S
T R A N S P O R T   O H O   M A P L E
S A L S A   S I E R R A   L I S T E N
      H L D   E R A T   D I S P O R T
  D R I V E   S S H   M A S S E
S E A P O R T   A H O Y   A N G E R
O P T S   I E R   L E N T I L   A X E
L O T   A D M I T   W A R N S   L P S
O R E   P E P L U M   D I S   S L O E
S T R A P   E L B A   P U R P O R T
    P R E S S   U S S   L E A N T
J E T P O R T   I N E E   T I C
O C U L A R   A M A N D A   G E N I E
R E B E C   A L P   D A V E N P O R T
U S A   H E L L O   O L A V   O V E N
M I T   E L D E R   F I N E   R A N A
S S E   S M A R T   F A T S   T E E S
```

101

```
P A T R O L   A N N A   M A R T Y
A S H O R E   B O O B   O L I V E R
T H E K I N G A N D I   R I V A L E D
H A H   G I R T   S E T T E E   P L Y
A M A   N A I L   R A N   L E A N
N E I G H   S N A P P E R   T O R T E
  R O A R   G R E A T   A M U S E S
V O Y A G E S   D A D   O L A N
O P A   S P A S   R U N N I N G M A N
L A P P   A N A S T A S I A   E I R E
T H E H U S T L E R   C O S A   L I V
  A S T A   T E A   N E B U L A E
C H A S E S   S T E L A   S A R I
H A T E D   L O O S E N S   S N O W S
A M T S   D O M   E N O S   N E A
M L I   R O D E O S   O A T S   A R S
P E R K I N G   M A R Y P O P P I N S
  T E E P E E   A G U E   S O I R E E
  S N E E R   R E E D   S T E E R S
```

102

```
B A R E S T   T A C H   O B O E S
A V O C E T   A C R O   P A S S E
N O M O R E   J H A W K S T A T E
  C A N A R D   E S S E   T Y E S
C A N   I T E S   S O R B I C
Y D O I L O V E U   R E A C T
D O V E   T O A S T   M A R N E R
    S E T T   K A L B S   U T E
B E L   N E E D   M E R S   C E Y
A R S   A R D E N   L A Y S
R O A S T S   T O R I C   A C I D
N O L T E   L A V E N R O S E
  V A S S A L   F R A U   U A R
S E A M   O R E O   E B B A N D
L C D I N S M O R E   L I C T O R
A T O N E   O N L Y   E A T E R S
T O R A H   R A Y E   U N S E A T
```

103

```
O K I E S   T O P E R   M A T T
B A N T U   O R A L E   A P R E S
O N T A P   T I C K L E D P I N K
E T O   E C H O   H A L   E T N A
    G R E E N M A I L   T O I T
A T H O M E   A R D   R I N S E
M O O R E   T E S T   P A T
B L U E N O S E S   A L G E B R A
L E S   D A N   P R O   R U M
E R E C T O R   W H I T E M U L E
    A I R   B A I L   N O T E S
S H A R P   R E S   I D L E R S
T O R T   R E D H A N D E D
A R E A   I C I   G A E A   D A B
B R O W N B A G G E R   R A I S A
S O L A N   P H O N E   E L V I S
R A Y E   S T A T S   D I A N E
```

104

```
S P I E D   B A L E   T O M A T O
A R O A R   E T O N   E P O D E S
N I T R O   L O O T   N E W E L S
A M A N W I L L N E V E R
    N E A L   R O T A T I O N
T E S T E R   H E W   A N N E
S T O O D   M O O D   D E L U D E
P A R C   O U S T   R I P E N E D
  C H A N G E H I S M I N D
S H E A V E S   E A V E   T A M E
H O R N E R   C A M P   M E T E D
A L E G   H A D   M O D E S T
H E R E F O R D   G A I N
    I F H E H A S N O M I N D
R E V O L T   N E T S   M I N E R
O R A C L E   C R E E   E M O R Y
B A T T E N   E A S T   R E N D S
```

105

```
S A G A S   R O T A T E   A T T A C K
P R I D E   A V A L O N   S H A R O N
A R N O L D P A L M E R   P O N C H O
R O Z   F R I L L S   O V E R   H O W
S W A P   E N S   C L A N   W O R N
  E A S E   K N O L L   L E F T
S P E E D S   C O E D S   W A R T
T O L L S   M O R A Y   M I N E R A L
R O B   M O N E T   B A L D   I D A
A P O   H A R D A S N A I L S   U R N
D E W   O L E O   F U L L Y   M O D
A D M I R E S   F O R K S   T A P I R
  A N D S   C R O S S   M I G H T Y
  A C M E   C R A T E   W E N T
B R A Y   C O I N   H O L   S E C S
A R R   M A N N   P A I R E D   N R A
W O O D E N   K N U C K L E U N D E R
D Y N A M O   L A S H E D   S A U D I
S O I R E E   E T H E R S   T Y P O S
```

106

```
ANTES   PETRO   PITH
BAHAI  LATHERS  RAHAL
OVERT  INCENSE  ENERO
LAS  ETRE  STORMS  MEG
THIS  HELLO   BOTTOMS
 OSCAR  SANA   MORT
 TILED  POMPOM  OHS
FIE  GEO  FOAMY  WEIR
LGR  ABEL  TRIAL  ERGO
OUSTER  OCHER  OBLONG
SAKI  OUTRE  SANE  FEU
SNAP  TRUER  UGH  TRE
 ART  HESTER  SLASH
 AONE  EGOS  ENDED
HAMPERS  ICING  ABET
ONA  ESTEEM  MUST  RAH
SIZED  ATTEMPT  AMICI
STOLE  TUNNELS  RADON
 AVID  NATTY  SCENE
```

107

```
POSER  TRACES   GHOST
UTILE  REGALIA  LUNAR
THEFIVESENSES  OPERA
TEN  DIMES  SHAW  NOD
SRAS  SOT  FATES  PINE
 WEAR  MORASS  EGGS
CITERS  GOUTS   BAHS
ANWAR  NITRE  SPILT
SPOT  EARTH  ONENESS
AUF  ONCLOUDNINE  TEC
 TOLLERS  NESTS  NAIL
 REESE  IDLES  PINNA
 STAS  CARET  SANDED
HUHS  STAGED  FILE
APET  HEROD  LID  RACE
SRS  LEAP  AONES  SAM
TEHEE  SEVENCARDSTUD
EMOTE  ETERNAL  ABASE
NEWER  STEELS  KAREN
```

108

```
MAMAS  SOHO  HOPI  LEG
AROSE  ODIN  EBAN  ETA
PETERANDTHEWOLF  THY
ACHAIR  MARNE  ABOIL
MAYO  GUYANA  NANCY
 FOURANDTWENTY
USE  HEEL  OLA  BRA
RUSTY  YEA  TRIB  FRAY
INTRO  GIOTTO  LATE
 BEAUTYANDTHEBEAST
HELP  RANEES  LISLE
ELLS  EGIS  YER  GRIEG
PTA  VET  SODA  ERG
 FAIRANDSQUARE
CABAL  ERASER  SHEM
OPERA  RACER  NICOLE
MAN  STICKSANDSTONES
URN  KANT  SPEE  IRONS
STY  AUKS  YETI  STRAY
```

109

```
MISC  ACE  AMP  IMPEL
ASTO  LOAN  NIE  NOLTE
LION  UNSETTLE  TROTS
LAWRENCEWHELK  HOYAS
 HEARSES  END  SEN
 DRED  SENATOR  VON
SOO  ARE  CLAMITYJANE
TRUST  SAR  DREAMER
PETTI  MOM  EAU  LORD
 COCKLEDOODLEDOO
ARUN  NIN  INN  RUSTY
BOREDOM  TAG  AXERS
MUSSELBEACH  ROC  SAL
STE  BLONDIE  EMUS
 BAS  DEN  TAILEND
COLIC  CONCHISTADORS
ATOLL  PROHIBIT  ATIP
STAGE  ASS  DINE  KIVA
HOMES  SEE  AGR  ATES
```

110

```
HEAL  SPAS  CWOS  REST
ALVA  WALK  HAMS  ILAY
LIAR  ALLIGATOR  BARK
TZIGANE  MOTTO  CAINE
SALON  SPATE  DUNNES
 SKIRT  TEAGARDEN
ARC  ALEE  SLUICE
LOUISIANA  TIA  DAS
MARC  ACCUSER  ALBERT
ODDER  TIRADES  LOSER
SELDOM  LARAMIE  NINE
TOE  WOE  MARDIGRAS
 DULLEA  REIN  ESS
 DIXIELAND  KNEES
PADRES  SNAPS  PLEBE
AREAS  STONY  BATEAUX
TRAY  JAMBALAYA  ETRE
NOTE  ORAL  ECRU  PURR
AWED  BANE  STEP  SPOT
```

111

```
AURAS  FRET   GATE
SLANT  RABID  OLLIE
ANITA  IRATE  PEARL
ALITTLENONSENSE
 OWL    TIN
PICARO  TSAR  POPE
IDOL  STEEL  SENOR
NOWANDTHEN  GENERA
 AIDE  THEM
ATTAIN  ISRELISHED
FRAIL  TRAYS  SURE
TEND  WEST  ASTERN
 GAS    SIP
BYMOSTGENTLEMEN
FREON  EERIE  EARED
BELLE  DEICE  DRIED
IDLE  SEED  SENDS
```

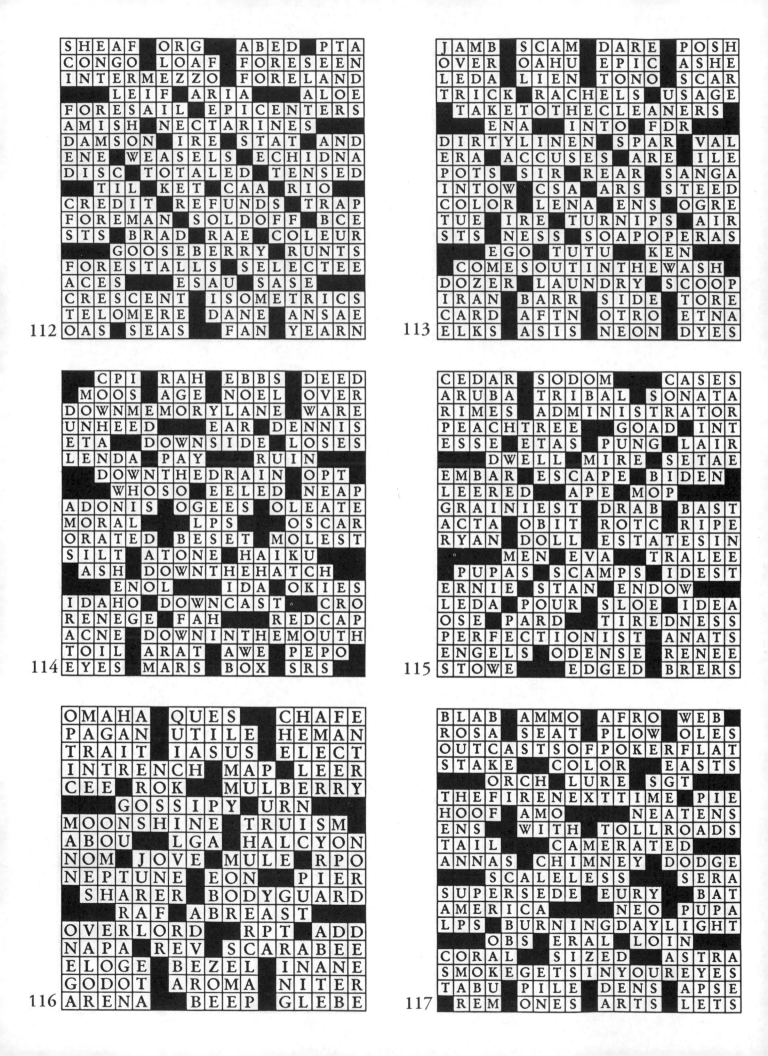

112

```
S H E A F   O R G   A B E D   P T A
C O N G O   L O A F   F O R E S E E N
I N T E R M E Z Z O   F O R E L A N D
      L E I F   A R I A   A L O E
F O R E S A I L   E P I C E N T E R S
A M I S H   N E C T A R I N E S
D A M S O N   I R E   S T A T   A N D
E N E   W E A S E L S   E C H I D N A
D I S C   T O T A L E D   T E N S E D
    T I L   K E T   C A A   R I O
C R E D I T   R E F U N D S   T R A P
F O R E M A N   S O L D O F F   B C E
S T S   B R A D   R A E   C O L E U R
      G O O S E B E R R Y   R U N T S
F O R E S T A L L S   S E L E C T E E
A C E S   E S A U   S A S E
C R E S C E N T   I S O M E T R I C S
T E L O M E R E   D A N E   A N S A E
O A S   S E A S   F A N   Y E A R N
```

113

```
J A M B   S C A M   D A R E   P O S H
O V E R   O A H U   E P I C   A S H E
L E D A   L I E N   T O N O   S C A R
T R I C K   R A C H E L S   U S A G E
    T A K E T O T H E C L E A N E R S
      E N A   I N T O   F D R
D I R T Y L I N E N   S P A R   V A L
E R A   A C C U S E S   A R E   I L E
P O T S   S I R   R E A R   S A N G A
I N T O W   C S A   A R S   S T E E D
C O L O R   L E N A   E N S   O G R E
T U E   I R E   T U R N I P S   A I R
S T S   N E S S   S O A P O P E R A S
      E G O   T U T U   K E N
  C O M E S O U T I N T H E W A S H
D O Z E R   L A U N D R Y   S C O O P
I R A N   B A R R   S I D E   T O R E
C A R D   A F T N   O T R O   E T N A
E L K S   A S I S   N E O N   D Y E S
```

114

```
  C P I   R A H   E B B S   D E E D
  M O O S   A G E   N O E L   O V E R
D O W N M E M O R Y L A N E   W A R E
U N H E E D   E A R   D E N N I S
E T A   D O W N S I D E   L O S E S
L E N D A   P A Y   R U I N
  D O W N T H E D R A I N   O P T
  W H O S O   E E L E D   N E A P
A D O N I S   O G E E S   O L E A T E
M O R A L   L P S   O S C A R
O R A T E D   B E S E T   M O L E S T
S I L T   A T O N E   H A I K U
  A S H   D O W N T H E H A T C H
    E N O L   I D A   O K I E S
I D A H O   D O W N C A S T   C R O
R E N E G E   F A H   R E D C A P
A C N E   D O W N I N T H E M O U T H
T O I L   A R A T   A W E   P E P O
E Y E S   M A R S   B O X   S R S
```

115

```
C E D A R   S O D O M   C A S E S
A R U B A   T R I B A L   S O N A T A
R I M E S   A D M I N I S T R A T O R
P E A C H T R E E   G O A D   I N T
E S S E   E T A S   P U N G   L A I R
    D W E L L   M I R E   S E T A E
E M B A R   E S C A P E   B I D E N
L E E R E D   A P E   M O P
G R A I N I E S T   D R A B   B A S T
A C T A   O B I T   R O T C   R I P E
R Y A N   D O L L   E S T A T E S I N
    M E N   E V A   T R A L E E
  P U P A S   S C A M P S   I D E S T
E R N I E   S T A N   E N D O W
L E D A   P O U R   S L O E   I D E A
O S E   P A R D   T I R E D N E S S
P E R F E C T I O N I S T   A N A T S
E N G E L S   O D E N S E   R E N E E
S T O W E   E D G E D   B R E R S
```

116

```
O M A H A   Q U E S   C H A F E
P A G A N   U T I L E   H E M A N
T R A I T   I A S U S   E L E C T
I N T R E N C H   M A P   L E E R
C E E   R O K   M U L B E R R Y
    G O S S I P Y   U R N
M O O N S H I N E   T R U I S M
A B O U   L G A   H A L C Y O N
N O M   J O V E   M U L E   R P O
N E P T U N E   E O N   P I E R
  S H A R E R   B O D Y G U A R D
    R A F   A B R E A S T
O V E R L O R D   R P T   A D D
N A P A   R E V   S C A R A B E E
E L O G E   B E Z E L   I N A N E
G O D O T   A R O M A   N I T E R
A R E N A   B E E P   G L E B E
```

117

```
B L A B   A M M O   A F R O   W E B
R O S A   S E A T   P L O W   O L E S
O U T C A S T S O F P O K E R F L A T
S T A K E   C O L O R   E A S T S
    O R C H   L U R E   S G T
T H E F I R E N E X T T I M E   P I E
H O O F   A M O   N E A T E N S
E N S   W I T H   T O L L R O A D S
T A I L   C A M E R A T E D
A N N A S   C H I M N E Y   D O D G E
    S C A L E L E S S   S E R A
S U P E R S E D E   E U R Y   B A T
A M E R I C A   N E O   P U P A
L P S   B U R N I N G D A Y L I G H T
    O B S   E R A L   L O I N
C O R A L   S I Z E D   A S T R A
S M O K E G E T S I N Y O U R E Y E S
T A B U   P I L E   D E N S   A P S E
  R E M   O N E S   A R T S   L E T S
```

118

```
I T I M E   I O P I N   S C A M P S
S O F A S   C R A N I A   T A K E I O
H O O T S   I O C E N T S A D A N C E
O K R A   A C N E   E M O T E   T A V
T A T   K I L O   I T A L   B A R E
    H A I L E   R U I N   P A R L O R
C L E V E S   D O P E   O S E
L A B E L   T R U S S   A S T R I D E
E N O S   C H A S M   O N T O   O U R
F O O   I O O Y E A R S W A R   G E R
T S K   O I L S   N A T A L   H A L O
S E S S I L E   A S T E R   M I L E R
    P O E   S H O O   W O R L D S
P L A C I D   S P I N   P O R T O
L A M A   A T I P   T R O T   N I L
A S P   T I T E R   C E I L   S H O E
T H E I O O I N I G H T S   R I A T A
T E R R E T   S N E E R S   A L T O S
E D E S S A   S T R A Y   E L S I E
```

119

```
C R E W S   G R A H A M   R E J E C T
L I M I T   L O C A L E   E N A M O R
A G I L E   O M E R T A   A D M I R E
P A R L E   B A R R O N   D R E A D
    I N F I N   I S T H M U S
S A L A   E N T R E   T I N F O I L
C L O M P S   I N T R U S T   E R L E
A V O C E T   C A B I N   U N C L E
N A T U R A L   E N O S   R I S E S
    L I L A   B E G   A R A M
A T A L L   T A L C   D E N O T E D
L A M E S   N O H I T   M I R A G E
A N O N   M A C B E T H   I C E M A N
S K Y B L U E   R E E F S   C E N T
    R E S T O N S   P E S T O
T R Y S T   R E T A I L   R O D I N
D E B A S E   A P O L L O   O P E R A
A L I N E R   L A W T O N   M E M O S
G E S T E S   S L E E T Y   P R I N T
```

120

```
L O C A L   A N G O R A   D E C A Y
I R A T E   T E R R A C E   O R A T E
B O R E D C H A I R M A N   P A S T A
E N G   A L E R T   D A L E   T A R
L O O P   I N S   C R E T E   A S I N
    R O M A   S H A M E D   M T N S
U R B A N E   S H A R E   F O E S
S E A T S   S A O N E   S P I N E
M A C E   C A B O T   S H I N G L E
A R K   N O P E T S A L O U D   S E T
    M A T A D O R   E M I R S   G O R E
    L O V E R   S L O P E   P L A I N
    B A T E   B O L U S   D R A P E D
T R U E   S O A R E R   B E E N
H A R M   U N D E R   D O N   D A D A
E V E   H E I L   B A L S A   H I P
T E A S E   C A W S A N D E F F E C T
A S T E R   E N H A N C E   A L A T E
S T E E D   D O D G E R   R A D A R
```

121

```
A B A N G   W R A P   M A Y
H O M E R   P I E T A   A G A
S N O W E D U N D E R   N I N
    D I S T E N D   A L O N G
    C A Y   I C E B E R G
S I L A S   S N A R L S
O D E S   H A S S L E   M A I
W E A T H E R T H E S T O R M
N A P   I N G R E S   H U M P
    A T R E U S   T R E Y S
    S O P H I S M   F R A
S P A T E   E G O I S T S
H A T   R A I N O R S H I N E
A C E   T A N T O   T E N E T
M E R   O A K S   E S T E E
```

122

```
F A L L S   A T P A R   S I M I L E S
A L I S T   P I E C E   K R A M E R S
I M B U E   O K E E F F E O R P I N E
R A E   R A K E D   R E N N E T
    R E N T E   E P P A   E L M A N
S A L U T   L E A G U E R   O L E
M A T A M A T A   R A D I O   A T O P
A D E N   A M M O   S A B R I N A
P A D D Y O R P I L A F   M A R V E L
    E C T A L   L O V E R
I P E C A C   S T U D Y O R B E T T Y
F O L D S U P   K A E L   A R O E
B O L E   L Y D I A   R E A S S E R T
E L I   T R E S S E S   S H E E N
T E N T S   B R E V   S T I R S
    G E N E R A   O R I O N   C A B
S E T T E R O R M A K E R   I G A V E
A D O R A N T   I R E N E   N A P E S
M O N A D A L   L A D E N   G O E R S
```

123

```
R O M E R O S   M E A R A   B R O K E
E V E R E S T   A L L A N   R E V E T
P A N A C H E   R U I N G   A T E A R
    S H E W A S L I K E A H O R S E
W B A   O A S T   L U M P S
H A F T S   B A S   R I D S   I N A
O N T H E T R A C K   I C E   I G O R
O T O E   N O T H I N G A N D T H E N
P U N D I T S   T A U   I S T L E
    O N S A L E   S P R A N G
A R T U R   I L K   E N T R A N T
T H E B E L L G O E S A N D   E R O O
O U S T   O O H   G R E T A G A R B O
M E T   R A P T   S I S   A T O L L
    A B E T S   O A T Y   W E S
S O M E T H I N G H A P P E N S
A T E T E   D O R I C   I S O L A T E
P I N T S   E L I D E   S T R I P E D
O C T E T   D I N E D   H A S T E N S
```

124

```
GAMBLER ▢ GALLS ▢ ADIOS
AVARICE ▢ ELIOT ▢ LANZA
PARATUS ▢ TIARA ▢ INGOT
▢ WHATWHENDRUNKONE
AHOLE ▢ HYENA ▢ NEEDED
DELS ▢ ROMP ▢ AKISS
MAE ▢ AMA ▢ BESET ▢ TRÉS
IRON ▢ VENTRALLY ▢ EXT
STROKE ▢ SEGOS ▢ CANOE
SEESINOTHERWOMENONE
INSET ▢ SEIZE ▢ OLIVER
VEI ▢ ACTRESSES ▢ LARA
EDNA ▢ TARTS ▢ ACE ▢ TAG
▢ PATNA ▢ PROS ▢ MOTE
ASHORE ▢ DARIN ▢ PORES
SEESINGARBOSOBER ▢
TEXTS ▢ IDEAL ▢ MATADOR
ANELE ▢ BASSI ▢ INALINE
BODES ▢ ESSEX ▢ CELEBES
```

125

```
WISER ▢ CALIF ▢ TABULA
IRENE ▢ AMORE ▢ CEDARED
PETTY ▢ RAPID ▢ OREGANO
EFTS ▢ TETES ▢ OLE ▢ SNIP
SUE ▢ THEIRHINDSI ▢ ONT
▢ LECHER ▢ SEWAGE
▢ AGNES ▢ LISA ▢ HASTE
SUNNI ▢ DARES ▢ TETCHED
KNEES ▢ HAD ▢ REDWHITE
ASA ▢ ELLEN ▢ DORSA ▢ NOS
TUTORIAL ▢ MOA ▢ STENS
ERELONG ▢ AITCH ▢ BOSSA
SERIF ▢ BASS ▢ HALER
▢ ORDERS ▢ RETAIN
GET ▢ IEHTNAHTRET ▢ NOM
OLEO ▢ LIS ▢ MARIS ▢ ALTO
LINCOLN ▢ PUREE ▢ DRAIN
FOOTPAD ▢ ESTER ▢ SINCE
STRAPS ▢ WEEDS ▢ CADET
```

126

```
ORGAN ▢ RAVI ▢ PAD ▢ CARB
MARNE ▢ ICER ▢ ARA ▢ HEAR
ENATE ▢ BETA ▢ LINGERIE
GOFORBAROQUE ▢ ERWINS
ANTI ▢ ALB ▢ IPSE ▢ ATEST
▢ NORDIC ▢ STARCH
ASSENT ▢ COAT ▢ TRIESTE
GIT ▢ TEA ▢ SNAG ▢ REFORM
ONEWORLD ▢ TRAM ▢ SLOOP
▢ APR ▢ STRAITMAN ▢ ANU
ETHAN ▢ AERO ▢ EXISTENT
TREPAN ▢ ECCE ▢ IGO ▢ RCA
CANSINO ▢ AHEM ▢ HISSED
▢ EVENED ▢ LITTLE
POSSE ▢ ASIS ▢ SHE ▢ LOBE
IHASTE ▢ CAWSFORALARM
MARIETTA ▢ ANIM ▢ RETIE
ARGO ▢ ASP ▢ LIRA ▢ IRENE
SEEN ▢ LEE ▢ ETES ▢ ASNER
```

127

```
GLAND ▢ SHEAF ▢ LEI ▢ SIR
AUDIO ▢ TERRAPINS ▢ ENE
MAYBENOTNANETTE ▢ MTD
INTS ▢ ONEAT ▢ RAREFIED
NDU ▢ ITER ▢ SINE ▢ AFRO
GAMUTFROMBTOY ▢ STING
▢ LEO ▢ ALAD ▢ BIEN
CAPT ▢ RASTER ▢ FORSALE
AGER ▢ MTHDEGREE ▢ LEG
NANA ▢ CIA ▢ AER ▢ BINE
EMU ▢ TENTHHOUR ▢ UZIS
SALTINE ▢ EARLET ▢ RENT
▢ TORT ▢ TARA ▢ AUK
AMILE ▢ TEPIDTEMPERED
DOME ▢ ARRS ▢ IRES ▢ ERR
ANATOLIA ▢ CARAS ▢ SAGA
GIT ▢ NEXTTOLASTSTRAW
ECU ▢ UNIONMADE ▢ SAUTE
SAM ▢ SEE ▢ TONES ▢ TYPER
```

128

```
FLOTSAMANDJETSAM
LAPIOTASLEENEURO
AMENMOTHRENOLESS
TENSEPIEBRAWLSET
SORBONNECONSIGNS
OVALFEEDISEETRAP
REMITLEGSHORTALE
TRASHLYETANGOBEE
SAPSERASPACESHOD
TROUSERSALLOWING
RIOTEDNASTEPELSE
AAREDOWNTOOTETTA
NETTAPEDOLDSNEER
GLUEYOREROOTENTE
ELBASEEDSPRYYARD
```

129

```
G E N A   R A W   P A N A M A
A D A M   A M O   I T A L I C
R I S E   P A R   C E T A N E
S T A R S A N D S T R I P E S
      I L L   S A U R O
R A S C A L   F I R E N Z E
O C T A   O S O L E   A O N E
S E A S   O R O   L O A D
E R I C   P A T R O   C M T E
  B R U T I S H   L O O S E N
    P O N T E   D R U
S Y M B O L O F A M E R I C A
P A Y O T E   L E A   A L O U
A N N A L S   A R I   G E N S
S K A T E S   G O D   E X I T
```

130

```
  D E W A R       S H I E D
H E X A G O N   S Q U A R E D
I N A N A M E   L U L L A B Y
R U M   S P A T I A L   S A N
E D I T   S T I N T   T E T E
S E N A T   A S K   B O R E S
  D E C A Y S   S T R E S S
    T H O       H E N
  O D I O U S   R E T A R D
A N I L E   E W E   T I E U P
L A V E   S C A L E   L A R A
I D I   A M E R I K A   V A S
F A N G L E D   V E R D A N T
T R E A D L E   E R U D I T E
  E R R O L       S T E L E
```

131

```
C L E F S   R A G S   B O O M
E A G R E   E C R U   A G R A
S C R A P E T H E B A R R E L
S E E M   D R E W   W E E S T
    S T E A D Y     H O D
    W R Y   W A I L   S P A
  S T O A   F A L L   N A I L
B E E R B A R R E L P O L K A
B A S K   P E T S   A N T E
L S T   F E E S   S I S
    F A D     F O R M A T
A S T E R   P A U L   O R R S
B A R R E L O F M O N K E Y S
L I A R   L O R E   S E N S E
E L M Y   B R O S   F R A T S
```

132

```
L A S E R   M O V I E   R O D
O R O N O   O V E R T   O R E
B E A T L E M A N I A   M A C
E S P I E D   T E S T   A T E
      C O O T I E   A N O N
O P I E   W O R R Y W A R T
D O N   P A I N   N A R C
D E F A U L T   M A R Y L O U
  O R M E   B O S N   E R G
D A R T A G N A N   E F G H
E L M S   E N T E R S
A M A   S P U D   L A S T E D
R O N   T O M A N D J E R R Y
I N T   U S A G E   A N I S E
E D S   B E N E T   H E X E S
```

133

```
D A N C E   A W E S   A C E D
O C E A N   M A Y O   V O L E
G R A N D H O T E L   A M I E
S E T T E E   C R U S T I E R
      A R C H   S C A N
A S K E R   L O S   A R G I L
G A I T   T E N T E R   H O E
O N T H E W A T E R F R O N T
O T T   M O T H E R   E M I T
D O Y L E   S E L   F L E A S
    F O E S   R E D O
F L O U R I S H   A R T I E R
R A Y S   G O I N G M Y W A Y
E L L E   N A N A   A R I S E
T O E S   S K E W   T O N Y S
```

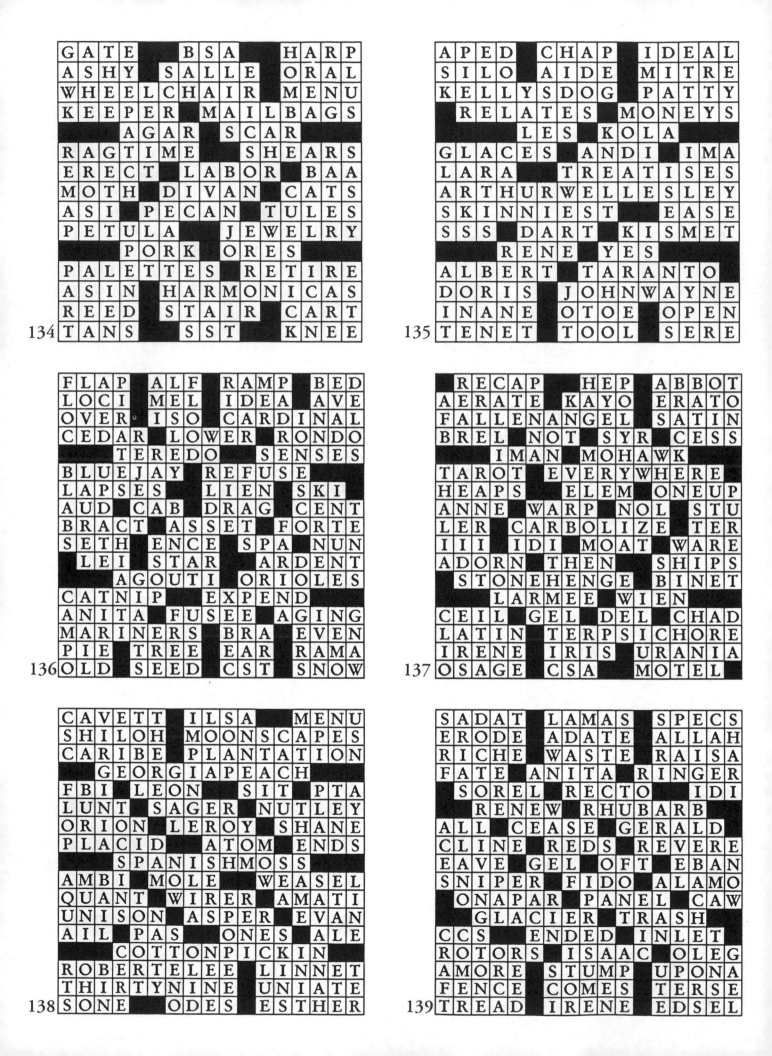

134

GATE · BSA · HARP
ASHY · SALLE · ORAL
WHEELCHAIR · MENU
KEEPER · MAILBAGS
· AGAR · SCAR ·
RAGTIME · SHEARS
ERECT · LABOR · BAA
MOTH · DIVAN · CATS
ASI · PECAN · TULES
PETULA · JEWELRY
· PORK · ORES ·
PALETTES · RETIRE
ASIN · HARMONICAS
REED · STAIR · CART
TANS · SST · KNEE

135

APED · CHAP · IDEAL
SILO · AIDE · MITRE
KELLYSDOG · PATTY
· RELATES · MONEYS
· LES · KOLA
GLACES · ANDI · IMA
LARA · TREATISES
ARTHURWELLESLEY
SKINNIEST · EASE
SSS · DART · KISMET
· RENE · YES
ALBERT · TARANTO
DORIS · JOHNWAYNE
INANE · OTOE · OPEN
TENET · TOOL · SERE

136

FLAP · ALF · RAMP · BED
LOCI · MEL · IDEA · AVE
OVER · ISO · CARDINAL
CEDAR · LOWER · RONDO
· TEREDO · SENSES
BLUEJAY · REFUSE
LAPSES · LIEN · SKI
AUD · CAB · DRAG · CENT
BRACT · ASSET · FORTE
SETH · ENCE · SPA · NUN
LEI · STAR · ARDENT
· AGOUTI · ORIOLES
CATNIP · EXPEND
ANITA · FUSEE · AGING
MARINERS · BRA · EVEN
PIE · TREE · EAR · RAMA
OLD · SEED · CST · SNOW

137

RECAP · HEP · ABBOT
AERATE · KAYO · ERATO
FALLENANGEL · SATIN
BREL · NOT · SYR · CESS
· IMAN · MOHAWK
TAROT · EVERYWHERE
HEAPS · ELEM · ONEUP
ANNE · WARP · NOL · STU
LER · CARBOLIZE · TER
III · IDI · MOAT · WARE
ADORN · THEN · SHIPS
· STONEHENGE · BINET
· LARMEE · WIEN
CEIL · GEL · DEL · CHAD
LATIN · TERPSICHORE
IRENE · IRIS · URANIA
OSAGE · CSA · MOTEL

138

CAVETT · ILSA · MENU
SHILOH · MOONSCAPES
CARIBE · PLANTATION
· GEORGIAPEACH
FBI · LEON · SIT · PTA
LUNT · SAGER · NUTLEY
ORION · LEROY · SHANE
PLACID · ATOM · ENDS
· SPANISHMOSS
AMBI · MOLE · WEASEL
QUANT · WIRER · AMATI
UNISON · ASPER · EVAN
AIL · PAS · ONES · ALE
· COTTONPICKIN
ROBERTELEE · LINNET
THIRTYNINE · UNIATE
SONE · ODES · ESTHER

139

SADAT · LAMAS · SPECS
ERODE · ADATE · ALLAH
RICHE · WASTE · RAISA
FATE · ANITA · RINGER
· SOREL · RECTO · IDI
· RENEW · RHUBARB
ALL · CEASE · GERALD
CLINE · REDS · REVERE
EAVE · GEL · OFT · EBAN
SNIPER · FIDO · ALAMO
ONAPAR · PANEL · CAW
· GLACIER · TRASH
CCS · ENDED · INLET
ROTORS · ISAAC · OLEG
AMORE · STUMP · UPONA
FENCE · COMES · TERSE
TREAD · IRENE · EDSEL

140

```
C L U M S Y   O S C A R   M E S S
R E L A T E   S P I R O   I N T O
A C T I O N   S I N T W I S T E R
T H I N K   S A T E     S W I N E
      R E N O   U M P   T O R O S
  R O A R I N G P A I N   R E S T
S O A K   B I O     S O L D
E A S E L   C O N C A V E   S Y S
A S T R O S   N O H   A N G L I A
M T S   G N O S T I C   A L I E N
      S O U P     L A M   U E L E
C L A W   B U M M I N G H E R D
R O S E S   S E A   A R A B
O C T E T     A R A L   R I A T A
W A R T Y F I N K S   F A L L O W
E T A L   C R E E P   A S L O P E
R E L Y   C A R D S   A S S E S S
```

141

```
H E R B   M A T C H     T R E N T
A P A R   A L O H A   R E V E R T
W I S E   N I T E R   I N A W A Y
  C H A N G E O F P A C E   H U P
      T E E N   I N K   D A M E
H I T H E R   I C E D   L I M A S
U N W E D   B R A S   H E M P
L A I R   L O O K   V A N E S S A
A N S   T U R N E D O U T   H U M
S E T B A C K   M U L L   P I S A
      E R S E   W I L T   A R R A S
V A D I S   F O X Y   P R E E N S
E R L E   G R R     S L I T
G E O   B R O K E N H E A R T S
A N G E L A   O C E A N   I R A Q
S A I G O N   F R O N T   A I D E
  S C O T T   F U N K Y   L O A D
```

142

```
P A N I C   S M E A R   A P O D S
I R A T E   P E A C E   S E P I A
N E V E R M I S S E S A T R I C K
U N E   T E N S E   T R A I N E E
P A S S A W A Y   B E T   L E S S
      H I L L   B E R E T
H A G E N   A R E   A R L O
A G U A   B A L I   A P P E A L S
T H E T R U M P O F T H E D U M P
S A S H A Y S   C L A D   D R E I
  S T E M   A H A   R E A C T
      S E R G E   F E E S
C A S A   T E E   B I D S T A N D
A G A R I T A   B I L G E   L O U
P U L L S A D O U B L E C R O S S
O S S E T   E N G L E   T E N E T
S H A N S   R E S E T   S E E D Y
```

143

```
C E R T I F Y       T H A M E S
O V E R S E E   W H O A R E Y O U
S I N A T R A   A I R L I N E R S
I D E S   S I G N A L     S E A
N E W H A R T A N D H O P E
E N E   L A Y N E   W A N T O N
S T R A I N   S R A S   L A R V A
      S A D E   A D O S   B E E P
  G I B S O N A N D F E L L E R
A R A L   M I L D   A L O E
D I G I N   D A D O   E N D E A R
A T O N E S   E D U C E   M S E
  D O L E A N D S T R A U S S
I O N   I M P I S H   S L U E
B R I G A D I E R   E N S N A R E
M A K E S I T S O   R O T A T E D
L E M A N S     S T A G E R S
```

144

```
  B A S S I   R I G   L I E T O
S A L O O N   S I S I   A L L I N
T S E T S E   W A L L A W A L L A
E S P   O R C A   E A R L   I D I
W E P T   T O R N   S T E E P E R
S T O A T   U T E S   A S S T
    M A R S H A L L   S M I T H
  P E P T I C   T O O T   E C R U
N A V   E N O S   E D I T   A U G
A P E R   G U T S   E T O I L E
P A N I C   S I N G S I N G
  H O L T   R O O T   G E N R E
E L A T I O N   W R A P   T I E D
M E N   E M E U   I R I D   A L E
B A D E N B A D E N   C A N C A N
E V E N T   P O N G   K R A I T S
R E D D S   S S T   S T Y N E
```

145

```
  A M B E R   T A M S   B V D
A V I A R Y   C O M E T   M E E R
M O N T R E A L T O R S   O R N E
E T C H   S N E E R   P O L I S
B R E L   N O M E C H A N I C S
A E D E S   I N S   R O X A N E
      T Y P E   W A T   N E M O
  R E S H   B A G D A D M A N
A P O   T A M P A R S O N   A N T
L I M A S S E U R   G A R N
A S A N   E R G     A S I E
  A N I L I C   O N A   S N A P S
M I A M I N I S T E R   O L A V
A L G A E   A I R O F   T A T E
N O E L   B O S T O N E M A S O N
G R R S   O A S I S   B A R K I S
O S S   S K Y S   S O Y A S
```

146

M	I	C	R	O		M	I	A	S	M	A		P	L	U	S
A	V	A	I	L		U	N	F	A	I	R		L	A	T	E
C	A	G	N	E	Y	S	J	I	M	M	Y		A	R	I	D
E	N	E		G	A	T	U	N			S	I	D	L	E	
			P	A	R	E	N	T		I	N	N	E	R		
B	B	L		S	P	R	Y		A	E	R	A	T	E		
E	L	E	C	T	E	D		H	I	R	A	M		R	P	M
S	A	V	I	O	R		E	A	S	T		O	S	L	O	
A	M	A	N	A		S	P	A	D	E		E	R	R	E	D
M	E	N	E		M	A	U	D		R	E	S	I	D	E	
E	S	T		T	O	N	G	S		B	E	L	O	N	G	S
		S	T	R	I	D	E		D	E	F	Y		G	E	T
C	H	O	R	E		S	T	E	E	L	E					
R	O	S	I	E			C	L	A	R	E		F	B	I	
E	N	C	S		B	A	I	L	E	Y	S	P	E	A	R	L
M	E	A	T		A	G	N	A	T	E		E	R	N	I	E
E	Y	R	E		T	E	S	T	E	D		E	A	S	E	D

147

N	I	G	H		P	A	J	A	M	A		B	O	Z	O
O	S	L	O		O	N	E	M	A	N		A	T	O	P
T	H	E	O	N	L	Y	W	A	Y	T	O	S	T	O	P
A	M	A	T	I		H	E	R	O		V	I	O	L	
B	A	N		B	O	O	L	A		W	I	N		O	S	S
L	E	E	S		A	W	E		H	I	D		A	G	A	L
E	L	D	E	S	T		R	O	A	N		A	L	I	N	E
			E	P	E	E		A	D	D		C	A	S	T	E
S	M	O	K	I	N	G	I	S	J	U	S	T	S	T	O	P
W	O	V	E	N		G	R	E		P	E	E	K			
E	V	E	R	Y		N	A	S	T		E	D	A	M	E	S
E	I	N	S		C	O	Q		H	O	P		N	A	V	E
P	E	P		F	O	G		F	I	R	S	T		N	I	X
		R	A	I	N		S	A	R	I		A	B	A	C	I
N	O	I	F	S	A	N	D	S	O	R	B	U	T	T	S
R	O	D	E		B	E	E	T	L	E		F	E	E	T
A	F	A	R		M	E	S	S	E	D		F	E	D	S

148

	S	S	W		C	H	A	D		H	A	T	E	R
T	A	T	I		G	L	O	V	E	S		A	D	O	R	E
A	M	O	N		R	E	M	O	V	E		R	I	N	S	E
L	O	O	K	H	O	M	E	W	A	R	D	A	N	G	E	L
C	A	L	L	O	W		R	E	L		U	S	A			
			E	L	E	C		D	U	P	E	S		R	A	P
C	E	S		I	R	O	N		E	R	N		L	O	G	E
A	R	T	I	E		F	A	A		I	N	F	I	D	E	L
T	E	R	M	S	O	F	E	N	D	E	A	R	M	E	N	T
S	C	E	P	T	R	E		Y	R	S		A	B	O	D	E
U	T	E	S		W	R	Y		S	T	E	M		S	A	D
P	S	T		C	E	S	A	R		S	N	I	B			
			M	A	L		W	E	E		S	N	E	E	Z	E
M	Y	D	A	R	L	I	N	G	D	A	U	G	H	T	E	R
M	A	R	N	E		L	I	A	G	R	E		E	U	R	O
E	L	I	S	E		O	N	L	A	N	D		A	D	O	S
S	U	P	E	R		G	E	R	E		D	E	S			

149

M	O	D	E	S		I	M	A	G	O		C	H	A	R
O	P	E	R	A		M	E	L	O	N		R	A	G	E
L	E	G	A	L		P	R	E	D	E	S	T	I	N	E	D
E	N	E		E	D	U	C	E		K	I	N	G	S	
S	E	N	T		A	R	I		S	T	I	N	G		
	D	E	R	I	D	E		G	A	R		D	E	F	E	R
	R	E	N	O		S	E	D	A	T	E		E	T	O	
M	A	S	K		B	A	N		I	E	R		R	A	W	
B	A	T	S		R	E	P	T	I	L	E		I	M	P	S
A	S	I		M	O	M		E	O	S		K	N	E	E	
I	S	O		A	C	U	M	E	N		K	I	L	N		
T	E	N	O	R		S	O	L		P	I	N	A	T	A	
			P	R	E	E	N		B	U	D		Y	A	R	D
	B	R	I	E	R		B	U	R	S	T		T	R	I	
G	R	A	N	D	R	A	P	I	D	S		A	L	I	E	N
S	O	R	E		L	A	R	G	E		M	O	O	S	E	
A	W	E	S		A	L	D	E	R		P	U	N	T	S	

150

	D	I	S	C		S	C	U	M		L	E	S	S	
L	O	C	A	L	S		S	H	A	M	E		A	L	A	E
I	N	A	R	U	T		H	U	B	B	A	H	U	B	B	A
N	O	R		B	E	L	A	B	O	R		O	D	E	U	M
G	R	U	B	S	T	A	K	E		A	P	S	E		
O	S	S	E	T		S	E	R	B		A	T	R	I	U	M
			D	E	P	T		T	E	A	L	S		S	R	O
A	P	P	E	A	R		A	S	I	D	E		A	I	R	
P	R	O		K	E	R	N		G	A	R	B		A	E	S
H	I	P		L	U	I	S	E		M	U	S	C	L	E	
I	C	E		B	A	N	T	U		R	O	B	E			
D	E	S	E	R	T		A	B	B	E		B	R	A	S	H
			D	I	E	T		J	U	B	I	L	A	N	C	E
P	L	A	I	D		O	N	E	L	A	N	E		C	O	G
R	U	B	B	E	R	N	E	C	K		I	G	N	O	R	E
O	R	E	L		M	I	S	T	Y		T	U	N	N	E	L
P	E	L	E		A	C	T	S			M	E	A	D	

151

A	T	B	A	T		L	I	B	E	L		E	M	I	T
R	E	E	V	E		O	D	O	R	S		N	O	N	O
R	A	V	E	N		N	E	O	N	T	R	O	T	S	K	Y
A	B	E		S	T	E	A	K		E	X	I	T	S	
Y	A	R	N		I	L	L		D	I	G	I	T		
	G	L	O	O	M	Y		M	O	N		D	Y	L	A	N
	Y	O	R	E		T	I	S	S	U	E		I	F	I	
A	S	S	T		S	I	D		E	S	S		N	I	N	
P	L	I	E		S	K	E	W	E	R	S		M	E	R	E
A	L	L		P	A	Y		E	A	T		L	O	S	E	
C	A	L		R	O	L	L	E	R		C	O	U	P		
T	H	Y	M	E		A	O	K		S	A	U	N	A	S	
		A	S	H	B	Y		M	I	S		D	U	A	L	
	S	P	R	E	E		S	A	G	A	N		L	I	E	
S	C	O	T	T	P	O	P	L	I	N		A	G	I	L	E
M	A	R	Y		D	I	A	N	A		S	E	N	O	R
U	B	E	R		E	X	P	E	L		A	N	G	R	Y

152

```
GEMMA  OWING  SADAT
AMAIN  BELIE  AGILE
BELLIGERENT   NESTS
BRIE  USE   SET  COT
EGG  LYE  BRAVADO
DENSE   LEYTE   ERMA
    HOSTILE   ANDES
BABY  KEEL  PORTALS
ADA  DISSIDENT  NEE
SATRAPS  CAKE  STET
ANTED   FORESEE
LOLL  AMUSE   FLOPS
  EYESORE  CUT  TAP
SOS  AHS   EAT  MOLE
ALOSS  QUARRELSOME
RAMIE  UTILE  OGLED
ANEND  EARED  STERS
```

153

```
ALTAR  MECCA   ITCH
LORNE  ALLAY  TOYON
FREDASTAIRE  ADDLE
ICY  LATIN  SOLACED
EAST  BENTS  GOTHS
   ISERE  CORNEA
KILLERS  RANEE  REP
ADELES  BORES  WINO
RISEN  TAPER  HASTE
MOLD  PAGED  DORSET
AMI  ARLES  RASPERS
  ERROLL  MELEE
SCOLD  SCAPE  DINE
STALEST  AGATE  NOL
KORAN  BARYSHNIKOV
INONE  ALLAT  IRENE
 ENDS  REARS  DARES
```

154

```
APBS  MAS  MAI  LASH
DRAT  ACT  ARM  OTTO
VERONICA  REPEATED
IFYOUDONTSTANDUP
SEEPS  SCI   ESTE
ERS   STET   SEDATE
  BITS  LASER  LOX
ACCEDE  EELY  HELI
FORSOMETHINGYOULL
OMIT  KNOT  LAOTSE
UTE  STEAL  SEPT
LESSEE   DOON   ITE
  TENA  ERN  OCREA
STANDFORANYTHING
RHETORIC  TEETOTAL
AONE  IRT  ETA  KINE
WEDS  LEO  SSR  ESTS
```

155

```
CHAMP  OPRAH  GLINT
AEIOU  SHAME  LAGER
PARER  LONER  AGAVE
EVE  PHONINESS  VEE
RESALE  ONS  ESTERS
    SEAL    RAYE
TIDY  DESCENT  LADE
ROOMS  SOUSA  DEGAS
INEPT   LST   SPINS
TITHE  SOPOR  THOSE
ECHO  TENSPOT  OSES
   NCAA    THAN
CRAYON  BOW  IMELDA
RAP  HOMOPHONE  AAR
ADAME  OTTER  RHINE
WIRER  THERE  CARTA
LOTTE  HADES  EDSEL
```

156

```
DAMAS  EAST  CREASE
ERICH  AMOI  HILTON
ANSER  SOUNDEFFECT
TISSUEY  STEVE  MII
HEB  BRAE  ELY  SPAR
SRS  SCLERA  STOLE
  OAK  ELASTICS
SMOTE  SER  ERA  HIC
TAKETH  RNS  ERRING
YES  TUN  ETO  FOLDS
  CLEANSER  SAD
OSSIE  PUTRID  MER
RULE  BON  EGOS  GOA
ARI  DOLCE  ICEBAGS
TEDDYWILSON  PERES
ETERNE  ETNA  ANDRE
DOSSED  SEAL  LIEST
```

157

```
FILED  ADLER   LOTS
ADELE  BRINE  JAPAN
NOVEL  OUTRE  OMAHA
LIVEHIGHONTHEHOG
  ETAL  ELTON  SES
SASSES    LEN
TEE  STABS  REDACT
URNS  ENATE  ACRID
BASKINTHESUNSHINE
STEAK  SPATE  SNIP
ESTEEM  SUETS  GET
    REB  TOTERS
SLY  CITED  HEIR
LEADACHARMEDLIFE
OGLER  ONEAL  ABIDE
PATER  DIANE  GENIE
SLAP  SEDAN  ESSEN
```

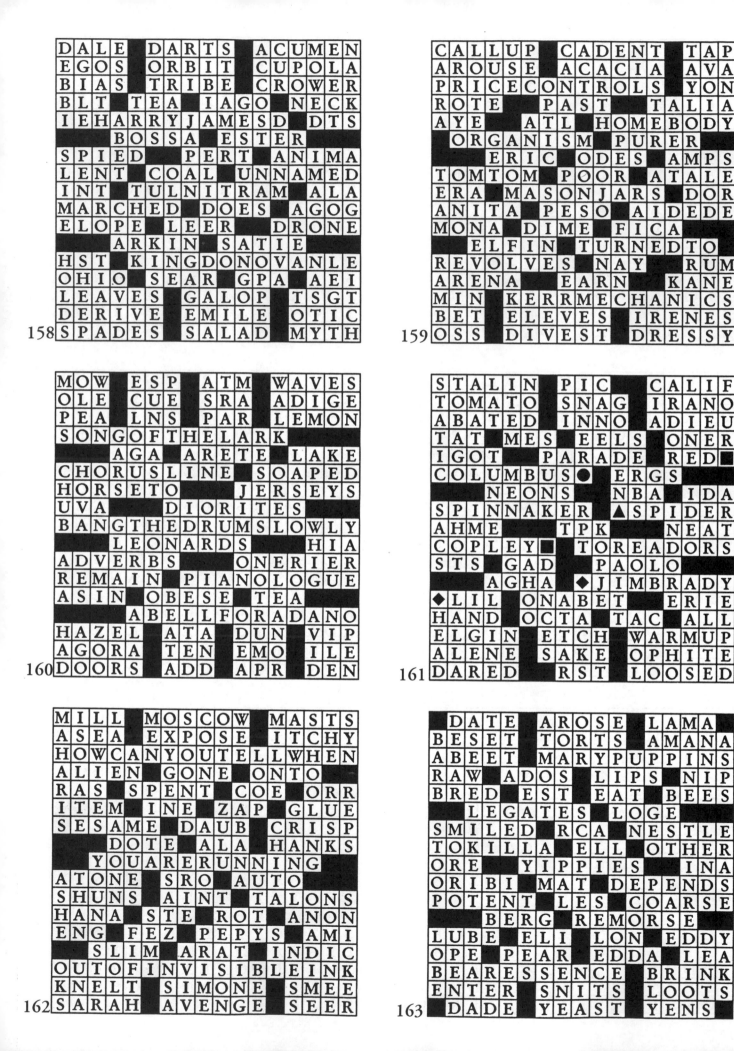

164

```
RAMPAGE  APISH  APHID
ALIENOR  RENTA  STONE
TALKINGTURKEY   SARGE
ISLE  DOOM  WREST  SOD
OKE  COTE  DEIST  NETS
NARIAL  STILL  ROOT
   STAG  RELEE  GORES
STEMS  ROUTS  SURNAME
ERAS  MOLES  SPEEDER
NEG  GOWER  CHESS  ERG
EVEREST  MOONY  URGE
CORINTH  COMIC  ASSES
ARBOR  SERUM  EARN
   ETES  MESAS  SEAMER
SPAS  EVADE  TWAS  EXO
CIV  OMANI  HEIR  ASTA
IGETA  RABBITPUNCHES
FIRES  ATLAS  ELEMENT
INSET  SEEDS  DETESTS
```

165

```
SHAMES  STELAR  SMASH
LEGUME  CICERO  HASTE
AMELIAEARHART  ELIAS
MODEL  EROO  ITALIANS
     YRLY  EVERT
UNROBE  HELENKELLER
SIERRA  SELF  REAVE
EPISODICAL  ATA  ACED
RANON  ROTE  TAMENESS
     TEARS  PORTS
CASSETTE  PALS  TAPAS
ARCA  HES  ILLITERATE
LEARN  ETES  RETIRE
MARIACALLAS  ALEXIS
     CODAS  GAMA
BACHELOR  SELL  UPSET
ETHEL  PRINCESSDIANA
SMELL  TUNICS  TENNIS
TORME  SPATES  BREEDS
```

166

```
ROBER  PURSERS  DECAL
APACE  EPAULET  ERATO
MARCS  SONGOFSOLOMON
PHILEMON  APS  WIDE
   ECUS  PRE  INSERTS
FEASTS  TRESTLE  SAHL
ALAI  IVIED  HERB  MIA
LIRA  CAPP  CUD  ALERT
LEES  ASSAILS  GRANDE
   TELE  ROO  MAAM
TOKENS  PERUSAL  ELEM
AVISO  SID  DONA  NICE
KEN  SITE  PILOT  TART
ERGS  RUSTLED  ICARUS
SAHARAN  HOR  WAIT
   ELAN  TAW  CANTICLE
PARALIPOMENON  ROMAN
AHOME  OPERATE  UNDID
CADIS  POSSESS  SSGTS
```

167

```
ABA  RIFF  FLUB  CHAD
BRIE  IGOR  LORE  ROME
EARLYTORISEAND  IRMA
   FLOAT  DOWN  SAMSON
BRIER  OAR  WIRE
AYE  EARLYTOBEDMAKES
BALI  PADS  MOSEY  RAT
ANDMEANS  SENT  RIGA
   PARC  PALE  HOLLY
JAMESTHURBERSFABLES
ALADY  PORT  TELE
CAFE  DOPE  TOLERANT
TRI  STONE  COMO  TREE
AMALEHEALTHYAND  BAN
   OMAR  OAS  ROOTS
BANDIT  HART  TOERR
ORIG  WEALTHYANDDEAD
ANNE  AVID  AERY  OAHU
TOAD  SERA  MANX  LAB
```

168

```
ARAGON  SPORE  AMERCE
REGIME  HUMID  ROMERO
SNARES  ELITE  TRIPES
   TRANSUBSTANTIATED
   STELAE  ISL  NEY
ESPOUSE  DIDNT  ETNA
REALM  GRINDS  ALECK
GARS  TERENCE  STERES
ONS  ARMING  WHOM
   SESQUIPEDALIANISM
   AUER  ORANGE  TIC
POPLAR  CANINGS  CIDE
ECOLE  HAGGLE  TONGS
ACRE  PETES  AVENGES
SUP  SAL  AERIES
   POSTIMPRESSIONIST
SAILOR  LICIT  LADLED
INSOLE  EPODE  AGEOLD
STEWED  ASNER  SERGES
```

169

```
PARDO  FLEW  HEAVE
AGORAS  MALICE  UNTIL
CEDARWAXWINGS  METAL
KNEW  APIECE  TAM  UNI
SAO  ASTI  KRA  FIENDS
   ART  LESS  ANTES
KINGFISHER  PARGE
INAT  KLUX  MER  BRAS
TUT  MAIL  PINT  INSTS
ERUGO  PARROTS  REMAN
SERAC  PHOO  RAND  ATE
DESK  EON  MELO  AREA
   MISDO  GREENSHANK
   AMANA  PORT  ARA
SLINGS  SRO  BAGS  SIL
ELD  BET  PUEBLO  IONA
NEGRI  WHISTLINGSWAN
SNEER  AENEAS  SELENE
ESSED  STES  MERES
```

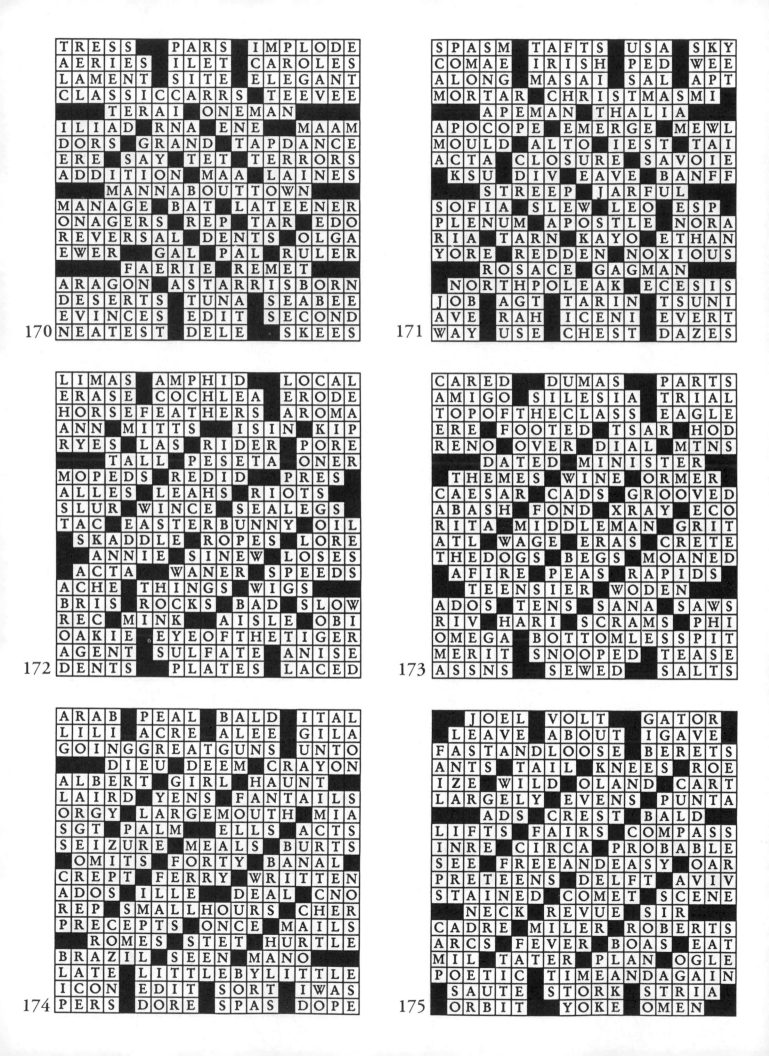

170

```
TRESS  PARS   IMPLODE
AERIES ILET   CAROLES
LAMENT SITE   ELEGANT
CLASSICCARRS  TEEVEE
    TERAI  ONEMAN
ILIAD RNA  ENE  MAAM
DORS   GRAND TAPDANCE
ERE  SAY TET  TERRORS
ADDITION MAA  LAINES
   MANNABOUTTOWN
MANAGE  BAT  LATEENER
ONAGERS  REP TAR  EDO
REVERSAL DENTS  OLGA
EWER  GAL  PAL  RULER
    FAERIE   REMET
ARAGON  ASTARRISBORN
DESERTS  TUNA  SEABEE
EVINCES  EDIT  SECOND
NEATEST  DELE   SKEES
```

171

```
SPASM TAFTS USA  SKY
COMAE IRISH PED  WEE
ALONG MASAI SAL  APT
MORTAR  CHRISTMASMI
    APEMAN  THALIA
APOCOPE EMERGE  MEWL
MOULD ALTO IEST  TAI
ACTA CLOSURE SAVOIE
KSU DIV EAVE  BANFF
    STREEP  JARFUL
SOFIA SLEW  LEO  ESP
PLENUM APOSTLE NORA
RIA TARN KAYO  ETHAN
YORE REDDEN NOXIOUS
    ROSACE  GAGMAN
NORTHPOLEAK  ECESIS
JOB AGT TARIN  TSUNI
AVE RAH ICENI  EVERT
WAY USE CHEST  DAZES
```

172

```
LIMAS AMPHID  LOCAL
ERASE COCHLEA ERODE
HORSEFEATHERS AROMA
ANN MITTS  ISIN  KIP
RYES LAS RIDER  PORE
   TALL PESETA ONER
MOPEDS REDID  PRES
ALLES LEAHS  RIOTS
SLUR WINCE  SEALEGS
TAC EASTERBUNNY  OIL
SKADDLE ROPES  LORE
 ANNIE SINEW  LOSES
 ACTA WANER  SPEEDS
ACHE THINGS  WIGS
BRIS ROCKS BAD  SLOW
REC MINK  AISLE  OBI
OAKIE EYEOFTHETIGER
AGENT SULFATE  ANISE
DENTS  PLATES  LACED
```

173

```
CARED DUMAS   PARTS
AMIGO SILESIA TRIAL
TOPOFTHECLASS EAGLE
ERE FOOTED TSAR  HOD
RENO OVER DIAL  MTNS
   DATED MINISTER
THEMES WINE  ORMER
CAESAR CADS GROOVED
ABASH FOND XRAY  ECO
RITA MIDDLEMAN GRIT
ATL WAGE ERAS  CRETE
THEDOGS BEGS MOANED
AFIRE PEAS  RAPIDS
   TEENSIER WODEN
ADOS TENS SANA  SAWS
RIV HARI SCRAMS  PHI
OMEGA BOTTOMLESSPIT
MERIT SNOOPED TEASE
ASSNS  SEWED   SALTS
```

174

```
ARAB PEAL BALD  ITAL
LILI ACRE ALEE  GILA
GOINGGREATGUNS UNTO
 DIEU DEEM  CRAYON
ALBERT GIRL  HAUNT
LAIRD YENS FANTAILS
ORGY LARGEMOUTH MIA
SGT PALM ELLS  ACTS
SEIZURE MEALS BURTS
 OMITS FORTY BANAL
CREPT FERRY WRITTEN
ADOS ILLE DEAL  CNO
REP SMALLHOURS CHER
PRECEPTS ONCE MAILS
 ROMES STET HURTLE
BRAZIL  SEEN  MANO
LATE LITTLEBYLITTLE
ICON EDIT SORT  IWAS
PERS DORE SPAS  DOPE
```

175

```
 JOEL VOLT   GATOR
LEAVE ABOUT  IGAVE
FASTANDLOOSE BERETS
ANTS TAIL KNEES  ROE
IZE WILD OLAND  CART
LARGELY EVENS PUNTA
   ADS CREST  BALD
LIFTS FAIRS COMPASS
INRE CIRCA PROBABLE
SEE FREEANDEASY OAR
PRETEENS DELFT AVIV
STAINED COMET SCENE
   NECK REVUE  SIR
CADRE MILER ROBERTS
ARCS FEVER BOAS  EAT
MIL TATER PLAN  OGLE
POETIC TIMEANDAGAIN
 SAUTE STORK STRIA
 ORBIT  YOKE  OMEN
```

176

```
DATA   SPASM  AMA   RIO
ORALS  HARTE  TARPONS
STRAWBERRYSHORTCAKE
 STEELE  SETA  ZEBRAS
    EADS     ANVIL
LAIT  YELP  SAP   ACHE
JUNKET  CARD  LAOCOON
ARSENIC  WEDDINGCAKE
BEA   EAT  PAID  ETTES
   BIRTHDAYCAKES
BESET  COIR  ETE   DOT
APPLESAUCES  EASTERN
NEUTRAL  KRIS  SORBET
DENS  NLF  SETH  LASS
    LISLE    DECO
ATOMIC  ARES  LIMBOS
CHOCOLATECHIPCOOKIE
REPINED  CRATE  NAILS
ENS   SSE  TUDOR  TELE
```

177

```
DELLA   FRAYED   IDAS
ELIAS   REDONE   SUET
BLACKEYEDSUSAN  ATOR
TEN  SPADS  IDES   CLI
SNAP  ERA  FELLOWSHIP
   APED  RILEY  EMMAS
SABLES  POLAR   IDEA
TRUMP  CADET  AMIENS
ETTE  PAR  DERMAS  SAY
PIT  HESSE  DOUGH  PIE
SSE  EATERS  USE  NIPA
 TRIALS  GOUGE  NOPAR
 ANTE  RALPH  SEVENS
CINCH  PETES  NAVE
ADDLEPATED  SOL  LIEB
NEE  RANI  SEAMS  NRA
NAGS  HENANDCHICKENS
ALGA  LARIAT  AERIE
ESSE  SLINKS  BYTES
```

178

```
TEAR  BANC  TAME  SMIT
ITEA  INCA  ANIL  LENA
PERDITION  RAILROADS
PRAISE   ACH   AIGLET
ENTOM  THREEON  PAINE
TEES  THEDEEDIS  NEED
   RHEA  SLICERS
 VINEGARY  NEVA   VCR
BATEAU  TARO  REPTILE
ONEIDA  SKULK  RIOTED
HEMLINE  SELL  YENTAS
RDS  LYNN  AUSTRIAN
   BYROADS  DAHS
WAGE  OLGEHTGNI  RCTS
ARRAS  ASPIRED  FAUST
TIARAS   ONO   BANTHE
ASCERTAIN  PAPERCLIP
PEER  AXLE  OVEN  HARP
ENDS  GELS  SENT  OSTE
```

179

```
LATHS   AROAR   TIDAL
ERROL  EMERSED  ARENA
DIAMONDBACKTERRAPIN
USN  WAGED  SIMON  ATE
PEST  PER  BORON  BRAD
   CHIPS  MOUES  MAT
 LEROY  HASTE  DERMA
SINES   BOP   BOLDEST
CODS  KOALA  RALE  NCO
ONEHUNDREDPERCENTER
PEN  NEED  SINGE  OAST
ESTATES   NEE  RULES
 SARIS  SCREW  FINIS
 LIE  SWANS  TOPAZ
ALID  FLIPS  PIN  LAMP
MES  HEAVE  SANDS  TAO
ANTIINTELLECTUALISM
STINT  SLEEVES  LOOSE
SOCKS   STEED   TONES
```

180

```
ALPS  PHAR  GAPE  COMB
LILT  LINE  IRES  ALAI
OMAR  ETNA  LARK  MEND
PANAMAHAT  BLUEJEANS
  POSE  AWES  REL
SWELTER  ERE  THOLE
CAMEOS  SALTATE  ARID
ALMS  GULLS  AVAILED
BEAST  ACTI  AVERRED
   HERRINGBONE
ANDANTE  GOAL  AGATE
TROUNCE  STATE  AMOK
AGON  ERINOSE  SABINE
BONGO   MAN  SOBERED
  ARF  IPSO  PAAR
OVERCOATS  SWANSDOWN
GALE  UTAH  CORD  IDEA
RIME  TOTO  AVES  NEBS
ENOS  SPET  REDO  ERST
```

181

```
PACE  MESTA  SKED  CTS
EDOM  ALTOS  INNO  HEP
EDWINBOOTH  AURA  ARE
PEELE  NOT  ANTI  OTRA
DREGS  GEORGECUSTER
  ZAP  ERIN  ROTTEN
DAKOTA  LOBO  UELE
OMELET  SHE  ACORN
DAMAS  JEER  SKINDEEP
ONA  HARM  BAND  ALI
SALTLAKE  COLE  SETIN
 HAGEN  APT  DILATE
 ODIN  LEAP  EDITED
MANANA  BRET  FEZ
WILLIAMBLIGH  SCADS
ONLY  MOLE  BAD  ABOUT
ROI  PETE  TELAWRENCE
DUE  ALTA  IRENE  TERN
SSD  DYAK  STRAY  HEED
```

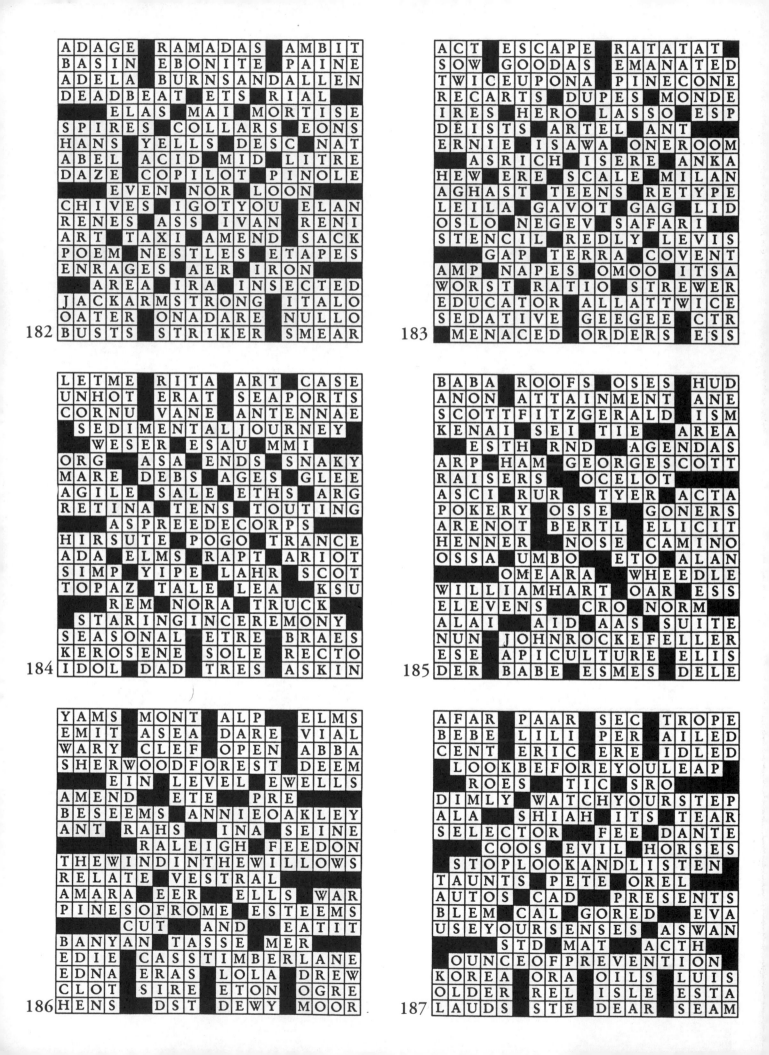

182

```
ADAGE  RAMADAS  AMBIT
BASIN  EBONITE  PAINE
ADELA  BURNSANDALLEN
DEADBEAT  ETS  RIAL
    ELAS  MAI  MORTISE
SPIRES  COLLARS  EONS
HANS  YELLS  DESC  NAT
ABEL  ACID  MID  LITRE
DAZE  COPILOT  PINOLE
    EVEN  NOR  LOON
CHIVES  IGOTYOU  ELAN
RENES  ASS  IVAN  RENI
ART  TAXI  AMEND  SACK
POEM  NESTLES  ETAPES
ENRAGES  AER  IRON
    AREA  IRA  INSECTED
JACKARMSTRONG  ITALO
OATER  ONADARE  NULLO
BUSTS  STRIKER  SMEAR
```

183

```
ACT  ESCAPE  RATATAT
SOW  GOODAS  EMANATED
TWICEUPONA  PINECONE
RECARTS  DUPES  MONDE
IRES  HERO  LASSO  ESP
DEISTS  ARTEL  ANT
ERNIE  ISAWA  ONEROOM
  ASRICH  ISERE  ANKA
HEW  ERE  SCALE  MILAN
AGHAST  TEENS  RETYPE
LEILA  GAVOT  GAG  LID
OSLO  NEGEV  SAFARI
STENCIL  REDLY  LEVIS
    GAP  TERRA  COVENT
AMP  NAPES  OMOO  ITSA
WORST  RATIO  STREWER
EDUCATOR  ALLATTWICE
SEDATIVE  GEEGEE  CTR
MENACED  ORDERS  ESS
```

184

```
LETME  RITA  ART  CASE
UNHOT  ERAT  SEAPORTS
CORNU  VANE  ANTENNAE
 SEDIMENTALJOURNEY
  WESER  ESAU  MMI
ORG  ASA  ENDS  SNAKY
MARE  DEBS  AGES  GLEE
AGILE  SALE  ETHS  ARG
RETINA  TENS  TOUTING
  ASPREEDECORPS
HIRSUTE  POGO  TRANCE
ADA  ELMS  RAPT  ARIOT
SIMP  YIPE  LAHR  SCOT
TOPAZ  TALE  LEA  KSU
   REM  NORA  TRUCK
 STARINGINCEREMONY
SEASONAL  ETRE  BRAES
KEROSENE  SOLE  RECTO
IDOL  DAD  TRES  ASKIN
```

185

```
BABA  ROOFS  OSES  HUD
ANON  ATTAINMENT  ANE
SCOTTFITZGERALD  ISM
KENAI  SEI  TIE  AREA
   ESTH  RND  AGENDAS
ARP  HAM  GEORGESCOTT
RAISERS  OCELOT
ASCI  RUR  TYER  ACTA
POKERY  OSSE  GONERS
ARENOT  BERTL  ELICIT
HENNER  NOSE  CAMINO
OSSA  UMBO  ETO  ALAN
   OMEARA  WHEEDLE
WILLIAMHART  OAR  ESS
ELEVENS  CRO  NORM
ALAI  AID  AAS  SUITE
NUN  JOHNROCKEFELLER
ESE  APICULTURE  ELIS
DER  BABE  ESMES  DELE
```

186

```
YAMS  MONT  ALP  ELMS
EMIT  ASEA  DARE  VIAL
WARY  CLEF  OPEN  ABBA
SHERWOODFOREST  DEEM
   EIN  LEVEL  EWELLS
AMEND  ETE  PRE
BESEEMS  ANNIEOAKLEY
ANT  RAHS  INA  SEINE
   RALEIGH  FEEDON
THEWINDINTHEWILLOWS
RELATE  VESTRAL
AMARA  EER  ELLS  WAR
PINESOFROME  ESTEEMS
   CUT  AND  EATIT
BANYAN  TASSE  MER
EDIE  CASSTIMBERLANE
EDNA  ERAS  LOLA  DREW
CLOT  SIRE  ETON  OGRE
HENS  DST  DEWY  MOOR
```

187

```
AFAR  PAAR  SEC  TROPE
BEBE  LILI  PER  AILED
CENT  ERIC  ERE  IDLED
 LOOKBEFOREYOULEAP
   ROES  TIC  SRO
DIMLY  WATCHYOURSTEP
ALA  SHIAH  ITS  TEAR
SELECTOR  FEE  DANTE
   COOS  EVIL  HORSES
 STOPLOOKANDLISTEN
TAUNTS  PETE  OREL
AUTOS  CAD  PRESENTS
BLEM  CAL  GORED  EVA
USEYOURSENSES  ASWAN
   STD  MAT  ACTH
 OUNCEOFPREVENTION
KOREA  ORA  OILS  LUIS
OLDER  REL  ISLE  ESTA
LAUDS  STE  DEAR  SEAM
```

188

```
HAFT  ABOARD    ABATE
ELLA  REFRIES   BURIAL
EDIT  REPASTE   ARISTO
DATEBASE  ION  BACHUP
    OAS  ASNUTTY  KAME
TAFFY  PROGRAHAMS
ADIT  SELF  ECU  TAI
GATHERS  THSD  ASIANS
   EMIT  WEED  RENTAL
OFGAB  SEERESS  UNITE
ARARAT  MANA  ARMS
SARTRE  BRER  BESTMAN
TUB  GAP  TOLD  RACE
   SOBROUTINE  PUTTY
STOA  EPITHET  SEC
CURSER  LOE  REELTIME
ABASER  EPININE  IGET
LATELY  RISEAND  OLLA
DEEDS  AMBLES  NUTS
```

189

```
CELLAR  BOARD  SHOAL
ORIENT  URANIA  CAPRI
CONSTELLATION  ALERT
ASK  OCC  TAIN  NIT
SESS  FREEWHEEL  CAVE
   STAIR  RID  LARDER
COTERIE  SON  PURIM
ORO  UNSOUNDNESS  ISM
INTACT  LEG  OPE  ESTA
LEAVE  BETHELS  CASAS
ERLE  RAN  ERA  CARIBS
DYE  RESTRAINERS  OLE
   CLOVE  ADE  RETUNES
OBLATE  LIE  KNEES
PAIR  ABANDONED  SETS
TUP  ALOG  AES  LIL
IBSEN  CONFRATERNITY
OLEAN  COOLED  BEFORE
NESTS  ENTAD  BOLTER
```

190

```
MARCH  SCHIST  ADOBES
ISERE  HOODOO  MORALE
THROWPILLOWS  AVALON
REASSURED  SIZE  LIS
ENNS  LES  SPIRE  RISE
   ROSS  TWINE  RUNES
BEGONE  BRING  PANT
ATLAS  BRENT  WRIGHTS
SHAD  SLANG  OHOS  ERA
HAS  STANDSASIDE  JAN
ENS  CARD  HEIRS  BALE
DEPLORE  FIDEL  VICES
   IANS  FIFER  MARKET
MATTE  BRATS  HOLT
ARCH  MOATS  MEN  HATE
NTH  SOON  SALTTREES
TEEMED  CATCHPHRASES
ARRIVE  IGNORE  ATONE
SYSTEM  SETTER  PEPYS
```

191

```
COSTAR  TITAN  AFRICA
ASTUTE  INONE  CROTON
WHATSCOMEYOU  COPSIT
SAY  ESKERS  TERM  NNE
   NBA  APT  DEFACTO
ALIE  BYA  PART  TUTOR
LEGUME  YEARS  FORYOU
ASHLARS  IST  BACKEND
SETAT  PARS  HAR  TAE
   HASONEABARREL
SOM  WON  GAME  ASHIP
CHOICER  EAR  DARLENE
ATONCE  CLING  CLEARA
MONTH  IRAN  EAT  ADES
   MOANFUL  DTS  UPS
ATI  ROAN  COHORT  FOE
UBANGI  CTOPERATIONS
RAMEES  HIRER  SECRET
ARIOSE  YSAYE  PRECIS
```

192

```
TURNOFTHECENTURY
ASIANLAOMARIEBOA
PALSCOPSSPATNOUN
ASEAERIEEASEMASK
CODLIARSARERITES
TALENTEDRESENTED
SPITARLONATOURGE
ARNOBIKETORNTAOS
SEENLESSAGESECON
TANAUDITIREISERE
ELSLEGALLETSTREW
RAREMEMOSTOLOAST
PROPOSALDILATION
ATOPOSLOATENESPY
DEMONOSYMOODNATE
```